Making

Liberalism

New

Hopkins Studies in Modernism
Douglas Mao, *Series Editor*

Making Liberalism New

American Intellectuals, Modern Literature, and the Rewriting of a Political Tradition

Ian Afflerbach

Johns Hopkins University Press
Baltimore

© 2021 Johns Hopkins University Press
All rights reserved. Published 2021
Printed in the United States of America on acid-free paper
9 8 7 6 5 4 3 2 1

Johns Hopkins University Press
2715 North Charles Street
Baltimore, Maryland 21218-4363
www.press.jhu.edu

Library of Congress Cataloging-in-Publication Data

Names: Afflerbach, Ian, 1986- author.
Title: Making liberalism new : American intellectuals, modern literature, and the rewriting of a political tradition / Ian Afflerbach.
Description: Baltimore : Johns Hopkins University Press, 2021. | Series: Hopkins studies in modernism | Includes bibliographical references and index.
Identifiers: LCCN 2020047921 | ISBN 9781421440903 (hardcover ; acid-free paper) | ISBN 9781421440910 (paperback ; acid-free paper) | ISBN 9781421440927 (ebook)
Subjects: LCSH: American fiction—20th century—History and criticism. | Liberalism in literature. | Literature and society—United States—History—20th century. | United States—Intellectual life—20th century. | Modernism (Literature)—United States.
Classification: LCC PS374.L42 A34 2021 | DDC 813/.5093581—dc23
LC record available at https://lccn.loc.gov/2020047921

A catalog record for this book is available from the British Library.

Special discounts are available for bulk purchases of this book. For more information, please contact Special Sales at specialsales@jh.edu.

Johns Hopkins University Press uses environmentally friendly book materials, including recycled text paper that is composed of at least 30 percent post-consumer waste, whenever possible.

Contents

Acknowledgments vii

Introduction 1
    What We Talk About When We Talk About Liberalism 1
    Modern Literature and Liberal Politics 7
    The Discursive Origins of American Liberalism 14
    Making Liberalism New 23

I A Liberal Modernism

1. Liberalism Incorporated: Intellectuals, Abortion, and the Critique of Possessive Individualism 33
    Tess Slesinger's Intellectuals and the Problems of Possession 37
    Wombs or Women? 46
    Modernism's Party Politics 57
    After the Party 63
2. Racial Liberalism: *Native Son* and the Problem of "Color-Blind" Law 67
    Social Psychology and the American Dilemma 71
    Color-Blind Justice 77
    Individualism and Reactionary Color Blindness 87
    Things Not Seen 96

II A Modern Liberalism

3. The Inward Turn: Tragedy, Documentary, and the Making of the Postwar Liberal Imagination 103
    Let Us Not Praise Liberal Documentary 107
    Lionel Trilling and the Tragic Liberal Imagination 115

Taking Tragedy to the White House 123
Arthur Miller and the Ends of Tragedy 130
4. Ending in Style: JFK, Nabokov, and the Apotheosis of a Liberal Aesthetic 137
Totalitarianism and the Democratic Character 142
Intellectual Style in an Age of Abundance 150
Lolita and the Liberal Ironist 159
"Liberal Totalitarianism" and the Problem of the Presidency 168

Conclusion: What's Left of Liberalism? (or What's So New about Neoliberalism?) 175

Notes 185
Bibliography 235
Index 263

Acknowledgments

Whatever faults or failings linger in these pages from the long process of their composition are solely my own responsibility. Whatever virtues this book might possess, however, owe their existence in large share to the generosity and goodwill of others. First, I have to thank Matthew Stratton for his inestimable occasions of sage counsel, guiding queries, and grounding cynicism over the years. If he had not taken a joke about Tess Slesinger's "sensus communist" so seriously, this book would not exist. At the University of California, Davis, Mark Jerng helped break and remake how I understood the act of reading, while also providing valuable professional mentorship. And every scholar of the liberal tradition should be lucky to have a radical interlocutor with the rigor of Nathan Brown, who made sure I had proper footing for the conceptual groundwork this project required.

Others at UC Davis played an important role in this book's development: Kathleen Frederickson, John Marx, Liz Miller, Beth Freeman, Greg Dobbins, Gina Bloom, and Hsuan Hsu. I would also like to thank the University of California for supporting my work with a Presidential Dissertation Year Fellowship Award and Semester Dissertation Awards. And I would hardly have made it this far without the companionship of my peers: Tobias Bates, who has been a hardy conversational foil for a decade now; George Porter Thomas, who seemingly never met a contrarian argument he didn't like; and Jessica Gray, whose capacious thinking and capacious friendship have been there for me when I needed them. Would that everyone had colleagues like Molly Ball, Ben Kossak, Thomas Hintze, Lisa Mendelman, Daniel Grace, Maria Kuznetsova, and Josef Nguyen.

As I worked on this project, I was fortunate to have been supported by several other institutions. I want to express my deepest gratitude to those at the Johannes Gutenberg University and the Obama Institute for Transnational American Studies, in Mainz, who enabled me to share my work with students and faculty, first as a visiting instructor, and most recently as an Institute Fellow. I cannot thank Oliver Scheiding and Alfred Hornung enough for these opportunities. My thanks also go to Maximilian Meinhardt, Tim Lanzendörfer, Damien Schlarb, Clemens Spahr, Anette Vollrath, and Stephan Braunschädel for the roles they played in these years of international collaboration; it truly has been a formative experience.

Here in Georgia, I am lucky to have a growing network who support me and my work: Michael Rifenburg, Lisa Yaszek, Kate Holterhoff, Joyce Stavick, and Matt Dischinger have all been instrumental in making these last few years come together. Elizabeth West deserves special thanks for offering superb advice at several stages of this project (and on two continents). My thanks go the University of North Georgia for a Presidential Summer Incentive Award and two Shott Awards in support of research for this project. I also want to thank all those who have provided feedback during panels and seminars at Modernist Studies Association, Modern Language Association, American Comparative Literature Association, and South Atlantic Modern Language Association conferences, and at the Dartmouth Futures of American Studies Institute.

I am enormously grateful to Doug Mao for the enthusiasm, composure, and guidance his editorship has lent to this project. I would also like to thank my readers at Johns Hopkins University Press for their incisive feedback on my manuscript and to thank Catherine Goldstead for all her work behind the scenes. Thanks, as well, to Johns Hopkins University Press and the Ohio State University Press for permission to reprint prior publications. An earlier version of much of chapter one appeared as "Liberal Use of Possession: Intellectuals, Abortion, and Tess Slesinger's Modernism," *ELH* 85.3 (Fall 2018): 803-24," and as a small piece of "Cocktails or Communism? *Vanity Fair*'s Belated Women of the 1930s," *American Periodicals* 29.1 (Fall 2019): 26-42. Portions of chapter 2 appeared in an earlier form as "Liberalism's Blind Judgment: Richard Wright's Native Son and the Politics of Reception," *Modern Fiction Studies* 61.1 (Spring 2015): 90-113. Finally, thanks to the Zentrum Paul Klee in Bern for helping secure a high-resolution photograph of "Das Konzert der Parteien."

A few more words for a few outliers. Special thanks go to Larry Heyl, who has likely read every word of this book twice as it emerged in drafts, and who approached this thankless task with joyous revelry in the foibles of others and admirable patience when the foibles were my own. And I have

Acknowledgments

to thank Fargyl, who always welcomed my excited chattering when things were going well and my reparative venting when they were not. Thanks for listening to it all.

Long before I had any notion of writing a book, the ideas that would grow into these pages first took root in an undergraduate classroom. When Dean Franco and Michaelle Browers co-taught a course on modern literature and political theory in 2007, they had each already done a great deal to shape my intellectual interests. But this joint seminar—no easy feat—helped me realize that I could use narrative form to pursue the conceptual questions that I found most captivating. These teachers also provided me with a model for the ambitions and possibilities of higher education, which continues to inspire and propel me today. I dedicate this book to them.

Making
Liberalism
New

Introduction

What We Talk About When We Talk About Liberalism

Few words in everyday American speech can match *liberalism* for seeming so obviously significant yet so resistant to simple definition. Each new essay or book adding to liberalism's endlessly growing archives tends to begin with an apology, justifying another account of what may seem a hopelessly overdetermined term, or else a disclaimer, defending one particular definition against its likely competitors and complaints. Compare several of these texts and one will find divergent, even conflicting meanings attached to this cultural keyword. In both academic and popular writing, liberalism will be identified with individual freedom but also with a strong welfare state; free market ideology but also a mode of governance; equal rights, or social justice; cosmopolitanism, or multiculturalism; humanist rationalism, or Western imperialism. Feeling impatient or inclined to nominalism, we might end up viewing liberalism as a vacuous term, an empty cipher for any conceivable position, an "amorphous . . . all-purpose word," as Judith Shklar has complained.[1] Feeling generous or inclined to expansive narratives, however, we might see liberalism instead as the organizing political grammar of modernity, a hegemonic set of categories that as political subjects we can struggle over and within, yet escape no more easily than capitalism. But sooner or later cultural critics, political scientists, and intellectual historians in the United States must all grapple with what Gary Gerstle aptly called the "protean character" of American liberalism, a term that seems ever present and yet constantly changing shape.[2]

This book takes up Wendy Brown's proposal to approach liberalism at once "as ideology and as discourse," as a deeply influential constellation of concepts shaping political life and as an evolving conversation about what these concepts mean and why they matter.[3] While discourse about liberalism and its priorities will vary in different places at different times, it is the relative consistency of a core network of concepts—the individual, the public, autonomy, equality, liberty, rights—that allows scholars to speak of liberalism as a three-hundred-year ideological tradition running from John Locke to John Rawls and beyond. As critics have long recognized, however, these core concepts in liberal thought carry with them a set of (often-unstated) subordinate or supplementary terms. Feminist thinkers like Brown, for example, have emphasized how liberalism's investment in (men's) rational discourse in the public sphere presumes a protected private sphere, sustained by (women's) domestic labor. Liberalism's privileged values suppress, yet depend on, this antithetical set of concepts: the social, the private, dependence, difference, necessity, needs. To understand liberalism's ideological dominance in modernity, as well as its profound failings, we must therefore learn to see it as at once historically and conceptually defined by what Brown calls its "constitutive dualisms." Adapting her original list to provide the broadest construction of liberalism's conceptual architecture, these dualisms would include:

> individual - social
> public - private
> autonomy - dependence
> equality - difference
> liberty - necessity
> rights - needs
> abstraction - embodiment[4]

Much of what has been called *critical theory* in recent decades—from feminist criticism to critical race theory to poststructuralism—has preoccupied itself with exposing these liberal dualisms, showing how efforts to promote the terms on the left have obscured or marginalized those on the right. Liberalism's investment in an autonomous individuality ignores the way that identities form collectively; its commitment to abstract equality impedes recognition of embodied differences, such as race, which continue to carry social meaning; its trust in rational discourse carried out in the public sphere depends on a private sphere, whose gendered domestic labor remains presumed yet unrecognized. Critiques of liberalism and its dualistic structure have to a large degree defined the theoretical commitments of the American academy.

Important as this work has been, however, its unfortunate by-product has been to promote a generalized sense that liberalism is a specious political tradition, without real ethical depth or aesthetic reflexivity, which has lumbered on through time despite all its injurious consequences. Amanda Anderson, the foremost chronicler and critic of this tendency, notes how today's "academic Left" and "Republican Right" show an unlikely partnership in their shared disdain for the term "liberal."[5] Since Ronald Reagan made the "L" word blasphemous, the denizens of right-wing radio have eagerly devoured screeds such as Ann Coulter's *How to Talk to a Liberal (If You Must)*, which cast liberals as an overeducated, predominantly white middle class, whose guilt makes them abandon family values and patriotism to champion instead abortion, affirmative action, and same-sex marriage. Meanwhile, liberalism's "key function" for Left academics—attacking from the other flank, as it were—"is negatively to define what counts as radical or antinormative" in their cultural studies and critical theories. This function, explains Anderson, unites "the Marxist critique of liberal bourgeois ideology, the Foucaultian critique of the liberal state, and the poststructuralist critique of the liberal subject."[6] For many American academics, liberalism quite simply names the not-radical. And ever since radical politics in the United States moved from the streets to the universities in the late 1960s, it has been liberalism—not an increasingly powerful conservatism—that has served as the preeminent antagonist in the political imaginary of the American academic Left. Writing with characteristic bluntness, Norman Mailer expressed this intellectual anathema already in 1962: "I don't care if people call me a radical, a rebel, a red, a revolutionary, an outsider, an outlaw, a Bolshevik, an anarchist, a nihilist, or even a left conservative, but please don't ever call me a liberal."[7] With Left, Right, and seemingly everyone in between taken to treating liberalism only as a political foil, Anderson and others have recently lamented that contemporary scholarship now displays "a significantly diminished, and often distorted, understanding of actually existing liberalisms."[8]

This book answers calls for a richer understanding of liberalism as a political and cultural tradition by charting the rise of a modern liberalism in the United States, which emerged as a definite intellectual culture between the 1930s and the 1960s. Liberalism only became a central term in American political discourse during the Great Depression—far later than is typically recognized—and yet by the early Cold War, liberalism was widely cited as the nation's only meaningful intellectual tradition, its consensus political language. The following pages argue that this rapid transformation cannot be understood without attending to a mutually formative relationship between liberal intellectuals and modernist culture. If modernism means an aesthetic response to accelerating change—in industrial production, communal relations, social geography, and so on—this book shows how modernist writers engaged changing liberal ideas in America, and how liberals in turn seized on aesthetic values from modernist cultural production, especially literature and literary criticism, to reimagine political life, in a reciprocal pattern of influence that shaped the meaning of modernism and liberalism alike. Although liberalism today may appear to name a steady tradition of writings stretching back to Locke, when this term first emerged in the United States, it was not simply used to name a classical tradition but to identify it as inadequate to the complexities of contemporary life, as having entered a crisis of modernity. Among those American intellectuals who first used the word, and sought to direct it on a new course, liberalism did not connote a set of institutions—not representative elections and the franchise, as it had signified in Britain during the nineteenth century nor "social welfare" programs and New Deal reforms, as it would come to signify for many Americans later in the twentieth century. Liberalism instead named a set of inherited conceptual problems, precisely those structuring dualisms that subsequent critical theories have interrogated in such detail. Modern American liberalism emerged as a reflexive investigation into its own inherited conceptual problems, and it is this intellectual enterprise, rather than the establishment of particular state institutions, whose story this book recounts.

To distinguish these modern liberal intellectuals, aware of their problematic inheritance, from those they came to see as predecessors (and so avoid some of the confusion that can envelop discussions of liberalism), I offer a few schematic definitions to help from the outset:

> I use *classical liberalism* to name a tradition of political thinkers, roughly from John Locke to Jeremy Bentham, broadly committed to the values on the left side of the columns above—individuals, rights, equality—and who were later understood to have relegated to inferior status, or simply ignored, those values on the right.

This notion of a "classical" liberal tradition, focused on individual rights, was crucially invented in the early twentieth century by Anglo-American critics who, as Helena Rosenblatt has shown in *The Lost History of Liberalism*, greatly oversimplified the work of earlier thinkers such as Adam Smith.⁹ When scholars treat all liberalism as synonymous with this classical tradition and its privileged values, they are reproducing this comparatively recent and reductive narrative. As this book shows, moreover, American intellectuals mapped this liberal lineage in the early twentieth century in order to define its responsibility for, and inadequacy in facing, the new century's crises. No study of John Locke, for example, described his political writings as "liberal" until a 1918 dissertation, a thesis supervised by John Dewey, who spent the next twenty years calling for a "new liberalism" that would move beyond Locke's possessive individualism.¹⁰ Classical liberalism was first consolidated in the United States as a broken tradition, and it was the need to move beyond this tradition that drove intellectuals to shape a modern liberal politics.

> I use *modern liberalism* to name a shifting intellectual network that came to see "classical" liberal thought as needing radical revision. To cope with the problems in political theory and practice created by liberalism's constitutive dualisms, these intellectuals turned to modernist aesthetic values, emphasizing the irony, conflict, and tension that inform political life.

This liberalism was modern in several senses: because it staged a rhetorical and ideological break with a classical tradition; because its proponents saw themselves as consciously responding to distinctive issues of modern social experience; and—central to this book—because these responses drew upon and were reciprocally expressed through an experimental literary culture. But modern American liberalism never completed this self-critical project, nor did it crystallize into one fixed form. Indeed, this book chronicles a pivotal shift in control over the meaning of American liberalism, from John Dewey's call for intelligence in social planning during the 1930s to Lionel Trilling and Reinhold Niebuhr's redefinition of liberalism as a tragic sensibility grounded by "moral realism" in the 1950s. Retracing this shift goes a long way toward explaining how liberalism became so fundamental and yet so variable a term in American political discourse. Trying to make liberalism new, American intellectuals repeatedly staged a break with the old.

In this book, I argue that modernist fiction proved an ideal vehicle for this emerging, reflexive critique of the liberal tradition. *Making Liberalism New* gathers an archive of writing representing major episodes in the development of modern liberal intellectual culture in the United States and shows how literary modernism consistently revealed intractable conceptual problems in liberal thought, as well as their material consequences. Through narrative irony, exposing aporias in the dualistic structure on liberal thought, modernist fiction dramatized ruptures between abstract individuals and lived identity, between formal equality and social difference.

> I use *liberal modernism* herein to name a set of midcentury fictions that expose liberalism's constitutive dualisms, and the practical problems in everyday life they create, through the ironies of narrative form.

Modernist writers pursued liberalism's conceptual and concrete problems beyond the ken or compass of liberals such as Dewey and Niebuhr, anticipating questions of gender, race, and representation that it would take later critical theories decades to pose anew. After World War II, however, liberal intellectuals began to appropriate modernism's organizing aesthetic values wholesale. Repeating the cry for novelty issued by Dewey during the Depression, figures such as Niebuhr, Trilling, and Arthur Schlesinger Jr. once again proclaimed a "new liberalism." Their postwar rewriting of the liberal tradition hinged on a set of interpretive protocols drawn from encounters with modernist culture, which affirmed the ironies and tensions of political life through aesthetic experience. Accepting conflicting values as a tragic insight into the limits of progressive reform, this new liberal aesthetic politics focused instead on private character-formation, subsuming liberalism's constitutive conceptual tensions into a modernist claim to individual autonomy, expressed through personal style. As this book's last chapter relates, liberalism and modernism paradoxically begin to fade as they achieve a shared orthodoxy in the early 1960s, their historical antagonism passing into reconciliation.

But the problems in political theory and practice manifested throughout this era endure. As this book describes the rise of a modern liberal culture in the United States and the literary responses it occasioned, its chapters focus on a series of volatile issues, which not only preoccupied midcentury intellectuals and modernist authors, but which largely continue to define the meaning of liberal politics in American discourse today: reproductive rights and abortion, race-blindness and legal equality, the moral questions raised by documenting social and personal tragedies, and the dangerous allure of presidential style. By restoring a richer sense of the discursive history of modern American liberalism—what liberals thought about, worried over, and why—this book aims to clarify the hold that liberal ideology and its constitutive dualisms still have over some of the most vital and divisive issues in contemporary American life. This book provides an intellectual history showing the entwinement of politics and aesthetics in midcentury liberalism, an archive of modern fiction that continually grappled with these developments in liberal thought, and a reading practice for using this fiction's ironic form to scrutinize our ongoing entanglement in the contested legacies of American liberalism.

Modern Literature and Liberal Politics

> That modernist literature apprehended with unrivaled power the collapse of traditional liberalism, its lapse into a formalism ignoring both the possibilities of human grandeur and the needs of human survival, is not to be questioned.
>
> —Irving Howe, *The Culture of Modernism*

Modernist culture grew amid classical liberalism's ruins. By the early twentieth century, the idea that liberalism's abstract, universalizing politics and laissez-faire economics had failed, leaving peoples around the world unable to establish shared communal values or control the growing inequities of industrial capitalism, constituted a rare point of agreement between otherwise adversarial literary camps. Mussolini's Fascism, which insisted that "all the political experiments of our day are anti-liberal," famously found an advocate in Ezra Pound, who saw democracy as a "running sore."[11] While T. S. Eliot did not share Pound's reverence for Il Duce, he did affirm in *After Strange Gods* (1934) that "the struggle of our time . . . to re-establish a vital connexion between the individual and the race" was "the struggle, in a word, against Liberalism."[12] For Eliot, as for so many others, abstract individualism and free market competition would inevitably lead to authoritarian control; by undermining the "traditional social habits of the people," Eliot laments, "Liberalism can prepare the way for that which is its own negation: the artificial, mechanized or brutalized control which is a desperate remedy for its chaos."[13] Similar diagnoses reappear among radical leftist writers of the age. In his essay "Why I Am a Communist" (1932), the preeminent proletarian author Mike Gold warned that American liberals would try to "patch up the master's failing fortunes" by electing "a Woodrow Wilson, a Franklin Roosevelt, and then a Mussolini; yes," insists Gold, "we know too well these liberals who are liberal in America, but now may be found in the Fascist ranks of Europe and the Orient."[14] The Second World War appeared to many to confirm a crisis in political liberalism augured by the First World

War and sustained through the intervening Depression. By 1941, even a moderate like W. H. Auden felt forced to concede that "the failure of liberal capitalist democracy" was "the most obvious social fact of the last forty years."[15]

Modernist scholars have long accepted classical liberalism's decline, recorded by figures such as Eliot and Auden, as an "obvious social fact," central to their understanding of the period.[16] Fifty years after Irving Howe insisted that modernism "apprehended with unrivaled power the collapse of traditional liberalism," the *Cambridge Introduction to Modernism* still grounds its period in a threefold crisis of "reason," "representation," and "liberalism."[17] Even as so many voices in the 1930s heralded liberalism's collapse, however, some intellectuals in the United States were issuing calls to make it new.[18] Eliot read his anti-liberal tract *After Strange Gods* as the University of Virginia's Page-Barbour Lectures in 1933; two years later, John Dewey received this honor and delivered papers published soon thereafter as *Liberalism and Social Action* (1935). There, Dewey challenged American liberals to modernize a classical tradition in the face of its historical failings and contemporary challengers. "If radicalism be defined as perception of need for radical change," he insisted, "then today any liberalism which is not also radicalism is irrelevant and doomed."[19] Similarly, Auden's lamentation that "it had taken Hitler to show us that liberalism is not self-supporting" appears in an otherwise enthusiastic review of Niebuhr's *On the Nature and Destiny of Man*.[20] Through his best-selling books and omnivorous editorial commentary, Niebuhr would assume a remarkable role as joint theologian and foreign policy advisor for postwar liberals, guiding a whole generation of Cold Warriors towards a tragic liberal sensibility. Dewey and Niebuhr held sharply differing visions for liberalism's future, which they debated for decades, yet their contest only reinforces how American intellectuals with complex aesthetic and ethical values felt a shared compulsion to reconstruct a failing liberal tradition against the growing authority of fascism and communism.

"Modernist anti-liberalism" was long taken for granted; Russell Berman, for instance, once insisted that modern artists responded to the "failures of a progressive liberal project" with either "a rejection of that project (fascist modernism) or its radicalization on the left."[21] But focusing only on radicals and reactionaries, complains Sara Blair, misrepresents modernism "as a project with only two logical endpoints . . . a people's revolution or the gas chambers of Auschwitz," a perspective that "fails to account for the broader range of experimentation in which responses to modernity were tried."[22] And few experiments in managing modernity shaped everyday life in the United States beginning in the 1930s more than those undertaken in the name of liberalism. Over the past twenty years, scholars have increasingly come to recognize the central role liberal culture continued to play in shaping modern American literature, part of a larger shift in the New Modernist Studies away from a coterie of avant-garde authors toward a more expansive view of modern literature's investment in everyday life, public institutions, and commonplace culture. Studies such as Michael Denning's *The Cultural Front* (1996) and Michael Szalay's *New Deal Modernism* (2000) broke new ground by showing how many American writers came to see their work as "related to the public activities of the modern welfare state," from the Works Progress Administration and its Federal Art, Theater, Music, and Writers' Projects, to "the federal 'insurance for all,' Social Security."[23] More work along these lines followed, from Bruce Robbins's *Upward Mobility* (2007), a literary history of the welfare state, to Sean McCann's *A Pinnacle of Feeling* (2008), exploring American literature's "fascination with the power of the presidency," to Szalay's *Hip Figures* (2012), which examines the racialized construction of "hip" culture in the postwar Democratic Party.[24]

This book would not exist without these important precedents; yet it departs from the tendency these studies share in equating liberalism primarily with state institutions, whether those be the Works Progress and Social Security Administrations, the Democratic Party, or the presidency.[25] While liberal politics today can often appear synonymous with various managerial agencies, their historical and conceptual relationship remains far from coterminous: explaining the Democratic Party's trajectory between 1948 and 1968, for instance, depends upon being able to identify moments when its representatives variously embraced or abandoned anything like a progressive platform or a liberal rhetoric. Certainly, no study of liberalism can neglect its institutional influence and articulation—and this book has good cause to refer to the New Deal, the Democratic Party, and the presidency at regular intervals, as well as the US Supreme Court and activist groups such as the Congress of Industrial Organizations, Americans for Democratic Action, and Congress for Cultural Freedom—but we cannot take the measure of liberalism's theoretical grammar and discursive history at any given point in time through the history of any one of these administrative bodies. When liberalism emerged as a keyword in American political life during the 1930s, it was not used to name any particular set of institutions, but rather to identify and remake an intellectual tradition, a classical inheritance that seemed unfit for the modern world. Those who sought thereafter to renovate the liberal tradition, from Walter Lippmann to Arthur Schlesinger Jr., were compelled by their awareness of the profound internal contradictions in classical liberal thought.

For this reason, as Christopher Lasch suggested some years ago, the emergence of a modern American "liberalism can best be understood as a phase of the social history of the intellectuals."[26] This book tracks these intellectuals, their awareness of and responses to liberalism's internal tensions, and the ethical and aesthetic complexities in modernist culture occasioned by this reflexive political project. In this way, *Making Liberalism New* joins other recent scholarship recovering the varied intellectual currents that shaped modernism's aesthetic politics, such as Lisi Schoenbach's *Pragmatic Modernism* (2012), Lisa Siraganian's *Modernism's Other Work* (2012), and Ben Mangrum's *Land of Tomorrow* (2019).[27] This book builds on these rich, revisionary studies by examining how American fiction recorded and responded to liberalism as it developed into a modern intellectual tradition. As the next section of this introduction explains in detail, liberalism only solidified its place in American political discourse during the Great Depression, far later than commonly recognized. It crucially emerged as a category of crisis, a term that intellectuals such as Dewey used to name a classical tradition untenable in modern society. By identifying the theoretical tensions and practical failings of this classical liberal tradition, Dewey and others sought to establish a distinctly modern American liberalism in its place.

This book argues that modernist fiction proved uniquely suited to exposing tensions in classical liberal political theory and practice. Decades before critical theorists began to interrogate what Brown calls the "constitutive dualisms" that structure liberal thought—individual/social, public/private, equality/difference, autonomy/dependence, liberty/necessity, rights/needs, abstraction/embodiment—modernist writers exposed these dualisms through the ironies of narrative form.[28] Their fictions metabolized these emerging tensions in liberal thought into aesthetic experience for midcentury readers, dramatizing the material consequences created by abstract problems in political theory. In the 1950s, however, postwar intellectuals eventually began appropriating the values of modernism wholesale, reimagining liberalism as an aesthetic politics of character-formation. The modernist interpretive protocols of this new liberal aesthetic, promoted through Trilling's criticism and Niebuhr's polemics, played a key role in shifting liberalism during the Cold War from a term signifying crisis to one signifying consensus. Showing how this remarkable writing, erasure, and rewriting of American liberalism was routed through intellectual encounters with modernist culture and its critical ironies, *Making Liberalism New* charts a mutually formative relationship between liberal intellectuals and literary modernism across midcentury American history. Liberalism and modernism were not blunt antitheses, but rather shared an ongoing entanglement that shaped the aesthetic and political contours of both these monolithic terms.

Because this book describes a twofold rewriting of the meaning of liberalism in the United States, it contains two halves: "A Liberal Modernism" and "A Modern Liberalism." All four chapters map the evolving relationship between modernist literature and liberal culture, yet the book's argumentative emphasis importantly shifts midway. Whereas the first half foregrounds how modernist fiction identified aporias emerging in liberal thought, the second half emphasizes how postwar intellectuals appropriated modernist culture to reimagine American liberalism. In so doing, this book aims to connect critical conversations still largely divided between modernist studies and American studies, fields that, as Will Norman recently lamented, "rarely speak to each other," because of a variety of institutional, disciplinary, and ideological differences.[29] Whereas modernist studies has been rediscovering the neglected role of liberal culture in shaping interwar literature, American studies has conversely spent recent years grappling with its own origins in the liberal consensus of the 1940s and 1950s. Perry Miller's *The New England Mind* (1939; 1953) and *Errand into the Wilderness* (1956) helped establish American studies around the Puritans and their worldview, adapting an approach to American intellectual history introduced by Vernon Parrington's foundational volume, *Main Currents in American Thought* (1927). For his later critics, Miller's work tethered the field to a holistic and heroic view of a singular, governing national ideology, an "American Mind" defined by "Individualism, Progress, Pragmatism, Transcendentalism, Liberalism."[30] Sacvan Bercovitch, who began working in this tradition with studies such as *The American Jeremiad* (1978), eventually proved a transitional figure, editing volumes such as *Ideology and Classic American Literature* (1986), which called for a broader understanding of the ideological pluralism that shaped early American letters. The New American Studies, like the New Modernist Studies, has since defined itself through a reflexive and ever more expansive conception of its domain.

For instance, in *Afterlives of Modernism* (2011), which aims to reach across these scholarly fields, John Carlos Rowe argues that "high modernism" contains more progressive responses to "marginalized issues of race, class, and gender/sexuality" than critics have allowed, and his book envisions "the literary *imaginary* as a possible means of calling for and proposing specific social, legal, and economic reforms."[31] This book likewise aims to draw modernist and American studies back into conversation by insisting that major midcentury US authors did not simply abandon liberalism in a retreat from some empty or malignant political center. Writers from Richard Wright to Vladimir Nabokov instead displayed a series of complex and critical engagements with contemporary liberal thought from the 1930s into the 1960s, an era when intellectuals from Dewey to Niebuhr oversaw a profound change in liberalism's meaning in the United States. But whereas Rowe's mode of cultural politics expressly rereads writing of the past for the progressive values of the present, this book hews to the rhetoric of midcentury American intellectuals, focusing on the theoretical and practical concerns that shaped liberalism during years when its meaning seemed uncertain but crucial and mutable.[32]

Each chapter in this book focuses on a major conceptual problem that emerged in midcentury liberal discourse: personhood and property relations, "blind" legal judgment, tragic political realism, and the notion of political style. Tracking these problems reveals how American liberals interrogated tensions in their own thought, a critical project that was at once echoed and amplified by modernist writing, which dramatized the concrete issues in modern American life structured by these conceptual problems: abortion and the dispossession of reproductive bodies, "race-blind" legal doctrine in the struggle for civil rights, social documentary's limits as a vehicle for promoting change, and the dangerous allure of heroic leadership. The fact that these issues remain profound obstacles for any contemporary progressive politics suggests one of the signal insights to be drawn from this book's intellectual history: the conceptual dualisms structuring liberal thought have yet to be resolved. For this reason, modernist narrative form offers a privileged site not only for mapping the historical development of American liberal culture but also for learning to see how the conceptual problems inherited from liberal thought continue to constrain some of the most profound legal, political, and social debates in American life.

By showing how modernist fiction engaged the evolving theoretical and practical concerns of American liberalism, this project extends what scholars have come to see as a complex and evolving relationship between political liberalism and print culture. In the eighteenth century, argues Elizabeth Maddock Dillon, early print culture helped render salient liberalism's constitutive divorce of public and private spheres. As "a medium in which bodies are, precisely, absent because only words remain present," print helped established "the writer as an abstract liberal subject."[33] Yet print culture also produced a sense of privacy by making it "visible, comprehensible, meaningful," through narrative representations of domestic space, consumed by readers at home.[34] Through this "recursive loop between privacy and publicity," Dillon explains, the literary public sphere enabled early American audiences to recognize, identify with, and even desire the structuring dualisms of liberal thought.[35] Nineteenth-century scholars, in turn, have long recognized how the realist novel frequently echoed the values of a prospering liberal society in Victorian England, especially the ambitions and sympathies of a burgeoning middle class. But as Anderson has shown, novels such as Charles Dickens's *Bleak House* and George Eliot's *Middlemarch* also contain more complex explorations of liberal thought than are typically acknowledged, often juxtaposing a skeptical ethos against dominant middle-class values.[36] By emphasizing this bleak temperament, Anderson demonstrates how literary form evokes an aesthetic and ethical depth often seen as missing from the liberal tradition, which was less self-certain about its own privileged values than critics sometimes think. If eighteenth-century literature generated desire for liberalism's dualisms, and nineteenth-century literature began to express ethical reservations about the limits of liberal thought even in its heyday, this book proposes that twentieth-century literature finally captures a breaking point in this increasingly strained relationship between print culture and political liberalism. Because of a storied partnership in shaping the history of the novel, notes Anderson, "liberalism is almost axiomatically seen as allied with realism," yet it is modernism—a cultural formation preoccupied with tension, conflict, and ambiguity, with reimagining the new from the ruins of the old—that served as a natural means for engaging the emerging crisis in twentieth-century liberal thought.[37]

This has been difficult to recognize, in part, because few modernist writers proudly self-identified as liberals, either when liberalism was widely seen as bankrupt or, mere years later, when it came to be viewed as middle-class orthodoxy. Perhaps no interpretive habit so much limits how we understand "the politics of literature" as the tendency to anchor this phrase to the expressed political values of an authorial subject. This book exposes the limits of this critical tendency by interrogating the reception of works typically read as emblems of fixed intention. Chapter 2, for example, shows how *Native Son* demands that its readers attempt to judge Bigger Thomas and yet interrupts any coherent judgment through its recurrent metaphor of "blindness." In this way, the novel's ironic narrative form offers a devastating critique of the race liberal coalition emerging in these years, which sought to combat segregation through an ideal of legal color blindness. Whatever Richard Wright intended for his novel, *Native Son* has undeniably produced more than eighty years of debate about who is really "blind" to the racialized conditions of Bigger Thomas's life, and why. Among the other authors who appear in these pages—including Tess Slesinger, James Agee, Arthur Miller, Vladimir Nabokov, and Norman Mailer—some had professional connections to the New Deal, and some were drawn into the Manichean struggle of the Cold War. Yet this project does not set out to vouchsafe their credentials as liberals but rather to show how the ironic form of their fictions offers an aesthetic critique of what American intellectuals were learning to see as liberalism's constitutive tensions. While fascism and communism may have had greater appeal for many experimental authors, liberalism and its conceptual legacy played an equally profound role in shaping the literary-historical parameters of American modernism. Most of the books surveyed herein have performed boundary work for scholars, cases that critics have used to define modern American literature through claims about gender (Slesinger), race (Wright), genre (Agee), radicalism (Slesinger, Wright, and Agee), or aestheticism (Agee and Nabokov). The interrogations of mid-century liberal culture by these authors, in other words, have helped shape what scholars understand "modernism" to mean. If often maligned, dismissed, and rebuked by writers and critics, liberalism nonetheless continues to exert a surreptitious influence on the interpretive practices of American literary studies. To tell the story of these entangled literary and political histories, however, one must first disambiguate liberalism as an intellectual tradition.

The Discursive Origins of American Liberalism

> Tradition forms at the moment those who perceive it regard themselves as cut off from it.
>
> —Susan Stanford Friedman, "Periodizing Modernism"

Tracing liberalism's contested and contentious history in midcentury America requires decoupling this term from a pair of values—individual autonomy and free market competition—too often taken as transhistorical constants in all liberal politics. Since the 1950s, American scholars from a variety of disciplines have routinely cited liberalism as a grounding national ideology or political culture, rooted in these twin values. Louis Hartz provided the most famous version of this narrative in *The Liberal Tradition in America* (1955), arguing that the United States had always already been liberal, committed since the Revolution to a Lockean theory of natural rights rooted in personal liberty and private property. Lacking a feudal heritage, Hartz proposed, Americans developed neither a reactionary aristocratic tradition nor a revolutionary left counterpoised to it, making liberalism the shared territory within which all of the nation's formative political disputes transpired.[38] Scholars such as J. G. A. Pocock challenged this narrative, pointing out competing ideological strands in the early days of the Republic and noting that Locke was not actually considered a liberal political philosopher until the early twentieth century. Yet the notions that American liberalism had been around since the nation's founding, and that it meant individual autonomy and private property, were rapidly accepted as truisms among postwar critics.[39] Tracking these values back through American history during the Cold War helped affirm the nation's political foundations at a time when many intellectuals, once drawn to Marxism, were now retreating to a militant anti-Communism, due not only to their growing awareness of the atrocities committed under the name of Soviet Communism but also to the Red Scare stoked by Joseph McCarthy and the House Un-American Activities Committee. For Cold Warriors, liberalism finally came to be synonymous with democracy itself, a *Vital Center,* as Arthur Schlesinger Jr.'s iconic book put it, offering the only secure ground against totalitarianism's encroachment from either side. In the 1960s, the New Left and New Right began stretching this reductive political spectrum through dynamic social movements, which, for all their differences, together helped alter liberalism's status in popular discourse from a vital center to a banal middle ground.

The 1960s also began an enduring tendency for left academics to define their politics in juxtaposition to liberalism, as Amanda Anderson has demonstrated. Once the liberal tradition came to signify a centuries-long defense of autonomous individuals and free markets, scholars influenced by Marxist theory, and by the social movements culminating in 1968, saw in liberalism the chief ideological obstacle to radical political action—more so than conservatism, which at least protested the erosion of communal solidarity brought on by liberal modernity and its abstractions.[40] After the landmark publication of John Rawls's *A Theory of Justice* in 1971, a whole academic industry sprang up among political scientists and philosophers debating the long tradition of social contract theory—now viewed as integral to a long tradition of liberalism—as a means to imagine public, procedural "fairness" in a democratic state.[41] Precisely as liberalism settled into a consensus discourse in such fields, scholars in the neighboring humanities came to see liberalism as little more than what Anderson calls a "structuring illusion" pervading Western philosophy, jurisprudence, economics, and politics.[42] Through all the waves of "theory" crashing on the shores of American universities in the 1970s, 1980s, and 1990s, liberalism remained a constant object of critique, whether that be "the Marxist critique of liberal bourgeois ideology, the Foucaultian critique of the liberal state, [or] the poststructuralist critique of the liberal subject."[43]

This vision of a hegemonic foe was only exacerbated with the fall of the Berlin Wall in 1989. That year, Francis Fukuyama announced the "End of History," drawing popular as well as academic notice to what he called "the unabashed victory of economic and political liberalism."[44] Of course, Fukuyama was speaking at Milton Friedman's home, the University of Chicago, at an event funded by Friedman's longtime industrial sponsor John M. Olin and celebrating the spread of Chicago's neoliberal doctrines since the 1970s.[45] His announcement at once testified to and exacerbated the semantic haze that had enveloped liberalism in the United States, which has only grown thicker after three decades of popular and academic writers continuing to conflate liberalism with neoliberalism—a problem that this book's conclusion addresses. Because liberalism so often gets depicted as a transhistorical commitment to free individuals and free markets, or as an ideologically bankrupt and vacuous tradition against which all meaningful politics must be defined, much scholarship today displays "a significantly diminished, and often distorted, understanding of actually existing liberalisms," of the situated responses to distinctive historical experiences made by liberals in nations like the United States and England, and the complex aesthetic and ethical commitments these responses entailed.[46]

It is now rarely acknowledged, for instance, just how recently liberalism emerged as a keyword in American political discourse, solidifying a place in this nation's intellectual writing and everyday speech only in the 1930s. It did so, crucially, not just to name a storied political tradition but also to grapple with this tradition's crisis, with what thinkers facing the Great Depression suddenly saw as a classical theory untenable in the modern world.

For traditions, as Susan Stanford Friedman once put it, are defined only when another group "regard themselves as cut off from it."⁴⁷ Dewey captured this impulse with characteristic rigor in his 1935 study *Liberalism and Social Action*, which clearly expresses the need to fashion a modern liberalism in the face of its historical failings. This desire corroborates what Anderson has recently contended: although the liberal tradition is continually misrepresented as unreflexive and naively optimistic, it actually constitutes "a philosophical and political project conceived in an acute awareness of the challenges and often bleak prospects confronting it."⁴⁸ Dewey opens his intellectual history by frankly admitting that the "ambiguities that cling to the career of liberalism" have left it "fallen between two stools," the subject of contempt by radicals and conservatives alike—a diagnosis as true then as it is today.⁴⁹ Setting out to determine whether "it is possible for a person to continue, honestly and intelligently, to be a liberal," Dewey retraces liberalism's history, identifies its contemporary crisis and attempts to imagine its future.⁵⁰ Associating liberalism with a self-critical intellectual enterprise, a need to break with the manifest failings of an inherited tradition, Dewey asserts that establishing a modern American liberalism hinges on three tasks: first, to recognize the "historic relativity" of its values; second, to grapple with the dualisms that have emerged around those values, tensions between individual and social, abstraction and embodiment, equality and difference; and finally, to promote creative intelligence as the necessary instrument for grappling with these problems, an intelligence Dewey defines as the capacity to fuse the old with the new. This book takes Dewey's tripartite project as an organizing premise, exploring how modernist writers and political theorists responded to his call for a reflexive, experimental liberal culture.⁵¹

In *Liberalism and Social Action*, Dewey takes the vital first step of historicizing the liberal tradition.⁵² Liberalism begins for Dewey, as for most subsequent scholars, with John Locke's claims upon individual liberty in the seventeenth century. Locke's theory of natural rights, originating in individual self-possession, protected labor and property against the intrusive claims of the state, or any other form of social organization. These ideas, Dewey explains, played a liberatory role in the English and American Revolutions, yet they also rooted liberalism in "a natural opposition between the individual and organized society," imagining an autonomous unit already possessed of rights and needing only minimal protections from the state (8). Over time, Dewey proposes, this dualism would eventually come to erode rather than protect individual liberty. In the eighteenth century, Adam Smith repurposed Locke's defense of natural individual liberty as the basis for securing what he saw as a more fundamental economic activity. Only through the unimpeded commercial activity of individuals, Smith maintained, could states direct self-interest toward collective progress. During "the great industrial and commercial expansion of England," summarizes Dewey, Locke's natural laws "lost their remote moral meaning" and "were identified with the laws of free industrial production and free commercial exchange" that had such palpable reality in everyday English life (10). Dewey's concise intellectual history emphasizes how liberalism has transformed across centuries, crucially revealing how the meaning of its core values carries a "historical relativity," with apparently universal terms like "liberty" adapted to the concrete social needs of the moment (291). In the nineteenth century, he proposes, Jeremy Bentham's utilitarian thought began to extend laissez-faire liberalism beyond the economic realm. Proposing to judge moral and legislative actions—that growing tangle of English laws and administrative customs present in *Bleak House*—by their consequences for individuals, Bentham and his followers saw any "restriction upon liberty" as "*ipso facto* a source of pain and a limitation of pleasure" (12). Through the utilitarian calculus, extended by Mill, liberalism regained an interest in the socially embedded nature of individual life.

It was in nineteenth-century Britain, moreover, when the term *liberalism* finally caught up to these evolving theories of liberty. Although the adjective *liberal* appears as a qualifier for humanitarian sympathy or aristocratic charity throughout the eighteenth century, the word only took on a definitively political meaning as anticlerical radicals in Spain started calling themselves *Liberales* around 1810; this usage spread to Italy and France before arriving in England, where Tories turned it into a pejorative for Whig reformers.[53] In the years leading up to the Reform Bill of 1832, when Whigs joined with Radicals to extend the franchise, "liberal" politics in England came to signify the interests and influence of a growing middle class. In 1859, the Liberal Party was founded, as political leaders like William Gladstone joined intellectual luminaries like Mill and authors like Dickens in making liberalism an organizing category for everyday life. In *Living Liberalism*, Elaine Hadley argues that the distinctive commitments and concerns of this liberal era are too often "refracted by earlier understandings of *Homo economicus* or later communitarian aspirations."[54] By offering a "synchronic study" of the political and aesthetic values of Victorian liberal culture, Hadley, Anderson and other scholars have sought to dampen the "roar of teleology" that often envelops narratives about liberalism, and to "amplify the period's specificity," an enterprise that informs and inspires this book.[55] Victorian liberalism was distinguished by trips to the ballot box, lowered government protection and taxation, religious non-conformism, utilitarian thinking, moral sentimentality, and a vibrant public literary sphere, which reflected and promoted this age's liberal commitments. The realist novel, a beloved medium in these decades, at once modeled and enriched the sympathetic moral character and active political citizenship promoted by liberal thinkers of the age.

But as "Victorian optimism" gave way to "the confusion, uncertainty and conflict that mark the modern world," Dewey explains, a crisis in liberalism burst forth.[56] Time had shown "that disparity, not equality, was the actual consequence of *laissez faire* liberalism."[57] What was more, the "Victorian idea that change is a part of an evolution that necessarily leads through successive stages to some preordained divine far-off event" had been revealed to be only "what psychoanalysis has taught us to call rationalization," a fantasy betrayed by the growing "conflict among nations, classes and races."[58] Facing an especially vocal labor movement, modern Britain entered what contemporary writer J. A. Hobson recognized as a "crisis in liberalism," a growing awareness that individualism and free trade could not adequately address mass poverty and industrial working conditions or curtail the runaway centralized wealth produced by English imperialism. In his classic study *Liberalism* (1911), L. T. Hobhouse called for a "New Liberalism" in England, based on more active state intervention and shaped by a dialectical understanding of individuation and social organization—a position resembling Dewey's own in coming years.[59] These calls for novelty, observes political theorist Duncan Bell, corresponded to the first professional efforts at consolidating a classical liberal tradition among British intellectuals, such as W. L. Blease's *Short History of English Liberalism* (1913).[60] Tradition crystallizes precisely as its practitioners fear it to have broken.

As Dewey remarks, however, the "United States lagged more than a generation behind Great Britain" in these intellectual developments.[61] With "no Bentham" to extend liberal values, Locke's possessive individualism remained firmly "embodied in the Declaration of Independence."[62] Natural rights, protecting individual liberty and property through bodily self-ownership, held sway over the experience of an agrarian nation with seemingly boundless territory, still proud of its break from colonial authority. After all, Locke himself had made this land a heuristic for the state of nature: "In the beginning," he writes in the *Second Treatise of Government*, "all the World was America."[63] Given this ideological lag, the use of liberalism as a political label in the United States was likewise delayed. While *liberal* could denote various charitable virtues in nineteenth-century America, there are only sporadic and unmemorable instances of the word indexing a political program— the most notable was the brief, futile run of the Liberal Republican Party from 1870 to 1872, unified by little besides an opposition to Ulysses S. Grant.[64] American reformers at the turn of the century of course identified instead as "Progressives," a slippery label in its own right, yet whose trust-busting and populist tendencies had to be distinguished at this time from the "negative liberty" and laissez-faire economic policies of the Manchester School, which had defined English liberalism since the 1830s.[65] Only in the 1910s, with Hobhouse's call for a "New Liberalism" in Britain, did Progressives in the United States slowly begin using this term as a synonym for their own reformist efforts.[66]

Just as Britain only consolidated its liberal tradition once it was widely recognized as being under threat, liberalism finally entered mainstream American discourse during the crises of the 1930s.[67] Entering the 1932 presidential election, Franklin Delano Roosevelt needed a new label to build popular support for his platform of "bold, persistent experimentation."[68] Because the Democrats had withered to a minority party during the Roaring Twenties, and Herbert Hoover was widely known as the "Great Progressive," Roosevelt opted for *liberalism*, a term vaguely evoking the reformism of Hobhouse and Gladstone across the Atlantic.[69] Yet because this term, and the English political philosophy behind it, was still young and untested in the United States, Hoover was willing to challenge FDR's claim to its use. Over the next few years, these two national representatives struggled to popularize antithetical definitions of American liberalism. In his speeches and election-year manifesto, *The Challenge to Liberty* (1934), Hoover defended "True Liberalism" as free markets and a freedom from government control, lamenting the "perversion and assumption of the term 'Liberalism' by the theories of every ilk—whether National Regimentation, Fascism, Socialism, Communism, or what not," whose desire for a strong state represented "the very negation of American liberalism."[70] Unfortunately for Hoover, the pseudo-Emersonian mantras of rugged individualism and laissez-faire self-reliance that had carried him into office in 1928 had far less appeal to voters struggling through the Great Depression. Roosevelt won the election of 1932, along with the battle to define liberalism, in this moment of crisis. Rebranding his opponent as a *conservative*, a term Hoover held in contempt, FDR effectively established for American politics the left-versus-right spectrum introduced by the French National Assembly's seating arrangement in 1789.

In the process, Roosevelt cemented liberalism's referential significance in American political discourse, claiming a position between the disastrous laissez-faire individualism of the nineteenth century and the threatening mass movements of the twentieth. Yet this claim to novelty was not defined by any fixed policies, programs, or agencies but by a method admitting experiment and uncertainty, a willingness to dwell in "discordances between confiscation and generosity . . . coercion and freedom."[71] When FDR addressed Congress in 1935 to introduce the welfare programs of the Second New Deal, notes Ronald Rotunda, the *New York Times* bureau chief covering this speech still framed his report with a telling conditional: "the President chartered a definite course for what may in time be known as twentieth-century American liberalism."[72] Journalists continued to show some confusion about the "liberal" label throughout the decade, yet no one missed the dynamic nature of FDR's changes in governance. One *New York Times* editorial from 1937 directly likens the aesthetic quality of his reforms—their speed, novelty, and daring—to modernist culture. Whereas the "former liberal approach to social problems was the moderate, gradualist approach," observes this editorial, President Roosevelt's new, experimental liberalism accelerated this desire for change beyond recognition: "The liberal temper" in Victorian years "was middle-of-the-road and a step at a time, and Tennyson described its ideal well enough as freedom slowly broadening down from precedent to precedent. But the new Liberal is in a hurry. The old, timid, one-step-at-a-time liberalism does not make a fine show against the dazzling modern formulas for storming the heights of Utopia overnight."[73] This editorial has less to say about what Roosevelt is doing than how he is doing it. Pining for a genteel tradition of reform, the editorial invokes Queen Victoria's poet laureate, Tennyson, who praised "A land of settled government, / A land of just and old renown / Where Freedom slowly broadens down."[74] And it cautions readers against FDR's speed and aggression in moving beyond steady "precedents," its invocations of "dazzling modern formulas" for Utopia making the president sound more like an assembler of avant-garde verse than an arbiter of federal budgets. George Santayana saw a similar cultural rupture beneath classical liberalism's decline: "I am afraid liberalism was hopelessly pre-Nietzschean," he writes; "it was Victorian; it was tame. In inviting every man to be free and autonomous it assumed that, once free, he would wish to be rich, to be educated, and to be demure."[75]

Because New Deal institutions, extended under the Great Society, eventually transformed life in the United States so profoundly, it can be difficult to recall that liberalism emerged as, and for years remained, a term defined not by fixed institutions but by a crisis in values. Yet in 1935, when Dewey acknowledged this crisis in American liberalism, his judgment was widely echoed not only by other philosophers such as Santayana and Lippmann but also by foreign dictators such as Mussolini and by modernist authors such as Eliot and Pound. Because of the lag in liberalism's development in the United States, Dewey explains, American liberals were slower to grasp "the historic relativity" of their values than their British counterparts, to see them not "as immutable truths good at all times and places," but as a continually developing political theory.[76] But modernity's sweeping challenges to traditional institutions and values since the turn of the century had finally brought this reality home. "Changes that are revolutionary in effect," observes Dewey, "are in process in every phase of life . . . in the family, the church, the school, in science and in art."[77] "The fact of change has been so continual and so intense," he admits, that "it overwhelms our minds . . . bewildered by the spectacle of its rapidity, scope and intensity."[78] Now liberalism, too, must change. For Dewey, liberalism's crisis lay in having halted its own intellectual development, frozen as a set of transhistorical values that, despite their claim to eternal validity, now appear "impotent or perverse."[79] Natural rights for individuals, which once protected a growing middle class against the remnants of feudal hierarchy, have "been given a definitely economic meaning by the courts, and used by judges to destroy social legislation passed in the interest of a real, instead of purely formal, liberty of contract."[80] Utilitarian philosophy, meanwhile, could speculate on "the abstraction of the legal and the political man," yet it "somehow . . . failed to touch man himself," an embodied existence that provides the "inner springs of personal sustenance and growth."[81] Liberalism, in short, had formed a set of hierarchical dualisms—individuals held above the social, abstraction above embodiment, formal equality above material difference—which served to promote specious political individualism and laissez-faire economics at the expense of the real "structure of human associations."[82] In coming decades, myriad critical theorists would echo this observation, identifying and interrogating what Brown calls the "constitutive dualisms" of liberal political theory.

To continue promoting human freedom, a broken classical liberalism had to be reimagined for the modern world. For Dewey, this task did not fall to institutions. Even in the 1930s, he held "no hope that either of the old main parties" would shake their ties to big business, nor the "mental habits" that kept them "property-minded" protectors of possessive individualism.[83] Dewey also saw how the enormous power acquired by corporations since the late nineteenth century, coupled with a recalcitrant legal system, represented serious obstacles to creating a more just social organization. For these reasons, he believed that modern American liberalism depended not on awaiting institutional reform from above but rather promoting creative intelligence, which Dewey defines as a "remaking of the old through union with the new."[84] Knowledge and habits, before being organized by any institutions, had to be "modified to meet the new conditions," to help mediate this era's dramatic social changes.[85] Liberalism, in short, had to learn to be relentlessly modern, to struggle against its "mental lag," challenging those inherited concepts that indirectly reinforce inequalities in existing institutions.[86]

Modernist studies may privilege the "ideology of rupture, opposition, and anti-institutionality" held by many modern artists, yet as Schoenbach has shown, Dewey's thought complicates any reductive contrast between radical novelty and pragmatic reform in the early twentieth century.[87] Across his interdisciplinary work, Dewey consistently aimed to make liberal thought new by challenging the old, invidious dualisms structuring it as political theory and practice. The "image of the antithesis" between individual and collective, personal rights and social obligations, or freedom and authority, he complained, preoccupied American intellectuals when they ought to be focused instead on the practical "*consequences*" of reconciling these dyads in one form or another.[88] To make it new, liberals first had to grasp the impasses of the old.

Making Liberalism New

Modernist fiction was ideally suited to this task. As Dewey affirmed in *Art as Experience*, written just a year before *Liberalism and Social Action*, art's role in a modern society had become "the problem of reorganizing our heritage from the past and the insights of present knowledge into a coherent and integrative imaginative union."[89] Important as intellectual speculation might be, Dewey insisted the "sum total of the effect of all reflective treatises on morals is insignificant in comparison with the influence of architecture, novel, drama, on life."[90] Art provides experience—a keystone word in

Dewey's thinking—through which competing values might be mediated and reconciled.[91] To recognize this reconciliation in the aesthetic experience of art, however, an audience needs creative intelligence to "provide them with an intellectual base."[92] Dewey, in other words, imagines a mutually formative engagement between artists and intellectuals, each necessarily modern inasmuch as they remain focused on experiences fusing the old to the new. And literature, Dewey insists, holds "an intellectual force superior to that of any other art," because language, being its raw material, carries overt social meaning—it "works with loaded dice."[93] "Literature conveys the meaning of the past that is significant in present experience," writes Dewey, "and is prophetic of the larger movement of the future."[94] This might sound like a call for social realism, yet Dewey insists that the task of literature is "not to set judgment," and certainly not to mimetically convey "a moral intent on the part of the poet and a moral judgment on the part of the reader."[95] Rather, aesthetic experience is strongest when art juxtaposes "possibilities that are unrealized" against "actual conditions," making an audience "aware of constrictions that hem us in and of burdens that oppress."[96]

Modernist fiction had a tried and true device for creating such critical juxtapositions: irony. Long before the New Criticism reframed it as a stable textual ambiguity, explains Matthew Stratton in *The Politics of Irony in American Modernism*, modernist authors saw irony as a "process of arriving at sub-certain aesthetic judgment" that might trigger a "reader's search for principles of causation and responsibility."[97] For modernist writers, as for Dewey, the "task of literature" was "not so much to delineate a blueprint for future action, nor simply to model mimetically the successes and failures of certain attempts at praxis, but to present 'facts' within a visible field of symbolic exchange that calls attention to its own manipulation of readers."[98] By exposing the gap between liberal values and lived experience—between abstract equality and embodied difference, or individual autonomy and social dependence—modern narrative form could reveal the failings of classical liberal theory, undermining this tradition via aesthetic experience while thinkers such as Dewey worked to establish an "intellectual base" for a modern American liberalism. Whether Richard Wright, subjecting one young black man to a relentless series of failed judgments by those around him in *Native Son*, or James Agee, disrupting the conventions of documentary reportage to reveal its tragic limits in *Let Us Now Praise Famous Men*, modernist authors employed a sometimes wry, sometimes scathing irony exposing the practical failings in liberal political thought. This ironic form did not dissolve politics into aesthetics or historical struggle into textual ambiguity but rather revealed the ineluctably aesthetic experience of political life, providing an experimental model for "citizens to embrace the fundamentally unstable interpretive nature of politics."[99]

Making Liberalism New maps a literary archive that pursued this task from the 1930s into the 1960s, with texts that represent major stages in the development of American liberal culture: from the class consciousness emerging among liberal intellectuals in New York during the Great Depression, through a newfound racial liberalism in the 1940s, to a tragic postwar sensibility, which led liberal intellectuals to a symbolic triumph during the Kennedy years. This episodic archive captures not only governing conceptual dualisms in liberal thought but also the material problems in lived experience they constrain: reproductive rights and abortion, race-blind judgment in a court of law, the ethical burden of documentary and tragedy, and the dangerous allure of style in political leaders. This book thereby tracks the developing relationship between liberal intellectuals and modernist culture through sequential historical eras and their lived concerns. Although all four chapters are roughly chronological, however, their causal flow crucially flips midway. Whereas the book's first half emphasizes how modernist authors recognized and exacerbated growing intellectual doubts about classical liberalism's core values, the book's second half emphasizes how postwar intellectuals eventually appropriated modernist values to refashion a modern American liberalism. The book's halves are titled "A Liberal Modernism" and "A Modern Liberalism" for this reason, yet these are once again meant only to foreground this broad narrative arc, not to imply a compartmentalization whereby no modern liberals appear in the first half or liberal modernists in the second. Each chapter rather demonstrates the mutually entwined development of American literary and political history.

Chapter 1 begins by recounting how widespread doubt about laissez-faire liberalism grew among American intellectuals as corporations solidified control over the economy in the first third of the twentieth century. By undermining traditional notions of personhood and property, corporations eroded classical liberalism's grounding commitment to individual proprietary relations. "Liberalism Incorporated: Intellectuals, Abortion, and the Critique of Possessive Individualism," shows how this newfound doubt about possessive relations generated a shared identity among modern liberal intellectuals such as Dewey, Lippmann, and Kenneth Burke in the 1930s. In her understudied modernist novel, *The Unpossessed*, Tess Slesinger provides "the best portrait we have of the intellectual ferment of the Depression years," using a roving narrative perspective, relentless verbal and structural irony, and various metaphors built around the word *possession* to illustrate how liberal intellectuals saw themselves as defined by their equivocal possessive relations.[100] But Slesinger also extends her critique of possessive individualism beyond the insights her male peers were expressing about class and property. Through its ironic form, *The Unpossessed* shows how a political economy of possessive individuals at once depends on and erases the gendered reproductive labor of the female body—an insight that anticipates feminist theory's foundational critique of liberalism. With her daring treatment of abortion, written during the brief window of reform that opened in the 1930s, Slesinger identifies a practice whose perennially contested legal status captures the aporetic structure of classical, Lockean liberalism: abortion cannot be coherently legislated through a claim to individual self-possession. Drawing on critical feminist and legal studies, this chapter reveals how struggles over how to define and protect women's reproductive rights have remained locked within conceptual problems inherited from liberal political theory.

Much as chapter 1 emphasizes how abortion poses a conceptual problem trapped in the wreckage of possessive individualism, chapter 2 examines how "color-blind" law has similarly emerged as an intractable conceptual problem for liberal thought. "Racial Liberalism: *Native Son* and the Problem of 'Color-Blind' Law" begins by explaining how midcentury liberals, awakening to the struggle for civil rights, made color-blind law their governing ideal for combating discrimination. Chronicling the oft-misunderstood history of this legal axiom, from John Marshall Harlan's dissent in *Plessy v. Ferguson* to the Warren Court's historical ruling in *Brown v. Board*, this chapter shows how Richard Wright's novel *Native Son* occupies a central if often unappreciated role in catalyzing an emergent racial liberalism, committed to combating prejudice through legal neutrality. While race liberals championed *Native Son* as a powerful testimony to discrimination, however, Wright's novel challenges their governing ideal of "blind" law. Built around a culminating trial, *Native Son* demands judgment of Bigger Thomas from its reader and yet Wright's narrative undercuts all judgments of his actions—by characters and critics alike—through its blanketing irony, which tellingly appears through the novel's governing metaphor of "blindness." In this way, Wright's novel presciently anticipates liberalism's inability to construct a

Introduction

stable theory of legal equality on the concept of color-blind law; this immanent critique of racial liberalism merits reframing *Native Son* as a modernist text. Drawing on work from critical race theory, this chapter demonstrates how "color-blindness" has come to represent an aporia in liberal thought, a concept alternately used to defend recognition of difference-based, embodied identities, on the one hand, and a universal, difference-blind neutrality, on the other.

These first two chapters emphasize how attempts to pass laws over bodies marked by difference provide an acute glimpse of the constitutive dualisms in liberal thought. As Alan Hyde explains, the body represents at once a real material space and a legal boundary where liberalism must navigate its organizing tensions: public and private, equality and difference, rights and needs.[101] This book deems abortion and color-blindness "aporias" because the legal and political debates that surround them remain riven by these dualisms; liberalism cannot parse these issues within its classical grammar. Chapters 1 and 2 draw upon work in critical feminist theory and critical race theory to express this conceptual predicament rigorously, yet they also show how these two critical schools—each founded on a critique of classical liberalism—had many of their key notions anticipated by modernist fiction.[102] Slesinger and Wright reveal, through narrative irony, how a commitment to protecting the abstract legal equality of subjects effectively imagines these subjects as bodiless, marginalizing the social realities of gender and racial difference. By privileging judgments about authorial intent during years when few modern writers self-identified as liberals, however, literary critics have frequently occluded the complex aesthetic critiques of liberal ideals present in American modernism, displacing the enduring conceptual tensions in political theory exposed by modernist form for the stable values of an authorial subject.[103] This book repeatedly demonstrates how authorial bodies have been used to regulate the unruly ironies of modernist texts.

After the project's first half has narrated the emergence of a modern liberal tradition, and emphasized how modernist fiction exposes signal aporias in liberal thought, the book's second half describes how postwar intellectuals appropriated concepts from modernist culture to reimagine American liberalism as an aesthetic politics, rooted in individual character formation. Chapters 3 and 4 continue tracking liberalism's constitutive dualisms, yet do so by focusing on a pair of concepts, "tragedy" and "style," which postwar liberals used to license an epochal retreat from debates about class, gender, and race. This shift hinged on a set of interpretive protocols that turned modern fiction's cardinal values into the means for cultivating a private sensibility. Chapter 3, "The Inward Turn: Tragedy, Documentary, and the Making of the Postwar Liberal Imagination," maps the rise of these modernist interpretive protocols by recounting the strange tenure of James Agee and Walker Evans's photo-textual volume, *Let Us Now Praise Famous Men*. This singular book performed an immanent critique of New Deal social documentary, depicting its reformist cultural politics as tragic, caught between dual imperatives to preserve the autonomy of its subjects or reduce them to integers for social change. Agee's tragic vision was all but ignored when the book was first published in 1940; when it was re-released in 1961, however, liberal intellectuals reeling from the horrors of Auschwitz and Hiroshima had widely come to embrace Agee's tragic sensibility, and *Famous Men* was now retroactively canonized as a cardinal work of American modernism. Tracking the use of "tragedy" and "tragic" in postwar liberal discourse, this chapter shows how these terms provided intellectuals with a narrative concept at once eminent and legible, through which they could reframe the catastrophes of World War II as an injurious yet vital insight into the blindness of the experimental, reformist liberalism of the 1930s. In so doing, these new liberals crucially rewrote the formative efforts of Dewey and his peers to establish a modern liberalism as the last flourishing of a naïvely optimistic liberal tradition in America. Making liberalism new, yet again, figures such as Trilling, Niebuhr, and Schlesinger Jr. popularized this revisionary narrative about the liberal culture of the 1930s, while promoting a "new liberalism" built around an aesthetic sensibility. Their tragic liberal imagination reached the nation's highest circles of executive power, where it influenced a generation of Cold Warriors and enabled many intellectuals to view progressive ideals as self-defeating, to accept political hope as doomed to tragic irony.

Liberalism's position in American discourse thereby shifted from a term signaling political crisis to one signaling political consensus. In these postwar years, the liberal subject was redefined as an agent capable of sustaining an aesthetic experience of tension and irony—defined, in short, as a reader of modernist literature, though here modernism was drained of its antinomian, critical force. As chapter 4 explains, this aesthetic sensibility was widely promoted by postwar intellectuals as the necessary bulwark against totalitarianism. "Ending in Style: JFK, Nabokov, and the Apotheosis of a Liberal Aesthetic" shows how the emphasis on cultivating personal character led liberal intellectuals to privilege an autonomous, ironic political style as the individual's best defense against totalitarianism and its banal, inflexible conformity. Reading Vladimir Nabokov's major American novels alongside the rise of John F. Kennedy's iconic presidency, this chapter shows how claims about style served as an interface between aesthetic and political discourses during the Cold War, mediating an ideological reconciliation between American liberals, modernist culture, and state power by the early 1960s. As postwar intellectuals settled into an age of abundance, the alienation previously expressed by modernist culture gradually dissipated. When President Kennedy welcomed modern artists into the White House, he symbolically announced a partnership between modernism and liberalism through their shared investment in autonomous individual style; the historical antagonism that had shaped these cultural formations since the 1930s now waned, as they shared a newfound power and legitimacy. Liberals such as Richard Rorty have continued to champion Nabokov's novels as totems for an aesthetic politics rooted in personal style; yet this chapter recovers in Nabokov's fiction a critique of this liberal aesthetic ideology, which warns that privileging a heroic personal style might license tyrannical cruelty. Placing studies of the modern presidency into conversation with Norman Mailer's writing on "Camelot," the chapter closes by showing how liberal enthusiasm for JFK's heroic style indeed legitimated a dangerous concentration of executive power.

By emphasizing moments when political, legal, and philosophical discourse by liberal intellectuals in the United States turned to claims on the aesthetic, or had its insights extended by modern fiction, this book insists on a richer interplay between literary practice and liberal culture in the twentieth century than scholarship typically recognizes. *Making Liberalism New* thereby answers recent calls for "a fuller understanding of the way liberal concepts, principles, and aspirations have informed novelistic art of the nineteenth and twentieth centuries," while also foregrounding how liberal thought has reciprocally required literary form, and a rhetoric of aesthetic values, to grapple with its own enduring tensions.[104] To balance these critical priorities, the reading practice in these chapters alternates between what might be called descriptive and diagnostic modes: at times recovering a constellation of concepts—possession, blindness, tragedy, style—and articulating their historical importance to American liberals, at times deconstructing texts to reveal how these concepts have produced or concealed intractable problems in political theory and practice.

This form of conceptual criticism reflects the book's underlying commitment to bridging literary studies and political theory through intellectual history, a method that shows, more than once, how more recent critical theories do not negate modern liberal thought, as is so often posited, but rather extend an interrogation of the liberal tradition begun by modern liberals themselves. In its conclusion, "What's Left of Liberalism? (or, What's So New about Neoliberalism?)," this book ends by offering one last intellectual genealogy, distinguishing modern liberalism from the neoliberalism with which it is often conflated. Too long overlooked as a mere foil, or a transhistorical constant, liberalism demands renewed attention today so we can not only recognize its historical influence on midcentury American literature and culture but also the ways its conceptual grammar continues to shape everyday political life in this nation. Modernist fiction, now as then, offers a singularly useful means to these ends.

1 A Liberal Modernism

1 Liberalism Incorporated
Intellectuals, Abortion, and the Critique of Possessive Individualism

Modern American liberalism did not come willingly into this world. A self-consciously modern generation of liberal intellectuals emerged in the United States only as they began to identify, and abandon, the classical framework that C. B. Macpherson has called "possessive individualism."[1] Beginning with Thomas Hobbes and John Locke, what has come to be called classical liberal political theory had traditionally justified the possession of rights and property through an account of the individual's self-possession, an immutable ownership and control over one's own body and its labor. This proprietary logic was justified by the authoritative force of "Nature or will of God" in the early modern period, explains Macpherson, and in the eighteenth and early nineteenth centuries, by a faith in the free market to reconcile private self-interest with public good.[2] Despite shifts in its governing discourse, this classical liberalism consistently treated the rational, acquisitive individual as the foundational unit of political life, the self-possessed and self-interested agent on whom all contractual and commercial relations depended. And while contemporary observers might well point out that these purportedly rational actors often behaved less than rationally, or that only a fraction of persons in most liberal states owned their bodies and property, neither of these significant qualifiers overruled possessive individualism as a theoretical defense of political organization and market behavior from the earliest years of commercial modernity through the Industrial Revolution.

This classical theory faltered, however, within the new political economy emerging at the turn of the twentieth century in the United States, which saw the boundaries of property and personhood troubled by the rise of corporate capitalism. Corporations, observes David Ciepley, "transgress all the basic divides that structure liberal treatments of law, economics, and politics: government/market, state/society, privilege/equality, status/contract, as well as liberalism's master dichotomy of public/private."[3] Throughout the 1890s, Progressive reformers fought against corporate monopolies —most notably those railroads vilified by Frank Norris's iconic novel *The Octopus* (1901)—and won several battles around the Sherman Act (1890). But by the 1910s, corporations had solidified their legal standing through a series of cumulative court cases, and this growing economic and legal entity shattered classical liberalism's political theory.[4] As the young critic Walter Lippmann observed in *Drift and Mastery* (1914), corporations fragment the integral pieces of possessive individualism by divorcing financial ownership from directorial control. Possession no longer describes a private relation of material holding, a control over physical goods, but rather a social organization, a contractual control over the capital of others and over its circulation.[5] With a keen sense of historical irony, Lippmann notes that the "trust movement is doing what no conspirator or revolutionist could ever do: it is sucking the life out of private property."[6] Meanwhile, cases such as *Santa Clara County v. Southern Pacific Railroad Company* (1886) had established that corporations were also legal persons, with rights protected by the Fourteenth Amendment like any individual—protected much more rigorously over coming decades, in fact, than those of women, children, laborers, and racial minorities.[7] This legal personhood likewise seemed to invert classical liberal theory. Rather than a market aggregating private interests toward public good, corporations subordinated public interests under private control; instrumental bureaucratic reason replaced rational individual choice. In this new political economy, where the meanings of "property" and "person" had fundamentally shifted, possessive individualism no longer appeared adequate as a theory of rights and obligations. "What was dearest to the heart of the historical, living liberal," summarizes Jeffrey Lustig in his study of the era, "was individualism of a possessive and acquisitive sort. When the units of possession and acquisition changed, the liberal changed with them."[8]

This chapter demonstrates how American intellectuals achieved a newfound self-awareness in the first third of the twentieth century by reframing possessive relations as a social problem rather than an individual right, inaugurating a break between classical and modern liberalism. Decades before Macpherson coined "possessive individualism," economists, philosophers, and cultural critics, such as Thorstein Veblen, Walter Lippmann, Lewis Mumford, John Dewey, and Kenneth Burke, were living through and diagnosing the emerging contradictions of this classical liberal political theory first-hand. After Progressives had their faith in corporate technocratic management shaken by World War I, the stock market crash and ensuing depression accelerated this intellectual self-scrutiny through the 1930s. Confronted with the material failure of state capitalism, and with Communism as a real political possibility in the Soviet Union, American intellectuals intensified their doubts about the tenability of existing property relations and about the possessive logic in political and social theory that had underwritten them. Responding to an escalating sense of crisis in their studies of the leisure class (Veblen), the corporation (Lippmann), technological history (Mumford), and, most explicitly, the intellectual's social role in a liberal state (Burke and Dewey), these figures interrogated possession as a concept binding together their disciplinary fields. A term that had long been used to index an individual's axiomatic right to property was gradually redefined as the mechanism of an invidious distinction between individuals, then as a category of class identity, and finally as a term conceptually bound to its antithesis: dispossession. Together, this work reframed a foundational political concept from within, defining one of nineteenth century liberalism's core values as one of twentieth century liberalism's structuring problems. By the middle of the 1930s, possession was recast as an aporia in liberal thought, and American intellectuals increasingly identified themselves and their social task through its equivocal terms.[9]

Published at the height of this era of critical self-scrutiny and from within these intellectual ranks, Tess Slesinger's modernist novel *The Unpossessed* (1934) employs competing senses of "possession" to show how intellectuals are defined by their equivocal relationship to possessive relations. Slesinger's novel, however, does not simply mirror the insights of her contemporary male critics, but also deploys its ironies to expose how possessive individualism structures questions of gender and sexual politics. The novel does so by juxtaposing two major plot lines: as a fledging group of academic intellectuals attempts to launch a radical literary magazine, one couple among them struggles with the idea of bearing a child. The magazine, never more than an idea, achieves its culmination and collapse in a fundraising party that serves as the book's climactic scene; Mr. and Mrs. Flinders conceive, only to have Miles convince Margaret into having an abortion—one of the earlier sustained treatments of the subject in American fiction. Written during a brief window of reproductive reform during the 1930s, *The Unpossessed* anticipates the conceptual problems that would keep legal debates over reproductive rights locked within the logic of possessive individualism for the next century. For abortions and corporations share more than an etymological link to the body. Just as corporations destabilize the traditional liberal conception of property by divorcing public ownership from private control, legal disputes over abortion pit public regulation against bodily privacy. Indeed, abortion debate produces a veritable roll call of liberalism's key dualisms: public versus private, abstraction versus embodiment, equality versus difference. *The Unpossessed* dramatizes what feminist critical theory would later argue: the question of abortion quite literally embodies liberalism's aporetic concept of possession. When two individuals are imagined as incorporated within one body, classical liberalism's account of the self-possessing individual once again collapses.

In this way, Slesinger's novel exemplifies the emerging pattern of shared conceptual work between liberal intellectuals and modernist literature in the United States, which this book traces from the 1930s into the early 1960s. This chapter repeats some of the origin story for American liberalism expounded at greater length in the introduction, but it principally focuses, as does chapter 2, on presenting an aporia in political liberalism, a point at which the constitutive dualisms in liberal thought became apparent in political theory and social practice in the early twentieth century.[10] As American liberalism discovered a newfound reflexivity, the modernist novel offered an ideal vehicle for confronting emerging tensions within its classical political concepts, reshaping an emergent critique by intellectuals such as Burke and Dewey into an aesthetic politics, wherein structural irony and free indirect discourse supplied the internal distance necessary to articulate and interrogate uncertain values. To map the emergence of a liberal modernism, this chapter's first section demonstrates how a generation of intellectuals, frequently mischaracterized as lacking reflexivity about liberalism's internal tensions, in fact defined their social class by interrogating the tensions within possessive relations. *The Unpossessed* captures the insights and anxieties of this moment; yet as the next section shows, Slesinger's inquiry also extends beyond class and property relations, scrutinizing gendered forms of possession that anticipate feminist theory and critical legal studies by decades. Situating this modernist novel between a generation of liberals and later radical scholars helps to clarify a surprisingly salient view of intellectual praxis across these divisions: to confront the tensions within liberalism's central values, the intellectual must provide an aesthetic experience of the lived contradictions they produce, the points of friction between abstract persons and embodied subjects; this intellectual ambition links many of the figures surveyed in the following pages, and it also defines the core interpretive practice of this book. This chapter's final sections address the counterintuitive position that literary modernism occupies in such an aesthetic politics, affirming the political seriousness of a novel that nonetheless ends with a ninety-page cocktail party. Reading for a liberal modernism, and recognizing its enduring concerns, requires reading across divisions between liberal and radical, modernism and social realism, ironic critique and political engagement, which conventionally compartmentalize criticism about and after the 1930s.

Tess Slesinger's Intellectuals and the Problems of Possession

Slesinger's readers noted early on the autobiographic echoes of her novel. Those Greenwich Village intellectuals depicted in *The Unpossessed* resemble the peers Slesinger found gathered around the *Menorah Journal*, edited by Elliot Cohen at Columbia. After graduating Swarthmore College, Slesinger entered the Columbia School of Journalism, and there met the charismatic Cohen as well as her future husband Herbert Solow, who remains best known for his central role in the Dewey Commission. With her 1928 marriage to Solow, Slesinger was firmly embedded within the journal's intellectual community, a predominantly Jewish group, including Clifton Fadiman, Anita Brenner, Henry Rosenthal, and Lionel Trilling, and which at times included associates such as Sidney Hook and Max Eastman. Over the next few years, Slesinger wrote a number of book reviews for the *Menorah Journal*, which also featured her first published story, "Mother to Dinner," later collected in *Time: The Present*, along with stories appearing in *Vanity Fair* and other prominent periodicals.[11] According to Alan Wald, Slesinger's most famous short story, "Missis Flinders," grew from her "experience of having an abortion at the insistence of her husband"; the story garnered praise, but her marriage to Solow crumbled.[12] Shortly after the divorce, Slesinger completed and published *The Unpossessed,* her lone novel, before leaving for California in 1935, where she would find a new career (and a new marriage) as an accomplished screenwriter. Although *The Unpossessed* has been praised by Morris Dickstein as our "best portrait . . . of the intellectual ferment of the Depression years," the novel appears to lampoon the community Slesinger inhabited.[13] In Trilling's words, "It passed judgment upon certain people."[14] The novel's curt epigraph, "to my contemporaries—," might easily appear as the parting shot of a confident, capable, and still young woman, escaping the cynicism of New York intellectual life to start afresh in a booming Hollywood scene.[15]

By fixating on the negativity and discontent in her novel, Slesinger's small but significant critical reception exemplifies the way literary histories of the 1930s have focused on condemning "fellow-traveling" intellectuals for their limited revolutionary energies and, in the process, overlooked the growing influence of a liberal culture among American intellectuals in this decade.[16] Because *The Unpossessed* concludes with a dual negation—no magazine, no baby—early critics such as Phillip Rahv, Murray Kempton, Lionel Trilling, and Alan Wald all identified the novel as a critique of parlor radicalism among New York intellectuals.[17] These biographic readings often displayed a coarse chauvinism, applauding Slesinger's insights into the psychosexual anxieties of her intellectual peers while denying her novel any substantive political content. For example, the pragmatist philosopher Hook, sometimes called "Dewey's Bulldog," once insisted that Slesinger "never understood a word about the political discussions that raged around her. . . . Her book shows that. There is no coherent presentation of any political idea in it."[18] Despite praising her command of modernist techniques, Rahv charged Slesinger's style with failing to direct intellectual action, concluding that her "writing suffers somewhat from a lack of economy," a choice phrase intoning at once Ernest Hemingway's terse masculine activity and Karl Marx's political-economic insight.[19] In the 1980s, feminist critics condemned the patriarchal tendencies of these early readers, exposed their false division of (feminine) sexuality and (masculine) politics, and recuperated Slesinger as a woman writer who bridged modernist and radical tendencies in the 1930s.[20] Yet these critics, still privileging a recovery of Left radicalism, upheld the organizing premise that an absence of magazine and child at the conclusion of *The Unpossessed* constitutes an unambiguous marker of failure. Even as she praised Slesinger's work in *Labor & Desire*, for instance, Paula Rabinowitz finally judges *The Unpossessed* against a radical benchmark, "the proletarian collective form, in which various individuals from different backgrounds come together for a common goal," reducing the novel's concluding negations into symptoms of its (predetermined) failure to imagine a revolutionary end.[21]

This literary-historical commitment to recovering radicalism has obscured the possibility that Slesinger's ironic negativity might not simply mark failed revolution but rather expose tensions in liberal thought through the formal capacities of the modernist novel. Slesinger's critics have consistently missed the complex conceptual relations traced by her varying uses of "possession" and, by ignoring contemporary interest in possessive relations, have unknowingly reproduced this liberal problematic. Astute readers such as Trilling, Wald, and Rabinowitz all take the "unpossessed" child and magazine as a pejorative lack, symbolizing the personal and political failure of intellectuals in the 1930s to consummate their era's revolutionary potency.[22] In these readings, the body of the intellectual becomes marked, even defined by this inadequacy. Wald suggests that "the intellectuals as a group . . . are sterile," a sentiment Rabinowitz amplifies, lamenting the novel's vision of "a sterile world in which neither words nor babies can add up to historical change."[23] Coming from a group of literary professionals, these judgments of "sterility" reveal how Left intellectuals often occupy a strangely pharmakonic status within their own critical discourse, acting at once as corruption and as cure. More to the point, however, this tendency to identify an unwillingness or inability to (re)produce possessions—babies and literary magazines—as a political failure also necessarily sustains a proprietary logic as the measure of individual political subjectivity. By locating agency in the capacity to reproduce possessions, even scholars explicitly invested in recovering the radicalism of the 1930s have implicitly reinscribed *The Unpossessed*, and the figure of the intellectual, within the gendered and proprietary logic of possessive individualism, reproducing a liberal framework that Slesinger joined an entire genealogy of cultural critics in scrutinizing as a political and legal obstacle. To recognize this conceptual work, however, we must be able to read the literature of the 1930s not just for unrealized radical possibilities but also for liberalism's realized contradictions.

Intellectuals in the United States began interrogating an inherited faith in possessive individualism before the new century dawned, before "liberalism" had emerged as a salient political term.[24] Thorstein Veblen's *Theory of the Leisure Class* (1899) may be best remembered for coining "conspicuous consumption," yet this seminal text from the Progressive era in fact establishes its grounding argument in a section entitled "Pecuniary Emulation." Imagining a heuristic moment of social behavior before the rise of a leisure class—before even capitalism—Veblen describes how "the prepotence of the possessor" emerges not from the objects possessed but from an "invidious comparison between their possessor and the enemy from whom they were taken."[25] Exposing a gap critics would later rediscover in corporations, Veblen distinguishes physical ownership of private property from possession's more elementary social function: satisfying a perpetual drive, motivated not by rationality or by a theory of the good, but by comparative lack.[26] This "invidious comparison," as Veblen calls it, serves as the mechanism for interpersonal distinction throughout his *Theory*, a social relation flatly opposed to classical liberal accounts that treat possession as a beneficial impulse and an axiomatic political right. Veblen's iconoclastic volume, if misread by some contemporaries, provided Progressives an important precedent in their later efforts to define and break with nineteenth-century laissez-faire liberalism.

Two major, interlocking issues facing Progressives in the 1910s—corporate power and World War I—intensified this underlying struggle with possessive individualism, a struggle that helped give shape to *liberalism* as a keyword in American political life. In 1912, the critics that would later cluster around the *New Republic*, such as Herbert Croly, Walter Weyl, and Walter Lippmann, supported Theodore Roosevelt's New Nationalism and his call to control corporations against Woodrow Wilson's efforts to reanimate a Jeffersonian individualism. For Lippmann, corporations had irrevocably undermined private property, creating a social "drift" that he called "liberalism."[27] This drift, Lippmann proposed, could only be halted by reasserting "mastery" over this new corporate form of social property, "combining popular control with administrative power."[28] Like Croly and Weyl, Lippmann "believed that the magnates who had overseen the corporate revolution should retain managerial control of the economy in the new society."[29] Faith in managing corporate capitalism through the state, which the War Industries Board would model during coming years, helped the *New Republic* Progressives eventually shift their support toward Wilson and war by 1916.[30] This shift triggered Randolph Bourne's famous attack in "The War and the Intellectuals" (1917), denouncing not only his erstwhile mentor John Dewey, and pragmatism, but also invoking terms like "war-liberalism" to drive home the irony of Progressives embracing such illiberal means in the name of "world democracy."[31]

Looking back on this moment in *Liberalism in America: Its Origin, Its Temporary Collapse, Its Future* (1919), Harold Stearns concludes that Wilson and his intellectual allies had been overcome by a blind faith in their "possessive instincts."[32] Even after the demonstrable collapse of laissez-faire economics, Stearns proposes, Americans had their proprietary drive stoked by narratives of rugged individualism, the frontier ethos, and Emersonian transcendentalism and still believed that they could marshal the organizational power of corporations.[33] Only after World War I, asserts Stearns, and witnessing the carnage abroad and oppression at home that such violence inevitably produces, did American intellectuals belatedly recognize the "horrible devastation our uncritical materialism and doctrine of success had wrought" and begin to doubt their ability to manage state power and direct corporate capitalism.[34] Stearns defines American liberalism through this inaugural crisis—a definition-through-negation recurring cyclically among liberal intellectuals thereafter. He suggests that intellectuals such as Bourne, Lippmann, and Van Wyck Brooks had begun to repair liberalism by going to "war with the dominant possessive impulses of the day."[35] These debates among Progressives about the relationship between state power, corporate property, and intellectual allegiance reanimated Veblen's skepticism about the drive for possession, while also gradually introducing "liberalism" into American political discourse. "Protest," concludes Stearns, "became articulate and critical in exact proportion as an increasing number of men discovered this appeal to the possessive instincts as a fraud."[36]

In the 1930s, this critique of possessive individualism would provide an organizing set of terms through which liberal intellectuals in the United States identified themselves as a social class. Behind this awakening lay the decade's defining anxieties: an intense scrutiny facing corporate capitalism during the Great Depression, along with Communism's rise to prominence as theory and, in the Soviet Union, as practice. In 1932, the Berle-Means thesis convinced mainstream economists of the corporation's constitutive divorce between ownership and control, which Lippmann had recognized almost two decades earlier.[37] By then, remarks Lustig, "the 200 largest corporations in the United States had acquired 50 percent of its corporate wealth," and the stock market crash cast serious doubts over their managerial self-regulation.[38] While Lippmann swung back to defending a free market individualism, those liberals who retained his earlier faith in scientific management and expert control showed a heightened recognition of proprietary inequality.

In *Technics and Civilization* (1934), for instance, Lewis Mumford pivots from a critical history of technology toward utopian social planning and argues that any technocratic future requires a reorganization of possessive relations. According to Mumford, America's "machine-dominated society" remains "oriented solely to 'things,' and its members have every kind of possession except self-possession," what Locke saw as an a priori right having been dissolved rather than secured by industrial capitalism.[39] Mumford's call to manage industrial production by reconciling scientific expertise with moral responsibility, if perhaps idealistic, seemed to him the only conceivable escape from class warfare, an attempt to evade the looming "struggle between the possessors and the dispossessed" through the intelligence of a few who might transcend this division.[40] Marxism's prevalence among American intellectuals in the 1930s obviously explains, in part, why Mumford would envision class conflict in this way. But treating his juxtaposition of "possessors and dispossessed" only as a watered-down "bourgeoisie and proletariat" not only risks reducing historical materialism to a set of loose, interchangeable categories but moreover erases the way that liberal intellectuals were shifting the conceptual status of possession within their own discourse, reframing one of liberalism's most privileged categories into a descriptor for structural social conflict, and defining themselves through these new terms.[41]

Perhaps no American intellectual was more aware of this shared critical and rhetorical project in the 1930s than Kenneth Burke. In *Attitudes Toward History* (1937), Burke distinguishes those persons "materially" dispossessed, without property or secure income, from the "spiritually" dispossessed, those intellectuals whose self-possession falters when they recognize how their material security depends on a system that deprives others of the same.[42] Describing ideology without ever calling it such, Burke argues that "the dispossessed tends to feel that he 'has a stake in' the authoritative structure that dispossesses him; for the influence exerted upon the policies of education by the authoritative structure encourages the dispossessed to feel that his only hope of repossession lies in his allegiance to the structure that has dispossessed him."[43] However, because intellectuals, that "peripheral class (of those spiritually alienated but still materially rewarded)," are uniquely fluent in the language of political authority, Burke insists, they "can contribute insight of a sort to which the wholly dispossessed are blinded." In a sly example, Burke notes that it was only because Marx was "spiritually dispossessed" from his observation of working class life, yet "given a fairly sufficient income from Engels' cotton mills," that he could produce his critique of capitalism.[44] In summary, then, what Christopher Lasch calls the "new radicalism" of American intellectuals, their class consciousness and sense of social purpose, emerged through a "twofold discovery: the discovery of the dispossessed by men who themselves had never known poverty or prejudice, and the mutual self-discovery of the intellectuals."[45] By the mid-1930s, liberal cultural critics such as Mumford and Burke increasingly defined themselves by their structurally equivocal position, trapped between a material privilege within existing property relations and a psychological alienation from this same system of possessive exploitation.

With *The Unpossessed*, Slesinger draws upon and extends this contemporary critical work, depicting intellectuals as at once defined and constrained by the inadequacy of possessive relations. The novel takes place in New York City, humming center of American liberalism and home to what Elizabeth Hardwick's introduction for the elegant New York Review of Books printing calls that "disorderly, self-appointed group: intellectuals, critical of society's arrangements and very critical of each other."[46] Bruno Leonard, a witty and cynical professor of literature, plans, at first quite half-heartedly, to start a literary magazine with his former college peers: Miles Flinders, a New England Calvinist racked by a profound sense of inadequacy before his friends' ambitions and his wife's affections, and Jeffrey Blake, narcissistic Don Juan, hack novelist, and self-described Marxist intellectual. The novel sets up gendered pairs, with Elizabeth Leonard, Bruno's cousin, joined by Mrs. Margaret Flinders and Norah, who remains attached to her unfaithful paramour Jeffrey. Most of the novel's surrounding characters are held in orbit by Bruno's magnetic and manic personality: the Black Sheep, a group of student radicals who idolize him; Emmett Middleton, an anxious but devoted student with archetypal Freudian issues, who competes with Elizabeth for Bruno's affections; and finally Mr. and Mrs. Arthur Middleton, Emmett's parents, whom Bruno uses to back a fundraising party for the magazine that will mark at once the energetic climax and the effective collapse of the narrative.[47]

Early in the novel, Bruno's urge for intellectual purpose remains held in check by a paralyzing fear of possession. Reclined in his university office, Bruno refers to "my Magazine," conveying a sense of satisfied ownership, which he quickly undermines by conceding that he had spent "about ten years ... playing with the Idea."[48] Unbeknownst to him, however, Jeffrey has ordered a first filing cabinet for the magazine, a sudden signal that Bruno's recurring daydream may finally take material form. But Bruno "almost groaned aloud as he saw his Idea turning on him and become reality embodied in a Filing Cabinet, emerging green and indisputable like fate under the salesman's crafty hands" (27). Frantically trying to refuse the cabinet, Bruno admits to the salesman that he does not actually own a literary magazine and suggests that he may not want to see this ownership realized: "I haven't *got* a Magazine; I'm not even sure that I want one" (27). Slesinger's italics unmistakably emphasize Bruno's anxiety as a fear of possession, a stylistic technique repeated on the next page: "To *have* the Magazine . . . But it was the Idea that Bruno was in love with" (28). Beneath his ironic posturing and confident oratory, Bruno's prose reveals his desire for the magazine to be fundamentally constituted by lack: as either Jacques Lacan or Thorstein Veblen might have put it, Bruno's desire remains a desire only for itself, a perpetual drive that he cannot stand to have satisfied. The terrifying possibility that his desire for a magazine might be realized turns this minor office delivery into a psychosexual drama, with Bruno's virginal flirtation reimagined as a degrading sexuality: "The Filing Cabinet was yesterday's blushing sweetheart turned coarsely to a bride" (28). Although he continually puts on the airs of confident, self-possessing masculine ownership, Bruno's ambivalence perverts the logic of possessive individualism, betraying a tenuous self-possession that risks collapsing should he possess the object of his desire.

Slesinger pushes this tension between masculine sexual conquest and a threatened individual self-possession further still with Jeffrey Blake. During a dull gathering of friends, where everyone seems to be waiting for Bruno's energizing wit, Jeffrey decides to seduce Mrs. Flinders. Margaret tolerates his advances only to avoid her husband, Miles, who is delivering a nervous excursus on economics in the other room. Jeffrey "fought for possession of her mouth which offered no resistance" (61) and "pressed himself against her bitterly" (62), but nothing comes from it: Margaret perceives the "falsely glowing eyes" that "failed to take possession of her" (62). A sexually aggressive male trying to "possess" a woman's body may hardly be an original trope; however, once Jeffrey detects that his advances will get him nowhere, the term's conceptual work suddenly changes: "when had both of his hands back in his own possession again he rubbed them one against the other as though he somehow washed them and forgave them" (62). This scene elaborates on the tenuous relationship to ownership exhibited by Bruno, capturing the way that the intellectual, bound to the drive for possession, comes to feel desecrated by this invidious desire. In his attempt to "have" Margaret, Jeffrey begins to lose himself, to lose that self-possession that constitutes liberal individualism's founding right. Jeffrey must perform ablutions to restore the propriety of his hands, to bring them "back in his own possession." Possession here describes not only the aggressive proprietary drive of male sexuality, but also a possessive individual whose drives alienate him from his own body. The "spiritually dispossessed" Jeffrey, to use Burke's phrasing, must ritually cleanse himself after giving way to his possessive impulses.

In a letter to her publisher, Slesinger addressed the difficulty of describing "the intellectual" as a category: "I can't attempt any dogmatic definitions because many intellectuals seem unintelligent; but let's say the doubters, the worriers, the weighers of the world; the class interested in things not essentially economically remunerative."[49] Rather than settle for any "dogmatic definitions," *The Unpossessed* joins Slesinger's contemporary cultural critics in identifying the intellectual as a class through their equivocal relationship to possession—a class whose self-awareness in these years had helped introduce "liberalism" into everyday American speech.[50] Whereas in the classical liberal tradition of Smith and Locke, Macpherson suggests, "freedom is a function of possession," Slesinger's intellectuals live by an antithetical axiom: "freedom's the password the byword the slyword, don't get possessed."[51] When Bruno remarks that "intellectuals engaged in a property war would lose their identity as intellectuals," this does not signal their freedom from property relations or class struggle but rather the liberal intellectual's structurally equivocal position within these questions.[52] During the novel's climactic fundraiser, when Bruno delivers the speech from which *The Unpossessed* draws its title, he elevates this equivocal position into a bombastic manifesto:

> Our party is of the intellectuals, by the intellectuals, and naturally against them . . . we are bastards, foundlings, phonys, the unpossessed and unpossessing of the world. . . . We have no class: our tastes incline us to the left, our habits to the right; the left distrusts, the right despises us. . . . Are you a tired radical? are you a parlor pink? are you a political pansy? are you a morbid individualist? are you a victim of the twentieth century social disease? do you have singed or clipped left wings? then climb right up and straddle with us. (281-83)

Slesinger's slippery irony tempts us to read this speech as a fatuous parody, a glimpse at Bruno's self-contempt. Yet this characteristic negativity, which defers any programmatic statement of values, also performs what contemporary critics such as Kenneth Burke saw as the essential task of the intellectual. In a passage entitled "Repossess the World," Burke suggests that once "relatively alienated or dispossessed" intellectuals recognize their position, they can challenge "allegiance to the symbols of authority," the concepts and attitudes governing social relations.[53] Neither capitalist nor working class, happy possessor nor wholly dispossessed, the liberal intellectual "straddles" these categories and calls attention to the terms of the conflict— terms such as "possession," which had structured classical liberal thought— thereby reshaping the vocabulary through which people understand what may be politically possible.[54]

When John Dewey, liberalism's foremost representative in the 1930s, cast a glance back on the crises of the first third of the century, he blamed prior generations of intellectuals for treating their expertise as a form of property: "just at the time when the problem of social organization was most urgent," he laments, "liberals could bring to its solution nothing but the conception that intelligence is an individual possession."[55] Those who are "obsessed by the need of protecting some private possession of belief and taste," he explains, "will remain hampered by fear lest something old and precious be destroyed," unable to become harbingers of the new, as Dewey believed modern intellectuals should be.[56] For the "method of democracy," Dewey believed, finally relied on an intellectual capacity for self-criticism and an embrace of novel, pragmatic experiment—a method he saw as modeled by aesthetic experience. "Intelligence in politics," Dewey insists, "means reliance upon symbols."[57] Despite differences in their disciplinary orientations and personal values, intellectuals such as Veblen, Lippmann, Mumford, Burke, and Dewey all helped undermine the symbolic authority of possessive individualism. By reframing possession as a political problem rather than an axiomatic right, these figures rewrote the status of a term permeating classical liberalism's economic, social, and political discourse. In the process, this reflexive intellectual effort helped introduce *liberalism* into American life as a term signifying the desire for some third way between Communist planning and laissez-faire individualism, as this book's introduction has related. With *The Unpossessed*, Slesinger continues the intellectual project introduced by these liberal critics: to reflect, alter, and replace the symbols that structure our aesthetic engagement with politics. As we have already begun to see, however, Slesinger's novel does not limit its interest in possessive relations to those issues of social class and property preoccupying her male peers. Recognizing and investigating the ways that possessive individualism also structures gender and sexual politics, *The Unpossessed* further explores the problems posed to liberal thought by the pregnant female body.

Wombs or Women?

> Women are discovering what reformers of all kinds are learning, that there is a great gap between the overthrow of authority and the creation of a substitute. That gap is called liberalism: a period of drift and doubt. We are in it to-day.
>
> —Walter Lippmann, *Drift and Mastery* (1914)

> I don't expect to be in the room or will I do anything to prevent you from obtaining a contraceptive. . . . However, once a child does exist in your womb, I'm not going to assume a right to kill it just because the child's host (some refer to them as mothers) doesn't want it.
>
> —Steve Martin, State Senator (R) Virginia (2014)

Before it became the closing chapter of *The Unpossessed*, "Missis Flinders" (1932) was published in *Story* magazine. It opens on the threshold of a New York City hospital, with a scene unavailable to American fiction ten years earlier and which will be impossible to restage ten years later. A nurse, Miss Kane, offers a brief focal point for introducing Mrs. Flinders, and her recent operation, after which this figure of institutional medicine disappears from the narrative. With her single hypotactic sentence, punctuated by short breaths, and ending with a subject coldly yet emphatically "dismissed . . . from her mind," the nurse's brief passage formally anticipates our knowledge of Margaret Flinders's terminated pregnancy:

> "Home you go!" Miss Kane, nodding, in her white nurse's dress, stood for a moment—she would catch a breath of air—in the hospital door; "and thank you again for the stockings, you needn't have bothered"—drew a sharp breath and turning, dismissed Missis Flinders from the hospital, smiling, dismissed her forever from her mind. (291)

Although Margaret's subsequent first-person narrative will take several pages to build up to the word *abortion*, revealing the dramatic irony of this opening scene, Miss Kane's appearance and retreat from the story preemptively models this medical procedure as a brief, impersonal effort, ending in simple and lasting absence. This model, of course, proves untenable. As Margaret and her husband, Miles, ride home, they fill the car with spiteful dialogue, fragmented memories, and growing resentment about the basket of fruit that Miles has offered his wife as a woefully misguided symbol of reconciliation.

As with other abortion narratives that began appearing in American fiction during the 1910s and 1920s, "Missis Flinders" opens *in media res* and explores the enduring psychological effects of a dangerous and illegal procedure on all those involved.[58] Nurse Kane's brief presence in "Missis Flinders," however, fixes this story at a distinct moment in the turbulent history of reproductive reform and repression in the United States. Even for an upper-middle-class white woman like Margaret, access to hospitals, nurses, and practicing physicians for a therapeutic abortion was impossible until the Great Depression, when the national economic crisis enabled reformers to recode a controversial issue in women's rights into a matter concerning the "needs of the family."[59] Antiabortion backlash would stamp out this brief era of tolerance within a decade, explains Leslie Reagan in her study, *When Abortion Was a Crime*, yet "the structural transformation that occurred during the 1930s" represented "the first time . . . physicians acknowledged that social conditions were an essential component of medical judgment in therapeutic abortion cases," conceding the broad benefits of relocating abortion from illicit and unsupervised private sites to publicly sanctioned medical institutions.[60]

Abortion's heightened visibility as a medical practice and political issue produced competing representational responses in the divided literary field of the 1930s. Meg Gillette argues that sentimental middlebrow writing depicted abortion as a moral deviancy requiring corrective emotional protocols, while a few radical feminist writers cast it as an issue tied to systemic class and gender inequalities; for modernists, Gillette contends, abortion was strictly a "rhetorical" problem: in stories such as Ernest Hemingway's iconic "Hills like White Elephants," men and women "lack a literary language to talk about babies."[61] This tripartite schema reproduces a familiar set of conceits about the politics of aesthetics in the 1930s, wherein modernism's stylized, reflexive ironies are presumed to be apolitical, removed from the material concerns of contemporary life and law with which middlebrow and radical women writers were each more intimately concerned.[62] By the time Slesinger repurposed "Missis Flinders" as the final chapter of her novel, however, she had indeed found a "literary language" for talking about babies, and about reproductive politics, in the concept of "possession" circulating widely through intellectual writing at this time. While critics have long described Slesinger's use of abortion as "a trope for loss and failed promise," this chapter argues that her novel's emphasis on lack, equivocation, and negativity function as essential components of a modernist critical praxis.[63] Other scholars have considered how realist literature of the 1930s instructed women about the methods and dangers of contemporary abortion practices or indexed this era's biopolitical fears about controlling and mixing racial populations; this section rather shows how Slesinger's novel anticipates the conceptual tensions, inherited from liberal political theory, which have continued to divide legal arguments over abortion during the last half century.[64]

As Walter Lippmann watched liberalism drift amid the corporate restructuring of ownership, he drew hope from the possibility that traditional gender roles, upheld by bourgeois property relations, might also dissolve. Rather than have women fight for entry into a socially corrosive capitalist marketplace, Lippmann in 1914 believed a nascent feminism might champion "a sense of social property," a cooperative rather than self-interested approach to collective ownership, which he saw as "the real antidote to acquisitiveness."[65] Over the next hundred years, feminism made enormous strides, yet the "sense of absolute possession" Lippmann hoped it might help combat has proved an intractable conceptual obstacle.[66] State Senator Martin's remarks on the difference between contraception and abortion illustrate how contemporary political discourse on reproductive rights remains locked within the logic of possessive individualism from the popular to the federal level. Martin implies that regulating contraceptives would require an impermissible interference with the marketplace, and yet he insists to his presumed audience of women that, "once a child does exist in your womb," you do not have "a right to kill it." Each step in Martin's reasoning reveals his assumption that one individual lives within the body of another: he replaces the fetus with "a child," gestation and development with what categorically "exists," and the creation of new life with the "right to kill." Martin concludes this performance by insisting that what "some call . . . mothers" are merely "hosts," defined by their wombs.[67] Despite his callous phrasing—which sounds like that of a sci-fi villain—Martin here offers a long-standing, indeed a classical liberal argument, depicting the fetus as a self-possessing individual with rights grounded in the ownership of its own body. This defense of one liberal subject's bodily integrity, however, irrevocably sacrifices that of another: protecting this purportedly self-possessing fetus requires alienating the mother from her body, from her own foundational self-possession as a subject. Possessive individualism cannot explain or protect the physical integrity of two individuals apparently located in one body.

The question of abortion exposes a friction between abstract notions of rights and the embodied differences of gender, which feminist theorists have identified as not incidental or local but rather congenital to liberalism's political grammar. Carole Pateman famously traces a "sexual contract" back to the origins of liberal thought in Locke. In the "standard reading of the theoretical battle in the seventeenth century between the patriarchalists and social contract theorists," she explains, Locke and his peers emerged victorious by arguing "that contract was the genesis of political right" rather than paternal authority.[68] But, in fact, "contract theorists had no wish to challenge the original patriarchal right," that is, the "sex-right or conjugal right" of the husband. So "they incorporated conjugal right into their theories and, in so doing, transformed the law of male sex-right into its modern contractual form," exemplified by the institution of marriage, which historically subsumed a woman's legal subjectivity within her husband.[69] As the grammar justifying social contracts between individuals, indeed justifying the existence of civil society and the state, possessive individualism remained conditioned upon and defined by this unstated sexual contract. The rights to free markets and choices for classical liberal subjects (men) depended on in practice, and yet erased in theory, the needs maintained by (women) ensuring family structure and reproduction. Admittedly, as Wendy Brown notes, in modern western societies "women are no longer required to enter a sexual contract—subordination in marriage—for survival or social recognition," and "liberal political orders no longer need refer to an imaginary social contract for their legitimacy."[70] Yet the "gender subordination Pateman identifies as historically installed in the sexual-social contract," Brown explains, has endured in the "*terms* of liberal discourse that configure and organize liberal jurisprudence, public policy, and popular consciousness," terms that "depend upon their implicit opposition to a subject and set of activities marked 'feminine.'"[71] Liberalism's constitutive dualisms—public/private, liberty/necessity, equality/difference—are constitutively gendered.[72]

While the abortion debate typically gets depicted "as a battle between opposed ideologies—one conservative and one liberal," remarks Pamela Haag—this discourse in fact represents "a battle between two strains of the same liberal values" or, rather, two attempts to interpret the constitutive dualisms that structure the theory of possessive individualism.[73] Whereas "pro-choice" advocates seek to be freed from the "physical constraints of the female body" and allowed "to share the voluntarist premises of liberal freedom with men," explains Brown, "pro-life" critics argue that a woman "necessarily loses this liberty when her body's 'natural processes' take over, when she is *taken over* by her nature, by nature, by necessity, by another."[74] Those defending a woman's right to "choose" and those defending the so-called unborn provide incompatible interpretations of individual self-possession; according to each camp, their opponents sacrifice the rights of one subject to protect those of another. Pro-life activists have systematically curtailed access to abortion across the United States not simply because they are better funded and better organized than their counterparts—though both are true—but because liberals remain unable to demarcate and defend rights within the pregnant female body without recourse to the same logic marshaled by their opponents.[75]

As Mary Poovey explains, the "two most common defenses currently advanced in support of legal abortion," the right to privacy and the claim to gender equality, each appeal to the Fourteenth Amendment's equal protection clause and a legal subject possessing individual rights.[76] The argument for bodily privacy, upon which *Roe v. Wade* (1973) was precariously built, rests on the notion of a "personal, intimate, autonomous, particular, individual," a liberal ideal, which, as Catherine MacKinnon puts it, comprises "everything that feminism reveals women have never been allowed to be or to have."[77] Moreover, once it becomes an object for debate in the legal public sphere, the "private body" can have some of its rights weighed against others, becoming, as Hyde puts it, a permeable fiction into which an aggressive (masculine) state will seek to "intrude."[78] The argument for equality, in turn, reifies gender as an implicitly heterosexual, biological difference, making it a fixed, individual possession, an either-or category once again legible for intervention—a dangerous precedent for those concerned with state efforts to regulate sex and gender identities. Either defense, in sum, asks women to adopt the classical liberal categories that have historically and conceptually constrained them, to become possessive individuals. This leaves progressives in the pro-choice camp trapped within the same logic that the pro-life camp deploys to defend the self-possession of an "unborn" individual, two sides holding inverse positions within one antinomous logic.[79] Despite the pragmatic compromise offered in *Roe*, possessive individualism has not contributed to the debate between pro-life and pro-choice camps a decisive interpretation of rights but a structuring contradiction.[80] Abortion has become an impassable limit case for possessive individualism, an ongoing social practice whose political illegibility reveals an aporia within classical liberal theory. When two individuals contentiously possess one body, this theory necessarily comes asunder.[81]

This aporia explains the peculiar imaginary work so often performed by the "womb," an overdetermined space, which, as Slesinger recognized, frequently gets figured as inside the woman's private body and yet subject to public discourse. As Miles, Margaret, and their friends mingle, Bruno quips that "male writers lay too much stress on women's secondary parts. The point about a woman, the salient point . . . is her womb."[82] Bruno makes womb a synecdoche for woman: the part that invokes her meaningful w/hole. This kind of conceit, suggests Drucilla Cornell, "thwarts the projection of bodily integration and places the woman's body in the hands and imaginings of others who would deny her coherence by separating her womb from her self."[83] As an "imaginary projection" located inside the woman, a container over which she does not have dominion, the womb makes women "transparent," a permeable body gazed on and regulated by the public sphere—that is, by men, law, the state.[84] Looking to build on Bruno's theme, Jeffrey literalizes the equivalence between a woman's value and her capacity to reproduce: "'Sure,' Jeffrey said; 'and by and large the better the woman the bigger the womb.' And Norah's, he thought, proud, affectionate, must be the size of Jonah's whale."[85] Although Jeffrey feels "affectionate" as he develops this comparison, his biblical reference transforms Norah's womb from a compartment for "hosting" babies into a man-swallowing behemoth, less the biological site for generating new life than a mythical enclave in which the doubter must confront his faith. Male intellectuals in *The Unpossessed*, though critical of property and class relations, revert to possessive insecurities over the female body when questions of reproduction arise, turning women, as Jeffrey's daydream makes clear, into their private property: "wombs, not souls—that's what women have, that's what Norah has. A lovely, brown—a great big comfortable home-like womb, a one-room womb; with room for me."[86] Jeffrey's possessive claim on Norah's body evicts her individuality, her very soul, and leaves his erstwhile partner little more than an apartment where he sometimes spends the night.[87]

Still hiding her pregnancy at this point, Margaret Flinders shows noticeable interest in this talk of wombs and women. Miles, taken aback, "eyed Margaret with resentment; covertly; with suspicion." Slesinger's free indirect discourse captures his surprise at realizing that the group's discussion pertains to his wife: "A womb (unpleasant thought!). She had never told him she possessed one. Was that where women went and sat, to brood, to count their injuries? Miles vaguely hated her." What does it mean for Miles to resent that Margaret "never told him she possessed" a womb? He can hardly need his wife to provide an anatomical inventory. This hyperbolic response rather emphasizes an anxiety in knowing Margaret possessed something independent of his control. Whereas Jeffrey imagines Norah's womb as a place for him to take shelter, Miles envisions the womb as a site of absolute female privacy, a room from which he is restricted entry—a womb of one's own. Margaret, without hearing Miles's internal fears, implicitly confirms them when she speaks up among the group, suggesting that all men must experience a comparative bodily lack: "'I think,' said Margaret slowly, 'that that's what men are scared of—what they haven't got.'"[88] Men pursue what they lack and yet fear it, an insight describing Bruno and his magazine as accurately as the marriage of Miles and Margaret. Like his male friends, Miles recognizes gender difference as part of his heterosexual male desire, where women are objects to be possessed. But he fears the womb as property of the female body, a space of interiority where women might "brood"—a word neatly collapsing reflection and reproduction, dual forms of labor possible for the intellectual woman. Sexual difference and psychological interiority overlap in Slesinger's modernist rendering of the womb, with this image of a self-possessing, intellectual female body troubling the relentlessly equivocal desire for and refusal of possession characterizing her novel's male intellectuals.

Throughout *The Unpossessed*, Slesinger subjects Bruno, Jeffrey, and Miles to such moments of irony, exposing how their anxiety over proprietary relations at once ignores and presumes the gendered labor of the female body. Her novel's aesthetic critique thereby extends beyond the analyses of property relations offered by contemporary liberal intellectuals, toward the insights of later feminist critical theory. When Bruno, arguing with the student radicals that he calls his Black Sheep, insists that an upcoming Hunger March must not be the extent of their group's political goals, his argument seems rather banal; yet his phrasing and recollections inadvertently turn this didactic moment into a striking tale of gendered intellectual genesis:

> "But the fight for full bellies—that can't mean everything to *us*; we come of a long and honorable line of full bellies—most of us," he added; "and we know damn well it's not enough; it's not the final object of the game." He thought with repugnance and pain of his father; reared in poverty and piety, his father had come to America to fight for a full belly for his family—and in the fight had dropped the piety along with poverty, in favor of a paunch: for himself, to pass on generously to his son. His father had turned from Jehovah to Mammon.[89]

A godlike father passes a "paunch" down to his son, a belly that testifies to the ease with which an escape from poverty can become an escape into luxury. But the novel's incessant talk of reproductive bodies makes it impossible not to have Bruno's class-conscious meditations on "full bellies" also invoke those pregnant women from which more than just "most of us" come. The ironic gap between Bruno's intended meaning and the effects of his figurative language calls attention to the erasure of women and their reproductive labor from this patrilineal narrative. Bruno's cautionary tale about the "fight for full bellies" ends up serving as a reminder of how consistently this gendered labor has been withheld from accounts describing the genesis of liberalism's public political sphere. Locke famously insisted that each (presumptively masculine) individual owns the "*Labour* of his Body, and the *Work* of his Hands."[90] This enabling premise for possessive individualism, however, depended on invisibly submitting the gendered reproductive labor of *her* body to male control. For Locke, explain Lorenne Clark and Lynda Lange, "The role of women is to bear men's children; the price of bearing children is loss of autonomy with respect to the acquisition, ownership, and control of property."[91] Bruno's speech at once performs Locke's patriarchal logic while also betraying its erasure of a gendered reproductive labor: "For that all bellies, being created equal, should be equally full, was an axiom; it needed no more thought."[92] And yet, by concluding with an abortion, *The Unpossessed* precisely negates this sentiment, suggesting that perhaps not all bellies "should be equally full," and insisting that we must give "more thought" to when and why this may be the case. Slesinger's narrative irony performs what feminist scholars would later insist: embodied sexual difference belies classical liberalism's axiomatic, genderless equality.

This critical negativity clarifies why the novel's final chapter, "Missis Flinders," focuses on Margaret's reaction to her abortion, without representing her and Miles arriving at the decision. Such a dialogue might frame the procedure as a choice, an agreement reached between classical liberal agents. Instead, the distance between thought and action in this final chapter emphasizes Margaret's unstable sense of self as she looks back on the hospital visit, her thoughts alternating between cold restatement and corrosive resentment, her narrative punctured by memories and unconscious verbal associations. Although this mode of representation—at once limited and overdetermined—must qualify any absolute claim about her motive for the abortion, Margaret and Miles have clearly evaluated the procedure from the standpoint of their identity as intellectuals. Margaret's thoughts draw directly from Bruno's speech about his "unpossessed, unpossessing" friends at the fundraiser: "intellectuals they were, bastards, changelings . . . giving up a baby for economic freedom which meant that two of them would work in offices instead of one of them only, giving up a baby for intellectual freedom which meant that they smoked their cigarettes bitterly and looked out of the windows of a taxi onto streets and people and hate them all" (296).

"By intellectuality are we freed," echoes Trilling, "from the thralldom of the familial commonplace, from the materiality and concreteness by which it exists, the hardness of cash and the hardness of getting it."[93] Miles and Margaret are defined by an equivocal relationship to bourgeois life and its possessive impulses—sustained by material wealth, yet opposed to the system that produces it; they recognize that having a child would inevitably lead them to labor and live like other middle-class Americans, with no time for "working out schemes for each other and the world," all their energy "concentrate[d] on the sordid business of keeping three people alive, one of whom would be a burden and an expense for twenty years" (300). As Margaret recollects it, "in a régime like this, Miles said, it is a terrible thing to have a baby—it means the end of independent thought and the turning of everything into a scheme for making money" (300). A child would make Miles and Margaret possessive individuals once again, and, inasmuch as the novel provides access to their motive, it seems they have justified the abortion as an attempt to preserve their social identity as intellectuals against this lapse into possessive behavior. The novel concludes with Mr. and Mrs. Flinders returning to their home: a property rented rather than owned, poised between high and low New York classes, which keeps them away from "both life of the Fifth Avenue variety, and life of the common, or Fourteenth Street, variety" (305). The lives they have refused define them.

Judith Butler has recently called for an embittered and embattled Left to "reclaim life," a call meant to transcend the fractious debate over abortion that has emerged since *Roe v. Wade* by eschewing the question of "where life begins and ends" for a relational account of "what makes life livable."[94] Butler, in other words, aspires to rehabilitate liberalism's foundational premise of equal protection by abandoning its dominant account of self-possessed subjectivity. But liberalism's aporetic logic of possession remains an intractable conceptual problem in this project. In a dialogue entitled *Dispossession: The Performative in the Political*, Butler and Athena Athanasiou trace a disconcertingly "aporetic" concept of "dispossession" through their shared theoretical commitments. On the one hand, they propose, dispossession names the vulnerability that comes with one's social, psychic, and bodily exposure to difference. They praise the notion of "dispossessed subjectivity" as a replacement for classical liberalism's notion of the self-possessed individual, challenging "the autonomous and impermeable self-sufficiency of the liberal subject through its injurious yet enabling fundamental dependency and relationality."[95] However, "dispossession" also names the "processes and ideologies by which persons are disowned and abjected by normative and normalizing powers."[96] Besides capturing an internal self-difference, "dispossessed subjects" clearly also refers to those materially deprived of land, loved ones, and bodily integrity. Butler and Athanasiou therefore face an equivocal task: how to protest this dispossession of populations, territory, and livelihood without "re-establish[ing] possession and property as the primary prerogatives of self-authoring personhood."[97] Although they rephrase and resituate their problem, "how to think about dispossession outside of the logic of possession (as a hallmark of modernity, liberalism, and humanism)," with consistent rigor over the next two hundred pages, the competing valences of *Dispossession*'s central concept remain fundamentally unreconciled.[98] As political subjects, it seems that we must remain at once constitutively and problematically dispossessed.

In the ongoing struggle to protect women's reproductive rights, some feminist theorists, such as Butler and Poovey, maintain hope that "we will be able to develop another set of arguments" outside of possessive individualism and its "metaphysics of substance."[99] For Barbara Johnson, however, the aporia structuring debates over abortion marks it as a truly political question: "It is often said, in literary-theoretical circles, that to focus on undecidability is to be apolitical. Everything I have read about the abortion controversy in its present form in the United States leads me to suspect that, on the contrary, the undecidable *is* the political. There is politics precisely because there is undecidability."[100] In a striking note to her essay on abortion, Johnson anticipates a predictable attack on this position as "liberal" and attempts to recuperate this pejorative label. Insisting that a "*liberal* is someone who stands *for* something that will ultimately put in question what s/he is standing *on*," Johnson identifies liberalism with a form of interpretive practice that links her poststructuralism to the thinking of early twentieth-century figures such as Burke.[101] Johnson's liberal, like Burke's "spiritually dispossessed" intellectual, exposes the conceptual foundations of her own socioeconomic position and its attendant values. If the story of modern American liberalism, as this book proposes, is that of a classical political discourse encountering its internal contradictions, Burke and Johnson might agree that liberals are those who pursue and expose these conceptual aporias, revealing how they structure the terms of popular debate and constrain embodied social practices.

This chapter has situated *The Unpossessed* as a vital point in liberalism's long intellectual engagement with the concept of possession. Slesinger's modernist novel, too long marginalized as a representative for the failures of the 1930s, in fact represents an unacknowledged intermediary between a generation of liberal intellectuals in the United States and more recent feminist critical theories. In the intervening years, feminist writers notably returned to the novel as a form suited to explore liberalism's possessive relations, the proprietary logic that continues to bind physical ownership, gender inequality, and sexual rights. In *Possessions* (1998), for instance, Julia Kristeva transposes her work on semiotics and psychoanalysis into fictional form. Her narrator, Stephanie Delacour—feminist detective, erudite journalist, and sounding board for Kristeva's musings—obsessively deploys versions of the term *possession* to describe not just the ownership of computers and paintings but also the complex network of family ties, sexual relations, and psychological neuroses texturing a murder mystery that remains suitably overdetermined. With her ruminative science fiction novel *The Dispossessed* (1974), in turn, Ursula K. LeGuin juxtaposes the "proprietarian" capitalists of a planet named Urras with the group of revolutionary anarchists relocated to its orbital twin, Anarres. LeGuin's story stages an ambivalent experiment in the competing appeal of "possessive" and "non-possessive" worldviews for the modern intellectual, as Shevek, an anarchist physicist who returns to Urras, finds himself tempted by luxury commodities and proprietary sexual relations. From Thorstein Veblen to Wendy Brown, through these feminist novels, writers interrogating possessive individualism reveal a common conviction: to expose and confront the tensions within liberalism's central values by providing an aesthetic experience of the lived contradictions they produce. Despite all their differences, the genealogy of intellectuals mapped in this chapter has consistently sought to expose American liberalism's intractable terms of possession, and in so doing, to undermine the privilege, violence, and exclusion they enable.

Modernism's Party Politics

In his essay "Commitment," Theodor Adorno defends an aesthetic politics rooted not in issuing programs but in adjusting attitudes: "Committed art in the proper sense is not intended to generate ameliorative measures, legislative acts or practical institutions—like earlier propagandist plays against syphilis, duels, abortion laws or borstals—but to work at the level of fundamental attitudes."[102] If "abortion," for Adorno, may code for legislative reform and crude propaganda, and if "Adorno," for some scholars today, may code for modernist aestheticism and political detachment, *The Unpos-*

sessed reconciles such supposed antitheses. Challenging possessive individualism through its ironic negativity, Slesinger's novel reshapes attitudes toward reproductive rights by exposing the aporetic liberal theory within which this ongoing legal and political contest transpires.

In a coy episode, *The Unpossessed* overtly dramatizes modernism's entanglement in the proprietary political struggles preoccupying liberal intellectuals in the 1930s. When Elizabeth Leonard decides to leave Paris and return to her Uncle Bruno in New York, she and her fling Dennis must divide their belongings. As the couple exchange parting banter, they reach an unforeseen impasse, realizing that "there's a book in the way" (99). The book in question is a black-market copy of James Joyce's *Ulysses*, which the couple purchased together and had bound in red leather, and which now sets off yet another ironic proprietary dispute (99). All at once, the two begin to shout, "It's mine . . . mine, mine, mine," eager to establish possession of this rare literary commodity.[103] But the book soon triggers memories of their time together, and the couple swiftly retreat from this possessive impulse, each insisting that the other keep it as a parting token of affection: " 'Take it, take the book, Elizabeth. It's yours, my dearest, my darling, my darling Elizabeth, it's yours.' 'No, yours, Denny, yours please, darling Denny, I am a nasty terrible girl, let it be yours, from me, Denny' " (100). Somewhat absurdly, the two reverse attitudes yet again and resume their contested claims; only now, the return of this proprietary drive generates a curious by-product, a hint of agency on the part of the book itself:

> The book in its fine red binding slipped to the floor as each one gave it to the other.
> "You dropped my book," she said and cried as if her heart would break.
> "You dropped my book," he scolded and his voice shook. "Elizabeth, we can't! Our book! We've only one of everything. Elizabeth! we're lost! we're saved."
> The book looked up hopefully from its ribald red cover. (100)

Between the ebb and flow of possessive drives, modernism comes alive. The fledgling pathetic fallacy in this "hopeful" glance turns into a full-blown anthropomorphism as the scene closes: "The red book that belonged to both of them burst into passionate weeping on the floor as over it they gravely said goodbye" (101). Famous for its sea-green cover, this *Ulysses* in "ribald red" removes the hue of silent, cunning, European exile from Joyce's iconic modernist novel and paints it with "red" questions of communal property and melodramatic sentiment—economic and affective concerns supposedly antithetical, then and now, to modernism's cosmopolitan aesthetic.[104] If admittedly bizarre, this scene in *The Unpossessed* finds a memorable way to color modernist literary production in the 1930s with liberalism's proprietary and gendered problems of possession, problems that defined the lives of Slesinger's contemporary intellectuals.

In the process, this scene identifies the political efficacy of the modernist artwork as rooted in aesthetic experience, with *Ulysses* provoking a series of reactions in Elizabeth and Dennis that expose their underlying possessive drives. After this episode, Elizabeth suggestively reflects on a simple yet trenchant question: "what matters enough to write about?" (118). *The Unpossessed*, as this chapter has shown, answers this query by exposing liberalism's possessive relations, and the way these constrain intellectuals, abortion, and our ability to talk about both. This final section seeks to explain why Slesinger chose to conclude this complex political project, and her own answer to Elizabeth's question, with a ninety-page cocktail party. As Kate McLoughlin's collection, *The Modernist Party* describes in rich detail, parties were an integral part of modernist culture, an important social institution as well as a trope for writers of fiction. Parties were "marriage markets and networking opportunities" for modern artists, a space for mixing and mingling across social boundaries that allowed for "extending patronage, forging creative alliances (and *mésalliances*), sparking productive disagreements and enabling knowledge transfer."[105] Parties also offered authors a dynamic narrative set piece, in which modernism's exploratory stylistic techniques could range across and dissect the preoccupations and behavior of contemporary society, conveniently gathered in one metonymic space.[106] In the final quarter of *The Unpossessed*, Slesinger offers one of the most elaborate, diverse, and immaculately crafted party scenes in Anglophone literature. Yet unlike the genteel precedent set by Woolf and earlier modernists, Slesinger's gathering does not explore the creative impulses of the host, nor does it titillate readers with the interpersonal quips of some famed clique. Refusing to privilege any person or group, Slesinger remakes the party into a space where clashing aesthetic and political values are all exposed to a blanketing narrative irony, a situational correlative for her own modernist intellectual praxis. Her modernist party, in short, models the aesthetic politics required for reading a liberal modernism, attentive always to its internal tensions, and so offers an ideal case study for articulating how this project will treat the ironies of literary form throughout its ensuing chapters.

Rendered in a hectic stream of conscious narrative, this extended party scene unfolds through a series of mistaken identities and pointed juxtapositions. Guests express continued confusion about the fundraiser's cause: it seems held in support for both Bruno's literary magazine as well as a Hunger March underway in Washington, DC. Uncertain of the motive for their meeting, those arriving add a litany of other, mistaken causes to this pair.[107] Our major characters all appear, yet soon recede into a crowd of unfamiliar socialites—the Miss Bee Powells, Mr. Tevanders, and Miss Hobsons of the City—whose self-important, dim-witted chatter fills much of each page. Bruno has procured funding from these elites by using Emmett Middleton's idolatry for him to leverage his wealthy parents into hosting. Al Middleton, owner of a luxury goods store, embraces his role as charitable capitalist with a self-deprecating irony. The two men playfully acknowledge their equivocal arrangement, "taking back with the left hand what the right hand giveth," as one of economic convenience rather than conversion: "I'm not trying to sell the revolution to you," Bruno insists, "The revolution needs the income from the nonessential Middleton Essentials" (163).

Such ironies—sometimes playful, often cruel—preside over Slesinger's party. Besides wanting to drive his son Emmett into activity, Al takes perverse delight in subsidizing the Hunger March with a decadent buffet: "'Remembah our stahving boys, Miss Powell honey.' He pointed to the banners behind the bar and crossed himself with the punchglass and the drumstick. The buffet girls sneered classconsciously" (212). Mocking the fundraiser with his best Boston Brahmin accent, Al angers the undernourished Black Sheep, who labor in angry silence. Slesinger's prose, however, does not pause to pity these poor students, who are all but mute throughout the party. Instead, she exposes the bitter truth behind Al's ironic jibes: "it ain't worth while, howling just for a bowl of soup; it takes caviar to make people really bloodthirsty" (233). Representations of soup kitchens, in liberal documentaries or the pages of a realist novel, might cause a few tears or a little indigestion for the middle class that deigned to look on them during the Depression. But Slesinger's party, with portly socialites devouring caviar as student workers stand in silent hunger, substitutes for complacent sympathy a corrosive irony, and thereby foregrounds a gap between classes within which the reader must find a way to position themselves. As two other guests note, their gathering appears to be a "study in contrasts" (219), like "society psychoanalyzed, all the cross sections exposed as in a tree" (218).

Slesinger's modernist party, in other words, grapples with political life not by endorsing values held by one person or class but through an aesthetic experience of irony.[108] No character steps forward to articulate this project, in some didactic moment that would undermine the message. Yet *The Unpossessed* does implicitly defend this aesthetic politics by negating a competing account of modern art, offered by one Arturo Teresca, composer and conductor for the party's band. His group's name, "Art Terry's Prosperity Boys," captures a lifelong struggle: Arturo has been torn between his desire to fashion immortal works of art, and his desire to heap luxury upon Mary, his wife, who "wore fur coats like a queen, bore him three fine fat sons ... and never knew she was married to that greatest of all tragic figures, a frustrated artist" (209). With but one symphony to his credit, it seems Arturo has chosen to privilege his domestic duties, yet for that he clings all the stronger to an ideology of autonomous, eternal art. Arturo imagines his entire life redeemed by the immutable virtue of a lone masterpiece:

> What man was a failure, thought Arturo strongly (the whiskey was good; the crowd was excellent) who had even one symphony to his credit? It might go unpublished; it might be played only at parties where no one listened to it; but it was music, it was eternal, it added to the sum total of beautiful music, to the unheard vibrating stream of perpetual music that surrounded the world, that would one day subdue the world to all its concerted rhythm. (226)

These musings, which read like a bad translation of Schiller, kindle Arturo's confidence, and he gathers his band to play "The Symphony," a prideful singular with which "he always referred" to his opus (227). Arturo believes in art as a universal formal achievement, an aesthetic ideology that has long been cited as modernism's creed, whether by its champions or detractors, by Clement Greenberg or Fredric Jameson.[109] Slesinger, however, handily dismisses this aesthetic ideology by subjecting Arturo's "Symphony" to a series of misrecognitions. After listening to the first few bars, Miss Hobson fires the opening shot: "Beethoven, isn't it?" (227). Causing Mr. Terrill to suggest "it's possible it's Brahms" (230) and, later, "Bach, perhaps?" (232). Unfortunately for Arturo, these guesses say less about his "Symphony" than about its audience; few admirers of classical music would mistake Bach's baroque arrangements with Brahms's high romanticism. By having the crowd grossly misrecognize Arturo's "Symphony," attributing it to the most revered of composers, the "Three Bs," Slesinger dissolves his vision of a transcendent, eternal artwork in the harsh tonic of an ignorant modern audience and its canons of fame.

Through these metafictional reflections on aesthetic experience, *The Un-*

possessed defines an art object not by its isolated moment of production, but by its social reception, by the effect it has on those who encounter it—a definition Dewey would have affirmed. Just as Arturo admits to himself that "he never played The Symphony without a faint belief that at its end some connoisseur would recognize it," someone taps him on the shoulder to make a special request (250). Mr. and Mrs. Ballister, privileged even among this privileged crowd, have arrived with fashionable tardiness, and an admirer wants to usher them in with some "old New York songs, you know, 1890 vintage" (250). Arturo obliges, cutting short his masterpiece, and leading The Prosperity Boys into an 1892 classic: "Af-*ter* the Ball was o-over" (250). The irony of Arturo conducting this particular Charles K. Harris hit is polyvalent and excoriating. "After the Ball was Over" of course puns upon the name of the "Ball-is-ters," and, unlike the Three B's to whom Arturo's Symphony gets falsely attributed, the crowd recognizes this Fourth B at once: when Merle Middleton hears the opening bars from the library upstairs, she immediately recognizes that "The Ballisters must have come" (252). Harris's track, moreover, was also an immensely popular single, the "nation's first certified million-seller," helping to spark Tin Pan Alley's growth by proving to record labels that they could sell sheet music en masse to middle-class Americans.[110] By having this stranger's request invoke at once restricted and mass cultural consumption, Slesinger dismisses the idea that art lives outside or beyond its reception, preserved in some ideal realm free from audiences; she locates art's import not in transcending the social but precisely in its audience's aesthetic response.[111] Lest readers miss the point, Mr. Terrill adds a parting shot at Arturo's "Symphony": "Thank God for that . . . I never really cared for Debussy anyhow" (250). Negating Arturo's aesthetic ideology, much as it negated Bruno's patriarchal speech on "full bellies," *The Unpossessed* forces readers to encounter the structuring tensions of modern political and artistic life through an aesthetic experience of irony.

For this reason, Slesinger's novel cannot be said to back any political party—such entities being corporations par excellence, which have historically claimed greater and greater representative power while also gradually eroding the authority of their public constituencies. Rather than encapsulate her values into any one privileged person, Slesinger embraces the modernist party's capacity for tension and irony, modeling the experience of politics as a contest structured by conflicts and failures rather than by centralized control. In a similar spirit, this book approaches "liberalism" not as one pre-given set of values or institutions but rather as constituted by a series of conceptual tensions and a historically developing discourse among intellectuals, which often merits attention for its ironies as much as its insights. Bruno Leonard's climactic speech, which claims for his intellectual friends the title of "unpossessed and unpossessing," comes at midnight, after the dusky hour when G. W. F. Hegel once said the Owl of Minerva should have flown, wisdom arriving with time's passing. But in *The Unpossessed*, as Mrs. Stanhope informs Mr. Merriwell, "you wouldn't know Minerva, G.F. . . . She's the Stable's Sunday School nag," a "blind-in-one-eye, spavined, consumptive creature with a rotten gallop like a Ford" (229-30).

Playing on Hegel's image of philosophy as the belated knowledge of an era, Slesinger's relentless irony suggest that a "spavined" and "consumptive" insight must fill the space between the ideal and the real—that the intellectual's embodied experience of struggle and inadequacy is precisely where wisdom, "blind-in-one-eye," must be found. As John Dewey had argued, whatever shape philosophy takes, it must speak "the authentic idiom of an enduring and dominating corporate experience."[112] Slesinger's party politics prevents readers from identifying with any position in its conflicted social field and thereby turns the act of reading into a search for the concepts that structure this contest of values—concepts such as "possession," which, as this chapter has shown, played a vital role in the evolving structure of liberal thought. Slesinger's novel cannot simply be labeled a "liberal text," if by this one means "written by a self-professed liberal" or "written to convey a liberal agenda." But like Burke's rhetorical criticism, and Johnson's poststructuralism, Slesinger's modernism prescribes and performs an intellectual project of interrogating liberalism's central concepts, revealing a corporate experience that complicates these classical abstractions and undermining the attitudes that sustain them.

After the Party

Only a few months after *The Unpossessed* appeared, Slesinger published a short story entitled "After the Party" in the *New Yorker*, which recapitulated many of her novel's interests: political unrest in the 1930s, "possession" as a figure troubling class and gender relations, and the party as a narrative space for channeling this social uncertainty into self-critique. But "After the Party" also dramatizes the reception of a certain book called "The Undecided." By inscribing her own novel back into the possessive drives it investigates, Slesinger emphasizes how modernist fiction, too, remains trapped by a possessive individualism, its ironic political aesthetic facing a necessarily equivocal fate. Her story focuses on Mrs. Helene Colborne, who "had given three cocktail parties a week in honor of various celebrities, ever since her nervous breakdown back in 1930," a depressive anxiety brought on by her husband converting to Communism.[113] At first, Henry Colborne had only worn "old clothes . . . wouldn't take her to the best places to dine, professed to be ashamed of his father's wealth—and all that," idiosyncrasies Mrs. Colborne finds charming. She saw no problem in his "Socialism," and "thought herself that it was what we were all drifting toward in the long run *anyhow*, the New Deal and the N.R.A. and after all the Republican Party was out, everyone was down on the bankers and about half the brokers had already committed suicide" (24, emphasis in original). Over time, however, Henry grew enamored with the working class, chatting with taxi-drivers and commiserating with a chauffeur who stole from them (23). "Obviously," records the wry narrative voice, "they were headed for disaster" (27). One day, Henry announces with a "mad smile, [that] he was *giving away every cent of money he had in the world*" to the "defense and propaganda organs of—*The Communist Party*" (30, emphasis in original). He explains, with "that supra-rational tone of one completely mad," that "as long as one possessed money, one was primarily concerned with it" (30). To atone for a lifetime of possessive individualism, Henry cedes all his accrued wealth.

As Helene watches her husband, he seems to her "a man utterly *possessed*" (32, emphasis in original). Yet it is Mrs. Colborne who will be visited by spirits after Henry's sudden departure from her life: she begins to see "beggars who continued to point their fingers at her from the walls," her home and mind now possessed by the dispossessed poor, haunted by the veritable specters of Communism (35). Mrs. Colborne's doctor convinces her she must get out of bed and get active; he suggests "dancing, social work, writing a novel, going round the world, being psychoanalyzed, studying economics, endowing a hospital" (37). This pragmatic belief in flexible action rather than firm program echoes the rhetoric of Franklin Delano Roosevelt's new liberalism. In his iconic inaugural address from 1933, in which he assured the American people that "the only thing we have to fear is fear itself," Roosevelt diagnosed their "common difficulties" as "concern[ing], thank God, only material things," and he offered a prescription parallel to Mrs. Colborne's: "This Nation asks for action, and action now."[114] By 1935, as this book's introduction explains, liberalism was emerging around FDR as a political category naming an experimental and, frequently, equivocal struggle to sustain a middle ground between inconceivable alternatives—continued capitalist profiteering, or Communist redistribution. "Happiness," as Roosevelt proclaimed and as Helene's doctor would agree, "lies not in the mere possession of money; it lies in the joy of achievement, in the thrill of creative effort."[115] After discussing plans of action with her physician, Mrs. Colborne decides to "give cocktail parties, and after still more thought and consultation, parties for celebrated writers" (24). This regime yields immediate results, her soirees for "authors of articles in the liberal weeklies" soon recognized as "a regular institution" in New York City (37).

As she scans reviews of recent fiction one day with her friend and secretary Miss Rand, her usual practice for gathering leads, Mrs. Colborne lights upon Ms. Regina Sawyer's book, "The Undecided," a clear analog for Slesinger's own novel. *The Unpossessed* was largely praised in the New York literary scene, yet Slesinger uses these imagined reviews to depict a markedly equivocal response to her book: while Mrs. Colborne reads one write-up noting the novel's "portrayal of New York intelligentsia . . . hmm hmm . . . promising newcomer . . . daring witty penetrating compassionate," Ms. Rand's review calls it a "wordy nightmare . . . hmm hmmm . . . trite dull unimaginative cruel."[116] These blurbs depict "The Undecided" as bound for opposite ends of the market, for mass and restricted fields of consumption that each reviewer describes as undeserved: "Unfortunate that such a book will probably fail to achieve success, read Miss Rand. Will probably sell widely because of specious air of 'truth-telling.' Mrs Colborne wound up" (44). These reviews, picking up where the "Art Terry's Prosperity Boys" episode from *The Unpossessed* left off, each evoke an implied antithesis between a novel's aesthetic impact and its market value, a tension that reappears once again during the party held for Regina. As part of her usual ritual, Mrs. Colborne asks the guest of honor to sign a copy of her book; before doing so, however, "LIttle Miss Regina Sawyer, whose eyes were a trifle blood-shot now with liquor and laughing," decides to reread some of her work (56). Emotions unexpectedly well up in Regina, and she jars the genteel gathering by crying out: "Oh God, I'll never do anything like it again, never, never! It's got everything in it I ever saw or thought or felt . . . Christ, will I ever do anything again? will anything ever mean so much again?" (57). This outburst perhaps evokes Slesinger's pride in completing her first novel, mixed with a (justifiable) fear that this might also be her last. But Slesinger quickly subsumes this affective display back into a governing focus on possessive relations. Having received at last her commemorative signature, Helene departs to look over this literary artifact, which now reads: "To Mrs

Colborne, with my very best wishes, Regina Sawyer, May 7, 1935" (60). As she retreats to her study to file the volume away, Helene reflects that these words are "the very same thing that Henrietta King had written in her 'Preambles and Constitutional'" (60). Whereas Regina's signature triggered for her an intense experience of the artwork's singularity, for Mrs. Colbourne, this written blurb only forms part of her consumptive routine, the book but one more accrued possession, a volume whose signature—which should capture individual autonomy—in fact "the very same" as another in a collection large enough to require its own room.

Only "The Undecided" never reaches its appointed place. As Mrs. Colborne sits down to rest, her last guests departing, she begins to feel a "sudden panic" as everything was "growing still" (61). Assuring herself that she is merely tired, "Mrs. Colborne's head began to shake from side to side, pleading *No, No, No* to all those shadows, to the many lifted fingers that suddenly pressed against her eyelids" (61). Her repressed poor now threaten to return. In this vulnerable moment, "Regina Sawyer's book slipped to the floor as Mrs Colborne turned the other cheek to day, to night, and rose to light the lamp that Henry's mother once had given her" (61-62). The not-quite suppressed political conflict concealed in this story reappears with Henry's name, here fittingly reintroduced to the narrative through an inherited possession. As Mrs. Colborne grasps at this ancestral lamp, however, it causes her to lose her proprietary grip on Regina's novel. When "The Undecided" falls to the floor, it crucially echoes that moment in *The Unpossessed* when *Ulysses* slips from Elizabeth and Denny's grasp, taking on a life of its own. Through this subtle doubling, Slesinger affirms that *The Unpossessed* must share the same dialectical reception as Joyce's masterpiece: modernist novels will inevitably be possessed and treated as property, commodities consumed in the market by collectors like Mrs. Colborne; yet precisely because of the relative autonomy that this status as commodities provides, the modernist artwork can also resist this possessive drive, challenging the values through which it is consumed by subjecting these to its ironic aesthetic form.[117] This internal distance from a world of proprietary individuals appears as these two novels slip from the hands of their owners, a quiet negation in which each visits upon their possessive reception a final moment of dispossession.

2 Racial Liberalism
Native Son and the Problem of "Color-Blind" Law

"In 1936," notes Eric Schickler, "no prominent political observer doubted that Roosevelt was a 'liberal' despite his steadfast refusal to talk about civil rights. By the time Harry Truman assumed the presidency" in 1945, however, "support for civil rights had become a litmus test for liberalism."[1] As Schickler shows in *Racial Realignment: The Transformation of American Liberalism, 1932-1965*, economic liberals gathered around the New Deal gradually fused with a new racial liberalism. Although national party elites would not wholly embrace this racial realignment until later—with the presidential contest between Johnson and Goldwater in 1964 acting as a watershed moment—liberal intellectuals, legal activists, and local politicians began a widespread ideological shift during the late 1930s and early 1940s by linking economic reform with civil rights. This effort was propelled by several key changes in the nation's underlying socio-political landscape: by African American migration creating a potentially decisive source of votes for Northern, liberal Democrats; by Southern Dixiecrats solidifying as an oppositional block to the New Deal; and especially by the rise of a network of activist and Intellectual groups that began to protest what they now saw as "the mutually reinforcing problems of economic and racial inequality."[2] These groups included the Congress of Industrial Organization, which replaced the openly racist American Federation of Labor by connecting support for the labor movement to anti-discrimination policies; the Labor Non-Partisan League, which published congressional voting records on issues such as lynching and labor rights; and the Union for Democratic Action, later Americans for Democratic Action, an influential circle that included figures such as Reinhold Niebuhr and Walter Reuther, who pushed for including civil rights in the platforms of local and national politicians. By "the end of the war," concludes Schickler, "support for civil rights had become a key marker of one's identity as a liberal."[3]

This racial liberalism championed "color-blind" law as a governing political ideal. While the metaphor had first appeared earlier in the nineteenth century, color blindness emerged as a guiding mantra after Justice John Marshall Harlan's famous dissent against the "separate but equal" ruling in *Plessy v. Ferguson* (1896), where he protested that "our Constitution is color-blind, and neither knows nor tolerates classes among citizens."[4] Until "the 1960s," argues legal historian Andrew Kull, "the profoundest claim of those who fought the institution of racial segregation was that the government had no business sorting people by the color of their skin."[5] This racial reform movement began to reshape the contours of American liberalism in the 1940s, when African American civil rights groups such as the NAACP at last found growing support for their quest to overthrow legal segregation. After several smaller legal victories, this race liberal coalition achieved its iconic achievement in 1954 with *Brown v. Board of Education*, which rejected, in Chief Justice Earl Warren's words, an educational system "based on color distinctions."[6] Almost immediately after *Brown*, however, conservative activists began to employ the same logic of color-blind law to oppose efforts at addressing racial inequality in the courtroom. What had been an ideal for racial liberals soon became a weapon in the hands of race reactionaries, who challenged affirmative action policies and undermined anti-discrimination measures on issues from education to housing through the same conceptual architecture that liberals had used to challenge segregation. Whereas midcentury reformers hoped that color blindness might redress racial inequity, this metaphor has become a major obstacle to building social justice, an aporetic legal phrase that conceals liberalism's constitutive tensions between equality and difference, abstract and embodied subjects, rights and needs. As scholars in critical race theory have shown, popular discourse and legal rhetoric on race in the United States gradually sank into a "color-blind racism," which shelters systemic inequalities by barring any judgments based on racial difference as a violation of formal equality.[7]

This chapter returns to racial liberalism's formative years to identify an immanent critique of color-blind law in one its foundational texts: *Native Son* (1940). Released to sensational acclaim in 1940, Richard Wright's novel expressed with brutal honesty the anger and fear that a black man in America could feel when discrimination led to desperation. With sales that "significantly exceeded those of any other black writer in American literary history," *Native Son* became a "mass cultural event," effectively establishing the race novel, or protest novel, as a socially urgent genre and a centerpiece in liberal culture.[8] Race novels and race novel discourse, explains Jodi Melamed, became the preeminent means of introducing white Americans to the realities and consequences of racism, which social scientists were now reframing as a problem rooted in individual prejudice. According to liberal intellectuals, the psychological complexity and emotional intensity of narrative form offered a "privileged tool that white Americans" could "use to get to know difference," a means to help middle-class readers recognize the results of their discrimination.[9] In the 1940s, institutions such as the Carnegie Corporation, the Rockefeller Foundation, and the Julius Rosenwald Fund began subsidizing black writers, along with research studies investigating the damaging social and psychological effects of segregation.[10] Gunnar Myrdal's *An American Dilemma* (1944), the most influential of these studies, helped to redefine racism in the United States as a moral problem, a hypocritical refusal by white Americans to uphold the values of their liberal democracy. Imagining that efforts to redress inequality might begin with fiction readers, and thereafter proceed into law, Myrdal hoped that "the literary product of a Richard Wright will achieve nation-wide publicity and acclaim and affect people as far down as the lower middle classes."[11] And, indeed, because of *Native Son*'s profound influence on social scientists, legal activists, and middle-class readers, Wright's novel has long been cited as the decade's definitive protest novel—a genre usually seen as anathema to modernism— and aligned with the ideals of this emergent racial liberalism.

And yet Wright's novel has also been the subject of perpetual dispute, as readers have offered sharply divided judgments about whether *Native Son* finally emphasizes the social conditions producing black rage or rather affirms Bigger Thomas's individual struggle for self-determination.[12] This tension appeared in the novel's earliest critical reading. When the Book-of-the-Month Club selected *Native Son* as the first work by an African American included in their program—and Wright consented to the deletions they required—Dorothy Canfield Fisher was chosen to write its first introduction. As a noted figure in the literary community and a pioneer in adult education, Fisher helped situate *Native Son* for its first readers as both a creative and a sociological text. According to influential Wright scholar Keneth Kinnamon, however, Fisher's liberal values render her introduction "innocently vapid," as she ends up "offering two opposed interpretations of Bigger."[13] Fisher identifies both an "environmental determinism" in the novel, prompting her to compare Bigger Thomas to a laboratory rat in a passage full of social scientific language, as well as a "spiritual sickness" she identifies with "Dostoeivski."[14] Naturalist fiction and its environmental determinism, Kinnamon suggests, cannot be reconciled with modern individualism and the search for self-identity. These incompatible literary modes produce competing judgments about the novel's protagonist: either Bigger Thomas's actions have been determined by his social environment and biological drives or else they represent a defining struggle for individual self-determination. While dismissed by Kinnamon at the time, these contested literary and political judgments—social conditions or autonomous will, abstract equality or embodied difference—have in fact continued to divide critical discussion of *Native Son* for more than seventy years, suggesting that Fisher's inaugural, liberal equivocation was far from "vapid."[15] Scholars recognizing this enduring interpretive tension have attempted to explain it through Wright's changing personal values, a shift in emphasis from naturalism to existentialism in literary studies and the institutional history of black aesthetics.[16]

Instead, this chapter shows how the divided critical judgments about *Native Son*, and divided political claims about Bigger Thomas, stem from a rhetoric of blindness that envelops the novel. This figurative pattern in the novel grows from a fledgling metaphor into a blanketing ironic negativity, which eventually undermines each character's attempt to form a conclusive judgment about Bigger's actions, and thereby produced nearly a century of contentious critical claims about the novel's political meaning. The first section begins by explaining how *Native Son* helped catalyze American racial liberalism through a shared investment in social psychology. While liberals believed that "color-blind" law could help combat racial prejudice, however, the second section shows how *Native Son* exposes the limitations of this key concept in race liberal thought through its rhetoric of blindness. By dramatizing how blind legal judgment fails to redress individual difference and collective equality—those competing values first identified by Fisher—Wright's novel exposes the aporetic structure of this liberal ideal, an aesthetic critique anticipating later challenges to liberal jurisprudence by scholars in critical race theory. Modern narrative form, as this book continually argues, was ideally suited to show how governing metaphors in the discourse of political liberalism in fact constitute aporias, concealing internal tensions within its conceptual grammar. Much as chapter 1 explained how liberal intellectuals transformed "possessive relations" from a governing value into a structuring problem, this chapter shows how liberal intellectuals made "blindness" into a governing value, only to have this same legal metaphor put in service of opposing ends.[17] By the 1970s, legal reactionaries began using "color-blind" claims to protect structural racism, insisting that equal protection of rights only entails an abstract individual formalism and precludes attention to racial difference. The color-blind law championed by midcentury reformers now constitutes a major conceptual problem in liberal thought, an aporia whose competing meanings emerge from liberalism's constitutive dualisms: Does equality mean formal symmetry or acknowledged social difference? Does it entail abstraction or embodiment? rights or needs? Although Melamed argues that protest novels "unify racial-liberal ideology" by producing readable encounters with difference, reinforcing "a liberal framework of legal rights," the most iconic of all race novels precisely undermines this framework by revealing how blind judgment fails to reconcile equality and difference through the law.[18] Having traced this prescient aesthetic critique of racial liberalism through *Native Son*, the chapter concludes by arguing that it should be positioned within the compass of literary modernism, a novel sharing important points of continuity with those works by James Baldwin and Ralph Ellison against which it is typically contrasted.

Social Psychology and the American Dilemma

With the publication of *Uncle Tom's Children* (1938), Wright seized the attention of white American readers. His collection of stories, which had been supported by the Works Progress Administration, received sweeping acclaim by liberals such as Eleanor Roosevelt, who later backed Wright's application for a Guggenheim Fellowship.[19] But this enthusiastic reception also made Wright realize that he "had written a book which even bankers' daughters could read and weep over and feel good about," and he famously "swore to myself that if I ever wrote another book, no one would weep over it; that it would be so hard and deep that they would have to face it without the consolation of tears."[20] *Native Son* succeeded in shocking Wright's liberal readership by offering a window into black hatred, fear, and alienation unprecedented in American fiction. "Until Bigger Thomas," explains Lawrence Jackson, "never had a black character, let alone the center of consciousness for a serious novel, been allowed to experience unfiltered disdain for and fear of whites."[21] By proving that a literary novel focused on race relations could yield enormous sales, Wright effectively launched the race novel as a genre, and was soon viewed as one of the nation's foremost authorities on African American social psychology. The "Bigger Thomas effect," as Jackson calls it, "stimulated an enormous growth in consciousness in American audiences and publishers."[22] Along with *An American Dilemma*, Myrdal's landmark study, *Native Son* helped to catalyze the formation of a racial liberalism among American intellectuals in the 1940s, which aimed to overthrow de jure segregation and eliminate discrimination, which social scientists now saw as rooted in individual prejudice among whites and as causing psychological harm to blacks. For these reformers, who imagined fighting discrimination first through literary culture, then through law, "People of the State of Illinois v. Bigger Thomas" was widely regarded as having prepared the way for *Brown v. Board of Education*.

This liberal appropriation of *Native Son* hinged on Boris Max, Bigger's attorney, and his extended protest during the novel's climactic trial. In his speeches, Max treats Bigger as an illustrative case of larger sociological conditions, subsuming his individual agency so thoroughly into environmental influences that the attorney's language at times seems to pass from literary naturalism into Social Darwinism. Max begins by insisting that the "complex forces of society have isolated here for us a symbol, a test symbol . . . like a germ stained for examination under the microscope."[23] By studying the biological disease or mutation that produced Bigger Thomas, he implies, the audience might gain some insight into "our whole sick social organism" (383). Treating Bigger's pathological violence not as a cause but as an effect, Max emphasizes the "instinctive nature of these crimes" (377). His client's murderous panic must not be judged under the rubric of individual responsibility, Max insists, but rather as "the case of a man's mistaking a whole race of men as a part of the natural structure of the universe and of his acting toward them accordingly . . . when he feels that he must defend himself against, or adapt himself to, the total natural world in which he lives" (396). Max does not expend any energy defending Bigger against the charges arraigned against him; they enter a guilty plea and only ask that his life be saved. Instead, Max struggles to make a white audience understand Bigger's psychological makeup, to recognize how his actions were shaped by discriminatory social conditions. Generalizing Bigger's case into a model for what afflicts "twelve million Negroes," Max bemoans how African Americans are deprived of "art, science, industry, politics" as "crystallized modes of expression" and suggests that even their religion exists "only in its most primitive form" (399). If sometimes condescending, Max clearly identifies Bigger's life as a symptomatic response to his environment and proposes that, to prevent future Biggers, the white audience attending to this scene must redress discrimination against African Americans as a whole. "Every movement of his body," Max insists, "is an unconscious protest" (400).

Max's liberal credentials have admittedly been the subject of some dispute, as early and influential critics such as Alfred Kazin, Robert Bone, and Irving Howe saw the attorney's speech as a statement issued by Wright on behalf of the Communist Party.[24] Wright had joined the party through the Chicago John Reed Club in 1932 and, after moving to New York in 1937, served as the Harlem editor for the *Daily Worker*. Disillusioned with party leadership, he broke with CPUSA by 1942 and, in 1944, published "I Tried to Be a Communist" in the *Atlantic Monthly*, later included in *The God That Failed* (1949). Critics have debated how to position *Native Son* within this biographic timeline for years, and yet the party's own reviewers were clearly ambivalent at best about Wright's literary and personal politics by 1940.[25] The novel, moreover, clearly identifies Max as a lawyer "from the Labor Defenders," and only the red-baiting prosecutor, Buckley, calls him a communist.[26] As Mark Decker has argued, Max's affiliation with the International Labor Defense rather makes him "representative of an important movement in progressive legal circles."[27] Wright composed *Native Son*, explains Decker, "at the high water mark of the Sociological Jurisprudence and/or Legal Realism movement," which he would have encountered through his mentors and friends at the University of Chicago's Sociology Department, Louis Wirth and Horace Cayton.[28] Building on arguments made by Justice Oliver Wendell Holmes, these progressive activists insisted that the law was not a stable ideal but a constructed and mutable discourse, which judges and lawyers should use as a vehicle for social change. By the 1930s, Decker observes, groups such as the ILD and the National Lawyers Guild had already "built impressive civil-rights credentials by attacking the Ku Klux Klan and fighting in the courts for racial equality and for an end to lynching," one important cluster of a broader racial liberalism taking shape at this time.[29] As Decker and others have noted, the structure of Wright's novel prepares its reader for such a progressive legal argument, offering hundreds of pages of sociological data, followed by Max's extended plea for the judge, jury, and reader to recognize the broader conditions underlying this case.[30]

Native Son's impact on liberals did not simply derive from Max's rhetoric, however, but also from a contemporary transformation in the way that intellectuals in the United States were conceptualizing race. By 1940, study of racial prejudice was replacing earlier biological and eugenic theories of race, which rapidly lost currency as Nazi Germany extended them to their brutal ends. Major volumes in the social sciences, such as Robert Sutherland's *Color, Class, and Personality* (1942), Theodor Adorno's *The Authoritarian Personality* (1950), and Gordon Allport's *The Nature of Prejudice* (1954), would recast race as a concept rooted in individual psychology. As Jay Garcia shows in *Psychology Comes to Harlem*, Wright devoted considerable energy in the 1940s to "exploring both the psychological conditions engendered by Bigger's environment and the unconscious structures of the racist social order."[31] Wright worked closely with the Lefargue Clinic, which offered psychiatric services for Harlem residents, and with the Wiltwyck School for Boys, which helped prevent juvenile delinquency; at these institutions, he collaborated with researchers studying the social psychology of urban black Americans.[32] Thanks to this social work, along with Max's protest in *Native Son*, Wright became "the most influential authority on black rage" in midcentury America.[33] Throughout the 1940s, prominent social scientists such as Kenneth Clark "habitually identified Wright as an expert in psychology" and began to focus on clarifying the psychosocial effects of discrimination, aiming, as Helen McLean from the Chicago Institute of Psychoanalysis put it, "to give validity to Wright's lay analysis."[34] During this decade, social psychologists, educators, and activists like Clark, McLean, and Cayton published essays such as "The Emotional Health of Negroes" and "The Psychological Approach to Race Relations," which followed the path laid out by Max's speech: introducing white Americans to the injurious effects of racial prejudice.[35]

Race novels like *Native Son* and social scientific research were thus widely recognized as mutually reinforcing projects. In his introduction for *Black Metropolis*, a study by Cayton and St. Clair Drake, which revealed racial discrimination to be as prevalent in the urban North as the agrarian South, Wright describes how all three figures had struggled as young men in Chicago, "pushed and pounded by facts much too big for us," until "science" helped him "discove[r] some of the meanings of the environment that battered and taunted me."[36] Later on, Wright explains, he found that "sincere art and honest science were not far apart," and that each could help capture "the environment out of which the Bigger Thomases of our nation come."[37] "If, in reading my novel, *Native Son*," he suggests, "you doubted the reality of Bigger Thomas, then examine the delinquency rates cited in this book."[38] As social scientific work testified to the urban conditions behind Bigger's life, meanwhile a whole generation of African American writers followed upon Wright's literary precedent, with *Native Son* sparking a national enthusiasm for the race novel. Known by a "variety of names," explains Melamed, "including the *sociological novel, problem novel, protest novel, psychological novel,* and *negro novel,*" the race novel emerged as a preeminent mean by which white American liberals could grasp the realities of racial prejudice documented by the social sciences, with more intimate detail and emotional force than any research study could convey.[39] African American novelists—often supported by the same institutions underwriting sociologists, such as the Julius Rosenwald Fund and the Rockefeller Foundation—took up the call to protest en masse, capturing urban poverty, discriminatory practices, and pathological behavior with a gritty narrative realism. Listing only first novels by new black writers seen as working in Wright's naturalist mode, Kinnamon catalogs Carl Offord's *The White Face* (1943), Chester Himes's *If He Hollers Let Him Go* (1945), Curtis Lucas's *Third Ward Newark* (1946), Ann Petry's *The Street* (1946), Alden Bland's *Behold a Cry* (1947), Willard Motley's *Knock on Any Door* (1947), William Gardner Smith's *The Last of the Conquerors* (1948), and Lloyd Brown's *Irony City* (1951).[40]

The racial liberalism coalescing around literary protest and sociological research found its organizing statement of values with the landmark publication of *An American Dilemma* in 1944. Gunnar Myrdal, brought to the United States by the Carnegie Corporation in 1937, had been "one of the architects of the Swedish welfare state," helping establish policies on public housing, reproductive rights, and economic planning.[41] Much as the New Deal had gathered together experts to build proposals for social engineering, Myrdal assembled a team of social scientists to build an authoritative study on race relations, one issue, as Walter Jackson observes, that Franklin Delano Roosevelt's "Brains Trust" had never turned into a "significant policy-oriented" project.[42] Myrdal's final product, seven years and a thousand pages later, "established a liberal orthodoxy on black-white relations and remained the most important study of the race issue until the middle of the 1960s."[43] *An American Dilemma* crucially reframed the "race problem" as a moral failure by white Americans, "an anomaly in the very structure of American society."[44] White Americans believed in the values of their liberal democracy, Myrdal explained, yet individual prejudice prevented them from extending these values to black citizens. Myrdal reaffirmed liberalism's core concepts, such as "abstract equality, individual rights, and market liberties" and, as Melamed observes, moreover defined these as "the substantive content of antiracism," ideals that needed to be reasserted and extended to black Americans.[45] American liberalism had all the necessary conceptual tools to combat racism, in other words, if only personal prejudice could be abated. *American Dilemma* expressed and promoted the era's salient conviction that race relations hinged on individual psychology, as social scientists such as Kenneth Clark, whom Mydal mentored, were concurrently affirming. The book also notably shows the influence of John Dewey, whose *Freedom and Culture* (1939), published as *Dilemma* was being written, argued that all social problems were at root moral problems and that "a contradiction between ideals and actions may produce psychological discomfort and lead to change."[46] Myrdal similarly proposed that black Americans metabolized discrimination into pathological behaviors, while white Americans experienced their moral hypocrisy as a "mental conflict," an internal dissonance between the liberal values they espoused and the illiberal practices they condoned.

Myrdal's ethical argument defined the priorities of racial liberalism in the United States, with his emphasis on moral hypocrisy echoed by prominent liberal intellectuals and politicians for more than a decade. Lionel Trilling, for instance, found in Wright's autobiography *Black Boy* a testament to "moral flaws of the dominant culture."[47] During the Cold War, segregation became a favored target for Soviet propaganda and an enduring embarrassment for American officials, who sought to champion the ethical, political, and economic superiority of liberal democratic capitalism. Even Arthur Schlesinger Jr. paused his polemic in *The Vital Center* to remark that the "sin of racial pride still represents the most basic challenge to the American conscience."[48] Racial liberalism, explains Melamed, made "African American integration within U.S. society and advancement toward equality, defined through a liberal framework of legal rights," a way to further "establish the moral legitimacy of U.S. global leadership."[49] Domestically, no group played a more important role in linking anticommunism to support for civil rights than Americans for Democratic Action, which Schlesinger, along with Reinhold Niebuhr and Eleanor Roosevelt, had helped launch from the pro-civil rights Union for Democratic Action in 1947. As "self-appointed guardian of liberalism," the ADA helped tie progressive racial views to this still fresh political label, most famously by forcing the Truman administration to include civil rights within the Democratic Party's national platform during the 1948 election.[50] A report by the president's newly created Committee on Civil Rights had identified a "pervasive gap between our aims and what we actually do," echoing Myrdal's moral dilemma, and it had called for major civil rights legislation, including regulations against discrimination in housing and transportation, an anti-poll tax law, an antilynching law, a division of the Justice Department devoted to civil rights, and a permanent Fair Employment Practice Committee.[51] With Southern Democrats fighting this proposed legislation, and Henry Wallace's Progressive campaign splitting votes on the left, Truman equivocated and sought to delay any civil rights proposal until after the Democratic Convention. But the ADA "carried the fight to the convention floor," and through pressure on individual representatives convinced party leadership to adopt the program in its entirety; by 1948, concludes Walter Jackson, American liberalism clearly meant racial liberalism, as "Democratic liberals were ready to risk splitting the party" to make civil rights central to their national political platform.[52]

Color-Blind Justice

> That Justice is a blind goddess
> Is a thing to which we blacks are wise.
> Her bondage hides two festering sores
> That once perhaps were eyes.
>
> —Langston Hughes, "Justice"

Because "race liberals . . . came to embrace the historically grounded understanding of white prejudice as a problem that corrupts political institutions and damages the psychological, social, political, or economic standing of African Americans," summarizes Murakawa, their principle objective was to make "institutions race-neutral."[53] Color blindness served as racial liberalism's legal ideal, a standard that might enable protection of the black franchise, equal economic opportunity for laborers and contractors, and desegregation of housing, schools, transportation, and public facilities. By removing any prejudice from institutional and individual judgments, color-blind law promised to resolve the moral hypocrisy at the center of the nation, fulfilling liberalism's promise of equal rights, without any favoritism.[54] When the Supreme Court handed down its unanimous decision in *Brown v. Board* in 1954, the race liberal coalition seemed to have secured a triumph decades in the making. Half a century before, *Plessy* denied that segregation "stamps the colored race with a badge of inferiority," yet Chief Justice Warren's opinion in *Brown* now insisted that the "modern authority" of the social sciences had "amply" demonstrated how segregated schools psychologically damaged black children.[55] In his famous "Footnote 11," Warren suggested that readers "see generally Myrdal, *An American Dilemma*," and cited work by Kenneth Clark, whose professed inspiration from Wright, in turn, "constructed a literary and cultural genealogy for the case that began with *Native Son*."[56] For many observers, *Brown* marked the righteous vindication of an idea extending back even further, an idea proposed by Justice Harlan some seventy years earlier: the US Constitution was "color-blind."

"Color-blindness," relates Kull, first appeared as a legal ideal during the Civil War, when activists like Charles Sumner and Wendell Phillips sought to defend African American rights by invoking this metaphorical demand for constitutional equality. In 1864, Phillips energized the Massachusetts Anti-Slavery Society by calling for a "government color-blind."[57] Later on, Albion Tourgée, the black writer and activist who served as lead counsel for Homer Plessy in 1896, would remark that "Justice is pictured blind . . . and her daughter, the Law, ought at least to be color-blind."[58] Yet it was Justice Harlan's dissenting opinion in *Plessy v. Ferguson* that "gave lasting form to an idea that might not otherwise have survived him."[59] "Our Constitution," wrote Harlan in 1896, "is color-blind, and neither knows nor tolerates classes among citizens," words which now stand as "perhaps the most quoted in Supreme Court history."[60] Though written in dissent for a case which signaled the end of the First Reconstruction and the rise of the Jim Crow South, Harlan preserved a legal concept in the public record and in the minds of liberal reformers, a metaphor that later lawyers and activists fighting for civil rights would enthusiastically embrace as a guiding ideal.

With the rise of a racial liberalism in the 1940s, this "once-radical idea" became "part of the governing liberal consensus of American political life."[61] Serving as a counsel for the NAACP in the 1930s and 1940s, for instance, Thurgood Marshall "repeatedly encouraged his colleagues to cite Harlan's famous injunction, seeking thereby to wield colorblindness against the racial degradation given constitutional sanction by Plessy."[62] The Supreme Court was characteristically slower to reflect this changing social temper, though between 1944 and 1948, Justice Frank Murphy did include the word "racism" in the court's opinions for the first time, protesting discrimination against Japanese Americans by associating such practices with authoritarian violence in Europe.[63] When the appellants in *Brown* submitted their brief, moreover, they directly affirmed an ideal whose discursive force had been growing over recent years: "that the Constitution is color blind is our dedicated belief."[64] After the court's historic ruling, a *New York Times* editorial declared that "not one word in Chief Justice Warren's opinion was inconsistent with the earlier views of Justice Harlan . . . the voice crying in the wilderness finally becomes the expression of a people's will."[65]

As Andrew Kull remarks, however, looking over the language of these two cases reveals "nothing of the sort."[66] If historians sometimes cast Justice Harlan as a lone prophet, awaiting a broader social movement that would turn his ideals into policy with victories like *Brown*, his complete remarks in *Plessy* reveal color-blind law to be less a liberal ideal than a liberal equivocation. Harlan did reject segregation of railway cars as a violation of the formal equality promised by the Fourteenth Amendment's Equal Protection Clause, yet he proposed that undoing this hypocrisy would in fact cement white supremacy in the United States by reaffirming the moral authority of the federal government. "The white race," writes Harlan, "deems itself to be the dominant race in this country. And so it is, in prestige, in achievements, in education, in wealth, and in power. So, I doubt not, it will continue to be for all time, if it remains true to its great heritage and holds fast to the principles of constitutional liberty."[67] Although his dissent "is customarily praised as a glowing affirmation of human rights," Harlan—a former slave owner who had originally opposed the Thirteenth Amendment—did not seek to redress racial inequality so much as limit the scope of judicial practice to formal interpretive protocols.[68] Whereas Myrdal and other race liberals believed that American liberalism's core values, enshrined in the Constitution, were inherently anti-racist, and simply had to dismantle people's prejudice, Harlan, who provided racial liberalism with its watchword, saw the Constitution as expressing rights that would secure white supremacy. Two years later, notes Ian Haney-Lopez, Harlan wrote a majority opinion on behalf of a whites-only high school, supporting the ruling that segregation in education was lawful.[69] Though later racial liberals embraced Harlan's axiom as an instrument for promoting equality, his original argument reveals how color-blind legal judgment represents a conceptual compromise rather than a universal ideal, a metaphor whose abstract equality disguises rather than redresses the tension between individual subjects and racial difference.[70]

While *Native Son* undeniably inspired a generation of racial liberals, the remainder of this section demonstrates how Wright's novel offers a prescient critique of blind legal judgment as a conceptual means of reconciling equality and difference. Readers have long noted that *Native Son* features "a constant play on blindness," mixed in with other imagery based on sight or perception.[71] Many critics have identified this thematic pattern as a didactic lesson in race relations, with Wright hoping to make his white audience aware of their failure to look at urban black life in America.[72] In *Native Son,* however, blindness does not consistently describe one attitude toward race, nor any stable set of values, but rather performs increasingly complex conceptual work as the narrative progresses, evolving from a humble metaphor to a sweeping ironic negativity, and eventually serving as a decisive interpretive framework for the novel's climactic trial. Introduced as a simple descriptor, blindness grows from a trope in Bigger's mind to define the texture of the narrative world, and during the trial scene finally becomes an allegorical figure for the difficulties of judging *Native Son* itself. As Ian Watt once remarked, reading a novel always bears some epistemological resemblance to the jury's role in a court of law; staging Bigger's trial as a finale to the novel effectively forces readers into this juridical register, gathering evidence for three hundred pages and then attempting to form a conclusive judgment.[73] But by the time the novel reaches this courtroom drama, every major character will have been marked by the narrative as "blind" to Bigger's life, in a formal irony that permeates the narrative so thoroughly as to render any final legal or readerly verdict deeply uncertain. Because the same novel that served as a foundational text for racial liberalism ultimately calls into question its defining legal mandate of blind judgment, *Native Son* offers an ideal site to rethink the history of this influential political and legal metaphor.

Though a vocabulary of vision permeates Wright's novel from its first page, when Bigger rubs his eyes against the light flooding his family's room, the word blindness does not appear until his encounter with the "ghostly" Mrs. Dalton, nor does it appear elsewhere in Book I (46). In this single instance—when Bigger realizes "She's blind!"—the word functions only denotatively, a linguistic mark registering Mrs. Dalton's disability (46). After observing the literally blind Mrs. Dalton, Bigger returns home and, turning new eyes upon his family members, fashions a modest metaphor: they, too, seem blind. He feels "in the quiet presence of his mother, brother, and sister a force, inarticulate and unconscious, making for living without thinking, making for peace and habit, making for a hope that blinded" (106). His conceit, crucially, is not about his family's ability to see—a limited sensation—but rather about their ability to understand—a limit on their judgment, their ability to reconcile particular and general. Bigger's metaphorical transmission of blindness from Mrs. Dalton to his family carries with it a realization that reaches across the division between white and black in the novel. Blindness is not merely a failure of empirical faculties, or a racially coded failure of sympathy, but rather expresses Bigger's growing sense that those around him are unable to judge themselves and their social conditions: "there was one way of living they preferred above all others; and they were blind to what did not fit" (106). For Bigger, self-interested and vulnerable, this blindness above all constrains the verdicts that others can form about him and his actions.

In Book II, blindness rapidly develops into the governing metaphor through which the narrative articulates Bigger's isolation from the world around him. Retroactively inscribing Mrs. Dalton within his enlarged figurative understanding of blindness, Bigger reels off a list of "blind" characters: "Jan was blind. Mary had been blind. Mr. Dalton was blind. And Mrs. Dalton was blind; yes, blind in more ways than one. . . . Bigger felt that a lot of people were like Mrs. Dalton, blind" (107). Bigger later adds Buddy to his list of blind figures, the bond between these two brothers apparent in his reluctance to implicate perhaps his truest friend in what Bigger now sees as a ubiquitous condition among those around him. When family, or those who pass for friends, attempt to approach Bigger and interpret his actions, he consistently responds with fear, anger, or apathy, unwilling to accept the roles he represents in their narratives. As Priscilla Ramsey puts it, the interpersonal demands black characters would put upon on Bigger "make him move psychologically further away from all of them. He places a barrier between himself and them so that they cannot know or see him fully. This partial hiding within his own skin becomes his only refuge" (58). Blindness serves as the presiding figure for this barrier, protecting Bigger and yet ironically marking the novel's other characters as unable to properly understand him. This interpretive contingency necessarily inflects the reader as well, watching helplessly and trying to understand as Bigger panics in the Dalton family mansion and accidentally suffocates Mary with a pillow to prevent discovery of his presence in her room.

Long before Bigger's trial in Book III, the narrative world itself has erupted with this pervasive blindness. When Peggy, the Irish cook, turns on the light in the furnace room, it comes on "blindingly bright" (117). Prefigured by the novel's opening page, this scene also points ahead to Bigger burning Mary's body, introducing an overtly tragic emphasis on blinded eyes, picked up again when the "humming fire" appears "blindingly red" (171). Finally, as Bigger walks outside, the narrative depicts "empty buildings with black windows, like blind eyes" (173). Wright's free indirect discourse at times implies that these visions come from an increasingly paranoid Bigger; at times, they also seem the observations of an intermittently present narrative voice, looking on with foreboding. In either case, the effect of this expanded metaphorical usage seems clear: Bigger's isolation has become absolute. Like the people in his life, these buildings encroach on him without recognition or understanding; Bigger no longer distinguishes between the human and inhuman entities around him: "He did not look at them; they were simply blind people, blind like his mother, his brother, his sister, Peggy, Britten, Jan, Mr. Dalton, and the sightless Mrs. Dalton and the quiet empty houses with their black gaping windows" (173). The transformation that this rhetoric of blindness has undergone is remarkable, not only for its acceleration but also in the growing implications it holds for interpreting the novel. A trope initially functioning as a defense mechanism in Bigger's mind now threatens it from without, defining the world that envelops him. After his brief and desperate flight from the law ends in capture, and Bigger stands on trial for murder, it can be none other than this blind world that judges him.

As the inquest begins, *Native Son* overtly allegorizes the notion of colorblind law. When the coroner summons Mrs. Dalton, legally blind mother of the deceased, as a key witness, she appears, at first, to model the classical representation of *Justitia*, who wears a blindfold to signify her impartiality. By removing "the temptation to see the face that comes to the law and put the unique characteristics of the concrete person before the abstract logic of the institution," justice's blindness has long stood as a metaphor promising equal, repeatable, and unbiased judgment.[74] And as the coroner's leading questions progress through Mrs. Dalton's remaining faculties, they appear to circumscribe her blindness as an ideal condition for impartial testimony. In a courtroom full of threats and sobs, Mrs. Dalton moves from sensory input to corresponding judgment without embellishment, calmly explaining her interpretation of the sounds she heard from Mary's room, the touch of Mary's body, and the smell of "alcohol in the room."[75] Because Mary's body has been burned beyond recognition, the deputy coroner asks Mrs. Dalton to confirm the victim's identity through an earring found in the bin below the furnace. "Justice's blindness," explains Martin Jay, sustains "the fiction that each judgment brought before her is a 'case' of something more general, equivalent to other like cases and subsumable under a general principle," and, despite her lone daughter being the victim in question, Mrs. Dalton manages to proceed with a remarkable equanimity.[76] At the same time, however, Mrs. Dalton's name crucially betrays the racialization of this legal ideal. "Daltonism" is a type of colorblindness, named after research by English scientist John Dalton in 1794.[77] To ensure the reliability of Mrs. Dalton's judgment, the faculty on which the court's claim to justice depends, it seems she must be not only blind but also color-blind, a supplementary marker ironically revealing that racial difference extends beyond the visual realm where it is often thought to reside.

Through Mrs. Dalton's apparently color-blind testimony, *Native Son* exposes the gap between removing individual prejudice through formal equality and addressing the material realities of racial difference in midcentury America. Suddenly interrupting their questions about the night of Mary's murder, the state asks Mrs. Dalton to swear that she "bear[s] no ill will toward the Negro people" and, to further reinforce her moral character, prompts her to admit that she and her husband have donated more than five million dollars to "Negro educational institutions."[78] These donations may affirm Mrs. Dalton's goodwill and generosity, yet they also betray the systemic racial inequality making them necessary in the first place. *Native Son*, in other words, dramatizes what critical race theorists would later argue: color-blind law promises to uphold formal equality by barring any individual prejudice, yet in the process refuses to address an underlying socioeconomic inequality, which it thereby preserves. And, indeed, Wright's novel captures just how easily color-blind judgment can slip from a barrier against racial prejudice into a shield protecting white supremacy. Though Bigger's inquest follows Mrs. Dalton's austere judgments, this procedure finally hinges upon her claim upon an inherited possession. Mrs. Dalton identifies the charred earring from the furnace as a "family heirloom," "made to order" and passed down by four generations of Dalton women.[79] With Mary's body burned beyond recognition, the state establishes Bigger's crime as a disruption in the continuity of white property: he has not simply violated the bodily integrity of a woman possessed of individual rights, he has violated a pattern of inherited wealth this white family has carried forward since the days of slavery, a socioeconomic privilege that permits their philanthropy toward impoverished black families.[80] While the liberal Mrs. Dalton may be without prejudice, moreover, the telltale signs of white supremacy unmistakably envelop Bigger's trial: the newspapers describe him as a "jungle beast"; outside the courtroom, a lynch mob curses his name; and the tenements where his family lives continue to crumble. These buildings are controlled by the "South Side Real Estate Company," owned by none other than the racially conscious Daltons, who in fact "*refuse* to rent houses to Negroes if those houses are in other sections of the city."[81] Mrs. Dalton's blindness does not finally ensure racial justice but rather ironically juxtaposes that which the law sees against that to which it remains willfully blind: the white bodies whose property must be protected and the black bodies whose lives remain expendable. When the coroner exposes the "raped and mutilated" body of Bigger's second victim, Bessie Mears, creating an "uproar" among the white crowd, Bigger recognizes how "it would be for the death of the white girl that he would be punished. The black girl was merely 'evidence.'"[82] In this moment at least, Bigger shows himself "wise" to what Langston Hughes called the "festering sores" hiding behind Justice's blindfold.[83]

Although *Native Son* undeniably played a central role in the rise of a racial liberalism devoted to color-blind law in the 1940s and 1950s, Wright's novel contains a troubling critical negativity, an excess of blindness that undermines liberalism's model for legal judgment.[84] As Harlan's dissent revealed, color-blind law has always represented an aporetic concept in liberal jurisprudence, less an ideal for reform than an equivocal metaphor, indexing the challenge of reconciling equality and difference. Carol Horton remarks that the formal equality enshrined by racial liberalism contained "critical blind spots that would, in time, prove enormously problematic," including the racial division of labor markets and labor unions; non-overt discrimination practices in housing, education, and employment; the redistricting and gerrymandering of urban populations; and white backlash against black migrants and those liberals who defended them.[85] These blind spots mar the seemingly heroic ruling in *Brown*.[86] By defining the illegality of school segregation through its psychologically injurious effects on African American children, explains Kull, the Supreme Court "implied that there was nothing wrong with racial segregation in and of itself."[87] Rather than identify segregation as an inherent moral wrong, or construe "equality" as requiring substantive socioeconomic reforms, the Warren Court instead defined the Equal Protection Clause as an abstract formal requirement, the struggle for racial equality as limited to a bar on racial classification, which might dismantle prejudicial institutional arrangements and undo the pathological consequences they produce.

Native Son prepared the way for this ruling in *Brown* by modeling race-liberal discourse in Max's sociological naturalism, his pathologization of black rage, and his condemnation of the moral hypocrisy in white Americans. "Multiply Bigger Thomas twelve million times," the attorney insists, "and you have the psychology of the Negro people ... a separate nation, stunted, stripped, and held captive *within* this nation, devoid of political, social economic, and property rights" (397, emphasis in original). And yet the rhetoric of blindness enveloping Wright's novel finally corrodes Max's race-liberal judgment as well. As his desperation grows, Max invokes the metaphor of blindness to explain Bigger's helpless relationship to his social environment, asking the jury to witness "a mode of life stunted and distorted . . . an existence of men growing out of the soil prepared by the collective but blind will of a hundred million people" (388). With this rhetoric, however, Max dissolves the boundary between the courtroom and the blindly deterministic world that shaped his client. Though he asks a jury to forgo mortal judgment on Bigger because of environmental influences, Max concedes that these white men, too, will act upon their "blind will." For racial liberals, blind legal judgment signified a personal and institutional neutrality, a reprieve from race prejudice, yet Max here implicates the judge, jury, and audience within the same "blind social forces" that drove Bigger to burn Mary Dalton's body: "Your Honor, in our blindness we have so contrived and ordered the lives of men that the moths in their hearts flutter toward ghoulish and incomprehensible flames!" (401). Max even likens Bigger to the mob gathered outside, insisting that both "are powerless pawns in a blind play of social forces" (390). Blindness no longer signals "neutrality," as the race liberals imagined, but rather an absence of agential responsibility, which includes the jury, lynch mob, and defendant alike. Max's capacity to identify and protest individual prejudice, let along systematic racism, collapses as he introduces blindness into his judgment of Bigger Thomas; as Paul de Man might have put it, Max's figurative language has undermined his propositional claims.

In a remarkable turn, Max actually rejects the idea that Bigger makes any claim on justice. With a second-person address, clearly meant to indict the reader as much as those in the courtroom, Max demands: "Let us banish from our minds the thought that this is an unfortunate victim of injustice. The very concept of injustice rests upon a premise of equal claims, and this boy here today makes no claim upon you" (388). By rejecting the premise of "equal claims," Max abandons the Equal Protection Clause of the Fourteenth Amendment, the single most important phase upon which the race liberal coalition's struggle for civil rights would rest. The blindness that spread across Wright's novel, it seems, now prevents any equitable judgments of Bigger's life. "If you think or feel" otherwise, Max warns, "then you, too, are blinded by a feeling as terrible as that which you condemn in him, and without as much justification" (388). By announcing that any thoughts or feelings about Bigger are blinded by the same social conditioning that produced his violence, Max effectively rebukes the empathetic reading protocols of

Native Son's white, race-liberal readers. To reduce Bigger, the savage crowd outside, and the courtroom to a common blindness concedes that those passing judgment on Bigger's actions must fail, just as his own family's efforts did. Convinced that the jury will condemn his client to death, Max warns that this inevitable judgment will only propagate more blindness: "The more you kill, the more you deny and separate, the more they will seek another form and way of life, however blindly and unconsciously."[88] Extending this logic to a brutal end, Max insists that "if we say that we must kill him, then let us have the courage and honesty to say: 'Let us kill them all. They are not human. There's no room for them.' Then let us do it" (405). A jury truly prepared to affirm blind judgment—to reject the racial difference that has informed Bigger's life from the tenements to the schools to the paltry philanthropy of the Daltons—must not merely remove Bigger from sight, Max suggests, but would need to destroy all the black men whose lives cannot be adequately seen and judged by white America. Resigned to the pervasive blindness around him, Max forfeits any claim on justice, preemptively dismissing the reformist politics of the racial liberalism that saw his speech as a triumphant call to arms.

Portions of Max's speech in *Native Son* certainly inspired social psychologists and jurists, and yet it is difficult not to see his rhetoric, in retrospect, as a crystalline expression of the increasingly apparent fault lines within a racial liberalism that clung to blindness as its governing juridical ideal. Whereas *Justitia*'s blindfold promises "that each judgment brought before her is a 'case' of something more general," blindness in *Native Son* represents neither equality nor a weapon against prejudice but rather a corrosively ironic rhetorical figure, which undermines any attempt to articulate the injustices shaping Bigger's life.[89] By extending blindness from Bigger's mind into the courtroom, Wright's novel anticipates this concept's growing importance to liberal jurisprudence in the twentieth century but then dramatizes how blind law must fail to reconcile social and individual responsibility, racial equality and racial difference, abstract rights and concrete needs. After the trial, Max's final exchange with Bigger makes it painfully clear that the attorney has failed to represent his client.[90] Bigger "had not understood" his attorney's protest and doubts that his own life is "worth the effort that Max made to save it"; yet Bigger finally sets aside the "meaning of the speech" to take pride in "the mere act of it" (406). Replacing Max's social determinism with a claim to self-determination, Bigger will attempt to affirm his individual identity: "what I killed for, I *am*!" (429). Hearing these words, "Max groped for his hat like a blind man . . . keeping his face averted" (429). Diminished from his hortatory position at the center of the courtroom and subjected to a negating blindness like all the other characters in *Native Son*, Max's liberal judgment of Bigger fails, marked as inadequate through the pervasive figural irony in Wright's novel.

Individualism and Reactionary Color Blindness

After World War II, a new generation of critics began to reframe *Native Son* around Bigger's budding individualism. This effort began with James Baldwin's iconic essays, "Everybody's Protest Novel" and "Many Thousands Gone," which cast Wright's novel as allied with white liberalism and its culture of social protest.[91] Baldwin rejected Max's speech, and the racial liberalism built upon it, for making Bigger into a mere symptom of social conditions: the failure of the protest novel, Baldwin insisted, "lies in its rejection of life, the human being, the denial of his beauty, dread, power, in its insistence that it is his categorization alone which is real."[92] Baldwin resented the pathological view of blackness he saw embodied in Bigger, and, like many other postwar intellectuals, saw such vulnerable, angry subjectivity as a breeding ground for totalitarianism.[93] "Bigger's tragedy," insists Baldwin, "is not that he is cold or black or hungry, not even that he is American, black; but that he has accepted a theology that denies him life."[94] By introducing an existential vocabulary into criticism of *Native Son,* Baldwin's essays provided a fulcrum for swinging the novel's reception away from an early emphasis on Max's sociological naturalism and toward an emphasis on Bigger's individual self-formation.[95] As Portelli puts it, the only way to redeem *Native Son* from what was increasingly seen as an orthodox and banal tradition of African American protest literature was "proving that it was no protest novel at all."[96] From the late 1950s through the 1960s, critics began to reframe *Native Son* as Bigger's quest for identity, an attempt to affirm his life, actions, and fate.[97] In the same years, conservative legal activists likewise began to reaffirm an abstract individualism by appropriating color-blind legal rhetoric, transforming an erstwhile liberal ideal into a means of rejecting any reparative racial classifications as an attack on (abstract, formal) equality. This section examines the rise of this reactionary legal movement alongside critical efforts to privilege Bigger's self-formation, demonstrating how Wright's novel preemptively challenges the color-blind individualism they share.

After Max's troubling speech in the courtroom, observes Donald Gibson,

Native Son's decisive "problem becomes not whether Max will save Bigger—the answer to that question is a foregone conclusion—but whether Bigger will save himself in the only possible way, by coming to terms with himself."[98] Gibson's apt locution, "coming to terms," captures a pervasive emphasis on language among critics invested in Bigger's individual identity. Surrounded by characters blind to his inner life, Bigger must create the terms for his own self-definition. Scholars such as Katherine Fishburn, Valerie Smith, and Joyce Ann Joyce emphasize how Bigger and Wright each "rely on their ability to manipulate language and its assumptions—to tell their own story—as a means of liberating themselves from the plots others impose on them."[99] As the novel progresses, Bigger indeed develops increasingly complex narratives for his actions: the stories (and lies) he tells to Peggy, Bessie, Mr. Dalton, Buckley, and Max are all shaped by the demands these listeners place on Bigger and what Werner identifies as Bigger's growing "awareness of the subjective element of sense-making."[100] And yet there are clear limitations to the process of self-formation valorized by this camp of critics. Bigger continually establishes his identity by ingesting the prejudicial judgments of those around him, risking his life for newspapers that describe him and his manhunt; even in jail, Bigger "insists on reading a newspaper because he cannot understand his position until he knows what others are saying about him."[101] As Dennis Baron demonstrates in an incisive syntactic analysis, moreover, Bigger's "inability to interpret and utilize sensory data" on his own in fact precipitates every one of his crises in *Native Son*.[102] Whereas Bigger normally perceives an object and then cognizes it, in certain moments, which Baron calls "indirect perceptions," the narrative formally instantiates Bigger's inability to perceive and articulate his own actions. In the most striking case, Bigger smothers Mary to death because he cannot recognize the effects of his holding the pillow over her face—or the fact that Mrs. Dalton cannot see him—until after the matron has left the room. Bigger "comes to terms" with his situation only too late. "Indirect perception" of such crisis events, argues Baron, become Bigger's "own personal type of blindness."[103]

Each of Bigger's pivotal scenes features a blindness to his own actions. His attempt to burn Mary's body gets discovered after Bigger cannot force himself to clean the ashes for fear of seeing her remains; he kills Bessie in the dark, after only a brief glimpse at her location with a flashlight; he cannot let himself recover the money left in Bessie's dress, once he has thrown her body down the air shaft, for fear of seeing her again; his vision fails yet again in the snowy escape from police; and he keeps his gaze in check throughout the trial, afraid to meet the glances of those around him.[104] While critics invested in Bigger's individuality would privilege a growing self-mastery, the language of the text subsumes this effort within its pervasive trope for ironic negation, illustrated in Bigger's habitual refusal to look upon his behavior. Only after he has indicted every other character, and even the surrounding world, within his metaphor of blindness does Bigger belatedly realize that he, too, may have suffered from distorted judgments. This awareness first appears after Jan forgives Bigger for murdering his girlfriend, Mary; Jan stuns Bigger, not just for his profound sympathy, but also because this sharp man admits that he had failed to judge Bigger appropriately: "Well, you jarred me," Jan explains, "I see now. I was kind of blind" (287). Trying to understand this admission, Bigger imagines himself "on a vast blind wheel being turned by stray gusts of wind" (287). Here, it is still the object-world that is blind, rather than Bigger himself, who remains helplessly trapped at its whim. But during the trial, as Bigger continually struggles to look at the events proceeding around him, he at last recognizes how his eyes betray him; Bigger realizes that he has become subject to the trope through which he shielded himself from the judgment of others: "Had he been blind all along? But there was no way to tell now. It was too late" (362). Max fails to produce a judgment that defends Bigger's equality; Bigger fails to produce a judgment that defends his difference.

Sitting in jail, Bigger does notably envision a new life, unmarked by blindness. In this hopeful moment, Bigger imagines that "the vessel was full again, waiting to be poured out. But no! Not blindly this time! He felt that he could not move again unless he swung out from the base of his own feelings; he felt that he would have to have light in order to act now" (311). When Bigger later imagines what this new, bright life would look like, however, his vision carries a final, vicious irony, dissolving any effort to affirm his individual self-formation:

> Another impulse rose in him, born of desperate need, and his mind clothed it in an image of a strong blinding sun sending hot rays down and he was standing in the midst of a vast crowd of men, white men and black men and all men, and the sun's rays melted away the many differences, the colors, the clothes, and drew what was common and good upward toward the sun. (362)

Under this "blinding sun," all distinguishing colors, all political difference, would melt away. But this is a flattening figurative equality, a world with so much light that everyone is blind. Just as the novel's trope of blindness ironically disarms Max's sociological protest, critics invested in Bigger's self-formation have often missed how this effort at redeeming his actions through an imaginative experience ends up erasing any trace of Bigger's personal identity, with racial difference or "the many differences" that otherwise distinguish individuals all dissolved into an abstract equality. This erasure, moreover, appears within a metaphor, precisely through Bigger embracing the linguistic expression seen by so many critics as the necessary ground for his existential self-discovery. Bigger does not gain self-mastery through this imaginative expression but rather demonstrates how his rhetoric of blindness, launched as a defensive mechanism to explain the failure of others to judge him, implicates his own attempts at self-judgment. Bigger heads to his death "feeling and thinking that they didn't see me and I didn't see them" (425).

Michael Szalay argues that the "resolutely aesthetic experience" imagined in Bigger's "blinding sun" represents his paltry "substitute for the personal welfare promised" by liberals under the New Deal.[105] "Wright identified 'the reality of the state' as the only mechanism for securing the Black body from the abrasions of history," Szalay proposes; "the fact that the 'abstract subject'" depicted in this scene "would later become the hallmark of all that was wrong with a White, homogenizing mass society had less to do with liberal philosophy writ large than with the counter culture's studied antagonism towards the New Deal."[106] Yet this chapter has shown how the blinding sun in Bigger's vision precisely enacts a central conceptual image of liberal philosophy, a blindness to racial difference that became the governing ideal for reformers by the end of the second New Deal. Chapter 1 showed how feminist theorists such as Carole Pateman and Wendy Brown identified liberalism's constitutive dualisms as having always been implicitly gendered, from Locke and the social contract theorists onward; providing a complementary critique, critical race theorists such as Charles Mills have argued that racial difference was likewise at once presumed and occluded within classical liberal thought. For Mills, liberalism's ideal social contract concealed a non-ideal "racial contract," which allowed the "differential privileging of the whites as a group with respect to the nonwhites as a group, the exploitation of their bodies, land and resources, and the denial of equal socioeconomic opportunities to them."[107] As the dominant political language in the United States, a nation whose history has been defined by evolving forms of racism and white supremacy, liberalism has always implicitly meant "white liberalism," a set of abstract concepts that gave color blindness "perverse philosophical sanction."[108] Baldwin once described *Native Son* as encouraging readers to "join hands and walk together into that dazzling future when there will be no white or black . . . the dream of all liberal men, a dream not at all dishonorable, but, nevertheless, a dream."[109] Whatever Wright may have thought about New Deal racial liberalism, however, his novel's ironies offer an immanent critique of its ideals, one that Baldwin and later critics have missed.

In the years following *Brown v. Board*, moreover, conservative legal activists appropriated the idea of "blind" legal judgment for their own ends, transforming this liberal dream into a practical tool for upholding white supremacism. Because *Brown* required only formal equality between individuals, rather than any reparative socioeconomic justice, Southern states immediately began to challenge the limits of its holding. In 1955, a South Carolina court ruled that "the Constitution . . . does not require integration. It merely forbids discrimination."[110] "From here," asserts Haney-Lopez, "it was but a short step to the contention that colorblindness affirmatively prohibited raceconscious integration measures"; North Carolina "grasped this in 1969, passing a law proclaiming that '[n]o student shall be assigned or compelled to attend any school on account of race, creed, color or national origin.'"[111] "By the late 1960s," Haney-Lopez concludes, "colorblindness had become a favored argument among those attempting to protect segregation."[112] Rejecting any racial classification as an unjust effort to discriminate among individuals, this reactionary color blindness employs the Equal Protection Clause to obscure the enduring socioeconomic inequities created by three hundred years of structural racism. In the 1980s, Supreme Court Justices Potter Stewart and William Rehnquist began directly quoting Harlan's dissent in opinions rejecting reparative racial classification; later on Clarence Thomas and Sandra Day O'Connor took up the same strategy.[113] Concluding a synoptic study of the subject, Neil Gotanda affirms that the "Supreme Court's use of color-blind constitutionalism" quite simply "fosters white racial domination."[114] And yet, as legal scholar Randall Kennedy observes, color blindness now represents "probably the most popular conception of what is thought to be commendable racial thought and conduct," a way to defend individual merit without betraying any overt racial prejudice.[115] What once served as a rallying cry for American liberals and an idealized end in the struggle for civil rights now serves as a means for conservative activists to constrain those same rights, and for middle-class Americans to avoid the unpleasant realities of racial inequality; this ironic reversal has exposed color blindness as an aporia in liberal thought, a concept at once enacting and undermining its privileged values, a metaphor that exposes the enduring challenge of reconciling equality and difference through a court of law.

By the end of the 1960s, the race liberal coalition had already begun to splinter, as the recalcitrance of white moderates and the militancy of Southern reactionaries drove African Americans struggling for civil rights to embrace new forms of protest, represented by the Rev. Dr. Martin Luther King Jr., Malcolm X, and Stokely Carmichael. These fault lines appear clearly in a 1963 roundtable entitled "Liberalism and the Negro," for which Myrdal made a rare public appearance in the United States to discuss race relations with Baldwin, Sidney Hook, and Nathan Glazer. Norman Podhoretz, editor for *Commentary* magazine and moderator for the roundtable, opens the discussion by identifying a "split among American liberals."[116] The traditional liberal, he explains, believes in "competing *individuals* who confront a neutral body of law and a neutral institutional complex," whereas a newer group, worried by "a widening split between the Negro movement and the white liberal community," have begun demanding "radical measures" to ensure racial equality, potentially even "preferential treatment."[117] The old liberal clings to formal equality among abstract individuals, the new liberal insists on the embodied experience of social difference, another iteration of the classical/modern split traced throughout this book. Myrdal equivocates in his response: he affirms his status as a liberal in the "first sense . . . both in believing that all formal discriminatory rules and laws must be eradicated and in looking forward to a society which is color blind," and yet he concedes that to "achieve anything more than formal equality" will require "remaking American society" wholesale, beginning with the growing rate of poverty among whites and blacks alike.[118] Baldwin, however, refuses either vision of liberal politics, and charges "white liberals" with being "unable to divest themselves of the whole concept of white supremacy . . . reinforced by all the institutions in which power is located."[119] The preeminent social psychologist Kenneth Clark, offering a comment from the audience, seconds Baldwin's fractious sentiment, confessing that "I now see white American liberalism primarily in terms of the adjective, 'white.' And I think one of the important things Negro Americans will have to do is learn how they can deal with a curious and insidious adversary—much more insidious than the out-and-out bigot." This threat, Clark explains, stems from "a peculiar kind of ambivalence in American liberalism, a persistent verbal liberalism that is never capable of overcoming an equally persistent illiberalism of action."[120] This chapter has argued that this ambivalence does not simply represent a personal, moral, or psychological failing on the part of American liberals but rather exists within the conceptual grammar through which liberalism has attempted to understand and remedy racial inequity over the past century.

In the 1970s, this liberal ambivalence in efforts to reconcile individual equality with racial difference would be neatly encapsulated in the debate over affirmative action. This now-contentious phrase was at first meant only as a warning against prejudice: in 1961, John F. Kennedy required that all federal contractors "take affirmative action to ensure that applicants are employed ... without regard to their race, creed, color, or national origin."[121] Over time, however, "affirmative action" came to signify not simply neutrality but reparative consideration for minority candidates. After the passing of the Civil Rights Act of 1964, conservatives began to lash out at Title VII, which prevented employers from discriminating based on race, sex, religion, or nationality, as demanding preferential treatment or even "quotas" based on race. Glazer, who had sat beside Baldwin and Myrdal for the *Commentary* roundtable, now inveighed against the federal government violating the equality of individuals with his book *Affirmative Discrimination* (1975). Citing Justice Harlan's call for a color-blind Constitution, Glazer branded race-conscious policies by liberals as reverse discrimination. Other neoconservative intellectuals, such Podhoretz, Daniel Patrick Moynihan, and Irving Kristol, joined Glazer in enrolling liberalism's privileged concepts and metaphors against what they saw as a sprawling welfare state, interfering with individual citizens and free markets.[122] The "trope of blindness," observes Robert Post, offered these neoconservatives a powerful metaphor to mobilize support around an individualistic market logic: "Blindness renders forbidden characteristics invisible; it requires employers to base their judgments instead on the deeper and more fundamental ground of 'individual merit' or 'intrinsic worth.'"[123] Of course, as Reva Siegel notes, it is precisely "the social condition of racial stratification that makes the concept of color-blindness intelligible as a distributive principle" in the first place; the call to ignore racial difference necessarily presupposes its social legibility.[124] The Supreme Court's most famous ruling on affirmative action, *Regents of the University California v. Bakke* (1978), attempted to split the middle of these ongoing debates, upholding the right to include race as a factor in admissions yet rejecting any specific racial quotas, a pragmatic solution resembling the trimester compromise of *Roe v. Wade*. In their opinion, Justices Brennan, White, Marshall, and Blackmun describe racial equality as an enduring "American Dilemma." For decades, they note, the Equal Protection Clause was "turned against those whom it was intended to set free," and even after *Brown*, "officially sanctioned discrimination is not a thing of the past."[125] The justices inveigh against recent "claims that law must be 'color-blind,'" noting that "no decision of this Court" has actually "adopted the proposition that the Constitution must be colorblind," and they warn that this politicized metaphor represents a "myopia which masks the reality that many 'created equal' have been treated within our lifetimes as inferior both by the law and by their fellow citizens."[126]

Despite this commendable plea, however, the Supreme Court has played an increasingly active role in promoting individualist color blindness since the 1970s. With cases like *Washington v. Davis* (1976), the court struck down its earlier ban on "disparate-impact" laws—in which a policy creates divergent outcomes based on race—ruling that discrimination only exists when the policy *intentionally* aims to produce such racially disparate effects.[127] One of the most egregious manifestations of this color-blind logic came with *McCleskey v. Kemp* (1987), where the plaintiffs provided a rigorous statistical study of bias in the State of Georgia's death penalty verdicts, which black convicts receive far more often than white ones, especially when they have murdered someone white.[128] The justices ruled against them. "Ensconced behind colorblindness," explains Haney-Lopez, the court reverted to a midcentury view of racism as an individual rather than a structural problem and "insisted upon exceptionally clear proof of racial bias by a particular bad actor."[129] The court's most fervent advocate for this color-blind individualism has ironically been Justice Clarence Thomas, who after filling Thurgood Marshall's seat, proposed that there is "a moral [and] constitutional equivalence" between "laws designed to subjugate a race and those that distribute benefits on the basis of race in order to foster some current notion of equality."[130] This, Kennedy insists, represents "one of the silliest, albeit influential, formulations in all of American law."[131] Scholars in critical race theory now identify "color-blind racism" as a dominant ideology in American law, politics, and public discourse, a paradigm that emerged from the organizing concepts of midcentury liberalism, yet reversed its reformist impulses.[132] Because the "normative climate in the post-civil rights era has made illegitimate the public expression of racially based feelings and viewpoints," explains Bonilla-Silva, color-blind racism explains away the enduring facts of racial inequality as the result of nonracial forces or decisions.[133] This interpretive framework repurposes the governing categories "of traditional liberalism (work ethic, rewards by merit, equal opportunity, individualism, etc.) for racially illiberal goals," naturalizing inequalities as the by-product of individual choices or varying abilities.[134] Efforts to seek racial justice are challenged by metaphors such as "playing the race card," which, as Kimberlé Williams Crenshaw explains, "presumes a social terrain devoid of race until it is (illegitimately) introduced."[135] When O. J. Simpson was charged with double murder during the "trial of the century" in 1995, his attorney attempted to point out that the white police officer who had arrested him had used the "N-word" repeatedly in the past. The prosecutor, however, rejected this information as a corrupting influence on those who were trying the case: "'It'll blind this jury. It'll blind them to the truth. They won't be able to discern what is true and what is not. It'll affect their judgment. It'll affect their ability to be fair and impartial.'"[136] Once thought to be a remedy for race prejudice, blindness now functions as a neutrality that reactionaries use to shield themselves against efforts to expose Americans to personal or national histories of racial inequity.

Color blindness, in sum, does not simply represent a rhetorical weapon belonging to those protecting white supremacy in the United States but also an aporia in liberal thought, a metaphor whose antithetical uses over the last hundred years exemplify liberalism's struggle to redress its constitutive dualisms—individual and social, equality and difference, rights and needs—through the law. Faced with questions about racial classification, observes Kennedy, progressive and conservative Americans each show a marked capacity to reverse their judgments, depending on the issue in question, inverting how they balance the conceptual dualisms that organize liberal political discourse. Those who reject affirmative action as promoting group needs ahead of individual merit will often flip sides on the subject of racial profiling by police, citing this as a practical necessity for protecting group safety; those who reject such police profiling, in turn, are likely to support such racial consciousness when it comes to college admissions practices.[137] These topics produce debate, in other words, not merely because of an ideological binary among the nation's citizens, or even a moral or psychological shortcoming among some of them, but because they reflect a more fundamental tension between protecting individual equality recognizing social difference. Transracial adoption exemplifies this tension and its practical gravity: should a child be placed among racially similar families, "in which their status as adoptees was less evident, in which they would avoid the prejudice that still targets multiracial families, and in which their own identities would perhaps be better supported by similarly situated parents," or does this represent a problematic return to ethnic segregation?[138] Colorblind law, as Wright's novel presciently grasped, does not resolve these enduring tensions within liberal theory and practice but rather contains them within an aporetic metaphor. While *Native Son* served a catalyzing role for midcentury racial reformers, this chapter has shown how the novel's ironic figure of blindness undermines its own appropriation. By juxtaposing Max's sociological protest and Bigger's individual self-actualization, *Native Son* dramatizes competing values in liberal thought, marks each position as blind through its pervasive narrative irony, and so anticipates the ongoing struggles to redress these values through blind legal judgment.

Things Not Seen

In 1963, Ralph Ellison published his review of *An American Dilemma*, which he had withheld for twenty years after the book's first release. It opens with a characteristic ambiguity: Ellison admits "joining in the chorus of 'Yeas' which the book has so deservedly evoked," yet he must also "utter a lusty and simultaneous 'Nay.'"[139] Myrdal "sees Negro culture and personality simply as the product of a 'social pathology,'" Ellison complains, as "the creation of white men" and their prejudice.[140] But black Americans have fashioned a vibrant culture, Ellison insists, have "helped to create themselves" despite the harsh realities of white supremacy.[141] Although social psychology and its protest novels dominated the 1940s, Ellison issues a distinctly modernist cultural call: adapting James Joyce's iconic phrase, he urges black Americans to give shape to "'the uncreated consciousness of their race.'"[142] Had it been published in 1944, Ellison's call might have seemed prophetic. By the 1960s, the racial liberalism built around *Native Son* had fractured, and several groups promoting cultural and political consciousness among African Americans had taken its place, from the Black Arts and Black Power movements to the Student Nonviolent Coordinating Committee. These shifting cultural winds also helped spread a compelling, yet reductive narrative about midcentury African American literature, in which Ellison and Baldwin stepped beyond the self-pathologizing protest culture embodied by Wright and embraced modernist notions of irony and craft to explore the complexities of black experience. The endlessly repeated stories of rupture between these iconic African American authors, laments Garcia, turned their "personal acrimony" into "the idea of inviolable literary camps" and in the process "obscured thematic and literary continuities" in their work.[143] If readers still regularly elide the complexities in *Native Son* through claims about Wright's biographic experience and authorial intentions, however, this chapter has shown his novel troubles any supposed program, any reading of the novel as a didactic work of naturalism, protest fiction, or liberal social psychology. Through an immanent aesthetic critique of blind judgment, the textual ironies in *Native Son* in fact undermine its ideological appropriation by midcentury liberals, challenging a central conceptual ideal in liberal political theory by exposing its failure to reconcile racial difference with abstract individuality. Given the interpretive ambiguity produced by this rhetoric of blindness, and the critique of liberal culture it entails, *Native Son* deserves to be repositioned within the compass of literary modernism and read alongside those works by Ellison and Baldwin against which it is usually contrasted.

Throughout much of their writing, Ellison and Baldwin follow Wright's precedent in employing tropes of sight, visibility, and blindness to explore how race creates ambiguities in individual self-formation and institutional recognition. *Invisible Man*, whose modernism has never really been in dispute, features a bounty of such images; some of the most memorable include Rinehart's opaquely green glasses, which transmute the dangers of Harlem into a realm of possibilities for a hustler, a lover, and a fighter; "Liberty Paints," whose trademark "Optic White" begins as a brown tarry hue, which it disguises with a precious few chemical drops; and of course the Battle Royale, in which ten young black men are blindfolded and made to lash out at one another brutally, competing for a prize offered by the town's white male elite. Similar figurative patterns reappear throughout Baldwin's prose. In *The Evidence of Things Not Seen*, for instance, Baldwin meditates on the Atlanta child murders, emotionally charged crimes in which, he insists, the "ability to suspend judgment" required for true legal equality becomes impossible.[144] Tracking the racial undertones in this case, Baldwin emphasizes how the conclusions to which so many observers were leaping only revealed the limits of their own capacity for judgment: "People can be defined by their color only by the beholder," he asserts, "who, in order to arrive at this definition, must will himself/herself blind."[145] Baldwin's poetry, barely touched by scholars, returns to this same notion of a will to blindness: in "Staggerlee wonders," the folk hero asks, "can blindness be desired? / Then, what must blinded eyes have seen / to wish to see no more!"[146] For Baldwin, blindness often signifies a tragic burden, an insight coupled with experiential pain and self-denial. D. Quentin Miller notes Baldwin's "frequent use of blindness as a metaphor" and yet once again cites this as part of his "alliance with the theme of invisibility that dominates African American literature from Ellison on," separating Wright from "the majority of African American literature following World War II."[147] Critics continue to install a break between *Native Son* and the richer connotative textures of modernist African American literature, despite the fact that Wright's novel employs a complex ironic figure of blindness to exposes pervasive conceptual tensions in liberal political thought.

Baldwin and Ellison did of course seek to differentiate themselves and their work from Wright, a onetime mentor to each and an unavoidable literary predecessor. Baldwin, as noted earlier, began this effort with essays linking *Native Son* to the sentimental, self-serving protest culture of white liberals. These aesthetic and political barriers were reinforced during Ellison's infamous debate with Irving Howe. In "Black Boys and Native Sons," Howe defended Wright against the charges of his two successors while rebuking what he saw as the broader ideological failings of literary intellectuals in the 1950s, who had maligned the social consciousness of the thirties by embracing modernism's purportedly apolitical aesthetic. Despite "all its crudeness, melodrama and claustrophobia of vision," Howe insisted, "Wright's novel brought out into the open, as no one ever had before, the hatred, fear and violence that have crippled and may yet destroy our culture."[148] Baldwin and Ellison "hoped to show the Negro world in its diversity and richness, not as a mere specter of protest," and yet Howe insists that if Wright's naturalism was mechanical, the anger and resentment in *Native Son* represent an inevitable social reality for any black writer: "How could a Negro put pen to paper, how could he so much as think or breathe, without some impulsion to protest, be it harsh or mild, political or private, released or buried?"[149] In his response to Howe, "The World and the Jug," Ellison rejects this pathological vision of blackness, echoing his review of *An American Dilemma*. "Howe feels that unrelieved suffering is the only 'real' Negro experience," Ellison writes, yet it "is not skin color which makes a Negro American but cultural heritage as shaped by the American experience."[150] To drive this home, Ellison adapts a time-tested metaphor: "Need my skin blind me to all other values?"[151] Racial difference, he implies, does not disqualify a black writer from addressing other human qualities, nor require them to make race their defining artistic priority. Ellison emerged a clear victor from his debate with Howe, whose pronouncements about the necessary suffering of black writers have not aged well. Yet again, their personal exchange only exacerbated the idea of an aesthetic and political rupture between Wright's didactic protest and the modern ironies of his successors.

Reframing *Native Son* as a modernist text would not only help repair an overstated gap between Wright, Baldwin, and Ellison but would moreover curtail the reductive aesthetic and political judgments about midcentury African American literature that contrasts between these authors inevitably produce. Despite its undeniable reception as a protest novel, this chapter has shown how *Native Son* undermines the same race-liberal ideology that embraced it as a founding text. Midcentury race novels, notes Melamed, "were presumed to concretize racial liberalism's ideologemes, including the power of sympathy, liberal whites as heroic agents of reform, and the moral hazards of racial prejudice," and yet racial liberals "never theorized what it was to read," never "depended upon acts of reading or the rhetorical performances of literary texts" to support their narratives about racial difference, its psychological origins, or its moral implications.[152] Learning to read Wright's novel as a modernist text, as this chapter has shown, means learning to interrupt the interpretive protocols that have allied it with racial liberalism and grappling with a color-blind legal paradigm now more powerful than ever. Melamed's discourse analysis, inspired by Foucault, allows her to identify the normative power of racial liberalism by tracking its network of institutional influence, yet this procedure risks reifying the bond between a set of novels and their ideological reception. No one could dispute the profound historical influence that *Native Son* had on midcentury American liberals; refusing to interrogate this appropriation of the text, however, allows this interpretive community to define the values through which Wright's novel continues to be read, taught, and discussed. Whereas Melamed effectively abandons those texts absorbed into race liberal discourse and recuperates a group of "race radical" texts, whose liberatory possibility lies in having been maligned by midcentury liberals, this chapter has shown how even a novel widely promoted by racial liberals might contain an ironic refutation of their organizing rhetoric. Indeed, it is precisely because *Native Son* attempts to articulate a liberal social psychology through Max's protest, anticipates a return to individualism through Bigger's self-scrutiny, and explores the failings of these efforts through a blindness that constrains rather than clarifies efforts to reconcile social and individual, equality and difference, that Wright's novel offers one of the most strident critiques of American liberalism in all midcentury fiction. For this critical purchase, manifest through an aesthetic politics of irony, Wright's novel deserves recognition as a modernist novel.

That *Native Son*'s unstable ironies have gone overlooked save by a few critics, however, provides an important reminder of the shifting relationship between modernist aesthetics and liberal politics at midcentury.[153] As the next chapter details, American intellectuals quickly rewrote the meaning of liberalism after World War II by juxtaposing the social protest culture of the thirties against a newfound investment in modernist culture and its emphasis on ambiguity, irony, and paradox. By attacking literary naturalism and the liberal culture that had championed it, argues Michael Nowlin, Lionel Trilling's epochal volume *The Liberal Imagination* (1950) "helped establish the terms for debunking Richard Wright" without ever mentioning his name.[154] Like other intellectuals in the *Partisan Review* circle—including James Baldwin, who had let the magazine publish "Everybody's Protest Novel" and "Many Thousands Gone"—Trilling rejected what he saw as the trite sentimentalism and didactic politics of social realism and instead privileged a "capacity to sustain irony through literary form," which became "the hallmark of the liberal imagination that both Ellison and Baldwin were seeking to engage and exhibit" in order to position themselves within the category of modernism being "canonized in the 1940s and 1950s."[155] Although they rejected Wright's novel as a symptom of the liberal culture of the thirties, Baldwin and Ellison would eventually find their psychological ambiguity and tragic irony embraced as governing values for a new liberalism emerging after World War II.[156]

II A Modern Liberalism

3 The Inward Turn
Tragedy, Documentary, and the Making of the Postwar Liberal Imagination

After World War II, American liberalism began a marked shift in political and aesthetic values, as intellectuals turned to modernist culture to explain the horrors that had enveloped liberal democracies around the world. Whereas earlier liberals such as Thorstein Veblen, John Dewey, and Charles Beard had trusted in the "rationality or common sense of men," suggests Daniel Bell, the leading voices of his generation, such as Lionel Trilling, Reinhold Niebuhr, and Sidney Hook, found their "wisdom in pessimism, evil, tragedy, and despair." This did not make them "better or greater," concedes Bell, but "sadder and perhaps wiser."[1] Bell's remarks display a recurring tendency to define postwar intellectual history through an affective experience of cynicism and doubt, elevated into a form of moral and political insight. Thomas Schaub calls this "the liberal narrative," a "Blakean journey from innocence to experience" triggered by the sense of betrayal among left intellectuals after Stalin's nonaggression pact with Hitler and the Moscow Show Trials, their disillusionment with technocratic political progress after facing fascism's camps and the devastation of the atomic bombs.[2] The liberal intellectuals who endured these existential shocks collectively assumed what Amanda Anderson has called a "bleak ethos" in the postwar years.[3] Chastened by crisis, these liberal thinkers display a more complex set of aesthetic and political investments than are typically recognized by studies that reduce liberalism's history in these years to a "conservative turn." Looking "to deepen the political debate on the left," explains Anderson, figures such as Trilling began introducing to liberal discourse the "aesthetic values of modernism": "pessimism, tragedy, irony, paradox, ambiguity, and complexity."[4] This tragic postwar sensibility belies the "widely held conception of liberalism as an optimistic ideology fueled by progressivist confidence."[5]

At the same time, however, it was precisely this generation of postwar intellectuals who popularized reductive narratives about American liberalism as a naïve and optimistic ideology.⁶ The most influential literary and political voices in the United States after World War II, such as Trilling, Niebuhr, and Arthur Schlesinger Jr., all identified themselves as liberal critics of liberalism and gained their iconic status by helping to canonize a popular understanding of American liberal culture as an overly optimistic middle-class faith in social reform and technocratic progress. Despite liberalism's relative freshness as a concept in American political discourse, these intellectuals called for a "new liberalism" after the war, better suited to the contradictions and ironies of modern political life. As previous chapters have shown, liberal intellectuals and modernist literary culture had in fact shared a mutually formative antagonism since the Great Depression. From the 1930s, when intellectuals began to scrutinize their relation to class and gender inequality, through an emergent racial liberalism built on "color-blind" judgment, modernism consistently engaged with—and was in turn delimited by—formative conceptual problems in liberal thought. Nonetheless, in the postwar years, figures such as Schlesinger successfully recast the liberalism of the 1930s as tragically overconfident in its explanatory power, doomed to ironic failure by a faith in fixed principles and naïvely unaware of the incompatible moral values and irreducible conflicts of political life. Reconstructing American liberalism around the critical impulses of modernist culture, these postwar intellectuals discovered in recent history a reminder of the ironies defining all human experience.

This book's first two chapters focused on identifying aporias in liberal political thought, showing how modern fiction proved ideally suited to exposing its constitutive dualisms. The second half of this book now examines how postwar intellectuals eventually appropriated modernist cultural values to redefine the meaning of American liberalism. This chapter argues that "tragedy," as an aesthetic concept, played a particularly vital role in the discursive reframing of American liberalism; chapter 4 focuses on "style." By "aesthetic concept," I mean the whole constellation of associations invoked by "tragedy" in intellectual discourse, rather than any particular texts or stable genre. In the postwar years, tragedy and the tragic served as widely legible and classically venerated terms for describing the increasingly pessimistic temperament of American intellectuals; more important still, these concepts also served a revisionary historiographic function, enabling figures such as Trilling and Niebuhr to legitimate an interpretive narrative that cast the liberal culture of the 1930s as having been blind to its own ironic limits and internal tensions. Launching his decades-long polemic against John Dewey, Niebuhr charged that his liberalism was "a kind of blindness" befalling those "who imagine that their intelligence has emancipated them from all the stupidities of the past" and "which does not see the perennial difference between human actions and aspirations, the perennial source of conflict between life and life, the inevitable tragedy of human existence."[7] Through his popular writings and institutional influence, Niebuhr instructed a whole network of powerful liberal thinkers, from Schlesinger Jr. to Hubert Humphrey, in the "basic incompatibility between self and society, ideals and self-interest, politics and ethics, culture and nature, love and justice, and private morality and public welfare."[8] Though Dewey and his contemporaries had made liberalism a salient category in American life precisely by attempting to grapple with the constitutive dualisms in its political theory and practice, Niebuhr juxtaposed a newfound moral realism about the intractability of such tensions against the supposed naïveté of a prior era of liberal thought. Tragedy provided Niebuhr and like-minded thinkers with an intellectually distinguished yet widely legible narrative framework within which they could situate the catastrophes of the 1940s as an injurious yet vital insight into the blindness of liberal thought in the 1930s.[9]

The postwar liberal imagination was in this way refashioned around a set of interpretive protocols drawn from liberalism's encounters with modernist culture. The liberal subject, reconceived as constitutively tragic, had to call guiding principles into question, to balance antithetical values and to recognize the ineradicable conflicts of political life. This liberal subject, in other words, required not just legal rights but an aesthetic sensibility honed by the ironies of modernist fiction. For Trilling, writing in his epochal volume, *The Liberal Imagination* (1950), the future of American democracy itself hinged on liberalism's engagement with modernist culture. "In the United States at this time," he asserts, "liberalism is not only the dominant but even the sole intellectual tradition," yet no "first-rate writer" takes liberal thoughts and sentiments as a motivating concern.[10] While the last two chapters argued that modernism had indeed exposed fundamental tensions in midcentury liberal thought—between private and public, equality and difference, abstraction and embodiment—Trilling influentially insisted that grappling with the illiberal urges of modern literature might help "to recall liberalism to its first essential imagination of variousness and possibility."[11] Trilling's widely popularized essays reframed liberalism's dualisms as part of a stable framework, a set of interpretive protocols that saw tragically conflicting values as the constitutive condition of individual subjectivity. Through the act of reading, postwar intellectuals subsumed modern American liberalism's tensions within a private self, internally divided yet self-consciously so, bearing what Trilling and Niebuhr each called a "moral realism." This tragic liberal imagination had at its center not the abstract economic values of classical liberalism, or legal rights of the Fourteenth Amendment, but an aesthetic subject forged from its encounters with the antinomian energy of modernist culture.

To narrate the rise of this reimagined liberal subject and its modernist interpretive protocols, this chapter examines a singular case study: *Let Us Now Praise Famous Men* (1941). As the first section relates, this iconic work of documentary modernism by James Agee and Walker Evans offered an immanent critique of New Deal social reportage. By insisting on a tension in the representation of tenant farmers, who can either index collective social ills or appear as autonomous individuals, but not both, Agee casts the liberal political aesthetic of 1930s social documentaries as tragically conflicted. Today, *Famous Men* serves as a privileged marker for the end of New Deal reformism and its dominant mode of cultural representation. At its first publication, however, the book was a "legendary flop."[12] As the next section explains, this canonical literary-historical narrative about *Famous Men* had to wait for a broad shift in American liberal culture, which made Agee's tragic sensibility, discomfiting in the 1930s, widely appealing to intellectuals in the 1950s and 1960s. Trilling, the preeminent literary champion for this tragic postwar liberalism, and for Agee's book, facilitated this shift by promoting an interpretive practice that privileged encounters with conflicting moral values, internalizing public crises, as Agee had, into a tragic personal insight.[13] When *Famous Men* was re-released in 1960, an epochal shift in liberal thought was found preemptively affirmed by the critical energies of modernist culture, and Agee's tragic sensibility was retroactively inscribed into American literary history. In these same years, tragedy's mediation between modernism and liberalism reached all the way to the White House through the writings and personal influence of Niebuhr, whose political theology shaped a generation of liberal elites. Finally, the chapter concludes by explaining why the rise of this tragic thinking among postwar liberals corresponded with a widespread worry that tragedy, as a dramatic form, was no longer possible. Midcentury literary debates about the "end of tragedy" reveal an underlying anxiety about the end of a unified liberal subject. As postwar intellectuals substituted a struggle within the self for the struggle against society, they also began to doubt whether a heroic individual agent could change the world.

Let Us Not Praise Liberal Documentary

In July 1936, Henry Luce, the publishing magnate behind *Fortune*, *Life*, and *Time* magazines, commissioned Agee and Evans to create a photo-textual account of three families of white tenant farmers in Alabama.[14] Agee, a writer for Luce since 1932, had recently provided *Fortune* with an insightful piece on the Tennessee Valley Authority and was a promising fit for the accomplished photographer Evans, on loan from the Farm Security Administration. The two seemed poised to produce another entry in President Roosevelt's nationwide effort to document rural poverty for the American public, whose sympathy in witnessing the shared conditions of the Depression would help buttress support for New Deal relief programs. As the cornerstone of New Deal cultural politics, this documentary work was generated by several agencies working to build national solidarity: the Federal Writers' Project produced its American Guide Series; the Federal Theater Project created "living newspapers"; and most prominently, the Farm Security Administration, with its Information Division led by Roy Stryker, generated more than a quarter-million photographs of rural poverty. Through this federal funding, images by Evans, Dorothea Lange, and Arthur Rothstein saturated American periodicals, from the *New York Times* and *Saturday Evening Post* to Luce's *Life* and *Fortune*. These photos, explains John Louis Lucaites, created a collective "portrait" of the Great Depression, a shared visual experience "of America's barren dust bowl, of bread lines and soup kitchens and street-corner apple vendors, of hoboes and destitute migrant workers" that continues to define the visual imagination of socioeconomic crisis in the United States.[15] This visual material remained in high demand for several years, and books such as Lange and Paul Taylor's *American Exodus*, Evans's *American Photographs*, and Margaret Bourke-White and Erskine Caldwell's *You Have Seen Their Faces* were runaway best sellers throughout the mid- and late 1930s. By the time Agee and Evans set out to Alabama, notes William Stott, the accrued material on Southern tenantry alone included "upwards of twenty books, hundreds of articles, a 'March of Time' film, a Hollywood melodrama, a 'National Sharecroppers Week,' and a commemorative stamp by Rockwell Kent."[16]

But what Agee saw and felt during the three weeks he lived among these tenant farmers led him to break with the established standards of social reportage. Weaving back and forth between direct descriptive passages on the families and a stream of conscious narrative, rife with guilt and anxiety, Agee's draft violated the boundaries between documentary realism and modernist aesthetics compartmentalizing the literary field the 1930s.[17] Luce's rejection would be but the first. When *Let Us Now Praise Famous Men* was finally published in 1941, its five hundred furious pages systematically undermined the reading protocols that liberal middle-class audiences had come to expect from social documentary under the New Deal. This antagonism appears from the very beginning: after its preface, Agee's first recto-verso pages infamously display two epigraphs and a footnote, which present a framing interpretive dilemma. On the left lies a portion of King Lear's speech on the heath; opposite that, the *Communist Manifesto*'s climactic lines: "Workers of the world, unite and fight. You have nothing to lose but your chains, and a world to win."[18] In his footnote below, Agee explains that these two passages represent the book's first and second "themes," arranged in "sonata form." "These words are quoted to mislead those who will be misled by them," warns Agee. "They mean, not what the reader may care to think they mean, but what they say."[19] These epigraphs—one a scene of tormented individual consciousness, the other a sweeping cry for collective struggle—model strikingly different responses to the ensuing documentary text, and yet Agee's note suggests that a synthetic reading of *Let Us Now Praise Famous Men* depends on accounting for these two divergent scenes of aesthetic reception and their potentially competing political outcomes.

Critics invested in reclaiming the radicalism of the 1930s have often tried to affirm the quote from Marx as a sign of the book's "revolutionary agenda," yet as Hugh Davis remarks, Agee soon abandons any sign of this agenda in his modernist exploration of "individual self-actualization."[20] At the same time, however, the "first theme" from *King Lear*, while clearly describing a form of individual self-formation, also raises serious problems for any reader interested in seeing the epigraphs as statements of authorial purpose. In this carefully excised passage, Agee reshapes Lear's budding catastrophe into a picture of enlightened empathy, a moment in which a privileged observer comes to recognize the need for economic reform:

> Poor naked wretches, wheresoe'er you are,
> That bide the pelting of this pitiless storm,
> How shall your houseless heads and unfed sides,

The Inward Turn

> Your loop'd and window'd raggedness, defend you
> From seasons such as these? O! I have ta'en
> Too little care of this! Take physic, pomp;
> Expose thyself to feel what wretches feel,
> That thou may'st shake the superflux to them,
> And show the heavens more just. (III.iv)

With his immersion in the raggedness of poverty, exposed "to feel what wretches feel," Lear belatedly perceives his failure to care for the poor of his realm—a transformative scene that seems to anticipate Agee leading his reader into rural Alabama. Through an overwhelming aesthetic experience, the passage suggests, even a king can recognize his callousness and come to embrace economic redistribution, to "shake the superflux" of excess wealth down to those less fortunate. This passage ends up modeling the empathetic reformism that made social reportage a central instrument in promoting New Deal policies. As readers soon discover, however, Agee will assault this liberal political aesthetic for the next five hundred pages, deriding the pity and charity of his middle-class readers, refusing to condescend to the farmers by turning them into abstract integers for social blight, and finally denying that any reform might alleviate the damage wrought by the tenant system. These epigraphs, in other words, do not offer programmatic goals but reading practices whose aesthetic and political values Agee anticipates and negates.

Agee thereby frames his project as an imminent critique of liberal documentary practice, exposing the form's constitutive tension between promoting collective political action and affirming autonomous individual experience. Addressing his presumptively liberal audience early on with a corrosive irony, Agee mockingly suggests his book "is written for all those who have a soft place in their hearts for the laughter and tears inherent in poverty viewed at a distance."[21] For Agee, comedy and pathos were criminally inadequate responses to the suffering of an "undefended and appallingly damaged group of human beings."[22] Charitable donations and support for reform would never amend their suffering; it was not enough that "the reader will be edified, and made to feel kindly disposed toward any well-thought-out liberal efforts to rectify the unpleasant situation down South, and will somehow better and more guiltily appreciate the next good meal he eats."[23] As Martha Rosler argues, documentary journalism had come "to represent the social conscience of liberal sensibility," presenting "information about a group of powerless people to another group addressed as socially powerful" and thereby rendering public blights as "a commodity to be experienced."[24] His book, Agee announces, is "intended . . . as a swindle, an insult, and a corrective" to these liberal reading habits.[25] In an appendix, Agee excerpts a review of Caldwell and Bourke-White's *You Have Seen Their Faces* to illustrate this "corrective" impulse. While the write-up fawns over Bourke-White's celebrity status, it casually mentions her "bribing, cajoling, and sometimes browbeating her way in to photograph Negroes, sharecroppers and tenant farmers in their own environments."[26]

Agee did not believe that the invasive, even abusive relationship between documentarians and their subjects could be wholly avoided, yet he saw the cardinal sin of liberal documentary as its tendency to dissolve the individuality of those it documented into sociological generality. Since its beginnings with Jacob Riis and Lewis Hines during the Progressive Era, photo-textual reportage had sought to represent public ills through synecdoche, with images and text about individuals standing in for collective populations.[27] Though such work was motivated by political reform, argues John Hilgart, Agee believed that reform could not amend the damage it surveyed and that the vogue for portraits of poverty-stricken men and women was finally more about "satisfying liberal and middle-class notions of what the rural poor must be and how utterly unlike themselves those people were."[28] Bourke-White's grotesque photos in *You Have Seen Their Faces*, for instance, carry legends that capture not the speech of those depicted, but "the authors' own conceptions of the sentiments of the individuals portrayed." This, Caldwell assures the reader, will "avoid unnecessary individualization."[29] Seeing this evacuation of autonomy as a moral failure, Agee refuses to reduce the tenant farmers to typological banality. His "Table of Contents" includes typical documentary categories such as "Money," "Shelter," and "Clothing," but through constant digressions and eccentric subsections, he dismantles the pretense that such categories can dissect these families for the comfortable digestion of readers at home. Playing on such conventions allows Agee to foreground what he sees as an ineluctable tension between the documentarian's descriptive urge and the autonomy of those persons documented. "How am I to speak of you as 'tenant' 'farmers,' as 'representatives' of your 'class,'" he exclaims, "as social integers in a criminal economy, or as individuals, fathers, wives, sons, daughters, and as my friends and I 'know' you?" (88). At one point, Agee lashes out against language itself, imagining how he might otherwise capture the raw materials of tenant life:

"If I could do it, I'd do no writing at all here. It would be photographs; the rest would be fragments of cloth, bits of cotton, lumps of earth, records of speech, pieces of wood and iron, phials of odors, plates of food and of excrement" (10). Treating human beings merely as "social integers" seemed to Agee a moral crime, a deprivation of their individual autonomy that betrayed the underlying hypocrisy in documentary's supposedly liberal mandate.

Agee instead demands that his audience encounter the tenants as irreplaceably individual entities. "George Gudger," he insists, "is a human being, a man not like any other human being so much as he is like himself . . . to what degree I am able it is my business to reproduce him as the human being he is; not just to amalgamate him into some invented literary imitation of a human being" (211). For Agee, this representational fidelity could never wholly succeed but might pass some sense of moral responsibility from the writer to the reader: "The most I can do—the most I can hope to do—is to make a number of physical entities as plain and vivid as possible," knowing that this will "leave to you much of the burden of realizing in each of them what I have wanted to make clear of them as a whole: how each is itself; and how each is a shapener" (97). Agee's neologism grants these farmers, who barely exist at a subsistence level, the status of shapers, or makers, defining their own existence and world. By insisting that Gudger and his family must be seen as "vividly and absolutely themselves," suggests David Denby, Agee becomes a "rhapsodist of things as they are," demanding that his reader encounter the Gudgers not with the urge to change them but to accept them in the plenitude of their brokenness. "There is a trap built into his kind of intensive receptivity," cautions Denby: "That a person or a thing is itself and nothing else, and is therefore worthy of notice and celebration, may be the beginning of morality, but it's also the beginning of tragedy."[30] Agee bestows a performative import on individual human life but in so doing accepts that these tenants face an unavoidable destruction; his tragic sensibility affirms their fate. For Susan Hegeman, this heroic effort at aesthetic individuation reveals Agee's "highly moralized, yet fundamentally antipolitical, outrage." By suggesting that "as individuals, even the humblest of us were both full of 'human divinity' and essentially *unknowable*," Hegeman remarks, Agee reveals less about the material conditions of tenant farmers than about the tragically conflicted sensibility of the liberal intellectual.[31]

Agee defends his tragic political aesthetic with a weighty reflection on "Beauty," tucked among descriptions of home life in his section on "Shelter."

Standing before the Gudgers' home, Agee proposes that his reader must try to see this impoverished dwelling not only as a symptom of lamentable socioeconomic conditions but also as a beautiful work of art. He frames this in a chiasmatic claim: "the Beethoven piano concerto #4 *IS* importantly, among other things, a 'blind' work of 'nature,' of the world and of the human race; and the partition wall of the Gudgers' front bedroom *IS* importantly, among other things, a great tragic poem."[32] Naturalism can perhaps help us understand how Beethoven's works were a product of his environment and not simply his creative genius. But how might the Gudgers' partition wall, which inserts some desperate privacy into their cramped living quarters, carry the stature of "a great tragic poem"? In *The Birth of Tragedy*, Nietzsche maintains that the world and all its horrors can only be justified "as an esthetic product," and Agee similarly insists that the "esthetic success" of the tenants' homes "seems to me even more important than their functional failure."[33] This Nietzschean moment, argues Paula Rabinowitz, reveals Agee's willingness to transmute the poverty of the tenants into a form of insight for himself and his reader, lapsing back into the same middle-class voyeurism he condemned in his liberal peers.[34] While Agee acknowledges that he and his reader will inevitably render the tenants into objects of aesthetic experience, however, he importantly does not see this as a simple pleasure. Whatever beauty lies in the Gudgers' home, Agee explains, represents the dialectical by-product of its damages: "it seems to me necessary to insist the beauty of a house, inextricably shaped as it is in an economic and human abomination, is at least as important a part of the fact as the abomination itself." And "one is qualified to insist on this," Agee adds, "only in proportion as one faces the brunt of his own 'sin' in so doing and the brunt of the meanings, against human beings, of the abomination itself."[35] By learning to see aesthetic autonomy and social blight as a constitutive tension in documentary practice, *Famous Men* would have its reader recognize an equally tragic dualism between freedom and necessity in their own subjectivity. For Agee, there can be no escaping the representational struggle between a morally adequate recognition of individual, autonomous beauty, and a politically efficacious recognition of collective suffering, because this conflict is rooted in the structure of reality. Yet through aesthetic experience, Agee imagines that his reader can recognize these incommensurable values and subsume them into a tragic personal insight, a revelation not simply about the limits of documentary practice but about the human condition, about our "sin."[36]

Agee's political aesthetic becomes decidedly tragic, in short, not because of some grounding Aristotelian belief in *hamartia* or *hubris*, but from his immanent discovery that documentary representation must remain trapped between two unimpeachable sets of values: the naturalizing impulse to use (and so abuse) these tenants as instruments for amending the social ills facing his audience, and a fidelity to the autonomous existence, and beauty, of these unique yet damaged lives.[37] Among theorists of tragedy, this internally divided sensibility falls closest to Hegel. In his *Lectures on Fine Art*, Hegel contends that, in classical dramas such as *Antigone*, a heroic individual collides with the state. While their antithetical values could each be independently "justified," each necessitates "the negation and the violation of the other equally legitimate power" and so each must "fall under condemnation."[38] This clash between equal drives, Hegel insists, also plays out within the mind. By witnessing an individual struggle with incompatible political and ethical values, and admit their corresponding guilt, Hegel argued that an audience might be purged of any one-sided perspectives, moving toward what he describes as a "feeling of reconciliation," a form of justice in which individual, family, and state are held in equilibrium through perpetual contest.[39] While Agee never defends such a tragic political vision directly, his blanketing irony refutes any potentially reparative hope for the tenants under a mass of syntactical hedging, pressing readers toward a tragic sensibility through the contradictions of his prose: "the discovery and use of 'consciousness,'" he writes, "which has always been and is our deadliest enemy and deceiver, is also the source and guide of all hope and cure, and the only one" (271). Agee's relentless negations keep his readers trapped within a tragic duality, denying them any comfortable experience through the internal tensions of his form: "I know there is cure, even now available, if only it were available, in science and in the fear and joy of God" (271). Writing under the auspices of social documentary, a genre dedicated to recording public crises, Agee ends up performing and promoting a private, tragic sensibility.

In so doing, Agee wholly undermines those liberal and radical reading protocols modeled by his epigraphs from *King Lear* and Karl Marx, offering an immanent critique of the political imaginaries that had made documentary a preeminent mode of cultural representation in the 1930s. Introducing a tragic, modernist reflexivity into documentary practice, Agee frames the call to collective action announced by Marx, and the call for individual awakening invoked by *Lear*, as equally valid yet ultimately irreconcilable urges for social reportage. Unsurprisingly, Agee supports neither progressive educational reform nor radical consciousness raising. Because the tenants' lives are defined by labor, he insists, intelligence and emotion are "all but entirely irrelevant" to their experience, leaving them "about as poorly equipped for self-education as human beings can be" (260). The farmers show "no attempt to counteract the paralytic quality inherent in 'authority,' no attempt beyond the most nominal and stifling to awaken, to protect, or to 'guide' the sense of investigation, the sense of joy, the sense of beauty, no attempt to clarify spoken and written words whose power of deceit even at the simplest is vertiginous" (259). Threatening even the best-intended political actions with a tragic irony, Agee shuts down the educational experience that John Dewey had seen as the engine for pragmatic liberal reforms, shuts down the class consciousness that Marxists like Georg Lukács had theorized as the foundation for proletarian revolution. All such efforts, he warns, are fated to be self-defeating: "I can appear too easily to recommend it, to imply, perhaps, that if these things were 'taught,' all would be 'solved': and this I do not believe: but insist rather that in the teaching of these things, infinitely worse damage could and probably would result" (259). Reconciled to the intractable limits this tragic irony installs in any politically reparative project, Agee only hopes that reading his book will strike his readers with sufficient force: "my self-disgust is less in my ignorance, and far less in my 'failure' to 'defend' or 'support' the statement, than in my inability to state it even so far as I see it, and in my inability to blow out the brains with it of you who take what it is talking of lightly, or not seriously enough" (271). Agee frames liberal and Marxian politics as constitutively tragic, as unable to protect the individual autonomy of the vulnerable while attempting to enroll them in collective sociopolitical action. *Famous Men* finally pushes the reader toward a tragic political aesthetic—not an Aristotelian catharsis of fear and pity, which might serve the liberal empathy modeled through *Lear*, but an internally riven consciousness, in which irreconcilable urges must remain in dialectical tension.[40]

In this way, Agee's book anticipated a newfound sensibility among postwar American intellectuals, who would likewise come to embrace a tragic perspective on the progressive political impulses of the 1930s. But *Famous Men* arrived too soon. After a series of editorial battles, it was published by Houghton Mifflin in 1941, and though admired by a handful of critics, it ended up selling fewer than six hundred copies in its first year.[41] The documentary practices Agee sought to challenge were rapidly falling from public notice, with photojournalism from World War II already replacing the formerly ubiquitous images of breadlines and sharecroppers. Despite the ferocity of Agee's invective against social documentary, writes Rabinowitz, by 1941 "this form and more importantly the concerns it embraced, no longer held the liberal imagination."[42] To occupy its current place of honor in literary history, Agee's book would have to wait for a wholesale reimagination of American liberalism.

Lionel Trilling and the Tragic Liberal Imagination

Between the 1930s and 1950s, a loosely connected group of literary critics began to transform modernism from an insurrectionary movement into an aesthetic standard by promoting interpretive practices that made its keywords—*ambiguity, irony, tension, contradiction, paradox*—into definitive values for the act of reading. With their landmark textbooks, *Understanding Poetry* (1938) and *Understanding Fiction* (1943), New Critics such as Cleanth Brooks and Robert Penn Warren made terms like *ambiguity* central to the literary education provided by American universities. Men returning home from World War II and seeking postsecondary training through the Serviceman's Readjustment Act of 1944, or GI Bill, learned to substitute the richness of paradox for the heresy of paraphrase. While groups such as the Southern Agrarians and New York Intellectuals did not share political views, argues Thomas Schaub, Allen Tate's belief in "tension" as "the central achievement in poetry," and Richard Chase's view that "unresolved contradictions" constituted the triumph of *The American Novel and Its Tradition*, reveal "an underlying agreement about the homologous structures of reality and art."[43] Because these critics, especially after World War II, broadly came to see reality as defined by ineradicable conflict and moral uncertainty, they asserted that art's meaning lay in its capacity to contain such tensions; modernism's formerly heretical view of experience as constitutively ambiguous, defined by tensions and tragically irreconcilable values, now defined the veracity of artwork at large. Some critics from this era cast their reading practices as "formalism," removed from political questions, but others recognized the ideological implications of this broad reorientation in interpretive priorities. Chase, for instance, boldly insisted that "if one had read and understood Melville one would not vote for Henry Wallace," the Progressive presidential candidate whose defeat to Harry Truman in 1948 signaled a shift from New Deal reformism to Cold War containment. "Literature tells us that life is diverse, paradoxical, and complicated," argues Chase, but "the tendency of modern liberal politics has been to bleed political ideas white, to deny them their roots in natural reality, to deny them their extension over the possible range of human experience."[44] Dewey would hardly have recognized or accepted this description of "modern liberal politics" in the 1930s, yet Chase insists that his fellow intellectuals had recently rediscovered a form political insight unknown to Dewey's generation, sequestered away in modern literature. By "sloughing off a facile idea of progress," he concludes, "Melville accepted . . . a tragic view of life," fashioning a chastened ethical and political sensibility that was now being reborn in the "new liberalism of the 1940s."[45]

This postwar belief in modern literature as a corrective to the purportedly naïve political progressivism of the 1930s found its preeminent champion in Trilling, who saw his central mission as challenging liberalism from within. A "criticism which has at heart the interests of liberalism," Trilling maintains, "might find its most useful work not in confirming liberalism in its sense of general rightness but rather in putting under some degree of pressure the liberal ideas and assumptions of the present time."[46] This critical pressure, Trilling argues, could be gleaned above all from modernist writers such as Proust, Kafka, Rilke, Joyce, Eliot, and Yeats, who show no "love of the ideas and emotions which liberal democracy, as known by our educated class, has declared responsible."[47] Modernism's "extravagant hostility to conventional patterns of civilized life," explains Adam Kirsch, offered Trilling an ideal vehicle to challenge what he saw as liberalism's undue faith in rational behavior, managerial expertise, and scientific progress.[48] Like Baldwin and other members of the *Partisan Review* circle, Trilling identified liberal culture above all with literary naturalism and the "protest novels" of the 1930s and 1940s, such as *Native Son*, which they rejected as condescending indulgences. A novel like Steinbeck's *The Grapes of Wrath*, inveighs Trilling, only "cockers-up the self-righteousness of the liberal middle class: it is so easy to feel virtuous in our love for such *good* poor people! The social emotions can provide a safe escape from our own lives and from the pressures of self-criticism and generously feed our little aggressions and grandiosities."[49] Against such a comfortable readerly experience, Trilling juxtaposed figures such as Baudelaire and Joyce, who sought to "shock us out of the way of seeing forced upon us by the political past and the institutional present" through their willingness to dwell in contradiction and paradox.[50] This view of modern art's tensions as a catalyst for perpetual self-reform sounds far more like his former professor Dewey than Trilling tended to admit; it also presumes an orthodoxy to liberal ideas belied by the coming Eisenhower years.[51] Yet *The Liberal Imagination*, which sold seventy thousand and then a hundred thousand copies in subsequent printings, nonetheless helped redefine liberalism as a set of optimistic cultural pieties, rooted in habits of reading, which had ignored literature's tragic insights into modern life.[52]

Because Trilling helped displace the social realism of the 1930s with modernism's ironies and ambiguities, explains Amanda Anderson, cultural histories often conflate his work with the New Criticism. And yet Trilling's project, Anderson explains, must be distinguished from the "close reading" systematized by Brooks and Warren based on "where the ambiguity and complexity is placed: for the New Critics, it is placed in the text itself, and for Trilling it is placed in the consciousness and temperament of the critic and the imagined reader."[53] This emphasis on a reader's aesthetic experience appears clearly in "the term that Trilling's oeuvre conspicuously adds to the group of terms favored by the New Critics: *tragedy*."[54] The modern writers Trilling held in highest regard—John Keats, Henry James, Sigmund Freud— all installed in their readers a tragic view of life, a "moral realism" about the perennially contested values in society and in themselves.[55] Keats famously identified Shakespeare's achievement in works like *King Lear* as a "negative capability," an urge to take "the dialectical view of any large question" and avoid any "final judgment." In Trilling's view, these remarks were also self-commentary.[56] "For all his partisanship with social amelioration," Trilling contends, Keats insisted on nature's hostility to humanity, on unpredictable historical circumstances, and "the ironic mutability of life;" he had "no hope whatever that life could be ordered in such a way that its condition might be anything but tragic."[57] By recognizing this tragic reality, however, Keats could remake "ugly or painful truth . . . as beauty."[58]

Among novelists, Trilling revered Henry James for inducing a similarly tragic social outlook in his readers. In *The Princess Casamassima*, James dangles Hyacinth Robinson between European aristocracy and political radicals; unable to carry out a revolutionary assassination in the novel's climax, Hyacinth turns the gun to his head instead. "Hyacinth's tragic fate," insists Trilling, forces us to recognize competing value systems in the novel and in society, with protagonist and reader each assuming "a certain amount of guilt" through their wavering convictions.[59] Trilling saw this conflict of values as the reality of human existence, a belief reinforced by his deep investment in psychoanalysis. According to Freud, each mind contains irreconcilable tensions, yet mediates these through the fundamentally creative process of the dreamwork, where the unconscious performs, with its messier methods, those artistic equivocations sublimated by Keats and James, instructing us in a "tragic courage in acquiescence to fate" that can dampen "the greater pain which life will force upon us."[60]

Trilling's essays, in other words, at once praise and perform the interpretive protocols of a tragic liberal imagination. Modern art displays psychological and political life as constrained by irony and ambiguity, and the reader internalizes this as a lesson in moral realism, converting public conflicts into private insight. Trilling's interpretive practice thereby reestablishes the priority of the individual subject in liberal thought, which Dewey had vociferously opposed; only this reimagined liberal individual no longer operates as a rationally self-interested actor but rather as a self-conflicted reader, tuned to the fractious complexity of modernist culture. Whereas Dewey and his generation of intellectuals struggled to modernize liberalism by grappling with the friction in its constitutive dualisms—individual and social, public and private, autonomy and dependence—Trilling aimed to reclaim control over these tensions by halting liberalism's critical project at the aesthetic level, subsuming public political tensions back into private experience. His interpretive protocols crucially allowed a generation of postwar intellectuals, disillusioned with both Communism and Senator Joseph McCarthy's scarlet brand, to retain their dialectical thinking, yet shifted this dialectic from a historical struggle between classes into an inescapable struggle within the liberal mind. For this reason, suggests Mark Schechner, *The Liberal Imagination* became "a handbook of intellectual survival" for the "stymied intellectual after whom Slesinger's *The Unpossessed* was named."[61] Trilling effectively reframed those intellectual equivocations, which Slesinger diagnosed in the 1930s as schisms in liberal political thought, into a form of self-knowledge. By "raising his own contradictions to the level of an explanatory principle," Krupnick concludes, Trilling made the liberal intellectual into "a possible redeemer of society," provided only they grapple with the tragic complexities of modernist art.[62]

This tragic political aesthetic explains why Trilling was one of the few critics who praised *Let Us Now Praise Famous Men* at its first release. Agee's insurrection against social documentary neatly matched Trilling's revolt from within American liberalism. In his original review, entitled "Greatness with One Fault in It," Trilling lampoons the "social consciousness" of Steinbeck, Odets, and Shaw as being "abstract and without fiber of resistance and contradiction . . . how essentially it was a pity which wonderfully served the needs of the pitier."[63] For mercilessly exposing such self-serving sentimentality and demolishing the documentary tradition that propped up this complacent liberal culture, Trilling proclaims Agee's book nothing less than "the most realistic and the most important moral effort of our American generation."[64] Its one fault, Trilling concedes, was that Agee's guilt about the tenants prevented him from seeing in them, too, the internal divisions he recognized everywhere else.[65] Trilling's one complaint about Agee's tragic sensibility, in other words, was that it was not absolute. While few other readers concurred with this sentiment in 1941, the next decade's horrors would seem to confirm belatedly the tragic outlook performed by Agee and defended by Trilling. Auschwitz and Hiroshima, as Daniel Bell puts it, conspired to make a generation of intellectuals "twice-born."[66] Writers "whose tragic view of history and whose conception of the destructive and irrational impulses in men would have seemed reactionary during the days of the United Front," proposed Daniel Aaron in 1954, now "seem to correspond more truthfully to the experiences of the last generation than the forecasts of the rational optimists."[67] Intellectuals began flocking to the "dark prophets of the continent," such as Kierkegaard, Dostoevsky, and Unamuno for melancholy comfort, while their bleak political and spiritual visions were "conveyed second-hand" to the American public "through such media as the Luce publications."[68] As American liberals reorganized around this tragic sensibility, which recast the experimental reforms of the 1930s as naïvely optimistic, the conditions gradually emerged for the critique of New Deal documentary in *Famous Men* to be legible as a meritorious literary intervention.

Meanwhile, Agee himself had passed away under circumstances that enabled his friends and admirers to proffer him as a heroic martyr, whose "talent was tragically wasted" before its time.[69] After ignoring a doctor's advice to quit his relentless smoking and drinking, Agee died from his second heart attack, suffered in the back of a New York taxicab in 1955. Three years later, his posthumous novel, *A Death in the Family*, won the Pulitzer Prize, despite or perhaps because of editorial changes lightening up Agee's bleaker, more experimental manuscript. Following this accolade, his close friend Dwight Macdonald published a moving tribute to Agee in the *New Yorker*, entitled "Death of a Poet." This essay began a transvaluation of Agee's vices, turning "the worst set of working habits in Greenwich village" into the virtues of a tragic hero, "spectacularly born in the wrong time and place," who passed away, Macdonald laments, as "the most broadly gifted writer of my generation."[70] Writing in a canny passive voice, Macdonald insists that "it is felt that Agee's life and personality, like [James] Dean's, were at once a symbolic expression of our time and a tragic protest against it," a sentiment few may have shared at the time, yet whose illocutionary force would help garner renewed attention to Agee's life and work.[71] It was "the Agee 'tragedy,'" observes Alan Spiegel, which reintroduced him into literary history.[72] His revolt against journalistic conventions resonated with midcentury intellectuals, whose fear of a symbiotic relationship between mass culture and totalitarian politics helped them see Agee as an early rebel against corporate America, typified by his former boss, Henry Luce.[73]

Agee's belated reception exemplifies a recurring pattern, tracked by this book, in which the unruly contradictions of a modernist text were tamed by locating a stable interpretive narrative in the body of the author. In this case, Agee's legacy was confirmed by a tragic liberal imagination, consolidated in the postwar years around a set of reading practices that subsumed tensions in public political life back into the sensibility of his private person.[74] Robert Fitzgerald, who was a friend and classmate at Harvard, tied Agee's insights directly to the reading practice taught to them by I. A. Richards. Not paying "the slightest attention" to Harvard's totem, "VERITAS," at first, Fitzgerald recalls how Richards one day separated "poem, referent, and reader" on the board, insisting that the relation between these determined the meaning of any artwork, yet they were not "stable, but variable."[75] From then on, concludes Fitzgerald, "VERITAS had become tragically complicated," and it "was destined to haunt us like a Fury."[76] When *Let Us Now Praise Famous Men* was reissued to widespread acclaim in 1960, Fitzgerald—now an illustrious translator of Homer, Euripides, and Sophocles—compared his departed friend's opus to the grandest of Greek myths: "Between them Agee and Evans made sure that George and Annie Mae Gudger are as immortal as Priam and Hecuba, and a lot closer to home."[77] In pouring honorifics on Agee's book, however, this newly enthusiastic generation of readers often ended up bypassing the tenant families altogether. This tendency was encouraged by Evans's new preface to the 1960 edition of *Famous Men*. Entitled "James Agee in 1936," it depicts the writer as a tragic martyr, whose "resolute, private rebellion" in the ensuing pages was "unquenchable, self-damaging, deeply principled, infinitely costly, and ultimately priceless."[78] As one reviewer for this new edition affirmed, throughout the book "we can see Agee worrying about a division in his own soul, a division much more important and tragic than that which we sometimes thought we saw in the

Decade."[79] Another review expressed this hierarchy in still blunter terms, declaring that the book was really "a study of its author, who—for my money—is in a much more tragic condition than any exploited sharecropper."[80] Whereas Agee's modernist form had drawn upon tragedy to confront readers with documentary's structuring tension between autonomous individuality and collective recognition, his recuperators reified this aesthetic experience into Agee's personal intellectual tragedy. Desperate to avoid a mass politics now tainted by Stalin, critics distanced themselves from the socioeconomic issues, state-sponsored cultural politics, and documentary culture that had originally shaped Agee's confrontational text, extracting only the tragic sensibility it left behind.[81]

Agee's canonization, which had to wait for an epochal shift in liberal culture, now retroactively inscribed that shift into American literary history.[82] His recovery illustrates how American liberalism reimagined its political values through aesthetic encounters with modernist culture and so reciprocally enabled the boundaries of literary modernism to be rewritten. Agee's tormented confessional, which his contemporaries had seen as a "literary freak," was enshrined in the 1960s as "the quintessential document of public culture of the 1930s," praised as "the decade's greatest literary achievement," and heralded as a central accomplishment of modernist literary culture, "the most important achievement in American prose, in or out of fiction, to appear between the publication of Faulkner's first great novels starting in 1929 and the emergence of the early writings of Bellow, Ellison, and Mailer in the late forties and early fifties."[83] In his touchstone study, *Documentary Expression in Thirties America* (1973), William Stott cites Agee's rebellion against liberal documentary as a seismic literary intervention. "*Let Us Now Praise Famous Men*," asserts Stott, "culminates the documentary genre and breaks its mold. It reveals the limitations, the tragic superficiality, of a way of seeing and speaking, of a perspective on life, and—in some measure, perhaps—of a time."[84] Middle-class readers in the thirties, Stott explains, could never have reconciled their "liberal optimism" with Agee's "tone of tragic resignation."[85] When that naïve optimism was shattered by the experiences of World War II, Stott asserts, Agee's schismatic and cynical book, which lacked the programmatic, experimental hope of New Deal liberalism, could be recognized for what it was—a monument to moral realism, a profound indictment of what postwar liberals were learning to see as the hubris of the 1930s Left. Stott praises Agee as "a tragic poet who had to see and magnify and beautify into art the suffering of any life" and suggests that history has validated Agee's doubts about repairing the system of tenantry: "in 1973, we know that the system and its victims are still with us."[86] As American liberals abandoned the reformist optimism inspiring social documentary work for a tragic sensibility, *Famous Men* was recovered as a punctual literary event, marking the passage between liberal epochs. In 1960, Trilling was able to release his original review with obvious pride, unchanged but for the title, which now read: "An American Classic."

Agee's recuperation, mediated by the concept of tragedy, exemplifies how American intellectuals sought to rebuild liberalism around a reflexive awareness of its internal tensions, turning the aesthetic critique at work in modernist fiction since the 1930s into a permanently divided subjectivity, tuned to ambiguity and contradiction. This transformative narrative gets lost in cultural histories that reduce the experience of postwar liberal intellectuals to a "conservative turn." In these years, liberals did not simply become more conservative but rather rewrote the meaning of liberalism itself. Tragedy played a decisive role in this discursive reframing by allowing critics like Trilling to situate the political failings of the 1930s within a powerful interpretive narrative, a rediscovery of timeless truths about the human condition. Struggles over class or gender or race—which Trilling's essays all but ignore—could now be glossed as but particularities subordinated within a more generalized condition: the ineradicably agonistic nature of political and moral life. If this was a conservatism, to adopt Walter Horton's terms, it was not a traditional or "fundamentalist" conservatism, rooted in an organic community and its shared values, but rather a "post-modern" conservatism, a response to tensions emerging from the fractiousness of modern political life.[87] Trilling's turn was less rightward than inward: by redirecting an ongoing intellectual effort to develop a modern liberal politics around aesthetic experience, Trilling retrenched into an individualism that prior thinkers like Dewey had seen as bankrupt. This was, to be sure, an aesthetic individualism of a higher conceptual order than classical liberalism had imagined, yet by allowing intellectuals to abandon social critique for a tragic resignation in the face of conflict, the postwar liberal imagination would prove easy enough to reconcile with free market capitalism and state power. By the 1950s, the tragic sensibility shared among American intellectuals would eventually enable liberalism to emerge as a consensus discourse, embraced by the nation's foremost brokers of power.

Taking Tragedy to the White House

For the cover of *Time*'s twenty-fifth anniversary issue in 1948, Henry Luce selected Reinhold Niebuhr, the nation's preeminent advocate for a tragic religious, philosophical, and political outlook.[88] Like Trilling, Niebuhr established himself as a liberal critic of liberalism. After beginning his career as a socially engaged Protestant minister in Detroit, Niebuhr rose to national prominence in the 1930s and 1940s through his polemic assaults against the "moral idealism" of American liberal culture. *Time*'s feature article on him in 1948—written by Whittaker Chambers, only months before he would accuse Alger Hiss of being a Communist before the House Un-American Activities Committee—summarizes Niebuhr's critique of liberal culture for the magazine's popular audience. "Man is essentially good, says 20th Century liberalism, because he is rational;" against this naïve vision "Dr. Niebuhr asserted: man is by the nature of his creation sinful; at the height of man's perfection there is always the possibility of evil. Against easy optimism, he asserted that life is inevitably tragic."[89] Three subtitled portraits, decorating *Time*'s pages, illustrate the intellectual tradition within which readers should locate Niebuhr's writing: "Sören Kierkegaard (*Tragic argument*)," "Karl Barth (*Tragic crisis*)," "Fyodor Dostoevsky (*Tragic drama*)."[90] Much like Trilling's effort to infuse the liberal imagination with a "moral realism," suggests Richard Wightman Fox, Niebuhr's insistence on the "inevitably tragic" conditions of moral and political life aimed "not so much to destroy liberalism" but "to transform it into a philosophy that was realistic . . . about the role of power, self-interest, and political mobilization in the social arena."[91] What Agee injected into documentary practice, and Trilling codified as a reading practice, Niebuhr justified as national policy. His ideas came to be grounding premises for a generation of Cold Warriors, such as Arthur Schlesinger Jr. and George F. Kennan, who collectively redefined liberalism in national political discourse around his tragic outlook. According to Kennan, architect of Truman's containment policy, Niebuhr "was the father of us all."[92] By the end of his remarkable career, Niebuhr brought a tragic liberal imagination all the way to the White House, his words influencing leaders as prominent as Vice President Hubert Humphrey and President John F. Kennedy.

And yet, like James Agee, Niebuhr had to wait for his time. In the 1920s, Niebuhr was a left-leaning minister at the Bethel Evangelical Church in Detroit, where he preached Social Gospel and supported autoworkers against

Henry Ford. Over time, Niebuhr came to believe firmly in original sin, an essential trait in human nature making individuals as capable of doing evil as good. Christian Realism, as Niebuhr calls it in *Beyond Tragedy*, sees the crucifixion as "a revelation of what life actually is. It is tragic from the standpoint of human striving" and only redeemed from this tragedy by Christ's sacrifice."[93] Disillusioned with his former political values after moving to New York in 1928, Niebuhr joined socialist organizations, drawn to what he saw as Marxism's more realistic recognition of power. With *Moral Man and Immoral Society* (1932), Niebuhr launched a decades-long insurrection from within American liberalism by taking aim at Dewey, its foremost representative.[94] Niebuhr charged liberals like Dewey with holding on to a naïve faith in individual intelligence as a mechanism for social change, failing to recognize how self-interest, irrationality, and outright evil could direct power far beyond well-intentioned intelligence.[95] Liberalism, in short, missed the reality of sin. Dewey's commitment to "'experimental procedures' in social life," guided by "human intelligence" and a "planned economy," could never overcome "predatory self-interest," an individual egotism Niebuhr believed to be only accelerated by collective organization.[96] With his talent for simplified paraphrase, Niebuhr often distorted beyond recognition Dewey's political theory—as even Niebuhr's biographer admits.[97] After World War II, however, Niebuhr's tragic worldview seemed validated by history. As American intellectuals sought to understand Germany's embrace of Hitler, Stalin's betrayal of Marxism, and the horrors of Hiroshima and Nagasaki, Niebuhr provided a blanketing interpretive narrative, written in digestible prose, which turned these historical traumas into a trans-historical lesson about the tragic structure of political life. Niebuhr reframed midcentury history as a cruel insight into the limitations of 1930s liberalism, whose "persistent blindness to the obvious and tragic facts of man's social history" had inadvertently led to this "tragic era of world catastrophe."[98] Through his characteristic gift for "emotionally potent oversimplification," as he himself called it late in life, Niebuhr drew postwar American liberals toward "a tragic perspective—stamped with a Christian imprimatur."[99]

In this way, Niebuhr played a central role in the rewriting of American liberalism. While Dewey and FDR had made liberalism a keyword in American political discourse during the crises in the 1930s, postwar critics now cast their effort to find a third way between laissez-faire individualism and communist revolution as "old liberalism," against which these intellectuals now called for a "new liberalism."[100] This modernist rhetoric staged a rupture with the past, a questionable break, dependent on oversimplifying a recent—and still quite active—intellectual tradition from which postwar liberals were now departing. To Niebuhr's credit, his liberal critique of liberalism often drew upon the same profound conceptual tensions addressed by this book's prior two chapters: he recognized, for instance, how Locke's theory of possessive individualism had collapsed with the "development from competitive to monopoly capitalism," a "historic refutation of the idea that property is primarily an ordinate and defensive power to be used against the inclinations of others to take advantage of the self"; and he recognized how liberal political judgments struggled to reconcile abstract equality with social difference without "confidence in the identity of particular and universal interests."[101] But whereas earlier liberal thinkers had sought to grapple with these conceptual problems, as modern writers like Slesinger and Wright demonstrated the practical issues they entail, postwar liberal thinkers now evaded these troubling questions of class, gender, and race by viewing all such political conflicts as tragically insurmountable realities. In his well-known 1958 lecture, "Two Concepts of Liberty," for instance, Isaiah Berlin distinguishes between "negative" and "positive" conceptions of liberty: a freedom "from" or a freedom "to." Berlin finally defends "negative" liberty, retreating into a classical liberal posture of rights above needs, autonomy above necessity, the individual above the social. He justifies this retreat by insisting that the negative conception of liberty is better suited to sustaining the fundamentally tragic nature of political life: "If, as I believe," writes Berlin, "the ends of men are many, and not all of them are in principle compatible with each other, then the possibility of conflict—and of tragedy—can never wholly be eliminated from human life, either personal or social. The necessity of choosing between absolute claims is then an inescapable characteristic of the human condition."[102]

Niebuhr eventually infused this widespread intellectual sensibility into the institutional power structure of the Cold War. In 1947, he helped establish Americans for Democratic Action alongside Schlesinger Jr. and in 1950 was appointed honorary chairman for the Congress for Cultural Freedom, which Schlesinger helped found. Together, these intellectual networks cemented liberalism's status as a consensus category in American politics, its "vital center," as Schlesinger dubbed it in his iconic treatise. This metaphor, oft-repeated, indicates a profound shift in what "liberalism" had come to mean for American intellectuals over just a few years; whereas Dewey's *Liberalism and Social Action* envisions a moving, experimental tradition, Schlesinger's *Vital Center* depicts a clear, stable space, which had to be protected against political movements encroaching from either side. Although he was a preeminent historian of American liberalism and a lifelong defender of the New Deal's reforms, Schlesinger had by 1949 come to believe that totalitarianism, whether of the left or the right, threatened "to liquidate the tragic insights which gave man a sense of his limitations."[103] Adopting from Niebuhr's writing a "moderate pessimism" about the tragic ironies of political hope, Schlesinger now maintained that Americans had to cast aside any "sentimental belief in progress."[104]

Even as it served to justify complacency at home, tragedy also offered Niebuhr and his followers a narrative that made Cold War realpolitik seem inevitable, a dramatic framework through which they imbued their global ideological program, and a growing military-industrial complex, with classical authority. In *The Irony of American History* (1952), for example, Niebuhr reframes the nuclear tensions between the United States and the Soviet Union as a sad necessity, "using the threat of atomic destruction as an instrument for the preservation of peace," an interpretation that obscures a whole history of military and diplomatic choices, granting a potentially apocalyptic standoff the semblance of fate.[105] "There is no more exciting time in which to live," echoes Schlesinger, yet "no time more crucial or tragic. We must recognize that this is the nature of our age: that the womb has irrevocably closed behind us, that security is a foolish dream of old men, that crisis will always be with us."[106] Between an inaccessible womb and an irrelevant senility lie a few, tough-minded liberal men. Numerous Cold War liberals cite Niebuhr's influence in these years, such as Hans Morgenthau, Adlai Stevenson, Perry Miller, Richard Hofstadter, Felix Frankfurter, Talcott Parsons, and Robert Coles. Niebuhr's work with the ADA helped promote this era's interventionist foreign policy, inspiring Eleanor Roosevelt, Hubert Humphrey, and John Kenneth Galbraith.[107] Even William Appleman Williams, in his revisionary study *The Tragedy of American Diplomacy*, framed his critique of Cold War interventionism around the proposition that US policy did not simply promote freedom, but "held within itself . . . several contradictory truths," which threatened to subvert its noble aims by ignoble means.[108]

Control over the term "liberalism" unmistakably changed hands at mid-century, passing from an intellectual network organized around Dewey to one shaped by Niebuhr. "Words suffer from the confused mixture of old and new from which all other human institutions suffer," wrote Dewey in an 1948 essay entitled "How to Anchor Liberalism," where he pleaded for a "cooperative effort towards something approaching a body of principles" for liberalism, rooted in "study of specific social conditions."[109] As postwar intellectuals embraced tragedy as an interpretive screen for promoting their political and aesthetic values, however, the modern liberal tradition in the United States shifted from a moving, critical force to an entrenched cynicism about the human condition. Drawn into the folds of the Cold War, liberalism came to signify a fundamental struggle against totalitarianism, a tough-minded realism within the governmental power structure, and a consensus category effectively synonymous with democracy. This change, to be sure, did not occur without protest. Sidney Hook and C. Wright Mills each famously accused their generation of intellectuals with a "failure of nerve." Mills saw the widespread turn away from pragmatism and toward "a tragic sense of life" as evidence that his peers had embraced institutional power rather than the responsibilities of critical intelligence.[110] Hook, writing alongside his mentor Dewey in *Partisan Review*, likewise defended pragmatism, science, and rational experiment against Niebuhr's "reactionary theology."[111] By 1959, however, even Hook had embraced a tragic worldview. In his presidential address at an American Philosophy Association conference, entitled "Pragmatism and the Tragic Sense of Life," Hook concedes that some moral choices involve two incommensurable rights, offering the "Israeli-Arab impasse" as an exemplar. While "many of the rights we presently enjoy we owe to our ancestors," Hook proposes, "who in the process of winning them for us deprived others of their rights . . . it would be a new injustice to seek to redress the original injustice by depriving those of their possessions who hold present title to them."[112] No reparations, no redistribution. As with Niebuhr's view of nuclear détente, Hook turns history into tragic fate. Dissolving pragmatic judgments into a tragic "irony," argues Cornel West, "serves as a way of morally condemning Thrasymachus' doctrine of might makes right yet politically accepting the historical verdict of the 'winners.'"[113]

Dewey had seen radical social action as necessary for any modern liberalism, yet this was soon forgotten as the newly tragic postwar liberal imagination came to justify status quo politics. Despite Niebuhr's early attraction to Marxism in the 1930s, in his mature years as a commentator on national policy he eventually accepted "that the 'oligarchy' was fluid, that inequalities of power were inevitable, that there was 'rough justice' in America, and that the private ownership of property was a 'relatively effective institution of social peace and justice.'"[114] This growing reconciliation between liberal intellectuals and executive power was proudly welcomed by Democratic Vice President Humphrey. Celebrating the twenty-fifth anniversary of Niebuhr's journal *Christianity and Crisis* with a White House banquet in 1966, Humphrey said:

> Dr. Niebuhr has always understood there is no easy way out of difficult dilemmas because there is no escape from the human situation. There is no painless remedy for racial prejudice and injustice which still exists in America. There is no quick or easy victory in war on poverty. And there is no simple solution to the complex, tragic situation facing America in southeast Asia. The challenge is to recognize and to accept the complexity and difficulties of these tasks, yet, nevertheless, to face them in the knowledge that they cannot be evaded. In the words of Keats, "to bear all naked truths and to envisage all circumstances—all calm."[115]

According to Trilling, Keats had praised negative capability as an urge to engage competing ideas and sentiments even if they remain tragically irreconcilable. Humphrey, however, invokes Keats to justify, with "all calm," the nation's ongoing "racial prejudice," the "war on poverty," and even the "tragic situation facing America in Southeast Asia," a "situation" that millions would soon have less hesitancy in calling the War in Vietnam; a situation in which the United States dropped more ordnance on southeast Asia than was detonated in all the military theaters of World War II combined. Humphrey might have stumbled into some of the complexity of this situation, and some of the ambiguity Trilling praised in Keats, had he quoted these lines in full:

> Now comes the pain of truth, to whom 'tis pain;
> O folly! for to bear all naked truths,
> And to envisage circumstance, all calm,
> That is the top of sovereignty. Mark well![116]

The "pain of truth," which Humphrey excised, returns in the ironic gap between these lines and their governmental appropriation. What began as a poet's passionate disinterest, calmly affirming circumstances so he can claim mastery over fate, now serves a means to endorse imperial aggressions, planned and executed at "the top of sovereignty," the executive branch of the American government. By turning state violence at home and abroad into "tragic situations," Humphrey and others removed these decisions from corrective scrutiny, from precisely the critical impulse Trilling imagined that tragic art could produce. As Anne McClintock observes, "the idea of history as tragic" always risks "allowing state violence to be shorn of historical complexity and political agency, so that ethical culpability is more easily cloaked, accountability concealed, and guilt disavowed."[117] Tragedy might compel liberal readers to recognize their personal internal tensions, yet tragedy also can also serve to legitimate the most illiberal abuses of public power by justifying violent conflicts as fateful necessities.

Because liberal thought, as this book continually insists, has been conceptually and historically defined by a set of constitutive dualisms, the question arises as to whether liberalism might be a fundamentally tragic politics, fated to remain constrained by its internal tensions. Dewey and Niebuhr represent two divergent responses to this question: Is the task of politics, as Dewey believed, to move beyond historical dualisms, using experimental procedures and novel aesthetic experiences to alter the meaning of our political concepts? Or as Niebuhr maintained, does intelligence provide no way out, with human agency forever limited by tragic fate and self-defeating irony? As previous chapters have shown, the questions raised by midcentury liberal discourse have often been rediscovered by more recent critical theories, and the notion that liberalism might be constitutively tragic has notably seen renewed attention by political philosophers. Over the past few decades, several critical schools have turned to tragedy to rethink liberalism and its relationship to democratic pluralism. William Connolly, Chantal Mouffe, and Richard Rorty have all praised liberalism, in different ways, for its "tragic" insight into the inevitable tensions produced by democracy enabling a plurality of values, suggesting that liberalism alone acknowledges and protects these competing goods and rights. Libertarian and conservative critics such as Berlin and Michel Oakshott, however, have argued the inverse, claiming that this same flexibility makes liberalism tragically doomed, unable to redress the competing values it admits into political life.[118] Facing these competing interpretations of the liberal tradition, scholars such as Bert van der Brink, Jonathan Badger, and Donald Moon have proposed that liberal politics represents a kind of meta-theoretical tragedy, one likely familiar to any scholars who have explored liberal commitments to multiculturalism, cosmopolitanism, or tolerance: liberalism must continue to affirm value pluralism, while recognizing that, in a pluralist world, this affirmation must itself remain perpetually contested.[119] This book does not presume to settle these theoretical questions. But it has aspired to show how the shift from Dewey to Niebuhr goes a long way toward explaining how the meaning of *liberalism* changed so rapidly in American culture and has argued that this transformative history depended on mutually formative encounters between liberal intellectuals and modernist literary culture.

Arthur Miller and the Ends of Tragedy

As modernist culture exposed tensions in liberal thought, American intellectuals reframed liberalism as a form of tragic subjectivity, tuned to the conflicting values and historical ironies limiting any progressive politics. By rewriting the meaning of modern American liberalism, this tragic postwar imagination not only created a climate ready to reclaim Agee's critique of New Deal documentary practice from the ashes of the 1930s but also fundamentally reframed the meaning of liberalism in American political life, shifting it from a category denoting Depression-era crisis to a category enabling Cold War consensus. This final section considers a marked irony in tragedy's role as a conceptual junction for these midcentury political and literary histories: over the same years when American intellectuals began describing liberal politics as constitutively tragic, literary critics began to worry that tragedy, as a dramatic form, was no longer possible.[120] These concerns crystallized around Arthur Miller's iconic work, *Death of a Salesman* (1949), which became the locus for midcentury debates about the end of tragic form. Beneath these anxieties about the exhaustion of tragedy and the tragic hero lay undeniably political anxieties about the exhaustion of individual agency, an inability to find shared social meaning in this new liberalism's vision of a constitutively divided subjectivity.

Facing industrial capitalism and wartime devastation, cultural critics in the early twentieth century began to doubt whether an individual might still alter society, or meaningfully protest its injustice, through heroic action or self-knowledge. In *The Modern Temper* (1929), Joseph Wood Krutch honed these doubts into a eulogy for tragic drama. Whereas Greek tragedy celebrated human will in the face of death and despair, Krutch suggests that affirming noble heroes has become impossible in a culture that associates humanity with "little people and issues," a vulgarity better suited to the novel.[121] Science, Krutch laments, has revealed humans to be creatures of social circumstance rather than a divine plan, stripping the universe of its mystery, removing from gods their former grandeur, and so emptying any cathartic power from accounts of individual suffering. As American readers sunk into a Depression in 1929, Krutch's pessimistic view of modern life made his book a timely best seller—his audience, as Fox notes, ironically embracing a tragic narrative despite Krutch's own claims that such an interpretive mode was exhausted.[122] Much as Agee's recuperators extracted an individual ethos from his critique of documentary practice, Krutch's book reveals how arguments about the end of tragedy internalize the interpretive power of a public dramatic form into a tragic personal insight. This pattern reappears with George Steiner's classic *The Death of Tragedy* (1961). Steiner echoes Krutch's claim that scientific rationality has left no room for a Hellenic sense of fate: "Where the causes of disaster are temporal," he writes, "where the conflict can be resolved through technical or social means, we may have serious drama, but not tragedy."[123] Social welfare puts a net below the tragic fall, and we cannot imagine "an old-age home for Lear."[124] Both Krutch and Steiner notably equate the dissolution of tragedy with a corresponding turn to documentary. Having lost the noble world of the ancients, Krutch argues, tragic texts now seem "halfway between the work of art and the document."[125] Once "we have ceased not only to write but to *read* tragic works," he argues, "then it will be lost and in all real sense forgotten, since the devolution from Religion to Art to Document will be complete."[126] Steiner similarly differentiates the "realism of the commercial theatre" from tragedy by suggesting that the former "is mere *reportage*, telling us what daily life looks and smells and sounds like in this tenement or along that wharf. The perspective of commercial realistic drama is blind as a camera."[127] For Steiner, as for so many other midcentury intellectuals, the modern culture industry was surreptitiously introducing the psychological and political distortions characteristic of a totalitarian state. Constantly bombarded by banal evils, broadcast across mass media such as radio and television, the public has grown too numb "to fresh outrage" to stir at anything imagined by a tragic poet, with catastrophes that "assail us in such vast, strident numbers, we no longer give them careful hearing."[128]

These attacks on the American culture industry found their most powerful articulation in Max Horkheimer and Theodor Adorno's *Dialectic of Enlightenment* (1947), which famously argued that consumer capitalism had dissolved a vital tension between individual and society, and less famously tied this to the end of tragedy. For Horkheimer and Adorno, commercial desire had overtaken the desire to struggle against social inequality, signaling an end to the classical art form predicated on this struggle: "Thus is tragedy abolished. Once, the antithesis between individual and society made up its substance. Tragedy glorified 'courage and freedom of feeling in face of a mighty foe, sublime adversity, a problem which awakened dread.' Today tragedy has been dissipated in the void of the false identity of society and subject."[129] "Everyone can be like the omnipotent society, everyone can be happy," capitalism promises, "if only they hand themselves over to it body and soul and relinquish their claim to happiness. . . . Their lack of resistance certifies them as reliable customers."[130] For these Frankfurt School thinkers, tragedy did not disappear from the loss of humanity's former nobility or experiential plenitude but from the loss of a constitutive tension between self and society, which supplied tragic art with its agonistic power.[131] Consumer capitalism dissolved this tension through a totalitarian control over everyday life, rendering all social relations unto the marketplace. Only the "vacuous semblance of the tragic" lingers on in the housewife's soap opera or the sensationalized newspaper story, which turn the miseries of modern society into "necessary suffering" and lend late capitalism the "aspect of fate."[132] This suffering no longer serves a cathartic function, or yields a heroic resistance, but rather testifies to the absolute identity between individuals and their consumer society: "The liquidation of tragedy confirms the abolition of the individual."[133] Those possessive individuals, who had formed the engine of classical liberalism now, as willing consumers, erode its foundation. The end of tragedy signals the end of liberalism.[134]

Raymond Williams suggests that this joint dissolution appears clearly in a set of dramas he calls "liberal tragedies."[135] In Henrik Ibsen's plays, such as *A Doll's House* and *Enemy of the People,* a heroic individual opposes a "false society," a principled struggle for change that destroys the protagonist.[136] These heroes, however, launch their struggle and meet their fate from an unshakable investment in the same social system they oppose, which for Williams appears thematically in the "concept of debt."[137] "What happens, again and again in Ibsen," he explains, "is that the hero defines an opposing world, full of lies and compromises and dead positions, only to find, as he struggles against it, that as a man he belongs to this world, and has its destructive inheritance in himself."[138] In liberal tragedy, individuals die knowing that their debt to a corrupting society remains intact, yet they achieve the stature of heroes by recognizing this truth and accepting the incumbent guilt, pursuing their desire for self-realization to a tragic form of knowledge. For Williams, liberal tragedy enjoys its last great flourish in the United States, with the plays of Arthur Miller. Although the modern, pseudo-naturalist dramas of Eugene O'Neill and Tennessee Williams, staged from the 1930s through the 1960s, also invoke a tragic mode at times, Miller's work alone produced sustained debate about tragedy's meaning and purpose, especially his most famous play, *Death of a Salesman* (1949), which became the

The Inward Turn

epicenter for midcentury disputes over tragic form and its relation to liberal politics.

From its opening run, the decisive question surrounding *Salesman* was whether Willy Loman's humble status and plight qualify him as a tragic hero. Critics such as Richard Foster, Eleanor Clark, George Jean Nathan, William McCollom, and Elder Olson all insist that Willy "is too commonplace and limited," the play "too ignoble for the arousal of total catharsis."[139] For critics such as John Gassner, Eric Bentley, and Dan Vogel, however, Willy displays a genuine tragic flaw, "man's innate, eternal, inevitable tendency to self-delusion, ironically induced by uncontrollable external powers."[140] This debate was fueled by the play's tremendous critical success: it won the Pulitzer Prize, the New York Drama Critics' Circle Award, the Theater Club Award, and the Antoinette Perry Award. As *Salesman* was playing on Broadway, Miller also wrote two essays for the *New York Times* in February and March of 1949, attempting to settle the question of tragic form. These essays, arguably the most influential criticism written by a modern American playwright, produced what Gerald Weales calls an "avalanche of genre-defining criticism."[141] "In the tragic view," Miller proposes, "the need of man to wholly realize himself is the only fixed star."[142] This notion would seem utterly alien to the societies that produced *Antigone* or *King Lear*; Miller here neatly encapsulate the governing ideology of what Williams calls liberal tragedy.[143] Tragic heroes need not come from "the well-placed and the exalted," argues Miller, but must only display a desire for "personal dignity," an "individual attempting to gain his 'rightful' position in his society."[144] Miller's liberal hero does not challenge a false society, but only desires his "rightful place" within it. In Miller's heterodox yet coherent view, tragedy preserves "the belief—optimistic, if you will, in the perfectibility of man."[145]

But Miller's iconic drama belies these liberal sentiments. *Death of a Salesman* depicts the last days of Willy Loman, facing his professional and paternal failures. Willy's inadequacy stems from comparing himself to his father and brother, who prospered as possessive individuals in an earlier age.[146] Willy's father, a "Great inventor" and a "rugged" man, made and sold his own flutes, and their trembling notes haunt Willy throughout the play with a nostalgic fantasy: working with one's hands, creating something other hands can hold, whose value comes not from abstract contracts but from metabolizing nature through physical labor.[147] Whereas Willy chases sales across America's highways, his pioneering father would simply "toss the whole family into the wagon, and then he'd drive the team right across the country."[148] To live up to this frontiersman, Willy's brother, Ben, took his possessive urges abroad, extracting value from African diamond mines: "Walked into a jungle, and comes out, at the age of twenty-one, and he's rich!"[149] Ben's death abroad hints at the violence behind these colonialist adventures, yet he haunts Willy much like their father's music, promising lucrative prospects in Alaska. These historical fantasies of possessive individualism are unavailable to Willy, yet he has internalized the invidious, competitive desire his consumer society demands, a desire ultimately destroying what it was intended to secure: the reproduction of his patriarchal economy.

Some critics have complained that the plot device triggering Willy's fatal fall—when Biff stumbles on his infidelity in a hotel room—lacks a clear motive, yet this scene acutely conveys how the same relentless individual desire that created prosperity and happiness for Willy's father and brother leads to his own self-destruction. Reeling with shame, Willy recognizes that he has passed on a doomed ideology of success to his sons, Biff and Happy, who talk of crushing opponents in business and sport, already steal and lie, and leap from one emotionally vapid relationship to the next. In "a false society which the individual alone cannot change," observes Williams, "the original liberal impulse, of complete self-fulfillment, becomes inevitably tragic."[150] With his infidelity discovered, his job lost, and his sons corrupted, Willy's composure cracks. As his haunted memories and need for action converge, he rushes to his backyard to plant a handful of seeds. Through this desperately symbolic return to the land, hoping to ensure some productive futurity, Willy signals his failure as an economic subject and as a father. In a final effort to justify his life through the pecuniary logic that has held him captive, Willy kills himself, intending for his wife Linda to claim his $20,000 life insurance policy. His suicide completes a lifelong struggle to legitimate his value-creating personhood.

Willy embodies a failed classical liberalism, a grasping after possessive individualism and the patriarchal family that sustains it, and so his death demands an ideological reckoning. *Salesman* closes with a *Requiem*, in which Linda, Biff, Happy, and their neighbor, Charley, all stand before Willy's fresh grave, trying to understand his actions. Much as Richard Wright cast one character after another's judgment of Bigger as "blind," the mourners attempt to interpret Willy's life through their own investment in the ideologies of possessive individualism, yet find their interpretations struck down sequentially by Willy's oldest son, Biff. Charley speaks first, affirming Willy as a rugged American frontiersman: "Willy was a salesman. And for a salesman, there is no rock bottom to the life. He don't put a bolt to a nut, he don't tell you the law or give you medicine. . . . He's a man way out there in the blue, riding on a smile and a shoeshine."[151] Not a laborer, who might "put a bolt to a nut," the salesman sells only himself, drifting "in the blue," in a financial market still imagined as a free, open space of possibility: "A salesman is got to dream, boy. It comes with the territory."[152] But Biff strikes this vision down: "the man didn't know who he was." Willy's rare moments of physical labor, Biff protests, provided more satisfaction than his actual job: "there's more of him in that front stoop than in all the sales he ever made."[153] Happy, the athlete, next attempts to reanimate Willy's competitive drive, which he sees as his proper inheritance: "He had a good dream. It's the only dream you can have—to come out number-one man. He fought it out here, and this is where I'm gonna win it for him." But Biff knows too well the self-destructive tendencies behind such invidious competition, having only recently halted his perpetual fighting with Happy. To prevent another scuff, Biff does not speak out against his brother, only looking up with "*a hopeless glance at Happy.*"[154]

When Linda finally speaks, she negates her own attempt to rationalize Willy's actions, unable to understand why Willy would take his life just as they paid off their home. "I search and search and I search," she cries, "and I can't understand it, Willy. I made the last payment on the house today. Today, dear. And they'll be nobody home. *A sob rises in her throat.* We're free and clear. *Sobbing more fully, release:* We're free."[155] In liberal tragedies, Williams argues, debt provides a central mechanism for identifying how pseudo-heroic individuals remain bound to a false society. Throughout *Death of a Salesman*, Willy complains about his debt: "Whoever heard of a Hastings refrigerator? Once in my life I would like to own something outright before it's broken! They time them so when you finally paid for them, they're used up."[156] With the mortgage paid off, Willy may be temporarily "free," yet his guilt still drives him to self-destruction. Willy has not struggled against a false society and fallen defending his principles. He struggles and dies because, despite escaping his debt, he has internalized this commercial society's insatiable desire—not a martyr for liberal values, but their victim. In this way, he embodies the dialectic traced by Horkheimer and Adorno: liberalism rose to dominance in the eighteenth century as an omnivorous instrumental rationality and market freedom, but in late capitalism, these same drives return to destroy the individual whom liberalism gave such totalizing license. Liberalism, despite its heroic effort at enlightenment, was for Horkheimer and Adorno ultimately a tragedy. And yet, as Anderson crucially points out, "the liberalism that serves as the defining other for the Frankfurt school" does not "accurately reflec[t] the existing liberalism" of their postwar era.[157] Even as Horkheimer and Adorno announced the end of a classical liberal project, Trilling and Niebuhr were reanimating American liberalism by marshaling a tragic sensibility much like the one displayed by these European exiles.[158]

In the last analysis, then, it was not tragedy as a metaphysical substance or representational mode that intellectuals were really mourning at midcentury but rather a certain interpretive narrative, a set of reading protocols about heroic individual agency that seemed threatened as these same intellectuals learned to see the modern liberal subject as constitutively tragic, internally riven. *Death of a Salesman* became the locus for disputes about tragic form because, whatever Miller's intentions, the play and its reception embodied this tension between the late liberal reading of tragedy as heroic resistance and an historical moment when American intellectuals doubted whether individuals could produce dramatic social change. Whereas Ibsen's protagonists are driven to destruction by resisting the inequalities of a mass market, Willy dies not because he resists an unbound market, but because his desires are blindly loyal to its destructive impulses. He achieves no insight into what has destroyed him, nor does the audience rise from the *Requiem* able to affirm some principle for social change behind his actions. Tragedy's tension between self and society has passed into a private, tragic sensibility. What Williams calls "the self-enclosed, guilty and isolated world," which comes from seeing individuality as a fractious "self against self," defines the tragic liberal imagination present in Agee and in Miller, in Trilling and in Niebuhr.[159] Even as critics saw tragedy reaching an impasse in Miller's drama, however, this tragic liberal imagination was reshaping the nation's political consensus, a historical irony that helps explain why some liberals went searching for a hero, a leader who might embody—and perhaps transcend—their newfound aesthetic.

4 Ending in Style
JFK, Nabokov, and the Apotheosis of a Liberal Aesthetic

Modernism always entailed a fierce devotion to style. From Flaubert, who aspired to write "a book about nothing . . . held together by the strength of its style," through the decadence of Pater and Wilde, to the innovations of Joyce and Eliot, modern artists regularly equated their work's merit with its distinguishing technique or manner.[1] By that *annus mirabilis* of 1922, J. Middleton Murray could affirm that "style is not an isolable quality of writing; it is writing itself."[2] "Can we not say," asked John Crowe Ransom somewhat later and quite rhetorically, "that fiction, in being literature, will have style for its essential activity?"[3] Long after Ransom's New Critical standards have been cast aside, theorists such as Jacques Rancière still mark the rise of a modern "aesthetic regime" by its scandalous "indifference of style with regard to subject matter."[4] Whereas style once meant a "choice of modes of expression appropriate to the different characters in a given situation and of ornaments proper to the genre," argues Rancière, with the moderns, style "becomes the very principle of art."[5] And yet sometime in the 1940s or 1950s, the story goes, style suddenly ossifies—modernism's experimental well runs dry. After Joyce's *Wake* and Samuel Beckett's *Endgame*, style no longer seems a shocking innovation but a desperate artifice, not a revolutionary assault but a self-conscious meditation on the limits of aesthetic experience. In his influential writing on postmodernity, Fredric Jameson links this apparent collapse in modernist style to the waning liberal individualism from which it had emerged: "the great modernisms were . . . predicated on the invention of a personal, private style, as unmistakable as your fingerprint, as incomparable as your own body. But this means that the modernist aesthetic is in some way organically linked to the conception of a unique self and private identity, a unique personality and individuality, which can be expected to generate its own unique vision of the world and to forge its own unique, unmistakable style."⁶ In the 1950s, argues Jameson, American mass consumerism eroded liberal culture's orienting commitment to a "unique self and private identity," leaving no autonomous individuality to make manifest in a singular style. Modern art soon passes into postmodern pastiche, cobbling together bits of its broken history, talking through "voices of the styles in the imaginary museum."⁷ Only a few "masterpieces of the late modern" such as *Lolita*, suggests Jameson, preserve the "formal splendor" of a modernist style against mass American culture, which Nabokov's "national allegory" memorably captures in its cross-country trips, motels, and soda shops.⁸

Familiar though this narrative of decline may be, however, modernist art and American liberalism in fact shared a newfound cultural orthodoxy during the Cold War, their ideological reconciliation precisely mediated by a mutual investment in individual style. As Greg Barnhiesel explains in *Cold War Modernists*, during the 1950s artists, intellectuals, and government agencies together "*redefined* modernism as an affirmation of Western bourgeois liberal values."⁹ No longer a "threatening, foreign, and fundamentally antibourgeois movement," modernism rather came to be seen as an expression of individuality and freedom, cardinal values in a struggle to promote American democracy—and capitalism—against its Soviet rival.¹⁰ Revisionary work by scholars such as Barnhiesel, Serge Guilbaut, and Frances Stonor Saunders has demonstrated how modernist art was turned into "a weapon" in the "cultural Cold War," a conflict ideologically and financially supported by institutions ranging from the Congress for Cultural Freedom, the United States Information Agency (USIA), and the Central Intelligence Agency (CIA), to the Ford Foundation, the Museum of Modern Art, and literary magazines such as *Partisan Review* and *Encounter*.¹¹ Through this institutional network, postwar liberals successfully taught American audiences to see modern artwork not as an aggressive social critique but as an autonomous aesthetic practice, "an empty vessel of style and technique that could then be filled with Cold War-specific meaning."¹² Guilbaut, for instance, shows how Abstract Expressionism and Jackson Pollock's action painting provided "a style equally aloof from the right and the left" that critics framed as an assertion of individual agency, with "a new standard of reference based on alienation and on the notion of the freedom of the artist as an individual."¹³ Through personal style, modernist art was seen to instantiate the freedom and self-expression permitted to individuals by liberal democracy in the United States, evidence levied by state agencies and cultural organizations of the nation's ideological superiority to a Soviet regime that rejected political liberties, capitalism, and modernism alike.

This chapter examines how claims about style, serving as an interface between aesthetic and political discourse during the Cold War, mediated an ideological reconciliation between American liberals, modernist culture, and state power in the 1950s and early 1960s. This completes the narrative arc traced by this book, which has moved from an exposition of aporias in modern liberal thought in its first two chapters to an emphasis on those intellectuals who sought to remake American liberalism by appropriating central concepts in modernist culture. As the last chapter explained, postwar liberals increasingly focused on cultivating an aesthetic sensibility tuned to the ineradicably conflictual nature of political life, a retreat from the socioeconomic struggles of the 1930s enabled by a booming postwar economy. This "new liberalism" made conceptual dualisms in liberal thought —between the individual and the social, rights and needs, autonomy and dependence—constitutive of a reimagined subjectivity, and made modern literature privileged material for documenting and facilitating the intellectual's private process of character formation. The last chapter showed how some postwar intellectuals, such as James Agee, sank into a permanently riven sensibility, often using "tragedy" to legitimate their interpretive protocols about political and social life; this chapter draws upon novels by Vladimir Nabokov to examine how other liberal intellectuals in the United States came to promote a heroic form of political agency rooted in individual style.[14] As with "tragedy" in the previous chapter, "style" did not so much provide postwar liberals with a conceptual solution to liberalism's internal tensions as a performative screen for concealing and containing them. Through readings of *Bend Sinister* (1947) and *Pnin* (1957), this chapter's first two sections show how liberals from Lionel Trilling to David Riesman reframed politics as an aesthetic practice, in which personal style was imagined to at once express and protect an individual's autonomous character. After World War II, social scientists distilled from Hitler and Stalin's regimes the blanketing category of totalitarianism, which became a pervasive threat not only to "liberal democracy" but also to the individual psyche.[15] To defend against this threat, government agencies, cultural critics, and mass-market sociology all began to promote an antithetical entity: an individuated, democratic character. With individual freedom now thought to be sheltered not simply in legal rights but in private character, liberal intellectuals increasingly placed a decisive import on personal style, understood as the visible manifestation of this democratic character's cultural and political autonomy.

During the same years in which Nabokov's American novels were being written, published, and praised for their idiosyncratic style, this liberal aesthetic reached the nation's highest levels of government. After Adlai Stevenson's presidential campaigns in 1952 and 1956 reorganized the Democratic Party around an intellectual character type, a liberal politics of style achieved its triumphant affirmation with the election of John F. Kennedy in 1960. What was ubiquitously called "the Kennedy style" during his campaign and iconic thousand days in the White House was not simply a personal formula of looks, charm, and wealth, but the culminating product of a long-term effort by midcentury intellectuals to reorient liberalism away from foundational values and toward a pragmatic politics of character formation, guided by heroic individual style.[16] Kennedy, argues John Hellman, was "strongly influenced by Reinhold Niebuhr's emphasis on original sin and the 'irony of history,'" and crafted his public persona as an intellectual around "a tragic sentiment similar to the modernist vision of life as full of the variety, possibility, complexity, and difficulty that Trilling was urging liberals to adopt."[17] Mixing masculine bravery, Brooks Brothers chic, and learned wit, however, JFK also emerged as a heroic figure for Cold War intellectuals, someone who promised—through the unifying force of his style—to transcend what many liberals had come to see as the tragic limitations inherent in political conflicts. JFK, in short, embodied the aesthetic ideology of Cold War liberalism.

While Nabokov remained unaffiliated with Kennedy's administration or most of the organizations sponsoring the cultural Cold War, he was singularly committed to an aesthetic ideology predicated on his autonomous personal style. And, over time, Nabokov's critics have gradually reanimated the same economy of values promoted by Cold War intellectuals to read his work, turning the ironic modernist style of this purportedly disinterested writer into an instrument for political liberalism. In his novelistic prefaces, his elegant autobiography *Speak, Memory*, his *Lectures on Literature*, and his interviews with magazines such as the *Paris Review* and *Playboy*, Nabokov relentlessly dismissed talk of any sociopolitical events, which he deemed mere "topical trash," and insisted that "it is the style peculiar to this or that individual writer of genius that is alone worth discussion."[18] Many of Nabokov's early, loyal critics accepted this premise, focusing on the patterns that texture his prose, in a practice Maurice Couturier deemed mere "annotation."[19]

No modern author, not even Joyce, has had his style praised as often, or accepted as often by critics as a marker of aesthetic autonomy.[20] Over time, however, scholars came to see Nabokov less as a disinterested aesthete than as a conscientious humanist, grappling with a hidden past, his achieved style a form of "control over history that life as an exile denied."[21] After Richard Rorty's major intervention in *Contingency, irony, and solidarity*, Nabokov's style was finally transformed into a resource for promoting political liberalism. According to Rorty, the ironic style in novels such as *Lolita* trains readers to be liberals by pivoting them from individual self-creation to social solidarity, from private autonomy to public welfare, from aesthetics to politics. Rorty's influential claims have since been buttressed by substantial biographic work, unearthing the deep liberal roots to Nabokov's family tree.[22] Illustrating yet again the entangled literary and political histories traced throughout this project, Nabokov's reframing as a liberal modernist reveals how Cold War efforts to make style an interface between liberal politics and modernist aesthetics have found an afterlife in literary studies.

But if Nabokov's novels do undeniably thematize central conceptual tensions in Cold War liberal discourse, this chapter shows how they reveal a growing skepticism about style's role as an interface between aesthetics and politics. This chapter's second half interrogates this problematic concept in liberal discourse by focusing on the troubled relationship between style and power. Taking up Rorty's reading of *Lolita* (1955), where he marshals Nabokov's modernist style as a way to negotiate between liberalism's constitutive dualisms, the third section argues that Nabokov's novel complicates any presumed affiliation between ironic style and liberal values. Moving from word to world, the final section then shows how critics such as Norman Mailer identified a similarly tenuous link between personal style and liberal values during Kennedy's presidency. For Mailer, the ironic style that freed JFK from dogmatism also enabled him to wield a potentially tyrannical power. Legal theorists and political scientists have more recently echoed this prophetic warning: JFK's presidency marked a dangerous escalation in popular support for unilateral executive power. By welcoming modern artists into the White House as no president had before, Kennedy not only valorized an ironic cultural style for American liberals but also drew intellectuals away from a critical alienation and toward a reconciliation with the state. Having lost their mutually formative antagonism, modernism and liberalism reach a shared apotheosis in Kennedy's stylized politics and, with his death, a symbolic end.[23]

Totalitarianism and the Democratic Character

Nabokov's first novel written in the United States, *Bend Sinister*, depicts a dystopian society amalgamated from various European regimes, in a manner reminiscent of George Orwell's *1984*. Paduk, the novel's tyrant, founds his "Party of the Average Man" on the theory of "Ekwilism." While "socialism had advocated uniformity on an economic plane, and religion had grimly promised the same in spiritual terms," Ekwilism traces human inequality back to a simpler problem: "there existed some individuals with more brains or guts than others."[24] Born with a hideous physical appearance, Paduk is from his childhood onward "dull, commonplace, and insufferably mean," and the novel leaves no doubt that his desire "to make the contents of the human vessel conform to an average scale" comes not from some ideal of racial supremacy or economic redistribution but from formative experiences with his personal shortcomings.[25] Gathering the brutal and unintelligent, Paduk assumes power through "the medium of the most standardized section of the inhabitants, namely the Army," and begins to stamp out all forms of individual distinction.[26] In his introduction, Nabokov describes cobbling together the source material for Paduk's police state from "bits of Lenin's speeches, and a chunk of the Soviet constitution, and gobs of Nazist pseudo-efficiency."[27] This lumping together of Nazis and Soviets does not simply reflect Nabokov's dismissive attitude toward politics but also a broader tendency among postwar intellectuals to abstract from Europe's wartime regimes a pervasive new threat to the liberal individual: totalitarianism.[28] Whereas "the catchword for political evil" had been "imperialism" in the years leading up to World War II, observed Hannah Arendt, totalitarianism took its place thereafter—a shift due in no small part to her own writing, especially the monumental *Origins of Totalitarianism* (1951).[29] Arendt developed a focused definition of this term, and yet totalitarianism soon slipped from a critical subject in political theory into an ideological bludgeon for anti-communist intellectuals, looking to mar the Soviet Union by associating it with the horrors of Hitler's Reich.[30] In his iconic treatise, *The Vital Center*, for instance, Arthur Schlesinger insists that his title "refers to the contest between democracy and totalitarianism," a threat coming from both the Left and the Right.[31] Though invented by European exiles to describe European regimes, notes David Ciepley, totalitarianism soon became a centerpiece in the postwar discourse of American intellectuals, a "photographic negative" for their "liberal democracy" in the Cold War struggle for ideological supremacy.[32]

Social scientists in the United States—many of whom had, like Nabokov, fled a war-torn Europe—came to see this geopolitical struggle between liberal democracy and totalitarianism as depending upon a prior struggle over the individual mind. Trying to explain how brutal dictatorial regimes could gain popular appeal, researchers envisioned a personality type who was vulnerable or even predisposed to ideological extremism. Theodor Adorno and his team received lasting credit for coining *The Authoritarian Personality* (1950), but it was Erich Fromm who first named this phenomenon ten years earlier in *Escape from Freedom* (1941), where he influentially argued that "a victory over the totalitarian forces" had to be won within "the character structure of modern man."[33] According to Fromm's dialectical account, the idealized value of freedom in liberal politics in fact names an ambiguous condition within modern society: as medieval traditions and hierarchies dissolve, individuals become "more independent, self-reliant, and critical," yet at the same time "more isolated, alone, and afraid."[34] What Fromm calls the "greatest achievements of modern culture, individuality and the uniqueness of personality," arise concomitant with a dangerous susceptibility to "feelings of inferiority, powerlessness, individual insignificance," which can drive individuals to escape from their freedom by clinging to figures of authority.[35] In *Bend Sinister*, Nabokov appears to provide an exemplary account of this Manichean struggle between individual autonomy and tyrannical authority. As the philosopher Adam Krug faces down Paduk's totalitarian regime, his attempts to remain a free individual result in a growing isolation and manipulation by those amassed against him. But if *Bend Sinister* seems to neatly reproduce the dichotomies pervading Cold War intellectual discourse—liberal democracy versus totalitarianism, individual character versus collective culture, autonomous style versus mass media—Nabokov's novel gradually betrays an anxiety that liberal intellectuals retrenching into one side of these binaries may end up enabling their antithetical other.

His nation's most esteemed thinker, Krug becomes a lone dissenter when he refuses to sign the loyalty oath that a group of academics intends to offer Paduk's regime. Krug notably opposes this collective coercion by claiming his signature as a marker of intellectual autonomy: "Legal documents excepted . . . and not all of them at that, I never have signed, nor ever shall sign, anything not written by myself."[36] In such moments, *Bend Sinister* defines Krug's integrity as an individual not by protective legal rights but by a presiding contrast in aesthetic and political values with his tyrannical leader, and old schoolyard rival, Paduk. As a symbol for his regime, Paduk chooses the Padograph machine, "a typewriter made to reproduce with repellant perfection the hand of its owner."[37] By demonstrating that "a mechanical device can reproduce personality, and that Quality is merely the distribution aspect of Quantity," Paduk's Padograph neatly reverses Krug's insistence on his personal signature as the formal marking of an autonomous intellect.[38] Their opposed values capture a salient fear among postwar intellectuals that media technologies might facilitate a totalitarian control of personality; as Frankfurt School exiles such as Adorno and Horkheimer were arguing at this time, mass media tutored the public in rote formulas, shaping them into a standardized character who would accept oppression and forget the burden of critical, individuated thought. Given this threat, private character or style, which Nabokov figures in Krug's graphical contours, could seem a bastion for that individual autonomy on which liberal democracy depends. By the 1950s, argues Fred Turner, "journalists and scholars" from varying traditions "agreed: Mass communication could turn the individual personality and, with it, the structure of society as a whole in a totalitarian direction."[39]

This fearful alliance between mass media and political tyranny saturates the cultural landscape in *Bend Sinister*, from the symbolic Padograph machine to the newspapers, movies, and posters of daily life. Paduk, for instance, draws his "sartorial sense" from a popular cartoon strip, "Mr and Mrs Etermon (Everyman)," who illustrate the banality and conformism of the authoritarian character (79). The Etermons aspire only to mundane, middle-class pleasures, "a visit to the movies, a raise in one's salary, a yum-yum something for dinner" (78), and their ubiquitous presence in Krug's society models a complacent citizenship, rooted in mass consumerism: "Poster pictures of Etermon showed him smoking the brand that millions smoke, and millions could not be wrong, and every Etermon was supposed to imagine every other Etermon, up to the President of the State" (78). For a generation of thinkers who came to believe that such cultural conformity would prepare the way for tyrannical power, intellectual independence assumed the status of political resistance. Reading, writing, and thinking alone, Krug's insistence on preserving his individual autonomy and style make him a dangerous outlier in Paduk's police state; an obsequious grocer, accompanying Krug to the university, voices the regime's anxieties about any such solitary behavior: "Less books and more commonsense—that's my motto. People are made to live together, to do business with one another, to talk, to sing songs together, to meet in clubs and stores, and at street corners—and in churches and stadiums on Sundays—and not sit alone, thinking dangerous thoughts" (20).

In this way, Krug seems to embody the "democratic character" that postwar liberals began promoting as an antithesis to the authoritarian personality. For "American intellectuals and government officials" who had come to see a contrast between totalitarian control and liberal democracy as hinging on a contrast in "personality styles," politics became a two-sided effort at "managing the psychological reactions of individual citizens and of whole nations."[40] As Turner explains, the notion of a democratic character—widely circulated among Cold War intellectuals, though never definitively defined—described a form of liberal subjectivity reimagined around the complexity and plurality of modern democratic life. Such individuals, summarizes Turner, were "psychologically whole and able to make rational, independent choices," "changed in response to life circumstances," and "recognized and accepted cultural and racial differences."[41] Governmental agencies, such as the Committee on National Morale, began promoting this character type, insisting that "every personality can be a citadel of resistance to tyranny."[42] This new liberal ideal was disseminated to a general reading audience through a booming paperback market, which not only featured political novels like *Bend Sinister* but also nonfiction coming from the emerging field of social psychology. Popular studies, such as C. Wright Mills's *White Collar: The American Middle Class* (1951), William Whyte's *The Organization Man* (1956), and Milton Rokeach's *The Open and Closed Mind* (1960) warned readers about the personal alienation and political drift caused by a growing homogeneity in American culture and promoted behavioral types that might reinforce individual autonomy. Perhaps the best known of these midcentury studies, *The Lonely Crowd* (1950), by David Riesman and Nathan Glazer, distinguished "tradition-directed," "inner-directed," and "outer-directed" individuals. Riesman and Glazer argued that politics had become but "one of the agencies of character formation," a site where individuals negotiated their relationship to the social whole by selecting among personality types, which came with distinct political "styles."[43] As with most studies in this vein, *The Lonely Crowd* champions an "autonomous man," a character whose private resistance to conformity and manipulation by propaganda would help secure a democratic, pluralist state.

US government agencies saw modernist art as an ideal vehicle for promoting this newfound investment in political and cultural autonomy. "Raised on modernist culture" at the nation's elite universities, explains Saunders, agents at the CIA and USIA "worshipped Eliot, Yeats, Joyce, and Proust," and believed "high culture was not only important as an anti-Communist line of defence [sic], but also the bastion against a homogenized mass society."[44] Easy to market as a medley of diverse yet unique styles, modernism was depicted by government propaganda—and by those cultural critics either directly or indirectly funded by the US government—as a by-product of the personal freedoms granted by liberal democracy in the United States. Nabokov himself had only tangential connections to this cultural Cold War, having opted for his own form of autonomy through exile at American college campuses.[45] However, Nicholas Nabokov, the novelist's cousin, was a pivotal actor in this ideological struggle, his career illustrating the pervasive entanglement of modernist culture and Cold War liberalism. During World War II, Nicholas served alongside figures such as J. K. Galbraith and W. H. Auden in the Morale Division of the US Strategic Bombing Survey Unit, using his musical training as a composer to "establish good psychological and cultural weapons with which to destroy Nazism and promote a genuine desire for a democratic Germany."[46] After the war, Nicholas was appointed Secretary General of the Congress for Cultural Freedom. Drawing on his "bewildering range of contacts and friendships," Nicholas organized international cultural events, such as the Masterpieces of the Twentieth Century festival, held in Paris in 1952.[47] Featuring artwork by virtually every major visual modernist, including Mondrian, Picasso, Seurat, van Gogh, Kandinsky, Klee, Cézanne, Brancusi, and many more, this event's billing emphasized how their creations "would not have been possible except in the climate of freedom in which the great artists, composers and writers of our time have worked," and visitors were offered public seminars on topics such as "isolation and mass communication."[48] "No one before," remarked Nicholas, "had tried to mobilize intellectuals and artists on a worldwide scale in order to fight an ideological war against oppressors of the mind."[49] Backed by the Congress for Cultural Freedom and the CIA, Nicholas waged this ideological war for years, within which modernist art served as a decisive weapon.

Because Adam Krug's intellect, autonomy, and personal style fit so neatly within the aesthetic ideology promoted by midcentury liberals, and because Nabokov constantly claimed these values as his own in his interviews and nonfiction writing, it is easy to see why readers of *Bend Sinister* might gloss the novel as a modernist author's defense of democratic character against the brutal philistinism of the authoritarian personality. Such an "invocation of aestheticism," as Ben Mangrum has shown, was indeed often imagined by postwar intellectuals as "a bulwark against the threat of political tyranny."[50]

And when Paduk's agents attempt to coerce the philosopher through increasingly violent means, they admit the division between their ideological dogmas and Krug's idiosyncratic style. Should he agree to deliver a speech on behalf of the tyrant, one of Krug's false friends encourages him, "The style, the *begonia* (brilliancy), will be yours, of course. Paduk will be satisfied with merely arranging the programme."[51] Far from requiring the erasure of his stubborn individuality, Krug's style—appearing formally in Nabokov's faux trans-lingual flourish *"begonia"*—is precisely what would make his endorsement of Paduk so valuable, legitimating what Eric Naiman has called Paduk's "aesthetic dictatorship."[52] This proposed partnership, however, also crucially implies that a tyrannical power might appropriate Krug's style to its own ends; style would no longer be a reliable site of resistance to tyranny, then, but an independent variable, which the state might learn to manipulate. This problem remains latent throughout most of *Bend Sinister*, buried beneath its heavy-handed contrast between a totalitarian power, spreading idiocy through mass media, and Krug's autonomous intellect, a shining symbol for individual freedom and self-expressivity. Within this Manichean logic, promoted by cultural Cold Warriors such as Nicholas Nabokov, a proper modernist novel would promote and indeed embody a form of aesthetic politics, resisting the tyranny of midcentury American consumer culture through its idiosyncratic style.

And yet readers looking to bind Nabokov and Krug through their stated values must confront the novel's decisive trap. For as often as Krug, like his creator, insists that he is "not interested in politics," politics remain interested in Krug (6). Confident that intellect and style will preserve his individual autonomy, Krug underestimates Paduk's willingness to wield a violent power. Agents of the state begin to tear Krug's friends from their homes and pressure those who remain into exploiting him. Though Krug naïvely goes on "believing that so long as he kept lying low nothing harmful could happen," he becomes more isolated and more afraid, recognizing, too late, how an individuating freedom carries a reciprocal vulnerability (153). When Paduk at last realizes Krug's greatest weakness—his son David—and seizes the boy, it precipitates the novel's climactic end. Mistaken for the child of another "Professor Krug," David gets turned into fodder for Paduk's "release games," an Ekwilist institution providing adolescents with an outlet for violence (218). David suffers a brutal death from this clerical error, which mocks not only totalitarian bureaucracy but also Krug's earlier insistence on his name as marker for individual autonomy.[53] Though stylized intellect seemed to place Krug on the right side of a set of salient Cold War binaries, his values finally provide him no autonomy from state violence, let alone the means to protect his loved ones. Krug discovers his son's mangled body cloaked in a grotesque costume, a scene surreptitiously disclosing once again how an autocratic violence might be hidden in the trappings of style: "The murdered child," now a neutered noun, "had a crimson and gold turban around its head, its face was skillfully painted and powdered: a mauve blanket, exquisitely smooth, came up to its chin" (224). As Krug struggles to process this horrific mixture of brutality and ornament, Paduk's minions train their guns on him.

Just as all seems lost, an authorial voice intrudes dramatically into this third-person narrative: "I felt a pang of pity for Adam and slid towards him along an inclined beam of pale light—causing instantaneous madness, but at least saving him from the senseless agony of his logical fate" (233). Because this authorial voice swaps out Krug's death for a palliative madness, critics have often framed this climactic metafictional gesture as Nabokov affirming, yet again, the heroic power of a stylized individual autonomy against the banality of totalitarian violence. Such a reading, however, misses the way this scene undermines the novel's contrasting political and aesthetic values. Claiming an overriding artistic power, this Nabokovian narrator evacuates Krug's political agency as a dissenting intellectual by reasserting the absolute power of style. As the authorial voice explains: "I knew that the immortality I had conferred on the poor fellow was a slippery sophism, a play upon words. But the very last lap of his life had been happy and it had been proven to him that death was but a question of style" (241). This narrative voice, in other words, transforms style from a marker of Krug's autonomous character into a vehicle for control over his fate. By reducing life and death to a mere "question of style," the narrator transvalues Krug's values, taking the stylized intellectual autonomy that seemed diametrically and democratically opposed to Paduk's tyrannical power throughout the novel's plot and collapsing this antinomy at the level of narrative. For Naiman, this sudden reconciliation of power and style makes *Bend Sinister* "the work by Nabokov that most conclusively establishes an affinity between totalitarianism and art."[54] In his famously prescripted interviews, Nabokov did boast of his tyrannical control as an author, calling himself the "perfect dictator" of his "private world" and his characters but "galley slaves."[55] "Artistic freedom and the ability of the author, unfettered, to work in perfect serenity turn out not to be the antitheses of dictatorship," Naiman concludes, "but its necessary complements. Artistic virtuosity requires unlimited control, and this aesthetic absolute power leads to a world with distinctly totalitarian contours."[56]

Except artistic virtuosity does not lead to political dictatorship, either in the world of our facts or in the world of Nabokov's fiction. Writers and painters were not responsible for Hitler and Stalin's regimes, which famously produced few lasting works of art. Nor, in turn, is *Bend Sinister*'s author responsible for creating an autocratic government, only a fictional dictator named Paduk. As Arendt once warned, the "ideal subject of totalitarian rule" is not "the convinced Nazi or the convinced Communist, but people for whom the distinction between fact and fiction (*i.e.,* the reality of experience) and the distinction between true and false (*i.e.,* the standards of thought) no longer exist."[57] There is a fundamental gap between tyranny in narrative and tyranny in government, and it is precisely where *Bend Sinister* invokes style to reach across this gap that it exposes the breach between aesthetics and politics. Introducing a higher-order narrative allows Nabokov to stage a symbolic resolution of the novel's tensions, with individual style apparently triumphing over the violent power of the regime. By shattering the narrative frame, however, this intrusive metafictionality reveals the contest between Krug's style and Paduk's tyranny to have been mere semblance, existing only within the domain of fiction. Style, in other words, gets decoupled from the political values it carried throughout the novel. Unbound to any underlying ideology, style now palpably fails to defend autonomous individuals against totalitarianism, or private character against public violence. As Paduk alone seems to recognize with his overtures to Krug, style might even be reconciled with violence and put to illiberal ends.

Whereas *Bend Sinister* appeared to reflect the dualistic structure of Cold War liberal discourse, posing an autonomous, stylized character against totalitarian mass culture, the novel's final irony undermines its own rhetorical structure. This climactic attempt to have style bind the world of private language with the world of public politics does not signal art's totalitarian impulses any more than it offers an ideological defense of liberal individualism. No longer an obvious allegory for the Cold War struggle between liberal democracy and totalitarianism, *Bend Sinister* instead concludes by foregrounding an asymmetric relationship between aesthetics and politics, offering an implicit critique of style as a performative illusion—a critique arriving just as this concept began to grow in importance as a mediator between these registers in postwar liberal discourse.

Intellectual Style in an Age of Abundance

The United States entered World War II amid political turmoil and financial instability; it emerged with a booming wartime economy, whose unprecedented growth rates were fueled by an ever-expanding spectrum of consumer goods. As J. K. Galbraith's best seller memorably put it, Americans now lived in an *Affluent Society* (1958) and with this newfound prosperity came changing political imperatives for American liberals. Whereas the "quantitative liberalism" of the 1930s had focused on "problems of unemployment, poverty, and want," argued Schlesinger Jr., Americans in the 1950s needed a "new liberalism, addressed to the miseries of an age of abundance," the "subtle and complicated problem of fighting for individual dignity, identity, and fulfillment in a mass society."[58] Lionel Trilling had found a historical precedent for this renewal of liberal politics in his study *Matthew Arnold* (1939). After the turmoil of 1848, Britain had entered a newfound stability with the 1850s; moving away from their prior radicalism, Victorian intellectuals came to embrace a form of politics rooted in individual character formation, leading to the consensus liberal culture of Gladstone, Dickens, and Mill. In these years, Arnold's emphasis on critical distance, many-sided thinking, and a cosmopolitan, cultivated agency found great appeal. Trilling observes—and through canny use of the present tense, promotes—a strikingly similar shift in values among postwar American liberals: "Style is character," explains Trilling, "it is the quality of a man's emotion made apparent; then, by an inevitable extension, style is ethics, style is government."[59] For Arnold and Trilling alike, self-fashioning and political agency were mutually constitutive projects. Much as Victorian liberals had a hundred years prior, midcentury American intellectuals settling into an age of comfort and consensus in the 1950s began to follow Trilling in seeing style not only as the legible form of "character" but of "government," an interface between individual experience and social life through which liberal subjects shaped themselves and their political values.

Nabokov's novel *Pnin* provides a singularly valuable textual reference for this era, when liberal intellectuals in the United States disarmed their historical alienation from state power by embracing a politics of style. As the last section explained, postwar American intellectuals increasingly reimagined politics as an aesthetic practice, wherein personal style protected an individual's autonomous character from mass culture and totalitarian politics. As the next pages explain, this liberal aesthetic finally found its symbolic hero in John F. Kennedy. Like his two personal advisers, Galbraith and Schlesinger, as well as Trilling, JFK distanced himself from the embattled ideological struggles of the 1930s. Reclaiming "liberalism" from this fraught decade, Kennedy recast it as a mode of governance guided by cultivated personal character: "liberalism is not so much a party creed or a set of fixed platform promises," he maintained, "as it is an attitude of mind and heart, a faith in man's ability through the experiences of his reason and judgment."[60] For those who praised it as well as those who condemned it, the omnipresent descriptor for Kennedy's cultured liberal leadership was *style*, a word that signified more than just his youthful good looks and Brahmin background. Kennedy's dramatic ascendance in national politics represented the signal victory for what Michael Trask calls a Cold War liberal "framework grounded on *stylistics*," an anti-essentialist politics of character, based on an "ironic social style," which replaced grounding principles with a tough-minded intellectual pragmatism.[61] Kennedy's style, though nebulous and contested, served a key discursive role in his brokering a symbolic alliance between modern artists, liberal intellectuals, and executive state power. Nabokov's fiction once again thematizes this contemporary constellation of values, showing how and why alienated intellectuals might take solace in a cultivated style.

Pnin plays out in the wake of those totalitarian regimes amalgamated by *Bend Sinister*. Having fled Revolutionary Russia, Timofey Pnin now teaches as professor of Russian at Waindell College, comfortably ensconced in small-town America, where he spends his life negotiating faculty, family, and the household commodities he can never seem to handle. Late in the novel, however, Pnin reveals that his apparently mundane life represents an ongoing effort to cope with the traumas of totalitarian violence. Amid other Russian émigré intellectuals at The Pines resort, Pnin relates how he and his first love, Mira Belochkin, fled from civil war. While he escaped, Mira slipped from the Bolsheviks into the hands of the Nazis. Her loss has defined Pnin's character: "In order to exist rationally, Pnin had taught himself, during the last ten years, never to remember Mira Belochkin" for "if one were quite sincere with oneself, no conscience, and hence no consciousness, could be expected to subsist in a world where such things as Mira's death were possible."[62] "To the extent that the rise of totalitarian governments is the central event of our world," wrote Arendt, "to understand totalitarianism is not to condone anything, but to reconcile ourselves to a world in which such things are possible."[63] Yet Pnin refuses to admit Mira's loss, refuses to recognize the regime that killed her: "One had to forget—because one could not live with the thought that this graceful, fragile, tender young woman with those eyes, that smile, those gardens and snows in the background, had been brought in a cattle car to an extermination camp and killed by an injection of phenol into the heart."[64]

Faced with "the incredible inhumanity of a world in which he is a perpetual exile," argues Stegner, "Pnin finds redemption from his suffering and loneliness through an adopted style" in the United States, land of plenty.[65] Every bit of this bumbling, lovable émigré's existence reverberates with singular mannerisms, from "the Russian-intelligenski way he had of getting into his overcoat," to his "constant war with insensate objects."[66] During driving lessons, for instance, Pnin struggles with "a harsh instructor who cramped his style" and "issued unnecessary directives in yelps of technical slang"; much as he fails to reconcile his idiosyncratic manner with his instructor's technical jargon, Pnin is "totally unable to combine perceptually the car he was driving in his mind and the car he was driving on the road."[67] Whereas alienation was once understood to be an injurious symptom of life under capitalism, remarks Richard Hofstadter, after World War II it increasingly assumed the status "of a cure or a prescription for the proper intellectual regimen."[68] With character now broadly accepted as a private line of defense against totalitarian politics, and its surrogate in mass culture, midcentury intellectuals felt compelled to render visible an individual, aesthetic identity, an impulse that recurs across otherwise divergent groups. "The spokesmen of the beatnik, and the hipster, and the left," may all have "quarrels about the proper style of alienation and the limits of its expression," Hofstadter observes, but they "all share a common conviction that there is some proper style or stance or posture to be recommended which will somehow release the individuality and creativity of the artist, or sustain the capacities of the social critic and protect him from corruption" in a consumer society.[69] *Pnin* likewise elevates style into an intellectual regimen, a mode of living that inflects the professor's every action. Nabokov's novel captures—through creative flourishes of its own—each "Pninian term" (41), marks the Russian exile engaged in "the pleasant task of Pninizing his new quarters" (35) and describes an office as "lovingly Pninized" (69). Pnin's "difficulty ('dzeefeecooltsee' in Pninian English)" (66) with spoken language produce, as one character puts it, a "nomenclature all his own. His verbal vagaries add a new thrill to life" (135). Pnin's idiosyncrasy extends even to his odd physical features: after a muscular upper body rises up from "a pair of spindly legs," his head seems to float above, so utterly bald that he lacks even eyebrows (7).

A ready epithet exists for balding intellectuals like Pnin—"egg-heads"— thanks to Stewart Alsop, the conservative journalist who first used this term to mock Adlai Stevenson during his run for the presidency in 1952. As the undisputed representative for a cerebral, left liberalism emerging among postwar Democrats, Stevenson fired back with a characteristically witty call to class consciousness: "Eggheads of the world unite, you have nothing to lose but your yolks!"[70] Stevenson fused eloquence with a coy cleverness and, as this retort reveals, a sometimes self-deprecating vulnerability. These same qualities, however, made him a target for the homophobia stirred up by McCarthy's "lavender scare."[71] Unable to garner mass support, Stevenson was defeated handily by the upright Dwight Eisenhower in 1952 and worse still in 1956. Nonetheless, by bringing an intellectual character into the arena of national politics, Stevenson's campaigns proved a vital intermediary step for Kennedy's election in 1960. Stevenson, as Schlesinger puts it, "remade the Democratic Party . . . largely in his own image," teaching American intellectuals to recognize themselves not simply in his Pninian looks but in the learned, witty style of his political character.[72] "Stevenson bewitched the intellectuals by miming from on high . . . their literary perception of politics," and they loved him "as much (if not more) for his style as for his restricted themes."[73] Sociologists like Riesman were helping to reinforce this mimetic association at the time by emphasizing "the process by which people become related to politics, and the consequent stylizing of political emotions."[74] "Stevenson had the dimensions and appeal of a major tragic hero," affirms Hofstadter, "and intellectuals identified his cause with their own. After the embarrassments of the Truman administration, it was refreshing to listen to his literate style."[75]

JFK built upon Stevenson's precedent by running what one observer called "a literary campaign" for the presidency.[76] Already a published historian, who had confronted *Why England Slept* (1940), Kennedy's *Profiles in Courage* (1956) won him the Pulitzer Prize. Though penned predominantly by his speechwriter, Theodore Sorensen, this collection of stories featured senators who defied political expectations and party lines, providing a powerful interpretive narrative within which audiences could understand Kennedy's character. "*Profiles*," explains Hellman, "avoids advocating a specific political cause or even his own Democratic Party's point of view" and focuses on establishing a "modernist vision of life as full of the variety, possibility, complexity, and difficulty that Trilling was urging liberals to adopt."[77] At the same time, however, JFK's personal bravery seemed to transcend the tragic sensibility that consumed postwar intellectuals like James Agee, and which Trilling himself often expressed in his essays. It also dispelled any suggestion of effeminacy, avoiding the specter of homophobia that had clouded Stevenson's campaigns. As a decorated war veteran, who had proved his courage carrying wounded sailors across miles of ocean, Kennedy made it possible to imagine a form of heroic action in government at "a time when Americans feared that their traditional individualism was threatened by the increasing size and scale of organizations."[78] For a generation of Cold War intellectuals, who had come to see liberal politics as anchored to a process of individual character formation, JFK's appeal lay not in his "what" but in his "how," not in his progressive positions—he had proved few in his time as a senator—but in his aura of "'masculine' risk-taking and autonomy."[79] In his iconic essay for *Esquire*, "Superman Comes to the Supermarket," Mailer proclaimed Kennedy "the Hipster as Presidential Candidate."[80]

Praise for the "Kennedy Style," as it came to be known, spread quickly across American media after his televised debates with Richard Nixon in 1960.[81] In these broadcasts, the first for a presidential contest, JFK famously benefited from his looks, charisma, and composure, standing beside a sweaty and somewhat discombobulated Nixon. Yet, as Kennedy's advisor Schlesinger emphasized to voters in a mid-election pamphlet—entitled *Kennedy or Nixon: Does It Make Any Difference?*—these debates also revealed a defining "contrast in political styles."[82] Invoking categories from Riesman's widely read study, *The Lonely Crowd*, Schlesinger identifies Nixon as an "other-directed man," with "no sure sense of his own identity," who acted only to create a popular image of himself. Kennedy, by contrast, represented that "autonomous" individual praised by Riesman and other midcentury sociologists, someone whose creativity and intellect were backed up by a tough-minded, independent character.[83] "Kennedy's personal manner," insists Schlesinger, "is studiously unemotional, impersonal, antihistrionic. . . . His is the world, not of the sob story, nor of the high school debater, but of serious men trying to find serious solutions to serious problems."[84] Had he turned to chapter 4 of *The Lonely Crowd*, Schlesinger would have found a searching description for this mode of political analysis: "in imitation of the marketplace, politics becomes a sphere in which the manner and mood of doing things is quite as important as what is done."[85] "Perhaps only a President who was at the same time seen as a war hero, a Roman Catholic, a tough politician and a film star," Schlesinger later mused, "could have infected the nation with so gay and disturbing a spirit. But Kennedy did exactly this with ease and grace; and, in doing so, he taught the country the possibilities of a new national style."[86] "As first Adlai Stevenson and then John Kennedy became the symbols of liberal politics," summarize Newfield and Grenfield, "Style became everything."[87]

The newfound emphasis on style within American liberalism, certified by Kennedy's election, made possible an unprecedented *"rapprochement between the intellectuals and their society."*[88] During the 1950s, middle-class Americans had enjoyed rising standards in income, luxury consumption, and secondary education; JFK's heroic leadership now modeled, at the highest level, a national desire for cultured intelligence. And as president, Kennedy sated the desire for recognition among artists and intellectuals, not only by founding the Advisory Council on the Arts—predecessor to the National Endowment for the Arts—but also by incorporating artists and intellectuals into the pageantry of his administration, "awarding them a kind of official recognition" in White House affairs.[89] Schlesinger, serving as special adviser, worked with Letitia Baldrige, Jackie Kennedy's social secretary, to fashion a cultural program that broke sharply with the stiff atmosphere of the Eisenhower years. As Baldrige's memoir, *In the Kennedy Style*, recounts, during their regular galas, the Kennedys served cocktails before dinner, procured a French chef for the kitchen, and invariably invited some of the nation's foremost literary figures. One dinner at the White House, honoring André Malraux, drew Arthur Miller, Saul Bellow, Archibald MacLeish, Robert Lowell, Elia Kazan, Robert Penn Warren, Edmund Wilson, and Tennessee Williams.[90] On another evening, Lionel and Diana Trilling, Robert Frost, James Baldwin, and John Dos Passos joined John Glenn, Robert Oppenheimer, and Linus Pauling for a dinner honoring Nobel Prize laureates, which one newspaper deemed the "President's Easter egghead roll on the White House lawn."[91] Proposing a toast, Kennedy proclaimed his guests "the most extraordinary collection of talent, of human knowledge, that has ever gathered at the White House, with the possible exception of when Thomas Jefferson dined alone."[92] Such a flash of ironic wit, thinly veiling the mutual flattery beneath, illustrates how Kennedy could win over such a serious and diverse range of figures. Irony, once a weapon wielded by modern artists, now flattered them. As Gore Vidal noted, "there were few intellectuals in 1960 who were not beguiled by the spectacle of a president who seemed always to be standing at a certain remove from himself, watching with amusement his own performance."[93]

In 1960, concludes Vidal, "politics and literature officially joined forces," ending what had been a mutually formative antagonism between American liberalism and modernist culture.[94] Through ceremonial participation in White House affairs, literary intellectuals shared vicariously in presidential power; through a symbolic allegiance with modern artists and intellectuals, JFK in turn displayed his cultured political character. Kennedy's most acute critic among the literati, Norman Mailer, observed how the style inflecting his campaign had appeared to reconcile the rebellious modernist irony of the 1920s with the advertising culture of the 1950s:

> It occurred to one for the first time that Kennedy's middle name was just that, Fitzgerald, and the tone of his crack lieutenants, the unstated style, was true to Scott. The legend of Fitzgerald had an army at last, formed around the self-image in the mind of every superior Madison Avenue opportunist that he was hard, he was young, he was In, his conversation was lean as wit, and if the work was not always scrupulous, well the style could aspire.[95]

Between 1952 and 1968, notes Michael Szalay, the Democratic and Republican Parties had indeed "turned to Madison Avenue for help in selling presidential candidates," part of the nation's larger shift to a post-Fordist economy, wherein advertising produces consumer desires.[96] For a young college graduate in the liberal arts, Kennedy's administration represented an irresistible mixture of cultured style and political power—so long, of course, as one was willing to leave behind a Greenwich Village model of intellectual praxis, which hoped to challenge established values from the outside, for a professional, white-collar life within the establishment, within postwar capitalism's new cultural markets. Any intellectual retreating from their constitutive alienation into a suspicious conformity would have been stigmatized in previous decades. But when sanctioned by a handsome young commander in chief, whose wry wit and Brooks Brothers glamour tapped into the dreams of more than one generation of Ivy-trained men of letters, the allure of privilege and public recognition proved irresistible. Even as sharp a critical mind as Arendt affirmed that by inviting in so "many eminent people in the notoriously 'unpolitical' field of the arts and letters," Kennedy "bestowed upon the whole sphere of government a new prestige and a new dignity." Having taken on the "awe-inspiring, solitary responsibility" of the presidency, Arendt insists, it was Kennedy's "style which elevated politics, as has been said before, to a new, higher level." After his assassination, "everything will go on just as before—except that it will be done in a different *style*."[97]

Not all intellectuals, however, were so taken with Kennedy's stylized politics. After being invited to the White House for a private interview, Alfred Kazin reportedly infuriated JFK with his essay "President Kennedy and Other Intellectuals," where he rebukes the partnership between modern intellectuals and executive power. "At this juncture," Kazin argues, "Kennedy's shrewd awareness of what intellectuals can do, even his undoubted inner respect for certain writers, scholars and thinkers, is irrelevant to the tragic issues and contributes nothing to their solution."[98] Clinging to a tragic sensibility described in this book's preceding chapter, Kazin lambasts the enthusiasm for Kennedy's leadership, viewing it, as other critics did, to be an "exaltation of managerial style over substance."[99] Whereas many midcentury intellectuals hoped that style might preserve some aesthetic and political autonomy against the encroachments of a mass market, Kazin saw how style and intellect had been decoupled from any political values, and subsumed into a market logic. "To be an 'intellectual,'" he insists, "is the latest style in American success, the mark of our manipulatable society."[100] Kennedy's "cultivation of the highbrow world as an executive taste and Presidential style" represents little more than a political ploy, Kazin charged, neutering the critical impulse of intellectuals through ceremonial illusion.[101] Whereas the intellectuals of the 1930s defined themselves as a social class through reflexive critique, "intellectual style" was now a means for literary and governmental figures to signal their shared cultural capital in a booming Cold War economy. Kennedy may have been "an ironist in a profession where the prize usually goes to the apparent cornball," but this precisely revealed how irony, tried and true weapon to peel away ideology for earlier modernists, had by the 1950s been reconciled with those entrenched forms of power they had once challenged.[102] "The liberalism of the fifties and sixties, with its unconcealed elitism and its adulation of wealth, power, and 'style,'" summarizes Christopher Lasch, "was firmly rooted in a social fact of prime importance: the rise of the intellectuals to the status of a privileged class, fully integrated into the social organism."[103] Caught up in the pursuit of personal success, America's liberal intellectuals abandoned their historical responsibility as agents of social critique, of speaking truth to power.

Pnin anticipates this intellectual failure. After the death of his beloved

Mira, Pnin withdraws from history, committed to cultivating a personal style.[104] In a striking moment, the chair of Pnin's department observes how the crematorium at Buchenwald where Mira was burned was only "an hour's stroll from Weimar, where walked Goethe, Herder, Schiller, Wieland, the inimitable Kotzebue and others" (135). Nazism's horrors took place in "the cultural heart of Germany," what "the President of Waindell College, renowned for his use of the *mot juste*," calls "that nation of universities" (135). These remarks offer a quiet but clear warning against intellectuals mistaking their cultured, alienated consciousness—each a Flaubert, searching after the perfect word—for resistance to political tyranny. But as with Adam Krug, Pnin refuses to use his intellect to engage with historical and political reality, and, as in *Bend Sinister*, style does not represent a simple vehicle for autonomy but also a potential vulnerability. Pnin's manifold quirks certify his aesthetic individuality in Waindell, a banal American college town, yet this distinguishing character also precipitates Pnin's routine abuse. At one point, he overhears Jack Cockerell, chair of the English Department, in the midst of his "famous act—he being one of the greatest, if not the greatest, mimics of Pnin on the campus," a description revealing this act to be common practice (36). Pnin has learned to absorb rather than react to injustice: "I hear every, every sound from downstairs, but now it is not the place to discuss it, I think" (37). Meek and gullible, Pnin makes easy prey for characters such as Liza Bogolepov, his manipulative first wife, who leaves him for a psychiatrist, then returns, seven months pregnant, and announces "it had all been a mistake," duping Pnin into paying her fare to America (47). Pnin's oppressive treatment by others, argues Stegner, makes him an Adam Krug "resurrected in America," only "in this democratic culture, rebels and oddfellows are not shot for their failure or inability to conform: they are simply ridiculed and subtly undermined into oblivion."[105]

Nabokov's campus novel, summarizes Michael Wood with characteristic acuity, was his way of "dueling with history," grappling with a traumatic past that "Pnin couldn't bear to think of" using half-hidden ironies.[106] Like Pnin, Nabokov fled Europe's tyrannical regimes and found comfort in American collegiate life; like Pnin, Nabokov committed himself to cultivating an idiosyncratic personal style, a marker of his intellectual autonomy. Yet unlike Pnin, and unlike so many of those who flocked to Kennedy's galas, Nabokov shows an awareness of style's limit as a political value and through his narrative ironies expresses a recurring fear that intellectuals embracing self-fashioning as a shield against political tyranny might end up isolated and vulnerable to a manipulative power.¹⁰⁷ By abandoning social struggle for stylized comfort, Pnin anticipates the failure of postwar liberals in the United States, who embraced Kennedy's cultured power rather than sustain the critical project that defined modern American liberalism with its emergence in the 1930s. In the final pages of Nabokov's novel, Pnin belatedly recognizes how his personal experience could have made him uniquely suited to grapple with political action. Issuing a rare burst of optimism, Pnin imagines turning his classroom next year into a sweeping forum on global injustice: "You and I will give next year some splendid new courses which I have planned long ago. On Tyranny . . . On all the precursors of modern atrocity. Hagen, when we speak of injustice, we forget Armenian massacres, tortures which Tibet invented, colonists in Africa. . . . The history of man is the history of pain!"¹⁰⁸ Just as Pnin recognizes his potential as an intellectual, however, Dr. Hagen informs the professor that he has been let go by the college. With this brutal negation, Nabokov throws into ironic relief an unfulfilled possibility, not simply for the novel but for midcentury American liberals: to push intellectual experience from private alienation into public engagement, to address the violence of the historical past and its continuity with the political present, to sustain critique even amid a newfound comfort.

Lolita and the Liberal Ironist

After Nabokov's death, scholars gradually displaced his self-professed aestheticism with a reparative emphasis on the moral and political values latent in his fiction. This shift was encouraged by Nabokov's son, Dmitri, who sought to dispel the early critical view of his father as a cold and indifferent aristocrat. Writing in a memoir, Dmitri invokes the death of another iconic midcentury figure to illustrate Nabokov's profound yet private moral character. While the nation mourned Kennedy's loss in November 1963, Dmitri recalls, his father's pity extended beyond the fallen icon to a suspect who seemed too "little" or "weak" for the crime committed:

> I recall his pang of pity upon seeing the grisly newsreels at the time of John Kennedy's assassination—not only for the dead president, but also for a still innocent (inasmuch as only suspected) Oswald, shown bruised and black-eyed; "if they have worked over (*zamoochili*) this poor little guy (*chelovechka*) needlessly . . ." he said, with the menacing tone he used only when defending the weak and blameless. . . . When the facts were established his attitude obviously changed. But I wonder how many people had such a first reaction.¹⁰⁹

Despite his "more obtuse commentators," Dmitri insists, the same "freedom from anything cruel, cheap, or mean" Nabokov displayed after Kennedy's death also presides over his novels.[110] To reinforce the moral continuity between author and fiction, Dmitri slyly cites a phrase, "pang of pity," drawn from the final episode in *Bend Sinister*, when Nabokov's narrative demiurge intervenes to save Krug after the death of his son. This climactic scene, and its echo in Dmitri's memoir, have since become signal moments in a major effort to reframe Nabokov's fiction as the work of a liberal humanist, a project taken up by scholars Brian Boyd, Leland de la Durantaye, Dana Dragunoia, Andrea Pitzer, and, most prominently, Richard Rorty. In its three short words—forming a fatherly acronym, "p.o.p."—this echoed phrase undeniably captures Nabokov's stylistic will: despite the morbid subject matter, a slight alliterative bounce betrays his controlled, yet unmistakable joy in the medium of language. For Rorty, however, this phrase more importantly signals Nabokov's "inability to put up with the thought of intense pain."[111] Nabokov interferes with Adam Krug's "logical fate" in *Bend Sinister*, Rorty maintains, because of the "intensity of his pity," a counterweight to that "capacity for bliss" usually treated as the characteristic feature of Nabokov's rapturous prose.[112] On these grounds, Rorty identifies Nabokov as a liberal: someone, according to the definition he adopts from Judith Shklar, who believes that "cruelty is the worst thing we do."[113] A renowned and controversial public intellectual, Rorty's efforts at fusing liberalism, pragmatism, and poststructuralism in *Contingency, irony, and solidarity*, by way of authors such as Nabokov, has generated diverse and contested responses.[114] Sidestepping many of the well-worn philosophical disputes that Rorty's work has occasioned, this section focuses on his attempt to put Nabokov's modernist style in the service of political liberalism. Nabokov's reframing as a liberal modernist reveals how midcentury efforts to make style an interface between liberal politics and modernist aesthetics have found an afterlife in literary studies, in yet another example of the enduring entanglement between literary modernism and liberal politics traced throughout this project.

Rorty begins his project by insisting that the constitutive dualisms of liberal thought cannot be reconciled, that public and private, individual self-creation and social solidarity, must remain "equally valid, yet forever incommensurable" ends.[115] As a replacement for this aim, which thinkers such as Dewey saw as the essential dialectical task of a modern liberalism, Rorty offers the ideal of the "liberal ironist." By "liberal," Rorty means someone who sets out to avoid being cruel to others; by "ironist," he means someone who accepts the contingency of their language, values, and sense of self, who accepts that politics will never mean convincing others through rational argument. Setting aside all the qualms one might raise about these definitions, if one accepts Rorty's terms, then the ironist who also aims to be liberal faces a decisive question: "Why not be cruel?"[116] Refusing any theoretical answer as inevitably essentialist or circular, Rorty insists that a sense of human solidarity must come through imaginative experience. Enter the novelists. According to Rorty, one can understand liberalism by reading Mill, Dewey, and Habermas, and one can understand irony by reading Nietzsche, Heidegger, and Derrida. But the vital task of stabilizing these inclinations through a sense of solidarity—the task, in other words, of bridging the divorced realms of public and private, of navigating the constitutive tensions in liberalism's political grammar—falls to writers such as Orwell and Nabokov, whose fictions "warn the liberal ironist intellectual against temptations to be cruel."[117]

But casting Nabokov as a cruelty-loathing liberal requires careful interpretive footwork. For as readers have long recognized, his fiction positively brims with cruelty: with betrayals, beheadings, assassinations, and, above all, with children dead or abused.[118] Despite the deus ex machina that closes *Bend Sinister*, notes Brian Walter, "Nabokov's novels feature numerous other victims of senseless and agonizing fate," and "no narrative deity intrudes to save Cincinnatus from Pierre or Lolita from Humbert or John Shade from Gradus."[119] According to Rorty, however, *Lolita* marks a sea change in Nabokov's values. Throughout his life, Nabokov fashioned a "private mythology about a special elite—artists who were good at imagery, who never killed, whose lives were a synthesis of tenderness and ecstasy, who were candidates for literal as well as literary immortality, and who, unlike his father," a reformer assassinated by reactionaries, "placed no faith in general ideas about general measures for the general welfare"; but starting with *Lolita*, Rorty proposes, Nabokov betrays an "inability to believe his own general ideas."[120] Abandoning the dichotomy between individual style and tyrannical power that (at least superficially) structures novels like *Bend Sinister* and *Pnin*, *Lolita*'s singular challenge, as well as its singular appeal, arises from internalizing these antitheses within one character: the pederast literary scholar Humbert. By entertaining the possibility that there might be "sensitive killers, cruel aesthetes, pitiless poets," *Lolita* pushes its reader towards an equivocal experience: drawn to the narrator's effusive style, yet aware of the violent power he inflicts on Lolita's bodily integrity and legal rights.[121] Trilling aptly described this experience in an early, celebratory review, published with the CIA-funded *Encounter* magazine: "we find ourselves the more shocked when we realize that, in the course of reading the novel, we have come virtually to condone the violation it presents . . . we have been seduced into conniving in the violation, because we have permitted our fantasies to accept what we know to be revolting."[122] As Humbert's style seduces his reader, it cloaks his infamous seduction of Dolores Haze. And, in his franker moments, Humbert admits this ploy. Awaiting trial for killing Clare Quilty, the man with whom Lolita escapes his grasp, Humbert quips: "You can always count on a murderer for a fancy prose style."[123] As Wood explains, Humbert uses his incarceration to claim "a sensational stylistic license" as a storyteller; he will "overwrite when he feels like it, parody himself whenever he wants, and we shall applaud, or at least put up with him" to hear his story.[124]

As he relates his tale, Humbert promotes an aesthetic ideology that would displace his desire for Dolores Haze from an issue of criminal abuse into the stuff "of aurochs and angels, the secret of durable pigments, prophetic sonnets, the refuge of art" (309). Most famously, Humbert describes the "indescribable itch of rapture that [Lolita's] tennis game produced in me—the teasing delirious feeling of teetering on the very brink of unearthly order and splendor" (230). His narrative captures Lolita midswing, frozen in space and time, and marks the organic unity of each corner of her body in a blazon that indeed seems to transform his unrelentingly lustful gaze into the art critic's eye for architectonics:

> My Lolita had a way of raising her bent left knee at the ample and springy start of the service cycle when there would develop and hang in the sun for a second a vital web of balance between toed foot, pristine armpit, burnished arm and far back-flung racket, as she smiled up with gleaming teeth at the small globe suspended so high in the zenith of the powerful and graceful cosmos she had created for the express purpose of falling upon it with a clean resounding crack of her golden whip. (231–32)

Humbert praises her serve's "beauty, directness, youth, a classical purity of trajectory" as if it had been painted by Rafael, and yet notes that "despite its spanking pace," it was "fairly easy to return" (233). "Her form," remarks Humbert, "was an absolutely perfect imitation of absolutely top-notch tennis —without any utilitarian results" (231). By dismissing effects in favor of form,

Humbert inculcates his reader in an aesthetic ideology that would reciprocally free his stylized gaze on Lolita's form from any vulgar complaints about moral decency or legal right.[125] Nabokov arguably echoes this project in his afterword, claiming that "a work of fiction exists only insofar as it affords me what I shall bluntly call aesthetic bliss."[126] As "one of the rare and unquestionable masterpieces of the late modern," concludes Jameson, Nabokov's insistence on aesthetic autonomy gets "acted out on the two levels of plot and style."[127]

Much as Cold Warriors had worked to reframe the jarring styles of modernist artwork into expressions of individual autonomy in a liberal democracy, Rorty aims to transpose *Lolita*'s cruel aestheticism into an instrument guiding the liberal ironist. To do so, he must provide a counterintuitive set of interpretive protocols. As readers lose themselves in Humbert's exuberant style, Rorty argues, they come to participate in his "cruel incuriosity," his inability to recognize how a personal pursuit of ecstatic autonomy might entail suffering for others.[128] Rorty's best example involves the "Barber of Kasbeam" episode, in which another father mourns for his lost son. By listening to Humbert's lengthy sentence, Rorty contends, readers partake in the pederast's surprise when he belatedly realizes what the Barber has been talking about:

> In Kasbeam a very old barber gave me a very mediocre haircut: he babbled of a baseball-playing son of his, and, at every explodent, spat into my neck, and every now and then wiped his glasses on my sheet-wrap, or interrupted his tremulous scissor work to produce faded newspaper clippings, and so inattentive was I that it came as a shock to realize as he pointed to an easelled photograph among the ancient gray lotions, that the moustached young ball player had been dead for the last thirty years.[129]

With this sudden recognition, insists Rorty, Nabokov intends for his reader to perceive how they have participated in an incuriosity about the barber's loss and to reject this behavior as cruel. Nabokov's style, in other words, springs its liberal irony on readers like a trap; cruelty becomes his currency, sensitizing readers to tendencies in their character through an interpretive circuit of exposure and retreat. In this way, Rorty argues, a novel like *Lolita* can help liberal ironists "see the effects of our private idiosyncrasies on others . . . how our attempts at autonomy, our private obsessions with the achievement of a certain sort of perfection, may make us oblivious to the pain and humiliation we are causing."[130] For Rorty, nothing can fully repair the breach between liberalism's constitutive dualisms, between private and public, between individual self-fashioning and social solidarity; yet modern literary form, he insists, allows the liberal ironist to sustain a subjectivity defined by these competing urges. Through the experience of narrative style, novelists like Nabokov provide the basis for a liberal political aesthetic, "a redescription of liberalism" into a force "poetic" rather than merely "rational."[131]

Although many of Rorty's premises, drawn from poststructuralist theory, would have been foreign to midcentury intellectuals, his drive to reimagine liberalism as a form of self-fashioning bears a striking resemblance to the ideas of postwar liberals such as Trilling, who likewise hoped that modernist literary style might help individuals—torn between their liberal goodwill and their tragic sense of irony—to sustain some form of social solidarity. As this book has continually insisted, much of what falls under the rubric of "critical theory" has been rediscovering tensions in the liberal tradition that prior generations of liberal intellectuals recognized. Like the "new liberals" who emerged after World War II, Rorty notably abandons any real demand for collective action, which his hero Dewey saw as the prerequisite for a modern liberalism, indeed as the veritable meaning of intelligence. In this way, Rorty's reading practice finally says less about Nabokov's fiction than about the insularity of the liberal intellectual since the 1960s, the only audience for whom his interpretive protocols really hold. For to read Nabokov in the manner Rorty prescribes, one must already be a liberal: not simply possessing the time, education, and desire to read Nabokov's work but also predisposed to recoil from having one's cruelty to others pointed out. As Trilling and Riesman would have appreciated, moreover, this interpretive circuit also hinges on the conviction that an author's style provides a clear index of their political character; only by believing that Nabokov's richly ironic prose conceals a stable pedagogic agenda can one dismiss his voluminous cruelties as a prop for his better liberal intentions. But this chapter has shown how novels such as *Bend Sinister* and *Pnin* precisely thematize the failings of such a blind ideological faith in style. Despite several generations of liberal intellectuals associating style with individual autonomy and creative intellect, style does not represent a steady value but rather an interpretive problem in Nabokov's fiction, which can enable precisely those tyrannical cruelties that liberal political thinkers and literary critics throughout the twentieth century have continually held it to oppose.

By dramatizing a fusion of style and power, Nabokov's most famous novel extends this immanent critique, exposing a gap between performed manner and private values only surreptitiously disclosed by his earlier work. As Trevor McNeely aptly puts it: "*Lolita* was written to prove a simple point in a complex way . . . that style can do anything."[132] This "anything" must be viewed dialectically: in Humbert's hands, style subsumes the reader's moral and legal concerns into aesthetic judgments; however, for Dolores Haze—surely the most frequently overlooked eponymous character in modern fiction—style also provides an enabling power through which she finally manipulates her manipulator, a performed manner disguising her private values. During her captor's tennis lessons, Dolores first begins to see Humbert's obsession with style as his greatest vulnerability. Humbert hinted at this weakness earlier on, as he describes prior erotic engagements. Searching for a first wife, or perhaps just a "soothing presence, a glorified *pot-au-feu*," he was suddenly taken by a woman named Valeria; what "really attracted" him, he admits, "was the imitation she gave of a little girl. She gave it not because she had divined something about me; it was just her style—and I fell for it. Actually, she was at least in her twenties."[133] He recalls "some fun from that nuptial night," but the spell is broken by morning, when her short blond curls reveal their bleaching. Valeria's momentary ability to deceive the novel's great deceiver, however, offers a lasting insight into *Lolita*: Humbert's need to view his own desire for nymphets as a strictly aesthetic judgment carries a corollary vulnerability to being deceived by style as an imitative performance of character. Dolores's tennis game seems, to Humbert, to offer an ideal display of style, a Kantian nymphet performing her "purposiveness without purpose," but as Bush notes, "Lolita's ineffective play has as much to do with her own resourcefulness as it does with Humbert's sway."[134] Far from being disinterested, Dolores's "easy groundstrokes form part of a deliberate ruse to lull Humbert into dropping his guard, swelling his ego so that he unthinkingly heeds a call to the telephone and allows her to plot her escape with Clare Quilty."[135] When Humbert proudly exclaims that Dolores's "tennis was the highest point to which I can imagine a young creature bringing the art of make-believe," his praise unknowingly intimates her deceptive motives.[136] Unaware of her budding resistance, Humbert "felt he could rest from the nightmare of unknown betrayals within the innocence of her style, of her soul, of her essential grace."[137]

Dolores learns to deceive and escape her "tyrannic old father" by reflecting the stylized character he desires (242). After she briefly slips from Humbert's sight, placing a call to Quilty, and reappears in a soda shop, Dolores announces: "A great decision has been made" (207). To disarm any suspicion about her time alone, she not only accedes to Humbert's wish for another lascivious cross-country trip but also crucially casts her acceptance in the manner of his speech:

> "But *this* time, we'll go wherever *I* want, won't we?"
> I nodded. My Lolita.
> "I choose? *C'est entendu*?" she asked wobbling a little beside me. Used French only when she was a very good little girl. (207)

Dolores's sudden embrace of a French language whose pretentiousness she has scorned has precisely its intended effect. Even in this retrospective narrative, recounted from jail, Humbert remains enamored of his "good little girl," the possessive "My Lolita" signaling how he still clings to her apparent embrace of his stylistic predilections. Humbert's fantasy has become Dolores's mask.[138] Shortly thereafter, she grants Humbert sexual license with a performed politeness and grace he finds irresistible: "In our hallway, ablaze with welcoming lights, my Lolita peeled off her sweater, shook her gemmed hair, stretched towards me two bare arms, raised one knee: 'Carry me upstairs, please. I feel sort of romantic to-night'" (207). Whereas Walter Pater called on fellow aesthetes to "burn always with this hard, gemlike flame," Humbert's eyes are blinded by Dolores's "gemmed hair," "ablaze with welcoming lights," indicting the aesthete not with a moral hedonism but with a tragic self-deception.[139] By posing as Humbert's ideal, Lolita lets him ignore the way he has corrupted and defiled her, while also keeping him blind to her deceitful intentions, to the mechanisms by which she executes her escape from his tyrannical control. Dolores betrays Humbert, but his suffering was requisite in her escape; what the man might call cruelty the child would call freedom. In the last analysis, style in *Lolita* does not simply illustrate the autonomous artistry of its author or narrator, nor, as Rorty hoped, does it show how an ironic style reliably leads toward liberal ends. By interrogating style's shifting relation to power, *Lolita* instead exposes an impasse in the liberal political aesthetic promoted by postwar intellectuals and later revamped by Rorty. With a "deep ambivalence about style" running through plot and narrative, through Lolita's actions as well as Humbert's, Nabokov's novel reveals how style represents a performative screen between private will and public accountability, a disjunctive performance of character that might be put to competing ends.[140] Style, in short, serves no master in Nabokov's masterpiece.

While Jameson cites *Lolita* as a last heroic defense of autonomous modernist style, this chapter has emphasized how Nabokov's fiction does not so much articulate as interrogate efforts to invoke style as a concept mediating between aesthetics and politics. Far from representing modernism's heroic last stand, moreover, his fiction appeared at a time when modernist art was achieving a newfound orthodoxy, among liberal intellectuals and state officials alike, in what scholars have come to call the Cultural Cold War. Indeed, it was only after this ideological appropriation that observers began to pronounce modernism dead; a cultural insurrection had been undone by cultural recognition. Reconciled with Cold War liberalism through the concept of style, summarizes Barnhiesel, modernism eventually "came to be used to *defend* the very societies and political systems that earlier modernist art had reviled," marshaled as evidence of the liberal democratic society that modern art had precisely emerged to challenge.[141] "Largely emptied of content," Barnhiesel concludes, "modernism as a style retained its prestige and status, particularly among intellectuals, which made it an appealing attribute for consumer products and middlebrow artworks that employed modernist techniques but without the seriousness, aesthetic unity, or moral depths of the best modernist works."[142] Critical studies that try to describe modernism's end through a shift in styles, perhaps toward some form of postmodernism, too often neglect this transformative era in American political history and how it altered the meaning of modernism. Nabokov has long served a key role in these periodization debates, due not only to his avowed aesthetic ideology, and distinguished style, but also a personal history that undeniably captures several signal changes in the life of modern literature: fleeing the violence of World War I, he was an expatriate in Berlin by 1922, a political refugee in the 1930s, an instructor in American universities during the 1940s and 1950s, and then an international celebrity in the 1960s. For some critics, the gap between *Lolita* (1955) and *Pale Fire* (1962) eventually came to serve as effective shorthand for the sense of an ending, for the gap between modernism and postmodernism.[143] In recent years, however, scholars have notably abandoned *postmodernism* as a term for organizing twentieth-century cultural history, instead displaying a growing interest in "late modernism," which acknowledges that modernist culture did not simply screech to a halt at midcentury.[144] Whereas postmodern critics saw modernism and liberalism as waning together, this renascent interest in modernism's endurance will hopefully produce more attention to the Cultural Cold War, to the way liberalism's constitutive dualisms have continued to define American politics and to a midcentury modernism that might still serve as a privilege vehicle for grappling with these enduring conceptual tensions.

"Liberal Totalitarianism" and the Problem of the Presidency

Kennedy's assassination, like Nabokov's fiction, has been regularly cited as a punctual scene of postmodernity. On November 22, 1963, millions of Americans watched as a devastated Walter Cronkite solemnly removed his glasses, a shared media event, argues Jameson, which "revealed what [television] could really do and what it really meant," ushering in a new age of "synchronicity."[145] Because JFK was venerated for his heroic, stylized leadership, which promised to transcend a nation's intractable conflicts, his sudden death necessarily seemed to intone the loss of more than just an individual life. In his speculative novel about the assassination, *Libra* (1988), Don DeLillo's protagonist describes it as "seven seconds that broke the back of the American century," a moment, Sean McCann suggests, which betrayed "the spiritual poverty of liberal society."[146] Depending on the account, then, modernism, liberalism, or some version of America itself may have died with the president. This chapter's final section, however, sidesteps the rhetoric of rupture that so often looms over JFK's legacy. Much as the last section showed how style's relationship to power has remained a theoretical problem for literary and political liberalism, these pages locate in Kennedy's presidential tenure an enduring practical problem for American liberals: how valorizing the heroic style of an individual leader has extended to dangerous lengths the power of the presidency.

No contemporary observer diagnosed this danger as presciently as Norman Mailer. Only a few years before he would join Abbie Hoffman's quest to levitate the Pentagon, Mailer genuinely came to believe that a liberal president might usher the United States toward revolutionary cultural change. Like so many other literary intellectuals, Mailer feared that the growing conformity of American mass culture in the 1950s was leading to a form of domestic totalitarianism, smuggled in by "corporate techniques," and "commercials on television," by "the jargon of educators" and "public-relations men."[147] "Since the publication of *Advertisements for Myself* in 1959," explains McCann, where he had depicted himself as "running for President these last ten years," Mailer "positioned his distinctive vision of the writer as self-created public combatant in counterpoint to the modern presidency," the climax of a long-standing fascination with executive power among modern American writers.[148] In JFK's political style—mixing masculine physical bravery with a cultured literacy—Mailer saw a potential hero, a narrative to renew the national imagination. Taking it upon himself to address a series of short missives to JFK, with "a desire to have its influence," Mailer composed the work later collected as his *Presidential Papers* (1963), including his famous essay "Superman Comes to the Supermarket."[149] The "unspoken thesis" of these papers, he explains, was that "no President can save America from a descent into totalitarianism without shifting the mind of the American politician to existential styles of political thought."[150] Echoing midcentury studies of character, Mailer believed that "historic ideas come to power" only when someone can "personify them or dramatize their qualities," someone whose aesthetic comportment might reflect for American citizens new desires and dreams.[151] After Kennedy's election, however, Mailer's initial enthusiasm waned, as he began to worry about the gap between the president's public persona and his private values. Pointing at JFK's capacity for self-contradiction, at the apparent void at the center of his charismatic character, and at his influence over American media, Mailer eventually came to see in Kennedy's mixture of style and power a potential fusion of liberalism and totalitarianism.

Kennedy's capacity for self-contradiction was integral to what Stephen Depoe calls his rhetoric of "transcendence."[152] Through his campaign for a "New Frontier," and in his subsequent public speeches, Kennedy defined politics as structured by opposing terms: "'perils' *and* 'opportunities,' 'threats' *and* 'hopes.'"[153] In his acceptance speech at the Democratic National Convention in Los Angeles, for instance, Kennedy did not propose to offer "a set of problems" but rather to articulate a "set of challenges."[154] By describing a Manichean world, shaped by "unsolved problems of peace and war, unconquered problems of ignorance and prejudice, unanswered questions of poverty and surplus," JFK created a need for heroic leadership, for a figure with the Olympian perspective necessary to navigate his nation between these poles.[155] Complex and divisive issues such as the nuclear contest with the Soviets, or what he called the "peaceful revolution" against racial discrimination, now seemed to hinge upon the character of the president, whose composed, ironic style elevated him above the apparent insolvency of these concrete issues in governance.[156] In an interview, Arthur Miller identified this quality as one reason why Kennedy "seemed so contemporary to people," why he could serve as a hero in an age that had largely stopped believing in them: "he never covered up the difficulties of existence. . . . He represented a kind of balance, or the potential of balance."[157] In *One-Dimensional Man* (1964), however, the Frankfurt School critic Herbert Marcuse was contemporaneously warning against the "unification of opposites which characterizes the commercial and political style" of advanced industrial societies. Through such a false dialectic, cautions Marcuse, businesses and government officials can foreclose "the expression of protest and refusal."[158] Their "harmony of contradictions" pretends to transcend social tensions through mere rhetoric, while enabling these individuals to consolidate a potentially totalitarian power: "People who speak and accept such language," observes Marcuse, "seem to be immune to everything—and susceptible to everything."[159]

Like Marcuse and other radical thinkers in the early 1960s, Mailer feared that totalitarianism would come to the United States not through the sudden action of a *Schutzstaffel* or other group of diehard believers, but through a creeping conformity, through Madison Avenue advertising firms emptying out the emotional potency of language and thought. "The concentration camps exist in the jargon of our souls," Mailer exclaims, "the storm troopers wear tortoise-shell glasses, and carry attaché cases to the cubicles in which they work on the Avenue of the Mad. The liberal tenets of the Center are central" (202). In his later *Papers*, Mailer depicts Kennedy not as a counterforce to this new threat but as its embodiment. Facing a "historic fork" in the 1960s, he proposes, the United States could either recover "its existential beginnings, its frontier psychology, where the future is unknown and one discovers the truth of the present by accepting the risks of the present," or else "America could continue to go on in its search for totalitarian security." JFK, Mailer insists, "chose to go in both directions at once," driven by "a similar paradox" in "his character" (183). Still admitting that JFK possesses "personal bravery, some wit, some style, and an aristocratic taste for variety," Mailer nonetheless notes that his "mind seems never to have been seduced by a new idea. He is the embodiment of the American void, that great yawning empty American mind which cannot bear any question which takes longer than ten seconds to answer" (183). As with most American intellectuals, Mailer saw in "the cavalier style of [Kennedy's] personal life and the wistfulness of his appreciation for the arts," a site of "Resistance to the American totalitarianism"; unlike most of his peers, however, Mailer also believed that "suffering his huge vice, his emptiness," the nation had "moved . . . deeper into totalitarianism" (183). Drawn though he was to the Kennedy style, Mailer came to see JFK as a split self: a heroic public character defined by the bravery and wit of his "cavalier" style, yet who conceals a private "void" beneath, an actor cloaked by his charming equivocations, yet who could potentially serve as an ideal locus for tyrannical power.

Beloved as a leader, if also largely unbound to guiding policy commitments beyond Cold War containment, Kennedy held tremendous power over American media.[160] Updating Roosevelt's fireside chats, JFK modeled a composed, cultivated character for the nation during televised speeches he held almost every week. Displaying what Mailer called "a potentially dictatorial nose for the manipulation of newspapers and television," Kennedy represented the executive office as a form of heroic leadership that inspired even when it erred (183). As critics noted, these public performances often served to cover up actions undertaken by his administration in secrecy.[161] After the Bay of Pigs Invasion in April 1961, for instance, Kennedy refused to elaborate on what had transpired in Cuba during his press conference. The CIA's operations are now remembered as a disaster, yet few may now recall that Kennedy's approval rating actually climbed to a staggering 83 percent afterward.[162] Indeed, Kennedy not only boasted the highest cumulative Gallup rating for any President since 1950 during his term in office, but has ever since retained the highest retrospective rating for presidential "greatness" among Americans.[163] Given Kennedy's reluctance to pursue civil rights, his aggressive foreign interventions, and the disclosures about his character revealed by books such as *The Dark Side of Camelot*, historians understandably disagree.[164] Kennedy's aura of infallibility, however, established a dangerous precedent for future presidents, as even his friend and adviser Arthur Schlesinger later admitted. During the Cuban Missile Crisis, explains Schlesinger, JFK's composure and personal bravery were justly praised, yet his "action, which should have been celebrated as an exception, was instead enshrined as a rule," for "it so beautifully fulfilled both the romantic ideal of the strong President and the prophecy of the split-second presidential decision in the nuclear age."[165] As an isolated leader, whose enormous popularity was contingent less on policy positions than heroic decision making, Kennedy modeled the liberal presidency as a performance of personal character, legitimating an increasingly centralized state power. In one speech, Kennedy finally took Schlesinger's seminal statement on Cold War liberalism, *The Vital Center*, and reframed its defining struggle against totalitarianism as transpiring within the presidential body: "We will need . . . what the Constitution envisioned: a Chief Executive who is the vital center of action in our whole scheme of government."[166] For Kennedy—if not for Schlesinger, and certainly not for the authors of the Constitution—liberal democracy in the United States would stand or fall through the guiding authority of its commander in chief.[167]

In this way, JFK crystallized a tension between American liberalism and the presidential office that had grown throughout the century. Looking to secure a public mandate for their reforms, argues McCann, progressive presidents in the United States gradually pushed political representation toward an aesthetic experience of individual heroism, "a new political mode built around the charismatic personalities of presidential candidates."[168] In his incisive literary history of the American presidency, *A Pinnacle of Feeling*, McCann has shown how Teddy Roosevelt's New Nationalism, Wilson's New Freedom, and FDR's New Deal all drew upon emerging media to establish direct access to the American public, employing and extending the power of executive orders to push forward their evolving visions of progressive politics.[169] For their supporters, a strong "chief executive would ideally serve as a national redeemer who could restore the sovereignty of the people and return America to its democratic mission," a heroic individual whose character and will might offer a "solution to a philosophical and nearly spiritual problem lying near the heart of American liberalism."[170] As critics point out, however, the growing authority of the executive office has also transformed "nearly every structural feature of US politics: the relations between federal and state governments, between the three branches of the federal government, and among voters, officials and parties," a reconstruction of American political life well suited to those with an "illegitimate appetite for power."[171] In *The Power of the Modern Presidency*, Erwin Hargrove observes that figures such as FDR, or Jackson and Lincoln still earlier, have had their actions retroactively legitimated by a liberal ideology in American political historiography, "a progressive interpretation of American history as a perennial battleground between entrenched forces of conservatism and private economic power and the mass of the people in search of greater social, economic, and political equality."[172] Kennedy's brief but heroic tenure in office further "altered the stylistic standards by which succeeding presidents sometimes measured greatness, and by which they were measured."[173] The lasting sense of "greatness" Americans associate with JFK, though seemingly superficial, registers a profound underlying belief: acts of individual heroism by presidents have been required to push the nation forward through moments of crisis, in an aesthetic relationship to politics replacing any concrete sense of national policy. Unable to reconcile liberalism's constitutive dualisms in our public discourse, citizens await a leader who will arbitrate over contested issues, and, with ever more direct access to the American public, this lineage of popular, heroic presidents has gradually corroded the system of checks and balances intended to establish procedural accountability for the executive branch.

Political scientists and legal scholars now warn that the dramatically heightened power of the presidency poses a serious threat to the political stability of the United States.[174] In an historical irony that Reinhold Niebuhr would have appreciated, those liberal presidents who have extended the powers of their office in the name of reform have inadvertently prepared the way for an illiberal tyrant. This irony flared up during the 1970s, with the disclosure of executive crimes in Vietnam and Watergate, and it has recently resurfaced with the jarring transition of power from Barack Obama to Donald Trump.[175] As countless observers pointed out, Obama's administration resembled "Camelot" more than any other presidential administration has since Kennedy's death. Propelled by a timely embrace of social media, Obama's enormous popularity among self-identified liberals signaled the renewed appeal of a vision of stylish individual leadership. Facing a bewilderingly inept and recalcitrant Congress, Obama frequently appeared a solitary hero, even if this agency in fact meant using executive orders to conduct international "police actions" and sustain an amorphous "War on Terror," and even if his credentials as a reformer were, like Kennedy's, dubious at best. Just a few years later, moreover, the same liberals drawn to Obama's leadership recoiled in horror before President Trump, as he likewise employed social media to inflame his celebrity status, displacing serious civic discussion of his reactionary policies with commentary about his character and the style of his administration.

Whether voting red or blue, many Americans have come to see the presidency as a heroic individual office, the only site—given a divided legislature, corrupted by corporate capitalism and its lobbyists—from which real change might come. With this entrenched corporate state, and a widespread desire for centralized, powerful leadership, some anxious commentators have begun to look back to the rise of authoritarian regimes at midcentury for guiding insight. Sheldon Wolin, for instance, has called the current political order in the United States "inverted totalitarianism," whose beginnings he traces back to Kennedy's cult of personality.[176] As a witness to Camelot, Mailer likewise sought an expression for the way American liberalism was foundering on its own internal tensions. To coin a name for this peril, Mailer collapsed the most sanctified dualism in midcentury political discourse: "Liberal Totalitarianism."[177] This paradoxical category today remains one possible end of American liberalism, and like many objects in the mirror of history, it may be closer than it appears. The constitutive dualisms in this book remain unresolved, as do the controversial political issues whose discourse they structure. If abortion cannot be legislated through claims on possessive individualism, if equal protection under the law can mean ignoring racial inequality as easily as addressing it, then liberal subjects may well try to escape these problems by subsuming them within one heroic individual, whose aestheticized politics promises an escape from these divisive problems through a unifying assertion of power.

Conclusion

What's Left of Liberalism?
(or What's So New about Neoliberalism?)

> The ideas of economists and political philosophers, both when they are right and when they are wrong, are more powerful than is commonly understood. Indeed the world is ruled by little else. Practical men, who believe themselves to be quite exempt from any intellectual influences, are usually the slaves of some defunct economist. Madmen in authority, who hear voices in the air, are distilling their frenzy from some academic scribbler of a few years back . . . soon or late, it is ideas, not vested interests, which are dangerous for good or evil.
>
> —John Maynard Keynes, *The General Theory of Employment, Interest and Money*

Milton Friedman, apostle for neoliberal policies across the Americas, recalls in his memoir a formative educational moment at Rahway High School. His teacher in political science, "or 'civics' as it was then called," also taught geometry. When this Mr. Cohan drew a proof for the Pythagorean theorem on the blackboard, recalls Friedman, he "stress[ed] what a beautiful proof it was by quoting from Keats's 'Ode on a Grecian Urn': 'Beauty is truth, truth beauty'—that is all ye know on earth, and all ye need to know.'"[1] In Friedman's anecdote, which he cites as an inspiring episode, literature's beauty confirms the mathematical laws that undergird a civic education. Fifty years later, Friedman would recite the same inspiring lines during a seminar on price theory at the University of Chicago. "The formal structure of price theory," Friedman insisted to his graduate students, "has an aesthetic quality that has always reminded me of the famous last lines of Keats's 'Ode.'"[2] Tucked among recollections of his profound influence on political leaders and financial magnates, this brief but instructive glimpse at a neoliberal's aesthetic education shows Friedman interpreting Keats's ambiguous couplet as a syllogism defending post-Keynesian economics: if the formal structure of price theory displays beauty in its equilibriums, and all beauty entails truth, then the theory's formalisms must be true. As Arnold Harberger, who taught alongside Friedman for years at Chicago, once affirmed, Friedman's neoliberalism indeed imagines a world of forces held in formal balance, "a very pretty but highly complex picture out there, which is perfectly harmonious within itself, you see, and if there's a speck where it isn't supposed to be, well, that's just awful . . . it is a flaw that mars the beauty."[3] By dissolving any tension in Keats's poem, Friedman's reading would of course disappoint any critic invested in the complexity of literary form, for, as these chapters have evinced, modern literature's ironies wholly rebuke the idea that art's truth lies in formal unity. Yet precisely in its reductive impulse, Friedman's reading displays in miniature the theory of reality informing his neoliberal thought: all the world's a market, knowable and harmonious.

Though of course it isn't. Despite much talk of freeing the natural forces of markets from government interference, neoliberalism's central aims— privatization, deregulation, and slashed social spending—all require aggressive state intervention. And despite Freidman's beauteous vision, these policies have produced economic hardship if not outright disaster for most citizens in countries where they have taken hold. Thinkers such as David Harvey, Naomi Klein, and Wendy Brown, while having some definitional disagreements about neoliberalism's contours, all agree that its policies have led to catastrophic consequences for global markets and local communities as they spread from experiments in South America in the 1970s, into orthodox governance in Britain and the United States during the 1980s, passed on to the former Soviet Bloc and "Asian Tigers" in the 1990s. Behind the viral growth of a market logic lurks, for these critics, profound dangers: for Harvey, neoliberalism represents a weapon wielded by corporate capitalists to extend and deepen class warfare; for Klein, neoliberalism's reliance on moments of crisis to take hold has created a self-perpetuating cycle of "disaster capitalism"; for Brown, the dissolution of all life into market activity intones a subtler but equally threatening loss of politics itself, of the forms of reason upon which democracy depends.[4]

Facing such vocal and incisive critics, neoliberalism occupies a curious discursive position in the United States today. Much like liberalism in the 1950s, neoliberalism appears ubiquitous in contemporary intellectual discourse, a keyword used to name varying political, economic, and social changes, and which at times appears to signify a hegemonic world order. Whereas postwar Americans routinely embraced liberalism as a political or intellectual label, however, virtually no one seems to identify with neoliberalism. Despite its omnipresence, the term has not been used as a slogan by those promoting deregulated markets or privatized resources but by hostile parties indicting these practices. Among Ronald Reagan, Margaret Thatcher, Augusto Pinochet, Boris Yeltsin, Bill Clinton, and Tony Blair, notes Harvey, not one described themselves or their actions as neoliberal.[5] And despite neoliberalism appearing in thousands of academic articles since the turn of the century, far more often than related epithets like "Washington Consensus," "market reform," or "monetarism," a quantitative survey by two political scientists from the University of California, Berkeley "did not uncover a *single* contemporary instance in which an author used the term self-descriptively."[6]

This book has traced liberalism's discursive history in the United States through midcentury fiction, arguing that by juxtaposing rhetoric about liberalism's novelty against its enduring ironies and ambiguities, we can better understand the ongoing ideological influence of this intellectual tradition. While committing to firm definitions of neoliberalism enables critics such as Brown and Harvey to maintain a stable analytic focus, whether it be on class struggle or democratic reason, these last pages once again call attention to the historical *instability* of a keyword in American intellectual life—for two reasons. First, as Bruce Robbins has recently insisted, "Everything is Not Neoliberalism;" returning to the discursive origins of neoliberalism can help restore a sense of historical contingency to a mode of market rationality that today too often seems like a teleological force, omnipresent yet faceless, which "always seems to be discoverable lurking behind or beneath whatever piece of culture happens to be under discussion," and even its sharpest critics seem unsure how to combat.[7] Calling attention to the rhetorical struggles that shape political life—the aesthetic experience of politics implicit in Friedman's anecdote and explicit throughout the preceding chapters—might open up space to resist contemporary changes that can sometimes feel irresistible. Second, this work can, in the process, help disambiguate neoliberalism from liberalism, which continue to be falsely equated. Because liberalism so frequently gets reduced in literary and cultural studies to a term of derision for left academics (mistakenly) reducing it to a transhistorical commitment to free market individualism, and because neoliberalism often (mistakenly) gets cited as simply being a renewed defense of laissez-faire capitalism, the profound ideological differences and historical relationship between these terms regularly gets effaced.[8] Attending to these differences provides a useful way to take stock of what American liberalism has left behind after its triumphant years in the twentieth century and what this might mean for literary studies.

Like modern liberalism itself, neoliberalism was shaped in the crucible of the 1930s. As Mirowski and Plehwe chronicle in *The Road from Mont Pèlerin: The Making of the Neoliberal Thought Collective*, throughout the 1920s a loose cluster of European intellectuals began sharing their worries over the dire condition of classical liberalism. In 1937, these thinkers at last came together around their enthusiastic reception of an unlikely ur-text: Walter Lippmann's *(An Inquiry into the Principles of) The Good Society*. Although writing in the heyday of the New Deal, Lippmann—who, as described in chapter 1, had been a vicious critic of corporate property rights—had begun promoting market freedom and cautioning against centralized state power.[9] The 1938 Walter Lippmann Colloquium in Paris, nominally held for its honored guest, today marks an origin point for neoliberal thought; its attendees included Friedrich Hayek, Ludwig von Mises, and thirteen other figures who would in 1947 found the Mont Pèlerin Society, the central intellectual network that has since largely shaped neoliberalism's various global strains. But while the conference attendees agreed in 1938 that classical liberalism had failed—as would have Dewey, Pound, or Mussolini—they held sharply differing views on how it might be rehabilitated. In "a quest for alternative intellectual resources to revive a moribund political project," suggests Mirowski, the colloquium members debated political identifiers like "positive liberalism" and even "left-wing liberalism" before opting for the now infamous "neo." Neoliberalism, in other words, began as but one more tenuous intellectual effort to make liberalism new in the 1930s. Working contemporaneously yet at inverse ends to figures like Dewey, who consolidated the meaning of modern American liberalism by reacting to the rise of corporate power, neoliberalism likewise began as an effort to reimagine classical economics for modern society, "a theory of how to reengineer the state in order to guarantee the success of the market and its most important participants, modern corporations."[10]

Although the Mont Pèlerin Society settled on neoliberalism as a unifying slogan, its advocates soon recognized the rhetorical power that came from identifying their revisionary doctrines with "liberalism" and its long-standing political grammar. Abandoning their neologism, the group's foremost thinkers now joined the ongoing midcentury struggle to redefine liberalism's meaning. In the United States, however, liberalism so clearly connoted the New Deal's welfare state programs—and the modern intellectual tradition traced by this book—that economists advocating a return to market liberalization doubted their capacity to reclaim this term and its constellation of related concepts. In his foreword to the American Paperback Edition of *The Road to Serfdom* (1944), a best-selling polemic that introduced neoliberal notions to mass audiences in the United States, Friedrich Hayek explains that while he uses "the term 'liberal' in the original, nineteenth-century sense in which it is still current in Britain," this runs against its usage in the United States, where the term "often means very nearly the opposite of this."[11] Hayek identifies this American appropriation of liberalism as "part of the camouflage of leftist movements in this country," who find their "leading philosopher" in Dewey.[12] Even as modern liberalism slipped from Dewey's hands into the Cold War discourse of Niebuhr and Schlesinger after World War II—as chapter 3 relates—the term remained palpably removed from the marketization demanded by neoliberals. When Ludwig von Mises had his *Liberalismus* translated into English in 1962, at the height of Kennedy's Camelot, the economist simply conceded that his intended meaning diverged too much from the expectations of readers and so changed the book's title to *The Free and Prosperous Commonwealth*. A year later, von Mises changed his mind, deciding that free market defenders should try to "reclaim 'the term "liberal."'"[13] While accounts of neoliberalism can sometimes make this movement appear to be an inexorable consequence of midcentury liberalism and its political failings, this textual archive preserves a clear struggle between modern American liberals and early neoliberals like Hayek and von Mises, who saw their project as obstructed by the conceptual reframing of liberalism that intellectuals like Dewey and Niebuhr had engineered in midcentury America.

The story of neoliberalism's eventual rise in the 1970s, beginning with Friedman's stunning overhaul of Chilean governance, has been recorded repeatedly and in great detail.[14] Yet these accounts rarely, if ever, stress the contested relationship between early neoliberals and modern liberals in the United States from the 1930s through the 1960s. For instance, Michel Foucault's influential 1978-79 lectures at the College de France, published as *The Birth of Biopolitics*, identifies the Lippmann Colloquium as a signal moment in the genealogy of neoliberalism, yet Foucault characteristically positions this event as but one representative node within a sweeping set of discursive changes across American and central European history. Written in the late 1970s, when collapsing rates of profit and declining manufacturing outputs were preparing the way for Reagan and Thatcher, Foucault's lectures have been justly praised for "their prescience and rich insights."[15] Yet, as Brown has shown, these lectures "largely comprise partial and speculative intellectual histories," which notably "vacillate between marking neoliberalism's distinctiveness and establishing its continuity with liberalism."[16] By leaping from the colloquium in the 1930s, to midcentury German Ordoliberalism, to the emerging world order in Britain and the United States in the 1970s, Foucault's narrative creates a driving continuity in neoliberalism's intellectual development. This narrative momentum, however, elides the modern liberal tradition traced by this book—an intellectual network defined, as were the neoliberals, by a governing struggle with the contradictions in classical liberal thought. Perhaps no other factor in the American academy clouds the historical influence and contemporary import of the modern liberal tradition as much as the teleological impulse to link the laissez-faire hypocrisies of classical liberalism directly to the contemporary blights of neoliberalism. Scholars on the American Left have too often been seduced by the Keatsian aesthetic appeal of Foucault's argument, its apparent transhistorical unity and driving narrative momentum precisely flattening out the vital tensions and ironies that define liberalism's history and conceptual architecture.

But in the last analysis, argues Mirowski, neoliberalism must be distinguished from any liberalism proper by its "*epistemic* commitments."[17] Whereas modern liberals like Dewey advocated for pragmatic experiments, guided by shared intelligence and aimed at social reform, neoliberals imagine a harmonious market order existing underneath government interference and individual error. Borrowing language from Hayek, Mirowksi describes this as a contrast between a "taxis," with "rationally constructed orders designed to achieve intentional ends," and a "cosmos," a "supposed spontaneous order that no one has intentionally designed or structured." Yet neoliberals, Mirowski explains, "do not in fact practice what they preach."[18] Whereas classical liberals like Adam Smith imagined market life as prior to and independent from the state, which simply needed to laissez-faire, neoliberals need aggressive governance to dismantle the existing regulations and public institutions that obstruct the market's supposedly natural harmonies, dissolving the boundary between market and state. While neoliberal theory imagines a market unified in Keatsian beauty, neoliberal practice requires

Conclusion

brutal "shock therapy" to take hold over national economies though deregulation and privatization, which create enormous new sources of exploitative profitability for corporations by exploiting the mass of citizens, who have naturally opposed these policies worldwide. Friedman may have found price theory confirmed as truth by Keats's beauty, but neoliberalism finally requires what Mirowski calls "a 'double truth' doctrine: one truth for the masses/participants and another for those at the top."[19]

Dewey, for his part, recognized the conflict inherent in modern political life and—*pace* Mr. Cohan's lecture to the young Friedman—knew that Keats did too. After praising Keats's notion of "Negative Capability" early on in *Art in Experience* (1934), Dewey turns to his famous last lines on the "Grecian Urn." Whereas Friedman's teacher saw beauty confirming a truth in laws of geometric composition, Dewey begins by emphasizing the reception of the poem, noting that "much dispute" has surrounded its final couplet. Ever the historicist, Dewey protests that readers have "carried on in ignorance of the particular tradition in which Keats wrote."[20] For a Romantic poet, insists Dewey, truth "never signifies correctness of intellectual statements about things," a claim that might have given pause to neoliberal economist and geometry teacher alike. More than a simple validation of propositional statements, Dewey explains, truth "denotes the wisdom by which men live."[21] Treating beauty and truth not as commensurate but as dialectically bound terms, Dewey insists that beauty stems from sensuous experience as much as formal abstraction—from literature as well as philosophy—and that imagination must conversely supplement reasoning in any quest for truth. "Ultimately," Dewey concludes, "there are but two philosophies. One of them accepts life and experience in all its uncertainty, mystery, doubt, and half-knowledge and turns that experience upon itself to deepen and intensify its own qualities—to imagination and art."[22] The other does not. In their readings of Keats's "Ode," Dewey and Friedman neatly encapsulate antithetical aesthetic theories, which clarify the competing views of reality, knowledge, and politics distinguishing neoliberalism from modern liberalism. The neoliberal imagines a world composed by harmonies of supply and demand, a natural set of forces organizing human behavior and knowable through systematic analysis—forces reflected in poetry, but not challenged by it—and yet hypocritically marshals this ideal to justify extreme violence and inequality. The modern liberal, by contrast, insists upon conflict, irony, and complexity as structuring conditions of political and economic life, and so turns to modern art seeking not confirmation of a worldview, but for renewed experience, insight at once sensory and reasoning, which might deepen and diversify efforts to build a more just society.

And yet what is left today of this modern liberalism? Many Americans would point first to welfare state programs created by the New Deal and Great Society, institutions that, despite perennial attacks by conservative and libertarian pundits, have indelibly transformed everyday life in the United States since the middle of the twentieth century. Beneath this institutional struggle, however, another story has unfolded at the level of language, with less visibility and yet equal import. Since modern liberalism's apotheosis in the early 1960s, its traditional conceptual grammar—liberty, equality, rights—has been gradually appropriated by the rhetoric of the American Right. Today, religious fundamentalists mobilize support against organizations like Planned Parenthood by reframing state control over women's bodies as a "right to life"; conservative lawyers protect white supremacy by casting efforts to promote racial equality as "reverse discrimination"; and the lobbyists behind *Citizens United* justify unlimited corporate spending in political campaigns as preventing a restriction on the "free speech" of these legal individuals. While the academic left has critiqued classical liberalism's values, the Republican Right has absorbed them, turning these concepts into a potent means of reinforcing what were once antithetical ends: traditional morality, patriarchal families, and ethno-national divisions. Backed by "think tanks" like the Cato Institute, the Heritage Foundation, and the American Enterprise Institute, this linguistic shift has spread from local levels of governance to the executive branch. When Ronald Reagan stepped into the Oval Office, the intellectuals at the Heritage Foundation provided him with a 1,093-page guidebook, entitled *Mandate for Leadership: Policy Management in a Conservative Administration* (1981), which, in laying out a capacious program for overhauling the priorities of American government, also captured the semantic erosion of American liberalism. "For 20 years," this volume announced, "the most important battle in the Civil Rights field has been for control of the language." Since the 1960s, "Americans and their laws oppose 'discrimination,' 'segregation,' and 'racism'; they favor 'equality,' 'opportunity,' and 'remedial action.' The secret to victory, whether in court or in Congress, has been to control the definition of these terms."[23] Liberalism's core values continue to hold real power over the political imagination of the American public, and yet they do so most influentially in the hands of those destroying liberalism's historical achievements.

For an American Left—often academic, often located in English Departments—that has struggled since the 1960s to establish solidarity against this resurgent Right, abandoning liberalism's core categories as a rhetorical resource represents a major pragmatic failure. By reducing liberalism only to its least reflexive classical tradition, and treating it only as a constant foil for critique, left academics have contributed to the waning of liberalism's efficacy as a grammar for collective political action, while producing no surrogate political grammars that might replace liberalism's investment in individual freedoms and equal rights to help organize democratic support among the mass American public.[24] As this book has shown, much critical theory focused on gender, race, and representation in fact continues a project of interrogating liberalism begun by midcentury liberal intellectuals. This is not to conflate John Dewey with Judith Butler but rather to suggest that reductive attacks on liberalism, which elide the complexity of modern liberal thought and distance contemporary intellectuals from liberalism's organizing concepts, do less good for a radical Left than for the forces of reaction. As intellectuals such as Dewey and Burke recognized in the 1930s, political action ultimately requires building shared allegiance to symbols. The challenge for cultural critics in the academy today, as evinced by the anxious reception surrounding a book like Rita Felski's *The Limits of Critique*, remains the same: how to move beyond a long-standing investment in dissecting liberalism's ideological failures and begin rebuilding attachment to shared political values.

Reconstructing American liberalism clearly represents a major task, given its conceptual aporias and enduring reprobation. But two steps appear manageable. First, the ongoing fight against neoliberal doctrine must not conflate this contemporary formation with modern iterations of liberalism, in a rhetorical gesture that inflates the intellectual depth of the former and undermines the historical richness of the latter. As a label claimed by no actors, *neoliberalism* might be shed as a term by critics altogether and the forces behind privatization and deregulation called by their proper name: corporate capitalism. Or, better still, let critics call this movement "corporate welfare," aiming to drive a wedge between corporate lobbyists and the working-class nationalists who have kept neoliberalism and neoconservatism in an uneasy alliance. Second, scholars in literary and cultural studies—especially those working to promote the public humanities—need to disarm the longstanding antipathy to liberalism, based on a reductive understanding of this capacious and diverse intellectual tradition, and to instead recognize how contemporary critical praxis might be aided by excavating the ethical challenges and aesthetic reflexivity that have informed liberal intellectual culture through its various historical eras.

How often do literary critics address liberalism's constitutive dualisms—individual/social, autonomy/dependence, rights/needs, abstraction/embodiment—not just as sites for critique but as values carrying authority, which literature might promote and enrich? Or, to resituate this question within the pedagogical scene that Friedman found so inspiring: how often do classroom discussions emphasize the practical need to reconcile these liberal dualisms, asking students to consider their attachment to such competing values? As this book has shown, debates over abortion, race-blind legal equality, and the style of political leaders all traffic in these conceptual tensions shaping liberal thought. For this reason, preparing a generation of young Americans to inherit such hotly disputed issues depends on their learning not simply to recognize liberalism's historical failures but also the ongoing influence of its central concepts and to practice negotiating for themselves the political conflicts structured by its organizing dualisms. Liberalism, to be sure, still demands critique. Yet any contemporary effort to produce and defend a vision of embodied individual identity, informed by participatory citizenship, communal solidarity, and experiential education, will necessarily draw upon liberalism's foundational grammar. For a progressive American politics, of any cast or creed, to continue gaining traction with the public, it will require this nation's intellectuals to renew the rhetorical power of the liberal tradition, while at the same time recognizing—as Dewey insisted—the dialectical constitution of liberalism's central terms.

This book identified modernist fiction as a privileged vehicle for such an enterprise, surveyed efforts to this end by midcentury American liberals, and modeled a reading practice whereby contemporary scholars—and teachers—might continue to grapple with the enduring theoretical and practical problems in the liberal tradition. Before institutions can be overhauled, or popular votes cast toward a radically democratic end, the symbols of allegiance through which people organize their relationship to political questions must be altered. Literature cannot help readers decide how governments should respond to collapsing rates of profit in the manufacturing sector. But as Dewey and Friedman each understood, the aesthetic experience provided by literature shapes how readers will understand truth and beauty, facts and values, reality and imagination—how they will find their way, in short, through a political world indelibly shaped by the contested legacies of American liberalism.

Notes

Introduction

1. Judith Shklar, "The Liberalism of Fear" 21. Shklar ends up anchoring liberalism to an aversion against cruelty, a notion this book returns to, via Richard Rorty, in chapter 4.

2. Gary Gerstle, "The Protean Character of American Liberalism" 1043. Woodrow Wilson, Franklin D. Roosevelt, and John F. Kennedy are all routinely identified as liberal presidents, for instance, yet the New Freedom, New Deal, and New Frontier differed markedly in program—while notably sharing the modern need for novelty.

3. Brown, *States of Injury* 142.

4. Brown, *States of Injury* 152. I have extended and amended Brown's original list beyond the specifically feminist project in *States of Injury*; my first chapter, however, notably returns to the feminist origins of her critique of liberalism.

5. Amanda Anderson, "Postwar Aesthetics: The Case of Trilling and Adorno" 418. Anderson's effort over recent years to urge a more complex, historically informed understanding of liberal intellectual culture has inspired and informed this book.

6. Anderson, "Postwar Aesthetics" 418.

7. Norman Mailer, "Letter to the Editor," quoted in Schultz, *Buckley and Mailer* 55.

8. Anderson, "Postwar Aesthetics" 418-19. John McGowan, who has defended liberal democracy as continuously and forcefully as any cultural critic in recent years, echoes Anderson's observation: "Contempt for liberalism characterizes the populist right and the academic left both." McGowan, *American Liberalism* 1.

9. By tracking liberalism's "word history," Rosenblatt emphasizes a major but forgotten emphasis upon "moral reform" in the liberal tradition, suppressed by a revisionary Anglo-American narrative that emphasizes possessive individualism—a narrative whose origins this book helps explains. Helena Rosenblatt, *The Lost History of Liberalism* 3.

10. Bell observes that the "first monograph on Locke's political philosophy" was in fact "a doctoral dissertation supervised by John Dewey." Duncan Bell, "What Is Liberalism?" 695. See note 39 below for more on the Lockean narrative.

11. Mussolini, *Fascism* 10. Pound, *Guide to Kulchur* 254.

12. Eliot, *After Strange Gods* 47.

13. Eliot, *Christianity and Culture* 12.

14. Gold, "Why I Am a Communist" 212.

15. Auden, "The Public v. the Late Mr William Butler Yeats" 6.

16. For a helpful survey of anti-liberalism in modernist writing and scholarship, see Janice Ho, "The Crisis of Liberalism and the Politics of Modernism."

17. Howe, "The Culture of Modernism" 17. Lewis, "Introduction" 3.

18. Michael North provides an instructive history of this phrase and its critical misprision in *Novelty*. Through a masterly contextualization of Pound's slogan "Make It New," North shows how modernist claims to novelty were never genuine ruptures from the past, but efforts to establish some recombination or recurrence rooted in tradition. Cries for a "new liberalism" throughout this book follow this same pattern. North, *Novelty* 162-71.

19. Dewey, *Liberalism and Social Action* 62.

20. Auden, "The Means of Grace" 131.

21. Berman, *Modern Culture and Critical Theory* 121, quoted in North, *Political Aesthetic* 5. North provides a sustained exposition of what modernist anti-liberalism looks like in his study of Yeats, Eliot, and Pound. North argues that the cultural nationalism, conservatism, and fascism embraced by these three canonical figures all grew from their attempts to escape fundamental tensions in nineteenth-century liberal thought. "As liberal society developed its contradictions," he writes, "the aesthetic was called upon more and more to resolve them . . . to rejoin subject and object, individual and community, fact and value." North, *Political Aesthetic* 15. These writers were all responding to the failures of classical liberalism, however, not the revitalized liberal culture that began with Dewey in the 1930s. For a fascinating study, which examines the equivocal reactions to a collapsing classical liberalism that exist within hard-boiled fiction, see Sean McCann, *Gumshoe Fiction* (2000).

22. Blair, "Politics of Culture" 156. Because so many modern artists embraced radical views—whether of the Left or Right—during the crises of the early twentieth century, political extremism has often been seen as constitutive of modernist culture. Fredric Jameson began a wave of studies on modernism's right-wing politics with *Fables of Aggression* (1979); for more recent studies, see Charles Ferrall, *Modernist Writing and Reactionary Politics* (2001); Roger Griffin, *Modernism and Fascism* (2009), and Annalisa Zox-Weaver, *Women Modernists and Fascism* (2011). Any catalog of scholarship on the American literary left must begin with Daniel Aaron, *Writers on the Left* (1961); scholars in the 1980s and 1990s later

began a more concentrated effort at recovering "radical" literature: see Cary Nelson, *Repression and Recovery* (1989); Paula Rabinowitz, *Labor & Desire* (1991) and *They Must Be Represented* (1994); Alan Filreis, *Modernism from Right to Left* (1994); and Harvey Teres, *Renewing the Left* (1996).

23. Szalay, *New Deal Modernism* 2. Despite their different backgrounds and ideological commitments, explains Szalay, authors from Wallace Stevens to Jack London searched for "compensatory mechanisms of risk management" in their lives and writing, leading to "new ways of conceiving literary labor." Szalay, *New Deal Modernism* 3, 5.

24. McCann, *Pinnacle* 36.

25. As Gabriel Hankins notes, a "larger institutional turn in modernist studies" has seen the field move "toward thinking about state institutions, international law, liberal politics, and literary aesthetics as interconnected rather than divided intellectual topographies." Hankins, *Interwar Modernism* 1. For other studies, such as Hankins's, focused on British or global literature and liberal governance, see Pericles Lewis, *Modernism, Nationalism, and the Novel* (2000); John Marx, *Geopolitics and the Global Anglophone Novel* (2011); and Janice Ho, *Nation and Citizenship in the Twentieth-Century British Novel* (2015).

26. Lasch, *The New Radicalism* ix.

27. Schoenbach looks beyond "the revolutionary ideology of the avant-garde" and its emphasis on discontinuity and rupture to examine how modernist writers also posed practical "questions about the relationship between tradition and innovation, habit and shock, continuity and transformation, means and ends." Schoenbach, *Pragmatic Modernism* 3, 5. Siraganian shows how claims about "the reader's or viewer's relation" to modern art "became a way to envision the political subject's ideal relation to a changing, rejuvenated, but essentially *liberal* state at a time when the discourse of threatened autonomy pervaded both high and mass culture." Siraganian, *Modernism's Other Work* 4 (emphasis in original). Her forthcoming book, *Modernism and the Meaning of Corporate Persons*, promises to resonate with and augment the intellectual history outlined in this book's first chapter. For now, see Siraganian, "Dreiser's Anti-Corporate Tools." And in *Land of Tomorrow*, Mangrum explores how postwar fiction "conferred cultural prestige on a cluster of new political sentiments within American liberal thought," such as existentialism, which eroded trust in an "'organizational liberalism' and the activist-managerial state it supported," eventually leading to the crisis of 1968. His book, appropriately enough, begins where this one ends: with Nabokov, aestheticism, and totalitarianism. Mangrum, *Land of Tomorrow* 2, 3. For an earlier study, which examines how canonical modernist fiction challenged Victorian notions of liberal subjectivity and narrative character, see Michael Levenson, *Modernism and the Fate of Individuality* (1991).

28. Brown, *States* 152. See note 4 above.

29. Norman, *Transatlantic Aliens* 15.

30. Wise, "Paradigm Dramas" 307. For another early, reflexive criticism from the field, see Bruce Kuklick, "Myth and Symbol in American Studies." For a look back on these formative years, see Donald E. Pease and Robyn Wiegman, "Futures."

31. Rowe, *Afterlives* 9.

32. Because *Afterlives* searches the past for the progressive viewpoint of the present, rather than historicize the liberal tradition either as ideology or as discourse, it ends up using "liberalism" in unclear and contradictory ways. At times, Rowe positions himself as a critic of liberalism coming from "the political left," as cultural studies focused on liberalism tend to do; yet at other times, Rowe recognizes how his interest in a reparative emphasis on racial, class, and gender equality clearly represents a contemporary iteration of liberal values. At times Rowe identifies authors such as Stein and Dos Passos as liberals because of their overlooked interest in marginalized groups; at other times, he speaks of "modernism's characteristic liberalism," a notion difficult enough to countenance on its own, but still more perplexing given the apparent historical refusal to read these authors in the reparative manner he prescribes. By the book's end, neoliberalism gets cast as one more iteration of liberalism, as does Philip Roth's "liberal middle," which "turns out to be far more conservative than he thinks." This semantic confusion illustrates the linguistic predicament that liberalism poses for critics today: a vital term, but an overdetermined one; its historical and present usages differing, even competing; and always producing an ambiguous affect, a mandatory hostility coupled with hesitant sympathy. Rowe, *Afterlives* 8, 10, 20.

33. Dillon, *Gender of Freedom* 25.

34. Dillon, *Gender of Freedom* 25.

35. Dillon, *Gender of Freedom* 35. For more on the construction of the public-private dyad in early print culture, see Gilian Brown, *Domestic Individualism*; and Annabel Patterson, *Early Modern Liberalism*.

36. For Anderson, the toggling between "first-person and third-person perspectives" in Victorian novels, "between embodied presence and impersonal critique, between ethics and politics," illustrates a reflexive tendency, facilitated by aesthetic experience, which recurs throughout episodes in the liberal intellectual tradition. Anderson, *Bleak Liberalism* 78.

37. Anderson, *Bleak Liberalism* 30.

38. Hartz frequently gets mischaracterized as championing the ideological conformity he describes. He and other "consensus" historians like Richard Hofstadter saw this liberal uniformity and its creed of "Americanism" as profoundly dangerous: "The decisive domestic issue of our time," Hartz writes, "may well lie in the counter resources a liberal society can muster against this deep and unwritten tyrannical compulsion it contains." Hartz, *The Liberal Tradition* 12.

39. See Pocock, *The Machiavellian Moment*. For other critical responses to the

Lockean narrative, see Gordon S. Wood, *The Creation of the American Republic*; Bernard Bailyn, *The Ideological Origins of the American Revolution*; and John G. Gunnell, "The Archeology of American Liberalism." Despite these important challenges, however, few may now recall that "it was not until after 1950 that there was even any extended discussion of Locke as a liberal"; more than a century after his death, Locke was still seen as a Whig metaphysician and not a liberal political theorist. Gunnell, "Archeology" 131. For a revised version of the consensus narrative, see James P. Young, *Reconsidering American Liberalism*.

40. Over time, Anderson remarks, the premise that liberals are really just conservatives without the requisite convictions has grown into an "axiomatic view on the left." Anderson, *Bleak Liberalism* 24.

41. Communitarian critics such as Michael Sandel, Charles Taylor, and Alasdair MacIntyre have notably charged that liberalism—at least the version espoused by Rawls—fails to recognize the shared conception of moral good that must unite any community. See their essays in Sandel, *Liberalism and Its Critics*. For an account of how political science emerged as a professional discipline through this growing liberal consensus, see Gunnell, "Archeology."

42. Anderson, *Bleak Liberalism* 19.

43. Anderson, "Postwar Aesthetics" 418.

44. Fukuyama, "The End of History?" 3.

45. Klein, *The Shock Doctrine* 230.

46. Anderson, "Postwar Aesthetics" 418.

47. Friedman, "Periodizing Modernism" 434.

48. Anderson, *Bleak Liberalism* 1.

49. Dewey, *Liberalism and Social Action* 5-6.

50. Dewey, *Liberalism and Social Action* 6.

51. Dewey's work has produced copious scholarship—if not all complimentary. For three studies sharing this book's focus on, and sympathy for, Dewey the modernist liberal, see Russell Westbrook, *John Dewey and American Democracy*; Alan Ryan, *John Dewey and the High Tide of American Liberalism*; and Ross Posnock, *The Trial of Curiosity*, esp. chapter 5, which compares Dewey and Adorno.

52. Despite stacks of books dedicated to liberal thought, J. G. Merquior could in 1991 plausibly assert that "there is a comparative scarcity of *historical* presentations of liberalism." Recent years, however, have seen several commendable efforts to historicize the liberal tradition. Edmund Fawcett's recently updated *Liberalism: The Life of an Idea* offers perhaps the most comprehensive single study of the tradition. Rosenblatt, in *The Lost History*, helpfully examines the forgotten German and French thinkers who influenced the tradition. And Merquior himself still deserves attention for chronicling the changing ideological propensities of liberal thought from its beginnings to the social liberalisms of the twentieth century in *Liberalism Old and New*. For a provocative, if often deeply reductive, account of the oppres-

sion and injustice that accompanied the liberal tradition, see Losurdo, *Liberalism: A Counter-History*. Losurdo begins with a commendable effort to identify the inequities present in liberal thought, and indeed openly advocated for by many liberal thinkers across history; yet the book continually lapses into a performative contradiction, characteristic of liberalism's less generous critics, who require and presume its conceptual grammar—liberty, equality, rights—in order to impugn liberals for, in effect, not being liberal enough. His criticism of individual thinkers and texts often remains valid, and yet one has not genuinely escaped or replaced or dismantled liberalism, as a political theory, when one's critical rubric (whether labeled equality or human rights or social justice) remains wholly defined by its own core concepts. Rhetoric suggesting otherwise, as this book's conclusion emphasizes, only serves to alienate intellectuals from a liberal grammar that remains vital for any progressive politics. Merquior, *Liberalism* xiii.

53. Rosenblatt, *Lost History* 61-62; cf. Rotunda, *Politics of Language* 18-19, and Bell, "What Is Liberalism?" 693.

54. Elaine Hadley, *Living Liberalism* 6.

55. Hadley, *Living Liberalism* 6. See also Hadley, "On a Darkling Plain"; Lauren Goodlad, *Victorian Literature and the Victorian State*; Daniel Born, *The Birth of Liberal Guilt in the English Novel*; David Wayne Thomas, *Cultivating Victorians*; and Kathleen Frederickson, *The Ploy of Instinct*.

56. Dewey, *Liberalism and Social Action* 23, 64.

57. Dewey, *Liberalism and Social Action* 29 (emphasis in original).

58. Dewey, *Liberalism and Social Action* 42, 40-41, 23.

59. Hobhouse, *Liberalism* ix.

60. Bell notes that Blease, a legal scholar, positioned this turn to social welfare as the next logical step after three prior revolutions—the industrial, the American, and the French. Bell, "What Is Liberalism?" 694.

61. Dewey, *Liberalism and Social Action* 16.

62. Dewey, *Liberalism and Social Action* 15-16.

63. Locke, *Two Treatises of Government* 319.

64. Rotunda records this episode and two other such attempts in the early twentieth century. In 1920, the "Forty-Eighters" attempted in vain to build a third party around Wisconsin Senator Robert "Fighting Bob" LaFollete, who had been a leader among Progressives since the turn of the century. In 1930, Samuel H. Church, president of the Carnegie Institute, attempted a fledgling effort at a Liberal Party based on repudiating prohibition, religious tolerance, and, rather notably, denying any discrimination based on "race or creed." Rotunda, *The Politics of Language* 32-43.

65. For an entry point into the problems of defining progressivism, see Richard Hofstadter, *The Age of Reform*.

66. The most notable instance of this political rebranding, and the first major

intellectual dispute about "liberalism" in the United States, occurred on the pages of the *New Republic*. Its Progressive founders, Walter Lippmann, Herbert Croly, and Walter Weyl, cultivated a largely intellectual readership, including Dewey, George Santayana, Charles Beard, and Learned Hand. In 1916, the *New Republic* supported Woodrow Wilson and thereby helped associate Wilson and his call for the United States to enter World War I with liberalism. Rotunda, *The Politics of Language* 38-41. After the disaster of Versailles, Randolph Bourne attacked the *New Republic*, and its pragmatic idol Dewey, for their "war-liberalism," for presuming they could direct such a conflict to intellectual ends, and failing to foresee the nationalist self-interest and xenophobia that this conflict had inevitably awakened. Randolph Bourne, "Twilight of Idols" 342. In his essays, however, Bourne still uses "liberal" and "progressive" interchangeably, and he often places "liberal" in quotation marks as if to mock this young term's pretensions. The same rhetorical tendency appears in Harold Stearns's *Liberalism in America: Its Origin, Its Temporary Collapse, Its Future*, although Stearns does importantly recognize a crisis in the liberal tradition.

67. Rotunda's *The Politics of Language* offers the best word history of "liberalism" in the United States. For a longer view of this term, largely outside of the Anglo-American tradition, see Rosenblatt, *The Lost History*.

68. Roosevelt, "Address at Oglethorpe University" 639.

69. Rotunda, *Politics of Language* 60.

70. Hoover, *The Challenge to Liberty* 7-8.

71. Green, *Shaping Political Consciousness* 123.

72. *New York Times* January 6, 1935, quoted in Rotunda, *Politics of Language* 70.

73. Anonymous, "Liberalism and Tempo" 16.

74. Tennyson, "You Ask Me, Why" 119.

75. Santayana, "The Irony of Liberalism" 183. "Culture requires liberalism for its foundation, and liberalism requires culture for its crown," Santayana maintained, sounding a bit like Dewey; sounding more like Eliot, he continues: "It is culture that integrates in imagination the activities which liberalism so dangerously disperses in practice." "Liberalism and Culture" 176

76. Dewey, *Liberalism and Social Action* 26.

77. Dewey, *Liberalism and Social Action* 40.

78. Dewey, *Liberalism and Social Action* 41.

79. Dewey, *Liberalism and Social Action* 25.

80. Dewey, *Liberalism and Social Action* 26.

81. Dewey, *Liberalism and Social Action* 24.

82. Dewey, *Liberalism and Social Action* 31.

83. Dewey, "The Need for a New Party" 158-59. Dewey remained one of FDR's staunchest liberal critics throughout the decade.

84. Dewey, *Liberalism and Social Action* 37.

85. Dewey, *Liberalism and Social Action* 37.

86. Dewey's agonistic vision sounds a good deal like Nietzsche, who writes that although "liberal institutions straightway cease from being liberal, the moment they are soundly established. . . . The same institutions, so long as they are fought for, produce quite other results; then indeed they promote the cause of freedom quite powerfully." Nietzsche, *Twilight of Idols* 94. Stratton glosses this passage in a similar way; see *The Politics of Irony* 51.

87. Schoenbach, *Pragmatic Modernism* 12. This book focuses on the political liberalism Dewey defended, rather than his philosophical pragmatism, whose influence upon modernist fiction has been chronicled by Schoenbach; her study's recuperative spirit and analytic rigor, however, inspire this book. "Without the recontextualizing component of social change," Schoenbach argues, "the energies of shock disperse, leaving mindless habits of thought essentially intact"; having understood this, "the gradualist politics of pragmatism" look "less like accommodationist capitulations to existing power structures and more like a refusal to take empty, radical posturing as a substitute for meaningful political change." Schoenbach, *Pragmatic Modernism* 8-9.

88. Dewey, *The Public and Its Problem* 355-56.

89. Dewey, *Art as Experience* 340.

90. Dewey, *Art as Experience* 348.

91. Morris and Shapiro, "Editors' Introduction" xvi. For Dewey, aesthetic experience served as a model for human experience writ large. Indeed, in his book, *How We Think*, Dewey outlines a theory of cognition that makes the governing coordinates of modern art—ambiguity, difficulty, novelty—into pivotal values for learning how to think for oneself. "Thinking begins in what may fairly enough be called a *forked-road* situation," Dewey proposes, "a situation which is ambiguous, which presents a dilemma, which proposes alternatives," after an initial "shock or an interruption needing to be accounted for, identified, or placed." The "familiar and the near do not excite or repay thought on their own account," he maintains; rather, it is "the new, precarious, the problematic," which drive our minds to work. Dewey, *How We Think* 122 (emphasis in original); 121, 350.

92. Dewey, *Art as Experience* 348.

93. Dewey, *Art as Experience* 348.

94. Dewey, *Art as Experience* 348.

95. Dewey, *Art as Experience* 349.

96. Dewey, *Art as Experience* 349.

97. Stratton, *The Politics of Irony* 184.

98. Stratton, *The Politics of Irony* 127-28.

99. Stratton, *The Politics of Irony* 187.

100. Dickstein, *Dancing in the Dark* 510.

101. The body, writes Hyde, "often mimetically represents a *private* world of domesticity, autonomy, and freedom, as well as a *public* world of politics, the social

order. It thus often symbolically polices the line between public and private." Hyde, *Bodies of Law* 135 (emphasis in original).

102. Critical Feminism and Critical Race Theory each emerged from schisms within critical legal studies, a rejection of classical liberalism's grammar, and a desire to move beyond the liberal political rhetoric that had respectively characterized the second-wave feminist and the Civil Rights movements. For a history of Critical Feminism, see Deborah L. Rhode, "Critical Feminist Theories." For a history of Critical Race Theory, see Richard Delgado, "Liberal McCarthyism and the Origins of Critical Race Theory," and Crenshaw et al, "Introduction." Chapters 1 and 2 in this book also engage with parallel critiques that emerged in social contract theory: see Carole Pateman, *The Sexual Contract*; and Charles Mills, *The Racial Contract*.

103. Chapter 1 argues that this interpretive tendency can often implicitly privilege a classical liberal vision of self-authoring, self-possessed individuals as the locus of political agency.

104. Anderson, *Bleak Liberalism* 1.

Chapter 1. Liberalism Incorporated

1. Macpherson, *The Political Theory of Possessive Individualism* v. Arguing for an original overlap between liberal politics and liberal economics, Macpherson suggests that liberal thought has always been intimately bound up in property relations.

2. Macpherson, *Possessive Individualism* 272.

3. Ciepley, "Beyond Public and Private" 140.

4. In *Chicago, Milwaukee & St. Paul Railway Company v. Minnesota* (1890), the courts ruled that due process limited states' ability to regulate railroads, acknowledging corporations had "the status of individual property." In *Allgeyer v. Louisiana* (1897), corporations obtained the right "to make all proper contracts" related to this property. And in *Smyth v. Ames* (1898), they obtained the right to "earning power." See Lustig, *Corporate Liberalism* 90-93.

5. In his 1924 treatise, *The Legal Foundations of Capitalism*, John R. Commons describes corporatization as entailing a "shift from the common law . . . meaning of physical things held exclusively for one's use, to the business-law meaning of property as . . . the exchange value . . . in one's business. It is the difference between . . . things owned, and the powers of acquisition residing in the ownership of things." Commons, *Legal Foundations* 163-65, quoted in Lustig, *Corporate Liberalism* 96.

6. Lippmann, *Drift and Mastery* 45.

7. "Corporate agency and its repercussions for morality were discussed widely in the late nineteenth- and early twentieth- century," remarks Lisa Siraganian, in an ongoing debate over "what was then termed corporate legal personality, and is

now labeled corporate personhood." "Dreiser's Anti-Corporate Tools" 251. For a survey of the literary responses this debate occasioned, see Siraganian, *Modernism and the Meaning of Corporate Persons*.

   8. Lustig, *Corporate Liberalism* 36. Lustig's incisive study informs this chapter throughout.

   9. For a conservative's view, defending private property against corporations, see Hilaire Belloc, *An Essay on the Restoration of Private Property*, originally published in the *American Review* from 1933 to 1934. Kenneth Burke notably offered a contemporary critique of Belloc in a review entitled "Synthetic Freedom."

   10. Chapters 3 and 4 once again present case studies in these liberal dualisms, but this no longer takes priority of exposition; instead, these chapters principally focus on conveying the second major step in this book's narrative: the appropriation of modernist culture by a new generation of liberals.

   11. This set of stories was later republished as the volume *On Being Told That Her Second Husband Has Taken His First Lover*.

   12. Wald, *New York Intellectuals* 65.

   13. Dickstein, *Dancing in the Dark* 510.

   14. Trilling, "A Novel of the Thirties" 5.

   15. Slesinger, *The Unpossessed* 3. Though she never published another novel, Slesinger wrote adaptations of Pearl S. Buck's *The Good Earth* and Betty Smith's *A Tree Grows in Brooklyn* for the screen, works which display her continued interest in socialist politics and gender equality; her activism on behalf of the Screen Writers' Guild also played a part in one of the early victories of the Popular Front. See Biagi, "Forgive me for Dying" 232-34.

   16. The most influential work on the literary culture of the 1930s has been biographic in nature, and nearly all of it focused upon the decade's radicalism: see Barbara Foley, *Radical Representations* (1993); Alan Wald, *The New York Intellectuals* (1987); Paula Rabinowitz, *Labor and Desire* (1991); and Carey Nelson, *Repression and Recovery* (1989). A few critics have addressed intellectuals who flirted with the oft-vilified category "liberal," such as Harvey Teres, *Renewing the Left* (1996), and Alan Filreis, *Modernism from Right to Left* (1994).

   17. See Rahv, "Review of *The Unpossessed*," 26-27; Kempton, *Part of Our Time* 121-23; Trilling, "A Novel of the Thirties," 3-24; Wald, "The Menorah Group Moves Left" 289-320. These claims served different functions as the standing of the Left changed over time: passing judgment on Slesinger's intellectuals for their false consciousness and Freudian hang-ups allowed critics like Rahv in the 1930s to berate liberals for their insufficient radicalism; in the 1950s and 60s, it allowed critics like Wald to distance themselves from an episode in the history of the American Left compromised by its prolonged attraction to Stalinism.

   18. Hook continues: "Tess could talk about Virginia Woolf, Jane Austen, some of the characters in Dostoyevski [sic]—not Ivan Karamazov—but the political isms

were something her 'obsessed husband and his odd friends' were concerned about. . . . Tess caught the psychological mood of some of Herbert's friends but she was a political innocent until the day of her death." Quoted in Wald, *New York Intellectuals* 40. According to Wald, *The Unpossessed* offers such a transparent view of the *Menorah* group's "cliquish and cultist and insular features," that he confidently names the person behind each character: "Murray Kempton accurately identifies Bruno Leonard with Elliot Cohen and Miles Flinders with Herbert Solow but incorrectly equates Jeffrey Blake with Lionel Trilling. Actually, Blake very clearly suggests Max Eastman, with whom Slesinger had an affair at the time." Wald, *New York Intellectuals* 68. Cf. Murray Kempton, *Part of Our Time* 121-23. In his brief, dismissive judgment, Lionel Trilling similarly charged Slesinger with a fault not of craft but of character: "Politics was not her subject." Trilling, "A Novel of the Thirties" 20. Such misogynist commentary provides a crude yet instructive reminder that basing the political analysis of literature on anecdotal biographic information invariably directs our attention away from the structuring concepts and conflicts organizing the social field of a text and towards the tenuous reproduction of an author's self-consciousness. That said, on Hook's status as "Dewey's Bulldog," see Greif, *The Age of the Crisis of Man* 51.

19. In his book review for *New Masses*, Rahv describes Slesinger's style as unhinged, her "psychological spite" a distinctly feminine failing: "Her knife slashes indiscriminately, and we get the impression that the hand that wields it is in frenzy." Rahv did, however, praise *The Unpossessed* as "undoubtedly a significant work" for pointing out "the ideological cul-de-sac in which the esthete-modernists of the twenties now find themselves." Rahv, "Review of *The Unpossessed*" 27.

20. The Feminist Press republished *The Unpossessed* in 1984, helping to propel this work. In her "Afterword," Janet Sharistanian dismissed the notion that Slesinger was simply recording the biographic foibles of the men around her: "all of the characters are either composites or clearly distinguished in some salient fashion from their sources, indicating that Slesinger considered herself to be writing fiction, not untransmuted autobiography or factual documentation." Sharistanian, "Afterword" 373.

21. Rabinowitz, *Labor and Desire* 142. Rabinowitz casts Slesinger as a radical woman writer participating in the "regendering of the 1930s revolutionary novel." Rabinowitz, *Labor and Desire* 141. But it is not at all clear what makes Bruno and his followers "radical." Founding a literary magazine does not necessarily constitute an "extra-institutional" or "extra-normative" political gesture: for every *New Masses*, there is an *American Review*; for every *Adelphi*, a *Criterion*; every *Menorah*, a *Dearborn Review*. Abbott similarly insists that Bruno's equivocal behavior symptomatizes a "generational failure of radicalism." Abbot, "Are Three Generations of Radicals Enough?" 604.

22. Dostoevsky's *The Possessed* often serves as a point of departure for this

interpretive tendency. I have elsewhere explained, however, that Constance Garnett's heterodox choices in translating the novel complicate such intertextual arguments. See Afflerbach, "On the Use and Abuse of Dostoevsky's *The Possessed* for Reading Tess Slesinger's *The Unpossessed*."

23. Wald, "The Menorah Group Moves Left" 315; Rabinowitz, *Labor & Desire* 171. Writing in the *Daily Worker*, Joseph Freeman called the novel "bourgeois" and "reactionary," and described it as "a study in social impotence without any real explanation of that impotence." Freeman, "Review of *The Unpossessed*" 7.

24. On the rise of liberalism as a keyword in American life, see this book's introduction, especially the section on "The Discursive Origins of American Liberalism."

25. Veblen, *Theory of the Leisure Class* 27.

26. Through all his ensuing examples, however odd—such as dogs being superior to cats as icons of leisure, given their servility and practical inutility—Veblen defines the behavior of a newly confident and increasingly wealthy American bourgeoisie as a function of possession: "the possession of wealth, which was at the outset valued simply as an evidence of efficiency, becomes, in popular apprehension, itself a meritorious act. Wealth is now itself intrinsically honourable and confers honour on its possessor." Veblen, *Theory of the Leisure Class* 29.

27. Lippmann, *Drift and Mastery* 126.

28. Lippmann, *Drift and Mastery* 50.

29. Lustig, *Corporate Liberalism* 212.

30. "By the 1920s," Lustig similarly suggests, "the New Nationalists were aware of the shortcomings of their theory." Lustig, *Corporate Liberalism* 222.

31. Bourne, "The War and the Intellectuals" 5.

32. Stearns, *Liberalism in America* 59.

33. Stearns invokes a distinction between "possessive" and "creative" impulses made three years earlier by Bertrand Russell in *Principles of Social Reconstruction* (1916). For Russell, these are the two decisive registers into which human activity might be sorted, "according as they aim at acquiring or retaining something that cannot be shared, or at bringing into the world some valuable thing, such as knowledge or art or goodwill, in which there is no private property." Russell, *Principles* 5.

34. Stearns, *Liberalism in America* 61.

35. Stearns, *Liberalism in America* 78.

36. Stearns, *Liberalism in America* 75.

37. Berle and Means write: "To Adam Smith and his followers, private property was a unity involving possession. He assumed that ownership and control were combined. Today, in the modern corporation, this unity has been broken. *Passive property*,—specifically, shares of stock or bonds,—gives its possessors an interest in an enterprise but gives them practically no control over it, and involves no

responsibility. *Active property*,—plant, good will, organization, and so forth which make up the actual enterprise,—is controlled by individuals who, almost invariably, have only minor ownership interests in it." Berle and Means, *The Modern Corporation* 346. While Lippmann anticipated this argument, O'Kelley points out, it was Veblen's important, if seldom revisited, *Absentee Ownership and Business Enterprise in Recent Times* (1923), which in fact provided Berle and Means with their vital antecedent: "Veblen's contributions had not been systematized" within the tradition of neoclassical economics, O'Kelley suggests, yet "we can be certain that *Modern Corporation* was intended by Berle and understood by his Columbia colleagues to be a work in the Veblenian tradition." O'Kelley, "Berle and Veblen" 1320. On the influence of the Berle and Means thesis, see Stigler and Friedland, "The Literature of Economics: The Case of Berle and Means."

38. Lustig, *Corporate Liberalism* 13.
39. Mumford, *Technics and Civilization* 400.
40. Mumford, *Technics and Civilization* 186.
41. Kenneth Burke saw his work as an intellectual as a kind of conceptual translation: in a letter to Malcolm Cowley, he explained, "I can only welcome Communism by converting it into my own vocabulary. I am, in the deepest sense, a translator. I go on translating, even if I must but translate English into English. My book [*Permanence and Change*] will have the communist objectives, and even the communist tenor, but the approach will be the approach that seems significant to me. Those who cannot recognize a concept, even [if] it is their concept, unless this concept is stated in exactly the words they use to state it, will think my book something else." Burke and Cowley, *Selected Correspondence* 202.
42. Burke, *Attitudes Toward History* 216.
43. Burke, *Attitudes Toward History* 229.
44. Burke, *Attitudes Toward History* 330.
45. Lasch, *The New Radicalism in America* 146.
46. Hardwick, "Introduction" vii.
47. Each chapter concentrates on one perspective or upon the interactions of these pairs; through Slesinger's deft hand at establishing psychological interiority, the episodes collate into a shared world.
48. Slesinger, *The Unpossessed* 27-28. The "literary magazine" was of course a principle vehicle for intellectual discourse at this time. For an incisive, granular look at how Slesinger parodied the language of contemporary periodicals, see Arvidson, "Numb Modernism" 242-54.
49. Slesinger applies this description to "intellectuals anywhere (but Russia) in the twentieth century." From the first edition dustjacket, quoted in Donald Adams, "Review of *The Unpossessed*" 6.
50. Of course, the simplest means of identifying the political status of the intellectual has always been to deny that this figure has any place in political life at

all. Many of Slesinger's reviewers were perfectly content to write off her intellectuals as having no vested interest in the political struggles of the moment, no real class position. Writing in the *Saturday Review of Literature*, George Stevens called "the intellectuals, uprooted, classless, unpossessed" the center of *The Unpossessed*. Donald Adams seconded the notion that intellectuals "have no class"; and Alan Wald likewise suggests that the New York Intellectuals "could not relate effectively to concerns of ordinary people or even fulfill their own aspirations. The group members are political only in drawing rooms and at parties, and have only a parasitic relation to the class struggle." Stevens, "Afraid to Grow Up" 701; Adams, "Review" 6; Wald, "Menorah Group" 316.

51. MacPherson, *Possessive Individualism* 266; Slesinger, *The Unpossessed* 115.

52. Slesinger, *The Unpossessed* 178. Bruno recalls his students borrowing copies of Veblen and Marx and wonders if "poverty, undercutting everything else, removed them a priori from the class of intellectuals." Slesinger, *The Unpossessed* 173.

53. First, he explains, the intellectual must acquire a "rationale of history . . . whereby the dispossessed repossess the world . . . a spiritual property that 'no one can take from them.'" Burke, *Attitudes Toward History* 315. This indirect account of Marxism neither looks to confirm nor refute historical materialism, but rather emphasizes the problem of securing its rhetorical appeal for those whom property relations have forsaken. For these persons, the otherwise absolutely dispossessed, Marxism offers one ineluctable piece of "spiritual property."

54. Burke defines "symbols of authority" as "courts, parliaments, laws, educators, constabulary, and the moral slogans linked with such," and makes clear that such symbols of authority are "[f]undamentally connected with property relations." Burke, *Attitudes Toward History* 329-30.

55. Dewey, *Liberalism and Social Action* 45.

56. Dewey, *Individualism, Old and New* 118.

57. Dewey, *Liberalism and Social Action* 71. Democracy cannot rely upon objectified individual intelligence, the "possession" of a privileged few, but rather depends on the social practice of negotiating and reframing the common symbols through which all of us encounter the most public, as well as the most intimate, issues of political life.

58. Meg Gillette, "Bedside Manners" 161. For a compendium of abortion plots in American fiction at this time, see Gillette, "Modern Abortion Narratives and the Century of Silence," and Weingarten, *Abortion in the American Imagination*.

59. Reagan, *When Abortion Was a Crime* 14.

60. Reagan, *When Abortion Was a Crime* 15; 132. For other histories of abortion, see Morh, *Abortion in America*; and Luker, *Abortion and the Politics of Motherhood*. On the role that race played in shaping abortion policy, see Weingarten *Abortion in the American Imagination*; Stormer, *Articulating Life's Memory*; and Beisel and Kay, "Abortion, Race, and Gender."

61. Meg Gillette, "Making Modern Parents" 63. Cf. Gillette, "Bedside Manners" 160-61.

62. But see also Gillette's "Modern Abortion Narratives," where she affirms that "modern literature created a significant abortion discourse during the early twentieth century, one that moved abortion into the realm of social reality, shattered the medical community's hold on abortion, and created interested publics ready and authorized to judge abortion for themselves" (680).

63. Castro, "My Little Illegality" 17.

64. See Gillette, "Modern Abortion Narratives" for realist engagements with contemporary abortion discourse. On the biopolitics of abortion, see Weingarten, *Abortion in the American Imagination*.

65. Lippmann, *Drift and Mastery* 130.

66. Lippmann, *Drift and Mastery* 130. For feminist accounts of the discourse surrounding choice, life, and reproduction, some of which receive direct treatment in this chapter, see Brown, *States of Injury* 135-65; Poovey, "The Abortion Question"; Cornell, *Imaginary Domain*; Petchesky, *Abortion and Woman's Choice*; MacKinnon, *Feminism Unmodified*; Siegel, "Abortion as a Sex Equality Right"; and Solinger, *Beggars and Choosers*.

67. Weiner, "V. State Sen. Stephen H. Martin."

68. Pateman, *The Sexual Contract* 3.

69. Pateman, *The Sexual Contract* 3.

70. Brown, *States of Injury* 137.

71. Brown, *States of Injury* 138. In *Consent: Sexual Rights and the Transformation of American Liberalism*, Pamela Haag argues that the shift from classical to modern liberalism proceeded through a redefinition of consent and coercion in which "the normative private relation—to be left alone by classical ideals of liberal laissez-faire—was displaced from the economic to the 'personal' relation." Modern liberals, she explains, "dismantl[ed] individualism in its economic renditions through the enshrinement of the association and greater state regulation," but at the same time "preserved 'personal' relations as the domain of choice and consent" by gradually turning "privacy" (historically the opposite of public, legal life) into a domain where the state can accord individuals protected rights. Haag, *Consent* 87, 97-99.

72. Brown unpacks the gendering of these dualisms, one pair at a time, in *States of Injury* 144-63.

73. Haag, *Consent* viii.

74. Brown, *States of Injury* 155 (emphasis in original). Weingarten also offers an important reminder that "use of terms *life* and *choice* is caught in liberal American ideals of individuality, autonomy, and self-responsibility, which work to obscure abortion's entanglement in larger questions about race, eugenics, economics, biopolitics, and, of course, gender." Weingarten, *Abortion in the American Imagination* 2-3 (emphasis in original).

75. In *Gonzales v. Carhart* (2007), the Supreme Court upheld the Partial Birth Abortion Ban Act, which not only restricted access for one particular set of cases, but also established "partial birth" as a descriptive category for framing subsequent discussion of abortion. Since the turn of the century, a number of states have passed laws mandating a waiting period between counsel and surgery, graphic "educational" information about the fetus's current state and potential risks to the mother, temporal and causal limitations on the justification for abortion, and intense regulations on the safety protocols and sanitation of institutions offering the procedure. As Lauren Berlant observes, even measures that do not prevent abortion outright surround it within "a state-sanctioned, morally pedagogical *zone of publicity*," further betraying the illusion of a woman's "right to privacy." Berlant, "The Subject of True Feeling" 118.

76. Poovey, "The Abortion Question" 239.

77. MacKinnon, *Feminism Unmodified* 99. The landmark verdict in *Roe* provided women access to abortion by subsuming it within a right to privacy, established as part of the Fourteenth Amendment's equal protection clause by cases like *Griswold v. Connecticut* (1965). But this claim to privacy remained unstable. In his majority opinion for *Roe*, Judge Harry Blackmun insists that a "pregnant woman cannot be isolated in her privacy"; unlike earlier cases involving "marital intimacy, or bedroom possession of obscene material, or marriage, or procreation, or education," he argues, the State can "becom[e] significantly involved" in protecting the "health of the mother or that of potential human life." During pregnancy, he concludes, a "woman's privacy is no longer sole and any right of privacy she possesses must be measured accordingly." *Roe v. Wade* 410 US 159 (1973).

78. Hyde, *Bodies of Law* 84.

79. Cf. Poovey, "The Abortion Question" 241.

80. In its most generous interpretation, the Supreme Court's decision in *Roe* was a pragmatic attempt to reconcile incompatible values by introducing the trimester system as an artificial timetable to balance competing accounts of privacy: a woman's right to control her body (and its privacy) against the state's right to protect the fetal life (and its privacy). On this divide, see Reva B. Siegel, "Abortion as a Sex Equality Right" 53.

81. Higher courts in the United States, observes Hyde, continue to toggle on a case-by-case basis between claims to the body's privacy, integrity, and status as property, yet possess no stable theory of any of these terms. In *Moore v. Regents of the University of California* (1990), for instance, the court decided that John Moore's spleen, removed during a surgical proceeding, was not his property—despite the fact that researchers at the hospital made enormous profits from studying its cells, and the fact that blood, for instance, is recognized as a salable commodity. In *Curran v. Bosze* (1990), meanwhile, the courts upheld a mother's right not to have her twins submit to a bone marrow test to see whether they might be able to save

a half-sister dying of leukemia. Such decisions, remarks Hyde, are frequently gendered: whereas the Court found "the body with bone marrow needed by a sibling . . . 'inviolable,'" he explains, "the pregnant body is constructed as 'private' in abortion cases." Hyde, *Bodies of Law* 15. On the argument for recasting the pregnant body as "inviolable," see Susan Looper-Friedman, "Keep Your Laws Off My Body."

82. Slesinger, *The Unpossessed* 83.
83. Cornell, *The Imaginary Domain* 38.
84. Cornell, *The Imaginary Domain* 49.
85. Slesinger, *The Unpossessed* 83.
86. Slesinger, *The Unpossessed* 84.
87. On the construction of the vagina as a space, see *Rodriques v. Furtado* (1991), which sought to review the legality, in a stunning phrase, of "Search warrants for appellant's apartment and vagina." Quoted in Hyde, *Bodies of Law* 166.
88. Slesinger, *The Unpossessed* 84.
89. Slesinger, *The Unpossessed* 174.
90. Locke, *Two Treatises on Government* 288.
91. Clark and Lange, *The Sexism of Social and Political Theory* 37.
92. Slesinger, *The Unpossessed* 175.
93. Trilling, *The Opposing Self* 163.
94. Butler, "A Carefully Crafted F**k You." See also Butler, *Undoing Gender* 225-26.
95. Butler and Athanasiou, *Dispossession* 2.
96. Butler and Athanasiou, *Dispossession* 2.
97. Butler and Athanasiou, *Dispossession* 6.
98. Butler and Athanasiou, *Dispossession* 7.
99. Poovey, "The Abortion Question" 250.
100. Barbara Johnson, "Apostrophe, Animation, and Abortion" 193-94.
101. Johnson, "Apostrophe" 215 (original italics).
102. Adorno, "Commitment" 180.
103. I cannot find any record of a legally published red leather binding for *Ulysses* until the first American edition of 1934, in its "Full Morocco Leather 'Art Deco' Binding" by Random House in New York. Given that *The Unpossessed* is likely set two years earlier, during the Hunger March on Washington in 1932, and that Elizabeth insists that she "chose the binding," it seems to me clear that this is a presumably illegal copy obtained in Paris and that the cover color was intended as a symbolic choice. Slesinger, *The Unpossessed* 100.
104. In "Numb Modernism," the one outstanding recent critical essay on *The Unpossessed*, Heather Arvidson explains how modernism and radicalism, "two of the era's most prominent, and purportedly antagonistic, discursive nodes," nonetheless share a "rejection of sentiment, pejoratively gendered as feminine, and the

deprecation of embodied personhood in favor of objectivity and intellectual autonomy," a tendency which she reads *The Unpossessed* as resisting. Arvidson, "Numb Modernism" 240. For an extended rethinking of this traditional juxtaposition of modernism and sentimentalism, see Mendelman, *Modern Sentimentalism*.

105. McLoughlin, "Introduction" 6, 9 (emphasis in original).

106. From the convivial connectivity that the Bloomsbury Group offered artists and critics, to Clarissa Dalloway buttressing her creative, feminine sense of self against the looming fact of death, the party provides a real and imagined space for modernism's "twin propensities to constructive enlightenment and destructive excess." McLoughlin, "Introduction" 2.

107. The Hunger March would seem to set the novel's events in 1932.

108. My understanding of modernist irony draws upon Matthew Stratton's *The Politics of Irony in American Modernism*, as I explain in the introduction.

109. For the two influential accounts I have in mind here, see Greenberg, "Modernist Painting," and Jameson, *A Singular Modernity*. For a more nuanced, dialectical study of modernist claims to autonomy, see Goldstone, *Fictions of Autonomy*.

110. Husock, "Popular Song" 52.

111. Precisely because the modern artist produces "objects defined as 'pure', 'abstract' and 'esoteric,'" explains Joaenne Winning in her contribution to *The Modernist Party*, these objects "rely upon an audience—a peer group—capable, intellectually and critically, of their consumption," making modernist parties exemplary of what Bourdieu called modern art's "field of restricted production." Winning, "Ezra through the Open Door" 128. For a more elaborate theoretical exposition of these ideas, see Bourdieu, *The Field of Cultural Production* 29-51 and *The Rules of Art*, passim.

112. Dewey, "Philosophy and Civilization" 10.

113. Slesinger, "After the Party" 21.

114. Roosevelt, "Inaugural Address" 11-12.

115. Roosevelt, "Inaugural Address" 12.

116. Slesinger, "After the Party" 44. To compare these blurbs to the enthusiastic advertising, blurbing, and print-runs Slesinger received for *The Unpossessed*, see Arvidson "Numb Modernism" 239.

117. Bourdieu's work on cultural production and Louis Althusser's brief contributions to Marxist aesthetic theory share a common conviction that modern art claims a relative autonomy from the realm of commodities, to which it nonetheless remains tethered, thereby offering some internal distance from its own formative ideology. Both theoretical traditions inform this project's interpretive method, although I do not reproduce the idiom that characterizes the writing of these thinkers and many of their disciples, for reasons analogous to Burke's

comments on Communism in note 41 above. See Bourdieu, *The Rules of Art* and Althusser, *Lenin and Philosophy*, especially "A Letter on Art" and "Cremonini, Painter of the Abstract."

Chapter 2. Racial Liberalism

1. Schickler, *Racial Realignment* 97. To trace the ideological shifts in American liberals, Schickler draws on a massive empirical archive, including national surveys, state party platforms, congressional reports and actions, and periodicals spanning some four decades. For a complementary account of these years, see Horton, *Race and the Making of American Liberalism* 121-38. Horton goes on to explain how postwar liberalism was later "uncoupled from any conception of the more economic dimensions of racial inequality, as well as from any form of class analysis more broadly," a retreat this book addresses in chapter 3. Horton *Race* 122.

2. Schickler, *Racial Realignment* 2-4. For a comparison of the anti-Jim Crow and pro-Jim Crow coalitions that formed in these years, see King et al., *Still a House Divided*, 62-92.

3. Schickler, *Racial Realignment* 14.

4. *Plessy v. Ferguson* 559.

5. Kull, *The Color-Blind Constitution* 1.

6. *Brown v. Board of Education* 496. Prior victories on the way to *Brown* included *Missouri ex. rel. Gaines v. Canada* (1938), which ordered the University of Missouri's law school to admit a black man, and *Smith v. Allwright* (1944), which rejected the "white primary" as a violation of the Fourteenth Amendment.

7. For important critiques of color blindness, coming predominantly from scholars in critical race theory, see Gotanda, "A Critique of Our Constitution Is Colorblind"; Guinier, "From Racial Liberalism to Racial Literacy"; Bonilla-Silva, *Racism without Racists*; Carr, *"Color-Blind" Racism*; Haney-Lopez, "A Nation of Minorities" and "Is the Post in Postracial the Blind in Colorblind"; Kennedy, *For Discrimination*; Murakawa, *First Civil Right*; Wise, *Colorblind*; and Crenshaw, "Color-Blind Dreams and Racial Nightmares."

8. Garcia, *Psychology Comes to Harlem* 27. On the rise of the protest novel see Melamed, *Represent and Destroy* 51-90. After its publication by Harper and Brothers on March 1, 1940, Wright's book broke a twenty-year record at Harper's by selling two hundred thousand copies within three weeks of its publication. Fabre, *The Unfinished Quest* 13.

9. Melamed, *Represent and Destroy* xvi.

10. The Rosenwald Fund notably took on Wright as an adviser and "attempted to sponsor the writing of similar novels throughout the 1940s." Melamed, *Represent and Destroy* 67.

11. Myrdal, *An American Dilemma* 656.

12. For an introduction to perhaps the most disputed final scene in American fiction, see Paul Siegel, "Conclusion of *Native Son*."

13. Kinnamon, "How *Native Son* Was Born" 123.

14. Fisher, quoted in Kinnamon, "How *Native Son*" 123.

15. For critics like Alfred Kazin, Robert Bone, and Edward Margolies, the "center of Richard Wright's art" is the "impulse to protest," making Bigger an exemplary victim of reprehensible social conditions, and *Native Son* a seminal case study of literary naturalism. Bone, *The Negro Novel* 157. Later critics, however, came to emphasize Bigger's identity and agency as an individual. These scholars, such as Robert Butler, Katherine Fishburn, and Houston Baker, replace Bigger's status as social symbol with a narrative in which "the evil he struggles against is identified with society itself and his exaltation is purely a personal one." Fishburn, *Richard Wright's Hero* 61.

16. Philip Goldstein attempts to explain this bifurcation in the novel's reception by tracking its chronological development alongside "Wright's changing beliefs . . . the changing status of the naturalist and modernist literary movements and the emergence of black aesthetics and black studies programs." Goldstein, "Richard Wright's *Native Son*" 120. For related accounts, see Portelli, "Everybody's Healing Novel" 255-65; Butler, *Native Son* 16-22; and Joyce, *Richard Wright's Art* 3-25.

17. As this book's introduction explains, chapters 1 and 2 focus on presenting aporias in political liberalism, conceptual nodes at which the constitutive dualisms in liberal thought became apparent in political theory and social practice. Chapters 3 and 4 once again present case studies in these liberal dualisms, but this no longer takes priority of exposition; instead, these chapters principally focus on conveying the second major step in this book's narrative: the appropriation of modernist culture by a new generation of liberals.

18. Melamed, *Represent and Destroy* 23, 53.

19. Jackson, *The Indignant Generation* 109. Several critics have discussed Wright's relationship to the New Deal: see Szalay, *New Deal Modernism* 215-17; Edmunds, "'Just Like Home," and Bell, *The Afro-American Novel*.

20. Wright, "How 'Bigger' Was Born 454. Jackson notes that *Uncle Tom's Children* was "the only time in his career" that Wright received "the combined praise of his black constituents, center-leaning white liberals, and the far Left." Jackson, *The Indignant Generation* 109.

21. Jackson, *The Indignant Generation* 114.

22. Jackson, *The Indignant Generation* 125.

23. Wright, *Native Son* 383.

24. These critics often rebuke Communism indirectly by expressing their disapproval for an apparently didactic turn in the novel; Bone, for example, insists that since there is "nothing in Bigger's life that corresponds to 'Communism,'"

Native Son "suffers from a major structural flaw, flowing from the fact that Wright has failed to digest Communism artistically." Bone, *The Negro Novel* 150. Summarizing these readings, Siegel states that the "conclusion of *Native Son* has perhaps caused more critics, distinguished and obscure, to go astray . . . than any other significant portion of a major work of modern American literature." Siegel, "Conclusion" 94.

25. Mike Gold, the leading Communist critic of the 1930s, praised *Native Son*, but only after nearly a month's delay, a wait long enough to make Wright—still a party member, but no longer in good standing and constantly having to defend his priorities—nervous about the political message being sent by Gold's apparent ambivalence. Fabre, *The Unfinished Quest* 185. More substantially, Ben Davis Jr., the party's coordinator and supervisor for Wright in New York, wrote a review for the *Sunday Worker* that flatly dismissed Max's speech as a representation of the Communist position. While Davis praised *Native Son* as a "terrific indictment of capitalist America," he resented the "characters who are not typical and who reflect distorted ideas which are far from adequately expressing the policies of the Communist Party." For Max "to give up Bigger, to abandon him" to the logic of the court, suggests Davis, "is to condone the system which crushed his social aspirations and enmeshed him in crime." Davis, "Review" 69, 74.

26. Wright, *Native Son* 290. Despite Max's attempt to convince Buckley that he, Jan, and Bigger are not in league in a Communist plot, Buckley sticks to Bigger's red herring: a ransom note for Mary signed with "the name of the Communist Party": "Red" (292). Explaining Bigger's deception to Buckley, Max retorts that "trying to blame the Communists for his crime was a natural reaction for him. He had heard men like you lie about the Communists so much that he believed them" (292). Max comes closest to a Marxist vocabulary when he offers a brief historical account of the progression from the "feudal age" to an era of "nations on a vast scale" in which slavery became "economically impossible" (389).

27. Decker, "A Lot Depends" 176.

28. Wirth helped promote sociological jurisprudence when he testified before the US Supreme Court in *Shelley v. Kraemer* (1948), a case concerning racially restrictive housing covenants. But while sociological jurisprudence was "prominent in the 1920s and 1930s," notes Decker, it was widely challenged after 1940, criticized by those who saw "the philosophy dangerous and even totalitarian because it allegedly allowed social scientists and social science too much influence." Decker, "A Lot Depends" 182-84.

29. Decker, "A Lot Depends" 180.

30. Decker, "A Lot Depends" 180.

31. Garcia, *Psychology* 49.

32. Garcia, *Psychology* 59-66.

33. Scott, *Contempt and Pity* 102.

34. Garcia, *Psychology* 19; Scott, *Contempt and Pity* 100.
35. Garcia, *Psychology* 84-86.
36. Wright, "Introduction" xvii.
37. Wright, "Introduction" xviii.
38. Wright, "Introduction" xx. Wright also cites work by the Chicago school of sociology, such as Louis Wirth's *The Ghetto*, Everett V. Stonequist's *The Marginal Man*; Frederick M. Thrasher's *The Gang*. Wright, "Introduction" xix.
39. Melamed, *Represent and Destroy* 63 (emphasis in original).
40. Kinnamon "Introduction" 24.
41. Walter Jackson, *Gunnar Myrdal* xi. The Carnegie Corporation, suggests Jackson, wanted the study conducted by someone from a country without a colonial history, lest any questions be raised about their racial impartiality. Jackson, *Gunnar Myrdal* xiii.
42. Jackson, *Gunnar Myrdal* xvi.
43. Jackson, *Gunnar Myrdal* xi.
44. Jackson, *Gunnar Myrdal* xlv. See also Horton, *Race* 124-26.
45. Melamed, *Represent and Destroy* 20.
46. Jackson, *Gunnar Myrdal* 105, 405.
47. Trilling "A Tragic Situation" 39, quoted in Garcia, *Psychology* 11.
48. Schlesinger, *The Vital Center* 190, quoted in Horton, *Race and the Making of American Liberalism* 121.
49. Melamed, *Represent and Destroy* 53. During testimony for *Brown v. Board*, the plaintiffs insisted that "It is in the context of the present world struggle between freedom and tyranny that the problem of racial discrimination must be viewed." *Brown v. Board* 6.
50. Brock, *Americans for Democratic Action* 30.
51. *To Secure These Rights*, quoted in Jackson, *Gunnar Myrdal* 276.
52. Jackson, *Gunnar Myrdal* 278.
53. Murakaw, *First Civil Right* 212n8.
54. In fighting for legal equality, observes Lawrence Jackson, civil rights groups such as the NAACP showed "strong resistance to any policy that 'set the Negro apart for special treatment'" (141).
55. *Plessy v. Ferguson* 551. *Brown v. Board of Education* 494. Warren was citing the language of the lower courts. He explains that the court "cannot turn the clock back to 1868 when the Amendment was adopted, or even to 1896 when *Plessy v. Ferguson* was written," and so must instead "consider public education in the light of its full development and its present place in American life." *Brown v. Board* 492. As Lucas Powe points out, Warren "astutely surmised that a brief opinion increased the probability that it would be reprinted in its entirety by a larger number of the nation's newspapers," and so he created a simple, direct statement of the court's decision to rule the segregation of schools in Kansas, Virginia, South Carolina, and

Delaware unconstitutional, knowing that it would increase the chances of the document's wide dissemination. Powe, *The Warren Court* 29.

56. *Brown v. Board* 494, 496. Garcia, *Psychology* 19. Clark's study, which claimed to show how some African American schoolgirls preferred white dolls to black ones and tied this psychological self-deprecation to racial discrimination, later became a target for scrutiny of Warren's opinion. On footnote 11 and the larger role of the social sciences in *Brown*, see Heise "Brown v. Board" 294; and Balkin, *What Brown v. Board* 51.

57. Phillips, *National Anti-slavery Standard*, quoted in Kull, *The Color-Blind Constitution* 61.

58. Tourgée, Brief for Plaintiff at 27, 46, quoted in Kull, *The Color-Blind Constitution* 119.

59. Kull, *The Color-Blind Constitution* 119.

60. *Plessy v. Ferguson* 559; Irons, *A People's History* 230.

61. Kull, *The Color-Blind Constitution* 2. Randall Kennedy notes that the *New York Times* first features an article quoting Harlan's dissent in 1942. Kennedy, *For Discrimination* 155.

62. Haney-Lopez, "Reactionary Color-Blindness" 988.

63. Haney-Lopez, "Reactionary Color-Blindness" 998.

64. "Brief for Appellants in *Brown v. Board*," quoted in Kennedy, *For Discrimination* 156.

65. "Justice Harlan Concurring," quoted in Kull, *The Color-Blind Constitution* 151.

66. Kull, *The Color-Blind Constitution* 151.

67. *Plessy v. Ferguson* 559.

68. Kull, *The Color-Blind Constitution* 130. The observation on Harlan's slave-owning past comes from Kennedy, *For Discrimination* 152.

69. Haney-Lopez, "Reactionary ColorBlindness" 993.

70. Kull, *The Color-Blind Constitution* 160. Although observers regularly affirm that *Brown* overthrew *Plessy*, insists Kull, the Warren Court rejected segregation based on color without offering a surrogate definition of what "equal protection under the laws" should constitute. *Plessy*, "in its broad holding as opposed to its particular application," Kull explains, "has never been overruled, even by implication." *The Color-Blind Constitution* 111.

71. Bone, *The Negro Novel* 147.

72. For such accounts of blindness in *Native Son*, see Bone, *The Negro Novel* 140-52; Margolies *The Art of Richard Wright* 117-18; and Nagel, "Images of 'Vision'" 86-88. For a broader treatment of the topic, see Ramsey, "Blind Eyes, Blind Quests."

73. Watt, *Rise of the Novel* 31.

74. Douzinas and Neads, "Introduction" 3.

75. Wright, *Native Son* 316.

76. Jay, "Must Justice Be Blind?" 26. For a wider view of *Justitia*'s problematic features, see Bennett Capers, "On Justitia, Race, Gender, and Blindness."

77. Gross quips that the title of Dalton's original paper, "Extraordinary Facts Relating to the Vision of Colors," could nearly "serve as the epigraph to *Native Son*." Gross, "Dalton and Color-Blindness" 76. In a remarkable psychoanalytic session with Frederic Wertham, published in the *Journal of Clinical Psychopathology and Psychotherapy*, Wright appeared not to recall the meaning of Daltonism, but then later suggested that he had learned of the condition through his time with a "medical research institute." Wertham, "An Unconscious Determinant" 114.

78. Wright, *Native Son* 316.

79. Wright, *Native Son* 315.

80. In her seminal essay, "Whiteness as Property," Cheryl Harris explains how the ruling in *Brown* "refused to extend continued legal protection to white privilege, yet it simultaneously declined to guarantee that white privilege would be dismantled, or even to direct that the continued existence of institutionalized privilege violated the equal protection rights of Blacks." Harris, "Whiteness as Property" 1751.

81. Wright, *Native Son* 326-27 (emphasis in original). Max later tells Mrs. Dalton, "Your philanthropy was as tragically blind as your sightless eyes!" Wright, *Native Son* 393.

82. Wright, *Native Son* 330, 330, 331.

83. Hughes, "Justice."

84. Melamed, *Represent and Destroy* 23.

85. Horton, *Race and the Making of American Liberalism* 138.

86. For a set of arguments about what *Brown* might have otherwise accomplished, see Balkin, *What Brown v. Board of Education Should Have Said*. Christopher Schmidt points out that while these shortcomings to *Brown* might be real, NAACP lawyers "recognized the limitations of anticlassification arguments" far more often than scholars like Kull have allowed. Schmidt, "Brown and the Colorblind Constitution" 207.

87. Kull, *The Color-Blind Constitution* 154.

88. Wright, *Native Son* 397-98. Paul de Man describes a text that creates a pattern of self-inflicted blindness, in which "the verdict repeats the crime it condemns," as an "allegory of judgment." de Man, *Allegories of Reading* 245. In an earlier version of this chapter, I framed *Native Son* as such an allegory; see Afflerbach, "Liberalism's Blind Judgment."

89. Jay, "Must Justice Be Blind?" 26.

90. Critics invested in Max's speech as a mode of realist or naturalist representation might dispute this claim; see, for instance, Tremaine, "Disassociated Sensibility" 102.

91. What Baldwin sought to condemn by pinning *Native Son* with the label

"protest novel" was less its craft—he called Wright's book "the most powerful and celebrated statement we have yet had of what it means to be a Negro in America"—but rather the liberal sentimentality it produced in its readers. Baldwin, "Many Thousands" 30. "The 'protest' novel," complains Baldwin, "far from being disturbing, is an accepted and comforting aspect of the American scene, ramifying the framework we believe to be so necessary. Whatever unsettling questions are raised are evanescent, titillating; remote, for this has nothing to do with us. . . . As long as such books are being published,' an American liberal once said to me, 'everything will be all right.'" "Everybody's Protest Novel" 19.

92. Baldwin, "Everybody's Protest" 23.

93. Baldwin worried that Bigger, who embodied the worst symptoms of black male life in America, would become a representative figure in the minds of white liberal readers, "a continuation, a complement of that monstrous legend it was written to destroy." Baldwin, "Many Thousands Gone" 28. Wright perhaps exacerbated this worry by threatening his readers with the image of a native totalitarianism, a mass of Bigger Thomases, angry, alone, and without direction, who cannot or do not care to understand the program behind a political party but are drawn to the power of action: "I've even heard Negroes say that maybe Hitler and Mussolini are all right; that maybe Stalin is all right. They did not say this out of any intellectual comprehension of the forces at work in the world, but because they felt these men 'did things,' a phrase which is charged with more meaning than the mere words imply." Wright, "How 'Bigger' Was Born," 440.

94. Baldwin, "Everybody's Protest" 22.

95. As the Cold War set in, existentialism provided a language to recover Bigger's individuality, for critics to insist on the importance of personal autonomy and self-expression against the dangerously tyrannical social determinism that seemed to take over Max's speech.

96. Portelli, "Everybody's Healing Novel" 255. For alternate takes on Wright's place in literary history, see Karem, *The Romance of Authenticity*; and Morgan *Rethinking Social Realism*.

97. For a thorough documentation of this shift in critical priorities, see Goldstein, "Richard Wright's Native Son." For an overview of the problems with "existential readings" of *Native Son*, see Afflerbach, "Liberalism's Blind Judgment." Wright's break with the Communist Party, his move to France, and the increase of existentialist themes in *The Outsider*, all clearly signal his growing admiration for a philosophical school that matched his disposition as a writer. But Wright did not read Camus or Sartre until the mid-to-late 1940s and so claims that existential thought proper influenced *Native Son* seem deeply tenuous. Fabre, *The Unfinished Quest* 320.

98. Gibson, "Wright's Invisible Native Son" 37.

99. Smith, *Self-Discovery* 70. The growing priority of self-expression in Wright

scholarship stems in part from the influential exchange between Ralph Ellison and Irving Howe in the 1960s. By linking control of language to a kind of "mastery" of the self and by placing his demand for aesthetic freedom within "an American Negro tradition which teaches one to deflect racial provocation and to master and contain pain," Ellison helped shift the terrain of discussion on the role of the midcentury African American novelist. Ellison, "The World and the Jug" 122.

100. Werner, "Bigger's Blues" 128.

101. Smith, "Alienation and Creativity" 112.

102. Baron, "Syntax of Perception" 17.

103. Baron, "Syntax of Perception" 21, 22.

104. Baron, "Syntax of Perception" 28.

105. Szalay, *New Deal Modernism* 218, 254.

106. Szalay, *New Deal Modernism* 22.

107. Mills, *Racial Contract* 11. These two scholars discuss their respective critiques of the contract tradition, especially John Rawls, in Pateman and Mills's *The Contract and Domination*.

108. Mills, "Racial Liberalism" 1385. Mills expanded this argument into his book *Black Rights, White Wrongs: The Critique of Racial Liberalism*. Carol Horton also offers a balanced historical study of the "complex and double-edged" relationship between race and American liberalism: "On the one hand," she affirms, "race has been instrumental in creating some of the nation's most radically democratic forms of liberal politics, which emphasize the inclusion of the disfranchised, the importance of socioeconomic equity, and, more recently, the value of cultural diversity. On the other," however, "it has reinforced the dominance of relatively inequitable forms of liberalism, which use the equation of equal rights and free markets to legitimate grossly unequal distributions of wealth, power, and status." Horton, *Race and the Making of American Liberalism* 4.

109. Baldwin, "Many Thousands Gone" 44-45.

110. *Briggs v. Elliott* 777, quoted in Haney-Lopez, "Post in Post-Racial" 810. In *Lassiter v. Northampton County Board of Elections* (1959), the Supreme Court upheld a literacy test for voters, noting no "evidence that it was discriminatorily applied" among different citizens. Powe, *The Warren Court* 176.

111. *North Carolina State Board of Education v. Swann*, quoted in Haney-Lopez, "Post in Post-Racial" 810.

112. Haney-Lopez, "Nation of Minorities" 1004.

113. Kennedy, *For Discrimination* 153-54. See also Brad Snyder "How the Conservatives Canonized *Brown v. Board of Education*."

114. Gotanda, "A Critique of Our Constitution is Colorblind" 2.

115. Kennedy, *For Discrimination* 147.

116. Baldwin et al., "Liberalism and the Negro" 25, 26.

117. Baldwin et al., "Liberalism and the Negro" 26 (emphasis in original).

118. Baldwin et al., "Liberalism and the Negro" 30.
119. Baldwin et al., "Liberalism and the Negro" 41. On Baldwin's disenchantment with efforts to combat racism through law, see Nabers, "Past Using."
120. Baldwin et al., "Liberalism and the Negro" 39.
121. "Executive Order 10925," quoted in Kennedy, For Discrimination 17.
122. See Horton, Race and the Making of American Liberalism 191-222. This neoconservative gospel spread through journals like *The Public Interest, Public Opinion* and *Commentary*, and massively funded "think-tanks," such as the American Enterprise Institute, the Hoover Institution, the Cato Institute, and the Heritage Foundation.
123. Post, *Prejudicial Appearances* 14.
124. Siegel, "Discrimination in the Eyes" 107.
125. *Regents of Univ. California v. Bakke* 327.
126. *Regents of Univ. California v. Bakke* 327.
127. See Kennedy, *For Discrimination* 168-71.
128. Bonilla-Silva, *Racism without Racists* 38-39.
129. Haney-Lopez "Is the Post in Post-Racial" 815.
130. *Adarand v. Peña* 240, quoted in Kennedy, *For Discrimination* 165.
131. Kennedy juxtaposes this staunch colorblind view with Justice O'Connor's moderate view, wherein race conscious policies serve an historical purpose but must be phased out over time. Kennedy, *For Discrimination* 165, 180.
132. See note seven above for a catalog of critical race studies on "color-blind racism."
133. Bonilla-Silva, *Racism without Racists* 11.
134. Bonilla-Silva, *Racism without Racists* 7.
135. Crenshaw, "Color-Blind Dreams" 104.
136. Darden, *In Contempt* 202, quoted in Crenshaw, "Color-blind Dreams" 126.
137. Kennedy, *For Discrimination* 159.
138. Kennedy, *For Discrimination* 160. On the legal and literary history of transracial adoption, see Mark Jerng, *Claiming Others*.
139. Ellison, "*An American Dilemma*: A Review" 328.
140. Ellison, "*An American Dilemma*: A Review" 339.
141. Ellison, "*An American Dilemma*: A Review" 339.
142. Ellison, "*An American Dilemma*: A Review" 340.
143. Garcia, *Psychology Comes to Harlem* 140.
144. Baldwin, *Evidence of Things* 1.
145. Baldwin, *Evidence of Things* 100.
146. Baldwin, *Jimmy's Blues* 11.
147. Quentin Miller, *Re-viewing James Baldwin* 241.
148. Howe, "Black Boys" 100-101.
149. Howe, "Black Boys" 100.

150. Ellison "World and the Jug" 159, 177.

151. Ellison "World and the Jug" 165.

152. Melamed, *Represent and Destroy* 23.

153. Craig Werner situates *Native Son* within the tradition of Afro-American modernism, as does Kimberly Benston, albeit via a more theoretical path. See Werner, "Bigger's Blues," and Benston, "The Veil of Black." Wright himself did not see a clear difference between the race liberal interest in social psychology and the insights of previous modernist writers; in his introduction to *Black Metropolis*, he wonders: "What would life on Chicago's South Side look like when seen through the eyes of a Freud, a Joyce, a Proust, a Pavlov, a Kierkegaard? It should be recalled in this connection that Gertrude Stein's *Three Lives*, which contained 'Melanctha,' the first long serious literary treatment of Negro life in the United States, was derived from Stein's preoccupation with Jamesian psychology." Wright, "Introduction" xxxi.

154. Nowlin, "Ralph Ellison, James Baldwin, and the Liberal Imagination" 118.

155. Nowlin, "Ralph Ellison" 126. As Matthew Stratton has shown, claims about irony were frequently mobilized to define opposing aesthetic and political values in midcentury African American fiction. Howe rejected the "unqualified assertion of self-liberation" at the end of *Invisible Man* and as a "vapid and insubstantial" gesture typical among postwar literary intellectuals, yet Ellison notes how this purportedly heroic assertion in fact comes from a speaker who still lives underground at the novel's end, with "Howe either missing the irony or assuming that *I* did." Howe, "Black Boys" 115; Ellison "The World and the Jug" 157, quoted in Stratton, *The Politics of Irony* 144-46 (emphasis in original).

156. "Ellison's work," as Robert Genter explains, "reclaimed the heroic subjectivity of modernism precisely at the moment when much of the American Left did so as well." Genter, "Toward a Theory of Rhetoric" 194. Howe proposes that Baldwin's essays, "bristling with dialectical agility," were the "fashionable" style of a "postwar liberalism not very different from conservatism." Howe, "Black Boys" 141, 141, 176.

Chapter 3. The Inward Turn

1. Bell, *The End of Ideology* 300.

2. Schaub, *American Fiction* viii.

3. Anderson, *Bleak Liberalism* 20-28. Anderson shows how a recurring "bleak" ethos has provided liberal intellectuals, throughout history, with a reflexivity and self-critical spirit, which some mistakenly believe the liberal tradition to lack. Her work provides an important point of departure for this chapter; the introduction also explains how such revisionary scholarship in Victorian studies has led the way in recovering a richer understanding of liberal culture.

4. Anderson, *Bleak Liberalism* 29.

5. Anderson, "Postwar Aesthetics" 419. For a reading of Trilling and his intellectual peers along the lines Anderson describes, see Kimmage, *The Conservative Turn*.

6. Despite the enormous importance of World War II in popularizing a tragic pessimism, critics often overemphasize the way that a "bleak" sensibility emerged as a causal response to catastrophe. As Richard Wightman Fox has shown, as early as the 1920s, a growing number of American thinkers already sought to reconcile a "tragic perspective earlier associated with Hawthorne, Melville, Twain, and Henry Adams" with their sense of intellectual responsibility. Fox notes how Reinhold Niebuhr, Lewis Mumford, Richard Wright, Joseph Wood Krutch, and Lionel Trilling all participated in a "marked rekindling of interest in the subject of tragedy and in . . . the 'tragic sense of life." Fox, "Tragedy, Responsibility, and the American Intellectual" 323–24. Fox's work in mapping this tragic sensibility, and as Niebuhr's biographer, informs this chapter throughout.

7. Niebuhr, "The Blindness of Liberalism" 45.

8. Naveh, *Reinhold Niebuhr* 23.

9. Despite near perpetual dispute about what "tragedy" means, the term has remained a remarkably consistent signifier for literary value; see Hugh Grady, "The Modernity of Western Tragedy: Genealogy of a Developing Anachronism."

10. Trilling, *The Liberal Imagination* ix, 98.

11. Trilling, *The Liberal Imagination* xv.

12. Spiegel, *James Agee* 3.

13. This chapter foregrounds these antinomies by emphasizing what Nikolopoulou describes as the friction between "tragedy's public, outward staging of conflict (the actual, the performative, the collectively experienced)" and the "interiorized . . . private, purely ethical provenance of the tragic (the speculative, the introspective, the singular relation to a singular Other)." Nikolopoulou, *Tragically Speaking* xxxvi.

14. Harper Publishing gave Agee a year's salary to complete the book, only to reject his draft in 1939, after Agee refused to make "deletions in the interests of good taste." Sun, *Succeeding King Lear* 128–29.

15. Lucaites, "Visualizing 'The People'" 271.

16. Stott, *Documentary Expression* 216.

17. The supposed division between modernism and documentary has been a critical commonplace, yet scholars such as Tyrus Miller and Jeff Allred have shown how this line was blurry at best during the 1930s, as authors such as John Dos Passos and Muriel Rukeyser created hybrid works fusing documentary journalism with modernist fragmentation. See Miller "Documentary/Modernism," and Allred, *American Modernism and Depression Documentary*.

18. Agee appears to have been concerned enough about quoting from the *Manifesto*, given what he calls the "topical dangers to which any man . . . is at

present liable," to insist in his note that "neither these words nor the authors are the property of any political party, faith, or faction." Agee and Evans, *Famous Men* xiii.

19. Agee and Evans, *Famous Men* xiii.

20. Hugh Davis, *The Making of James Agee* 140. While the book begins with photos by Evans in uninterrupted succession, suggesting a fidelity to the objective conditions of tenant farming, it ends with Evans and Agee projecting themselves onto foxes crying in the night. As Rabinowitz puts it, "the movement from the documentary image of the tenants to the narrative of his own subjectivity is complete, and with it, the movement from visual to descriptive, from the people to the self." Rabinowitz, *Labor & Desire* 41.

21. Agee and Evans, *Famous Men* 11.

22. Agee and Evans, *Famous Men* 5.

23. Agee and Evans, *Famous Men* 11-12.

24. Rosler, "In, Around, and Afterthoughts" 176, 179, 190.

25. Agee and Evans, *Famous Men* xv.

26. Agee and Evans, *Famous Men* 339.

27. For a thorough account of this tension between individual and collective in *Famous Men*, see Lucaites "Visualizing the People."

28. Hilgart, "Valuable Damage" 85.

29. Caldwell, *You Have Seen Their Faces* x.

30. Denby, "A Famous Man."

31. Hegeman, *Patterns for America* 178 (emphasis in original), quoting Agee and Evans, *Famous Men* x (emphasis in original).

32. Agee and Evans, *Famous Men* 179.

33. Nietzsche, *The Birth of Tragedy* 42. Agee and Evans, *Famous Men* 177.

34. "Agee," she insists, "cannot escape the confessional narrative of bourgeois selfhood: the story that encodes the middle class as the subject and object of its own narcissistic and self-loathing gaze." Rabinowitz, *They Must Be Represented* 45.

35. Agee and Evans, *Famous Men* 178.

36. Lest his reader mistake this as advocacy for "art," Agee cites Beethoven, along with "Christ, Joyce, Kafka," as some of those betrayed by "official acceptance" and pleads for his own book: "Above all else: in God's name don't think of it as Art." Against the "equilibrium" of being sanctioned as Art, Agee continually insists on a discomforting aesthetic experience: "If it hurts you, be glad of it." Agee and Evans, *Famous Men* 12-13.

37. Agee invokes tragedy at several suggestive moments throughout his book. Emily Sun, Robert Coles, and David Humphreys have all noted his affinity for *King Lear*, and three such points of connection merit acknowledging. First, in a poem dedicated to Walker Evans just a few pages after his epigraphs, Agee imagines Evans and himself in an adaption of the play where they are the "younger sons, the

fools." Agee casts himself as the King's jester—who knows more than he can say—while turning Evans into "Edgar," maligned son who must lead his blinded father Gloucester toward a tragic insight. He and Evans, Agee implies, walk among those who should not have trusted them; they might lead a blinded reader toward a begrudging, even fatal vision. Later, Agee issues a hortatory apostrophe drawing upon King Lear's favored metaphor of old age: "O, we become old. . . . In what way were we trapped? where, our mistake? what, where, how, when, what way, might all these things have been different, if only we had done otherwise? if only we might have known." Agee and Evans, *Famous Men* 70. By leaving unanswered this bitter catalog of journalistic prompts—what, where, how, when—Agee signals the impossibility of objectively representing, or escaping, the all-encompassing "trap" in which he now places himself, and his reader, along with the Gudgers, the Ricketts, and the Woods. He likens this fate to "growing old," and *Lear* is of course the great drama of aging: the King casts himself as a "poor, infirm, weak, and despised old man . . . old and white as this. O! O! 'tis foul!" Shakespeare, *King Lear* 3.2.21-26. Finally, Agee also rewrites Lear's famous scolding of the heavens, "Crack nature's molds, all germens spill at once / That make ingrateful man," when he describes reproductive life as a perpetuation of humanity's damage: the "germens they carry at their groins," he writes, are "strained, cracked, split, tainted, vitiate to begin with, a wallet of cheated coinage." This "cheated coinage" captures not only the unjust privation, pecuniary and sexual, of the tenant's life of labor, but also the declining value of reproduction, wherein the spilling of genes only perpetuates a "crime soaked world." Shakespeare, *King Lear* 3.2.10-11; Agee and Evans, *Famous Men* 90.

38. Paolucci, *Hegel on Tragedy* 48.

39. Paolucci, *Hegel on Tragedy* 51. This movement from two competing subjects to one internally divided subject of course resembles (and arguably informs, via *Antigone*) an episode in the *Phenomenology of Spirit*; see Hegel, *Phenomenology* 109-19.

40. Hegeman recognizes how the "anodyne of charity" in Lear's speech on the heath is incommensurable with Agee's profound doubts about his ability to represent the "wretched" conditions of tenant life. Hegeman, *Patterns for America* 178.

41. Spiegel, *James Agee* 3. Nearly all early reviewers saw *Famous Men* as a failure. Even Selden Rodman, who admired the book, suggests that "part of the greatness and unique quality of 'Let Us Now Praise Famous Men,' then, is its structural failure, its over-all failure as the 'work of art' it does not aim or presume to be and which from moment to moment it is." Rodman, "The Poetry of Poverty" 6. *Time*'s write-up calls *Famous Men* "the most distinguished failure of the season." "Experiment in Communication" 667.

42. Rabinowitz, *They Must Be Represented* 43.

43. Tate, *Reason in Madness* 72, quoted on Schaub, *American Fiction* 35. Chase, *American Novel* 49, quoted on Schaub, *American Fiction* 37.

44. Chase, "A Novel Is a Novel" 590-91, quoted on Schaub, *American Fiction* 23.

45. Chase, *Melville* viii, 209.

46. Trilling, *The Liberal Imagination* x.

47. Trilling, *The Liberal Imagination* 98.

48. Kirsch, *Why Trilling Matters* 99.

49. Trilling, *Speaking for Literature and Society* 189.

50. Trilling, *Speaking for Literature and Society* 216.

51. In "The America of John Dos Passos," Trilling singles out the modern novel as especially useful for triggering pragmatic evaluations of character, and he notably acknowledges Dewey's thought along these lines: "The moral assumption on which Dos Passos seems to work was expressed by John Dewey some thirty years ago; there are certain moral situations, Dewey says, where we cannot decide between the ends; we are forced to make our moral choice in terms of our preference for one kind of character or another: 'What sort of an agent, of a person shall he be? . . . The modern novel, with its devices for investigating the quality of character, is the aesthetic form almost specifically called forth to exercise this modern way of judgment. The novelist goes where the law cannot go." Trilling, *The Liberal Imagination* 109-10.

52. A second reprint in 1953 sold seventy thousand copies, and the Doubleday Anchor paperback sold one hundred thousand. Rodden, *Lionel Trilling* 12.

53. Anderson, "Postwar Aesthetics" 435. See also Anderson, *Bleak Liberalism* 112.

54. Anderson, *Bleak Liberalism* 112 (emphasis in original).

55. In early work, Trilling describes "moral realism" not as "the awareness of morality itself but of the contradictions, paradoxes, and dangers of living the moral life." Trilling, *E.M. Forster*, 11-12. He uses the phrase, observes Krupnick, "as he does 'liberalism,' to suggest a large tendency"; it generally "stands for the tragic sense of life." Krupnick, *Lionel Trilling* 65.

56. Trilling, *The Opposing Self* 31.

57. Trilling, *The Opposing Self* 39.

58. Trilling, *The Opposing Self* 31.

59. Trilling, *The Liberal Imagination* 80.

60. Trilling, *The Liberal Imagination* 80, 56.

61. Schechner, "The Elusive Trilling" 355.

62. Krumpnick, *Lionel Trilling* 67, 69.

63. Trilling, "Greatness with One Fault in It" 99.

64. Trilling, "Greatness with One Fault in It" 102.

65. Recalling his "last conversation" with Agee, Trilling proposed that Agee had "to affirm, if not actually to believe, that the human soul could exist in a state of

radical innocence which was untouched by any contrary," and remained unwilling to recognize that "poverty and suffering are not in themselves virtue." Trilling, *Speaking of Literature and Society* 379.

66. Bell, *The End of Ideology* 300.

67. Aaron, "Conservatism" 99.

68. Aaron, "Conservatism" 100.

69. Hegeman, *Patterns for America* 177. Hegeman notes how Agee's employment in the Luce empire and commercial flop with *Famous Men* made him a focal point for the emerging hierarchization of culture developed by intellectuals around the *Partisan Review*. His tragic loss buttressed "a new emphasis on the necessity of preserving the modernist aesthetic culture of the avant-garde against the onslaughts of mass culture." Hegeman, *Patterns for America* 159.

70. Macdonald, "Death of a Poet" 216.

71. Macdonald, "Death of a Poet" 214. The cover of the McDowell paperback edition of *Death in the Family* echoes Macdonald's high praise, calling Agee "the most prodigiously talented writer of his generation, and one of the most tragic figures of our time."

72. Davis has recounted how this canonization was a deeply personal affair: Macdonald's interest in making Agee representative for the "cultural decline" of his era, Robert Fitzgerald's excision of Agee's political poems from his collected work, and David McDowell's wholesale reconstruction of *A Death in the Family* all helped sanitize Agee for the annals of literary history. Davis, *The Making of James Agee* 30-50.

73. Henry Luce's *Fortune* magazine, argues Michael Auspurger, was a "crucial document of the rise of what has been called 'corporate liberalism' from an idealistic minority view in the teens and twenties to the dominant American social force of the postwar years." Auspurger, *Economy of Abundant Beauty* 2. Agee's remarks on his profession have helped to reinforce the cultural hierarchy this narrative entails: "I do not wish to appear to speak favorably of journalism. I have never yet seen a piece of journalism which conveyed more than the slightest fraction of what any even moderately reflective and sensitive person would mean." Agee and Evans, *Famous Men* 234. But while some continue to suggest that Agee was a journalist only of necessity, his career spanned an enormous range of forms, and he excelled in many of them. Agee wrote poetry, short prose, a novel, screenplays such as *The African Queen* and *The Bride Comes to Yellow Sky*, film reviews for *The Nation*, and a series on Lincoln for CBS's *Omnibus*, a major achievement in television programming for its time. Some of Agee's early poems, such as "Ann Garner," and his later wartime journalism, evoke the same tragic sensibility displayed in *Famous Men*. Cf. note 88 below.

74. "Of the ten full-length books on or about, or at least significantly associated with, Agee," Spiegel notes, "only four represent sustained critical treatment of what

he wrote . . . two are critical biographies, two compendiums of reminiscence, one an estranged son's memoir . . . and one a psychological portrait of the artist's personality." Spiegel, *James Agee* 13. In explaining rather than merely reproducing this reception formation, Spiegel's monograph rises above its peers.

75. Fitzgerald, "James Agee" 589, 605.
76. Fitzgerald, "James Agee" 605.
77. Fitzgerald, "James Agee" 618-19.
78. Evans, *Famous Men* vii.
79. Erling Larsen, "Let Us Not Now Praise Ourselves" 92.
80. Cort, "Contemporary Social Problems" 499. Maharidge and Williamson tried to sell a sequel to *Famous Men*, which compares Agee's wracked consciousness to George Gudger's now-mature daughter: "James Agee, the urbane writer, poet, man-about-town, and Hollywood celebrity, and Maggie Louise Gudger, Alabama cotton picker, lived strangely similar lives. They were both dreamers and, deep down, tragic people who yearned for something they could not define even as they came to know finally that it had irretrievably escaped them." Maharidge and Williamson, *And Their Children after Them* 136.
81. Some white reformers sought to synthesize the racial liberalism described in this book's previous chapter with Agee's tragic sensibility. For Northern, white reformers who headed South during the struggle for civil rights, Agee's guilt in *Famous Men* made it a kind of a handbook for responsible social action. John Hersey—author of *Hiroshima* as well as an influential article on John F. Kennedy's wartime bravery—later recalled how in the summer of 1964 Agee's book appeared in the hands of "northern white college kids who had risked their lives—and those of their black hosts—by invading the state that summer to help with voter registration." Hersey, "Agee" 81. Robert Coles similarly recalls how one white "invader" during the civil rights era described Agee as someone who "makes you realize how troubled you are, and how troubling everything is, because he is brave and honest enough to expose himself, and show us how mixed up he was." Coles, *Agee* 98. Coles aligns Agee with great tragedians of the past: "He is addressing questions of justice, of fate, even as playwrights from the beginning of (our) time have done so—Sophocles and Euripides, and then Shakespeare. Why do some live so well, while others starve? Why do Christians forget Christ's words, His very life? And as the Greeks wondered before Him, what does suffering do to people, not only to the sufferers themselves, but to the rest of us, witnesses in greater jeopardy than we (mostly) want to realize?" Coles, *Agee* 81-82.
82. Rodman's review, "The Poetry of Poverty," predicted the book's fate. He suggests that Agee's "feeling that this is the tragedy of most of the two billion inhabitants of the planet" would create a "guilt . . . shamelessly exposed in its most raw and unattractive shape" that guarantees the book "will be spat upon—and years hence . . . read." Rodman, "The Poetry of Poverty" 6.

83. Scott, "Most Famous" 6; Pells, *Radical Visions* 246; Lucaites, "Visualizing" 269, paraphrasing Warren Susman, "The Thirties."

84. Stott, *Documentary Expression* 266.

85. Stott, *Documentary Expression* 311.

86. Stott, *Documentary Expression* 312-13.

87. Horton, "New Orthodoxy" 4.

88. Luce had rejected Agee's draft of "Cotton Tenants," yet Agee continued to infuse the Luce magazines with his tragic sensibility. In *Time* magazine, for instance, on October 15, 1945, Agee writes: "The fall of the year shone gently upon the broken cities and the exhausted fields of Europe. On Berlin's Keurzberg, frost stiffened upon the worm-wrought, illegible features of an exhumed, Gestapo-killed cadaver to which someone had attached a tag reading, *Homo sapiens*." Agee's image reduces this human being to its corporeal shell—as if to say "that is all we are"—while also indexing the staggering historical violence that had produced such bodies by the millions—bitterly insisting that "this is what we are." Agee, "Europe: Autumn Story" 149.

89. Chambers, "Faith for a Lenten Age" 70.

90. Chambers, "Faith for a Lenten Age" 71.

91. Fox, "Emergence of the Liberal Realist Faith" 246.

92. Fox, "Emergence of the Liberal Realist Faith" 264.

93. Niebuhr, *Beyond Tragedy* 20.

94. For a chronicle of the direct and indirect polemics between these figures, see Daniel F. Rice, *Reinhold Niebuhr and John Dewey*.

95. In his review of Dewey's *Liberalism and Social Action*, Niebuhr has a great deal of praise for the social diagnosis offered, but then insists that it is "in his discussion of the function of intelligence in the process of social change that the limitations of Professor Dewey's liberalism appear." Niebuhr, "The Pathos of Liberalism" 303. Cf. Rice, *American Odyssey* 61.

96. Niebuhr, *Moral Man* xv, xiii.

97. "Niebuhr's version of liberalism," as his biographer Fox puts it, "was a caricature of the position of a thinker like Dewey—who was far less naive about power than Niebuhr thought." Fox, "Self-Made Intellectual" 49. Dewey certainly knew this, and even Niebuhr admitted in later life that his "polemics" were excessive. Rice, *American Odyssey* xvii. Dewey and Niebuhr notably served as successive chairs for the Congress for Cultural Freedom, each enrolled in an establishment Cold War liberalism against which they had respectively rebelled.

98. Niebuhr, *Children of Light* 18; 22.

99. Fox, "Emergence of the Liberal Realist Faith" 247. West, *Pragmatism* 150.

100. Schaub, *American Fiction* 7-9.

101. Niebuhr *Children of Light* 109, 27.

102. Berlin, "Two Concepts of Liberty" 214.

103. Schlesinger, *Vital Center* 56.

104. Schlesinger, *Vital Center* 165, 38.

105. Niebuhr, *Irony of American History* vii.

106. Schlesinger, *Vital Center* 10.

107. Naveh, *Reinhold Niebuhr* 100. See also Morgenthau, "The Influence of Reinhold Niebuhr."

108. Williams, *Tragedy of American Diplomacy* 2.

109. Dewey, "How to Anchor" 8, 9, 10.

110. Mills, "The Powerless People" 16. "Many who not long ago read John Dewey with apparent satisfaction," he observes, "have become vitally interested in such analysts of personal tragedy as Søren Kierkegaard." Mills, "The Powerless People" 14.

111. Hook, "The New Failure of Nerve" 13. See also Dewey's essay in *Partisan Review*, "Anti-naturalism in Extremis" where he attacks the supernatural speculations of Christian Realism.

112. Hook, "Pragmatism and the Tragic Sense" 18.

113. West, *Pragmatism* 121.

114. West *Pragmatism* 163.

115. *Address of Vice President* 4504.

116. Keats, "Hyperion" 298.

117. McClintock, "Imperial Ghosting" 821.

118. Badger, *Sophocles and the Politics of Tragedy* 172.

119. In *The Tragedy of Liberalism*, a study that grapples with major liberal political theorists such as John Rawls, Jürgen Habermas, and Will Kymlicka, van der Brink argues that "liberalism's tragic predicament" arises from asserting itself as a "universalist and egalitarian doctrine," and yet inevitably making "some conceptions of a valuable and good life appear to be more valid than others," notably excluding "traditionalist and religious world views and social practices that seem to be of genuine value to some people." As a result, van der Brink concludes, liberalism will continually "be a party to sometimes irreconcilable conflicts—over, for instance, public justice, cultural authenticity, and the definition of a good life." He notably identifies abortion as an exemplary "tragic" political conflict. van der Brink, *The Tragedy of Liberalism* 1; 34. See also Badger, *Sophocles and the Politics of Tragedy*, esp. "The Tragic Politics of John Locke," 148-73, and Donald J. Moon, *Constructing Community*.

120. Tragedy's generic boundaries have of course been perpetually contested, from Aristotle imposing his immeasurably influential, yet belated and reductive taxonomy onto Athenian drama, to Chaucer and the appearance of the English word "tragedy" in the thirteenth century, through Elizabethan and Jacobean theater, to the German philosophers of the nineteenth century, from whom the adjective "tragic" emerges first as a philosophical category, and later as a vernacular

descriptor for everyday events. As a genre or representational mode dependent on displays of human suffering, moreover, tragedy has always had enormous political currency: disputes between radical or conservative readings of *King Lear*, for instance, are among other things a dispute over how its vision of property, power, and dispossession will affect an audience. For an overview of this history, see Rita Felski's "Introduction" to *Rethinking Tragedy*.

121. Krutch, *Modern Temper* 82.

122. Fox incisively notes that the "book refuted itself: the modern temper had not prevented Krutch from creating *The Modern Temper*, an anti-modern text informed by the tragic sense of life." Fox, "Tragedy" 327. He lists a number of other books in the first quarter century in which critics who mourn the loss of tragedy end up performing their own narrative of tragic collapse: F. L. Lucas's *Tragedy in Relation to Aristotle's Poetics* (1928), Walter Lippmann's *Preface to Morals* (1929), and Lewis Mumford's *Herman Melville* (1929).

123. Steiner, *Death of Tragedy* 8.

124. Steiner, "Tragedy Reconsidered" 32.

125. Krutch, *Modern Temper* 80.

126. Krutch, *Modern Temper* 97 (emphasis in original).

127. Steiner, *Death of Tragedy* 305 (emphasis in original).

128. Steiner *Death of Tragedy* 315.

129. Horkheimer and Adorno, *Dialectic of Enlightenment* 124, quoting from Nietzsche, *Götzendämmerung, Werke* viii, 136.

130. Horkheimer and Adorno, *Dialectic of Enlightenment* 124.

131. Importantly, the tendency to associate tragic drama with individual autonomy is itself a bias of the liberal era. "Greek tragic action was not rooted in individuals," explains Raymond Williams, "or in individual psychology, in any of our senses. It was rooted in history, and not a human history alone." Williams, *Modern Tragedy* 87. For a grounded, historical introduction to tragedy's role in Greek culture, see Charles Beye, *Ancient Greek Literature and Society*. For a provocative argument about the tragedies as a kind of political mythos, see Jean-Pierre Vernant and Pierre Vidal-Nacquet, *Myth and Tragedy in Ancient Greece*.

132. Horkheimer and Adorno, *Dialectic of Enlightenment* 122. "Just as totalitarian society does not abolish the suffering of its members, but registers and plans it," they write, "mass culture does the same with tragedy," which does not disappear outright, but rather gains "permanent employment as routine." Horkheimer and Adorno, *Dialectic of Enlightenment* 122-23.

133. Horkheimer and Adorno, *Dialectic of Enlightenment* 124.

134. At several moments, Horkheimer and Adorno notably refer to "the liberal era" as a thing of the past, or describe "late liberalism" in its waning moments. Horkheimer and Adorno, *Dialectic of Enlightenment* 113, 106.

135. Williams sets out to defend the possibility of modern tragic drama and its

capacity to catalyze revolution. Our intuitive opposition between tragedy and revolution, he maintains, stems from the "great current of liberalism" that has animated tragic drama for more than a century, making the individual the center of social action. Whereas Steiner saw Marxism as "anti-tragic" in its promise of future redemption, Williams insists that Marxism, Freudianism, and Existentialism, being the "characteristically new systems of thinking, in our own time," are "all, in their most common forms, tragic. Man can achieve his full life only after violent conflict." Williams, *Modern Tragedy* 68, 323, 189.

136. Williams, *Modern Tragedy* 97.

137. Williams, *Modern Tragedy* 97.

138. Williams, *Modern Tragedy* 98.

139. Vogel, "Willy Tyranos" 58. Eleanor Clark's "Old Glamour, New Gloom" stands out as an extended attack on *Salesman*'s tragic stature. For readings that treat the play as Linda's tragedy, rather than Willy's, see Gassner "First Impressions" and especially Stanton, "Women and the American Dream."

140. Vogel, "Willy Tyranos" 59–60.

141. Weales, "Introduction" xiv.

142. Miller, "Tragedy and the Common Man" 5.

143. Miller's lifelong liberal values are well established. He began his playwriting career with the Federal Theater, a New Deal program; he was blacklisted by Joseph McCarthy during the witch-hunts; he protested Vietnam during Lyndon Johnson's presidency; and he served as a delegate for Eugene McCarthy in 1968. Motram argues that Miller's work was consistently "aimed at a critical clarification of the already existent attitudes of liberal-minded American theatergoers." Motram, "Arthur Miller" 23. Bentley concurs, suggesting that "Arthur Miller is the playwright of American liberal folklore." Bentley, "Innocence" 206. See also Warshow, "Liberal Conscience in *The Crucible*."

144. Miller, "Tragedy and the Common Man" 4.

145. Miller, "Tragedy and the Common Man" 7. By the time he composed his preface for *A View from the Bridge* (1955), Miller seems to have grown skeptical about modern tragedy's capacity to stage an enlightening conflict between individual and society. Much like Krutch and Steiner, he now describes the "debilitation of tragedy" as rooted in "machine technology," and, instead of casting the common man as a heroic martyr, he acknowledges the difficulty a person faces trying "to maintain a fruitful kind of union with his society." Miller, "On Social Plays" 62.

146. Bates argues that Willy's private imagination contains "four anachronisms: he is the archetypal cherisher of the pastoral world, the pre-industrial-revolution artisan, the ham-handed outlaw frontiersman, and the dutiful patriarchal male intent upon transmitting complex legacies from his forbears to his progeny." Bates, "The Lost Path" 164.

147. Miller, *Death* 49.

148. Miller, *Death* 49.
149. Miller, *Death* 41.
150. Williams, *Modern Tragedy* 105.
151. Miller, *Death* 138.
152. Miller, *Death* 138.
153. Miller, *Death* 138.
154. Miller, *Death* 139 (emphasis in original).
155. Miller, *Death* 139.
156. Miller, *Death* 73.
157. Anderson, *Bleak Liberalism* 102.
158. For an incisive comparison of Trilling and Adorno, see Anderson, *Bleak Liberalism*, 99-114.
159. Williams, *Modern Tragedy* 100.

Chapter 4. Ending in Style

1. Flaubert to Louise Colet, Croisset, 16 Jan. 1852. On these modernist views of style, and the narrative of decline summarized in this paragraph, see Ben Hutchinson's *Modernism and Style*.
2. Murray, *Problem of Style* 77.
3. Ransom, "The Understanding of Fiction" 197.
4. Rancière, *The Politics of Aesthetics* 5.
5. Rancière, *Mute Speech* 51.
6. Jameson, "Postmodernism and Consumer Society" 17.
7. Jameson, "Postmodernism and Consumer Culture" 18.
8. Jameson, *A Singular Modernity* 201, 205, 201, 201.
9. Barnhiesel, *Cold War Modernists* 10 (emphasis in original).
10. Barnhiesel, *Cold War Modernists* 2.
11. Barnhiesel, *Cold War Modernists* 10. See also Saunders, *Cultural Cold War*; and Guilbaut, *How New York Stole the Idea of Modern Art*.
12. Barnhiesel, *Cold War Modernists* 39.
13. Guilbaut, *How New York Stole* 2, 155.
14. As with "tragedy" in the prior chapter, I approach "style" pragmatically in these pages, open to all the (potentially conflicting) usages and associations made by postwar intellectuals about this aesthetic concept. Trilling notably features prominently in both chapters, as his work straddles both discursive formations. More than any other figure, Trilling gave sustained expression to the belief that narrative style might serve as a means for liberals to fashion an aesthetic sensibility that would help them cope with the tragic conditions of modern life.
15. Slippage between liberalism and democracy, or character and personality, was ubiquitous during midcentury intellectual writing. A postwar invention,

"liberal democracy" erases liberalism's non-democratic history and democracy's illiberal origins to provide a unified front, as it were, against totalitarianism. Similarly, "character" and "personality" were often used interchangeably at this time, though intellectual investment in these terms emerges from different disciplinary traditions. "Character" invokes a cultivated manner of being in the world, an achieved set of values or attitude traditionally associated with a more conservative, aristocratic vision of political life. Claims about "personality," by contrast, grew in popularity through socio-scientific research that carried wide intellectual respectability at the time, yet which today appears highly problematic, such as Adorno's "F-Scale," measuring the "authoritarian personality" through empirically quantifiable preferences, including sexuality. For an illustrative criticism of Adorno's method, see Glazer's "New Light on the Authoritarian Personality."

16. For measured yet critical views of the Kennedy style, see Hellman, *Kennedy Obsession*; Henggeler, *Kennedy Persuasion*; and Wills, *Kennedy Imprisonment*.

17. Hellman, "Kennedy and Postwar Intellectual Culture" 141, 138.

18. Nabokov, *Lolita* 315; Nabokov, *Lectures on Literature* 59. Little Jo's death amid the squalor of poverty in *Bleak House*, Nabokov informed his students at Cornell, "is a lesson in style, not in participative emotion." Nabokov, *Lectures on Literature* 94. Elsewhere, he suggests "style constitutes an intrinsic component or characteristic of the author's personality. Thus, when we speak of style, we mean an artist's peculiar nature." Nabokov, *Lectures on Literature* 59–60.

19. Couturier insists that "the specialists of Nabokov, myself included, have allowed themselves too often and too long to be intimidated by Nabokov's 'strong opinions.' They have preferred to annotate his works, without always realizing how much they were abiding by Nabokov's avowed or unavowed hermeneutics or following their own unconscious ones." Couturier, "Annotating vs. Interpreting Nabokov." "No writer since Dr. Johnson," concurs Newman, "has so predetermined the tone and concern which his critics shall bring to him, no writer in English more controls those personages who serve doubly as his characters and his ideal readers." Appel and Newman, *Nabokov* 354.

20. Style has been the common denominator for praising Nabokov's work—many see him as "the pre-eminent English prose stylist of post-war letters"—while also providing a term of opprobrium for those who find in his technical mastery a lack of "substance." Norman and White, *Transitional Nabokov* 1. In his review of *Lolita* for the *New Republic*, John Wain typifies the early sense among Nabokov's critics that this commitment to style corresponded to a necessary lack of sociopolitical substance: "Nabokov has expended a lifetime's devoted effort on the task of developing and refining an absolutely individual style, which will convey the thousand and one idiosyncratic *nuances* suggested by his imagination. . . . And yet it is remarkable that he has never troubled to develop a style in which ordinary generalized thought (political opinions, for instance) can be conveyed." Wain,

"Review of *Lolita*" 114 (emphasis in original). Whereas the *Oxford English Dictionary* defines "Joycean" as "pertaining to, or characteristic of Joyce or his work," its entry on "Nabokovian" makes a more emphatic claim: "Of or relating to Vladimir Nabokov; resembling or characteristic of his writing, esp. its ironic, witty, or erudite style." "Nabokovian, *adj.*"; "Joycean, *adj.* and *n.*"

21. Bethea, "Style" 701. Nabokov scholars tend to speak of a formalist school that gave way to an ethical turn. For the former, see Page Stegner, *Escape into Aesthetics*; Leona Toker, *Literary Structures*; Jessie Lokrantz, *Underside of the Weave*; and W. W. Rowe, *Deceptive World*. For the latter, see Ellen Pifer, *Nabokov and the Novel*; Leland de la Durantaye, *Style Is Matter*; Maurice Couturier, "Annotating"; and Michael Wood, *Magician's Doubts*.

22. Bryan Boyd's two-volume biography *Vladimir Nabokov* opens with a chapter entitled "Liberal Strains: The Patterns of the Past," in which he traces an emerging moral sensibility from Alexander Nabokov, military leader, to Dmitri Nabokov, minister of justice, to V. D. Nabokov, Vladimir's father, a passionate defender of liberal juridical rights, who was shot and killed by right-wing assassins. See Boyd, *Vladimir Nabokov*, esp. 8–35. Dragunoia later developed this line of thinking, arguing that "Nabokov's manifold debt to the discourses of pre- and post-revolutionary Russian liberalism" appear in his resolute commitment to anti-tsarism, trial by jury, and opposition to the death penalty. Dragunoia, *Vladimir Nabokov and the Poetics of Liberalism* 6. Such biographic criticism has drawn much-needed historical air into the stale annotative practices that have kept Nabokov's novels isolated from shifting currents in modernist and twentieth-century Americanist studies. Yet this work has continued to identify the politics of literature only as the politics of the author, reducing the political from a dynamic field of conflicting values into the stable values of a self-possessing authorial subject. This has left liberalism, in turn, signifying only a minimal (and basically incontestable) abhorrence for cruelty, or the admirable but antiquated bourgeois reforms of the nineteenth century. As prior chapters have emphasized, biography tames the unruly ironies of modernist texts by pinning them down to stable interpretive narratives located in the authorial body.

23. For more traditional historical accounts of liberalism's decline—focused on the collapse of a progressive coalition that had temporarily united urban bosses, farmers, racial minorities, labor unions, and intellectuals—see Brinkley, *The End of Reform*; Fraser and Gerstle, *The Rise and Fall of the New Deal Order*; and Matusow, *The Unraveling of America*. For a provocative if also more theoretical consideration of how pluralist "interest-group" liberalism led to the collapse of this order, see Lowi, *The End of Liberalism*.

24. Nabokov, *Bend Sinister* 75.
25. Nabokov, *Bend Sinister* 68, 77.
26. Nabokov, *Bend Sinister* 76.

27. Nabokov, *Bend Sinister* xiii.

28. Nabokov was notorious for his declared indifference to all contemporary social plights. In the 1963 introduction to *Bend Sinister*, he dramatically exclaims, "Politics and economics, atomic bombs, primate and abstract art forms, the entire Orient, symptoms of 'thaw' in Soviet Russia, the Future of Mankind, and so on, leave me supremely indifferent." *Bend Sinister* xii.

29. Arendt, "Understanding and Politics" 311.

30. Arendt cautioned against a tendency to conflate totalitarianism with more traditional forms of tyranny and authoritarianism. Tyranny names the rule of one against all, Arendt explains, and authoritarian government resembles a pyramid with hierarchical power in layers. Totalitarianism, she proposes, instead resembles an "onion, in whose center, in a kind of empty space, the leader is located." With each strata possessing its own psychological self-deceptions, from the secret police to the party bureaucracy to the professional societies, totalitarian society becomes "shock-proof against the factuality of the real world." Arendt, "What Is Authority?" 99–100. Slavoj Žižek, however, argues that totalitarianism's ideological function was "dismissing the Leftist critique of liberal democracy as the obverse, the 'twin', of the Rightist Fascist dictatorship," and he cites Arendt's influence on contemporary political theory as "perhaps the clearest sign of the theoretical defeat of the Left—of how the Left has accepted the basic co-ordinates of liberal democracy." Žižek, *Did Somebody Say* 3.

31. Schlesinger, *The Vital Center* xiii.

32. Ciepley, *Liberalism in the Shadow* 1.

33. Fromm, *Escape from Freedom* vii.

34. Fromm, *Escape from Freedom* 124.

35. Fromm, *Escape from Freedom* vii, 163. Fromm approvingly quotes Dewey: "The serious threat to our democracy is not the existence of foreign totalitarian states. It is the existence within our own institutions of conditions which have given a victory to external authority, discipline, uniformity and dependence upon The Leader in foreign countries." Dewey, *Freedom and Culture,* quoted in Fromm, *Escape* 44.

36. Nabokov, *Bend Sinister* 56.

37. Nabokov, *Bend Sinister* 69.

38. Nabokov, *Bend Sinister* 70.

39. Turner, *Democratic Surround* 38.

40. Turner, *Democratic Surround* 214.

41. Turner, *Democratic Surround* 60.

42. Turner, *Democratic Surround* 44.

43. Riesman et al., *Lonely Crowd* 209.

44. Saunders, *Cultural Cold War* 249.

45. His duel with Edmund Wilson over Pushkin did transpire in part on the pages of *Encounter* magazine, flagship organ for the Congress for Cultural Freedom,

and pet project of the CIA. Nabokov's rebuttal was published in the February 1966 issue; he also published a later response to criticism by Robert Lowell and others in the magazine. See Andrea Pitzer, *The Secret History of Vladimir Nabokov* esp. the chapter "Speak, Memory."

46. Saunders, *Cultural Cold War* 13.

47. Saunders, *Cultural Cold War* 220.

48. "Masterpieces of the XXth Century," 1952, Allen Tate Papers, Box 16,"Congress for Cultural Freedom" folder, quoted in Barnhisel, *Cold War Modernists* 144-45.

49. Nicholas Nabokov, quoted in Saunders, *Cultural Cold War* 100.

50. Mangrum, *Land of Tomorrow* 23. Mangrum's study notably begins where this book ends, "showing that the period of 'apex'" for liberalism "was in fact rife with tumultuous changes within American intellectual culture." *Land of Tomorrow* 2. See his first chapter for a broader account of aestheticism in postwar liberal thought.

51. Nabokov, *Bend Sinister* 90.

52. Naiman, "Hermaphobia" 133.

53. David has been mistaken for "Arvid Krug, son of Professor Martin Krug," a dual slight to Adam's belief in the autonomous intellect carried by his name. Nabokov, *Bend Sinister* 215.

54. Naiman, *Nabokov, Perversely* 47. See also Baxter, "Nabokov, Idolatry, and the Police State."

55. Nabokov, *Strong Opinions* 69, 95.

56. Naiman, *Nabokov, Perversely* 72.

57. Arendt, *Origins of Totalitarianism* 474.

58. Schlesinger, "Future of Liberalism" 8.

59. Trilling, *Matthew Arnold* 30.

60. Kennedy, "Definition of a Liberal" 106.

61. Trask, *Camp Sites* 4. Trask argues that this "politics of performance aligns liberalism with camp," and his book shows how "a vision of closeted homosexuality" was pivotal in making this era of liberal cultural policies, and later, in the New Left unmaking it. But while Trask recognizes that the "liberal personality" grew oriented around a "renovated masculinity, a manhood that combined 'tough-minded' pragmatism with a sensitivity to nuance and a distance from all isms," his book, somewhat perplexingly, ignores Stevenson and Kennedy. He does, however, provide a reading of *Bend Sinister*. Trask, *Camp Sites* 13, 1, 4, 71-79.

62. Nabokov, *Pnin* 134-35.

63. Arendt, "Understanding and Politics" 308.

64. Nabokov, *Pnin* 135.

65. Stegner, *Escape into Aesthetics* 90.

66. Nabokov, *Pnin* 65, 13.

67. Nabokov, *Pnin* 113.

68. Hofstadter, *Anti-Intellectualism* 420.

69. Hofstadter, *Anti-Intellectualism* 423.

70. McKeever, *Stevenson* 247.

71. In his seminal study *Anti-intellectualism in American Life*, Hofstadter emphasizes how Stevenson's 1952 campaign re-introduced the appeal of intellect in American politics, and yet marks how an "association of intellectuality and style with effeminacy" that had been common in Gilded Age political discourse resurfaced with his presidential runs. Hofstadter, *Anti-intellectualism* 226.

72. Schlesinger, *Kennedy or Nixon* 34.

73. Newfield and Grenfield, "Disrupted History" 41.

74. Riesman 164; qtd. Szalay 80.

75. Hofstadter, *Anti-intellectualism* 221. "If Jack and Robert Kennedy seemed to symbolize style in politics," echoes David Halberstam, "much of that was derived directly from Stevenson." Halberstam, *Best and Brightest* 27.

76. Herbert Parmet, quoted in Hellman, "Kennedy and Postwar Intellectual Culture" 134.

77. Hellman, "Kennedy and Postwar Intellectual Culture" 138.

78. Hoberek, "Introduction" 8.

79. Hellman, *Kennedy Obsession* 82. Hellman notably ties the contemporary vogue for such a persona to the tragic heroism on display in Ernest Hemingway's decorated novel *The Old Man and the Sea* (1952). On Kennedy's record as a liberal, see Mackenzie and Weisbrot, *The Liberal Hour* 74. Members of the ADA, including John Kenneth Galbraith and Arthur Schlesinger, notably signed and circulated a missive entitled "An Important Message of Intent to All Liberals," on the eve of the Democratic Party convention, intended "to convince progressives of Kennedy's liberal credentials." Gillon, *Politics and Vision* 133. But see also Robert Mason, "Kennedy and the Conservatives" for the ways JFK has served as an icon for politicians on the Right.

80. Mailer, *Papers* 44. Szalay argues that "hip" became a "fetish" for the Democratic Party beginning with Kennedy's administration. As a "range of predominantly white fantasies," which Szalay ties to blackface minstrelsy, hip enables "otherwise multicolored bodies possessed of different economic interests" to share a style—real or imagined. This common cultural imagination, Szalay proposes, was crucial to the Democratic Party's effort "to consolidate the voting constituencies of postwar liberalism." Certainly, there can be no question white-black relations at this time were instrumental to the Democratic Party's success, and that "the popularity of the Catholic, Irish American Kennedy signaled a new relation between minorities and the administrative apparatus of industry and state." Yet, as with other studies of the era, *Hip Figures* often conflates the Democratic Party as an institution and liberalism as an intellectual tradition; it did not take the struggle between Humphrey and McCarthy during "the election of 1968" to put "this formula into question." Truman and Wallace had clearly signaled this schism

as early as 1948, when Kennedy had barely begun his tenure in the House. *Szalay*, Hip Figures 2-4, 24, 143.

81. On this media event, see Mary-Ann Watson, "Kennedy-Nixon Debates."

82. Schlesinger, *Kennedy or Nixon* 27. Kennedy's pragmatic character was widely noted when the candidates were asked about their foreign policies concerning Quemoy-Matsu. Whereas Nixon insisted that these small islands, caught between China and Taiwan, lay within the "area of freedom" and should be defended against the Red threat, Kennedy encouraged a more cautious approach, depending more on personal judgment than fixed policy.

83. Schlesinger, *Kennedy or Nixon* 15. After Nixon's election some years later, Gary Wills would confirm that Nixon "lacks the stamp of place or personality because the Market is death to style, and he is the Market's servant." Wills, "Richard Nixon" 25.

84. Schlesinger, *Kennedy or Nixon* 27-28. Schlesinger constantly affirms Kennedy's tough masculinity, such as when he insists that JFK stood behind his positions "not because political market research told him that the electorate cared about them, but because he, John F. Kennedy, thought they damn well ought to care." Schlesinger, *Kennedy or Nixon* 22.

85. Riesman et al., *Lonely Crowd* 188-89.

86. Schlesinger, *Thousand Days* 729.

87. Newfield and Grenfield, "Disrupted History" 37.

88. Hofstadter, *Anti-intellectualism* 394.

89. Hofstadter, *Anti-intellectualism* 228.

90. Bowles, *Jacqueline* 9.

91. Baldridge, *In the Kennedy Style* 93.

92. Baldridge, *In the Kennedy Style* 93.

93. Vidal "Holy Family" 235.

94. Vidal *United States* 44, quoted in Szalay, *Hip Figures* 7.

95. Mailer, *Presidential Papers* 54-55.

96. Kennedy notably hired Doyle Dane Bernbach (DDB) to run his campaign, the firm later responsible for Lyndon Johnson's iconic "Daisy" ad. Szalay, *Hip Figures* 113, 119.

97. Arendt, "Reflections on the Fate of the Union: Kennedy and After" (emphasis in original).

98. Kazin, "President Kennedy" 516.

99. Shannon, "Kennedy Administration" 487. Mattson similarly notes that Schlesinger's intimate role in promoting "JFK's cultural leadership" often led him to confuse "intellectual style for concrete policy accomplishments." Mattson, *When America* 169. Supporters, however, insisted that Kennedy's "style" was all-important to the continuing success of his political, legislative, diplomatic, and presidential efforts. Sorensen, "Introduction" 1.

100. Kazin, "President Kennedy" 516.

101. Kazin, "President Kennedy" 507.

102. Vidal, "Holy Family" 235.

103. Lasch, *New Radicalism* 316. Lasch quips that "what liberals called Kennedy's style consisted largely of a Harvard education, a certain amount of conscientious concert-going, and a feeling, never very precise, that the arts ought somehow to be officially encouraged." Lasch, *New Radicalism* 311.

104. When Pnin arrives to present a paper for the Cremona Women's Club, after much delay and disorder, he briefly looks out onto the audience and discovers that the club's dignified ladies have been joined by a crowd of the dead from Pnin's past: "Murdered, forgotten, unrevenged, incorrupt, immortal, many old friends were scattered throughout the dim hall among more recent people." Nabokov, *Pnin* 27.

105. Stegner, *Escape into Aesthetics* 90.

106. Wood, *Magician's Doubts* 17.

107. As European exiles like Arendt and Fromm insisted, totalitarian government precisely aims to alienate each citizen from any solidarity: "Only isolated individuals can be dominated totally." Arendt, "On the Nature of Totalitarianism" 356.

108. Nabokov, *Pnin* 168.

109. Nabokov, Dmitri, "Father's Room" 78.

110. Nabokov, Dmitri, "Father's Room" 78.

111. Rorty, *Contingency* 155.

112. Rorty, *Contingency* 155.

113. Rorty, *Contingency* xv. See also Shklar, "The Liberalism of Fear" 23.

114. For orienting responses to Rorty's work, see Brandom, *Rorty and His Critics* and Malachowski, *Reading Rorty*.

115. Rorty, *Contingency* xv.

116. Rorty, *Contingency* xv.

117. Rorty, *Contingency* 144.

118. There are reasons for dismissing Rorty's reading of Nabokov outright and seeing cruelty as an essential feature of his fiction and authorial persona; see de la Durantaye, "The Pattern of Cruelty"; and Pitzer, *Secret History* 4-5.

119. Walter, "Two organ-grinders" 34.

120. Rorty, *Contingency* 168.

121. Rorty, *Contingency* 157.

122. Trilling, "The Last Lover" 331-32.

123. Nabokov, *Lolita* 9.

124. Wood, *Magician's Doubts* 110.

125. Kingsley Amis noted that *Lolita*'s contested publication might offer a decisive episode in the ongoing struggle for freedom against censorship: "The long battle against style still hangs in the balance, and a reverse over 'Lolita' could be damaging." Amis, "Review" 104.

126. Nabokov, *Lolita* 314. Nabokov's afterword identifies *Lolita*'s tennis episodes as one of "the nerves of the novel . . . the subliminal co-ordinates by means of which the book is plotted." Nabokov, *Lolita* 316. Critics have often concurred; see Ellen Pifer, *Nabokov*, and Bush, "Tennis by the Book," esp. 272.

127. Jameson, *Singular Modernity* 201, 204.

128. Rorty, *Contingency* 158.

129. Nabokov, *Lolita* 213.

130. Rorty, *Contingency* 141.

131. Rorty, *Contingency* 53.

132. McNeely, "Lo and Behold" 185.

133. Nabokov, *Lolita* 25.

134. Bush, "Tennis" 275.

135. Bush, "Tennis" 277.

136. Nabokov, *Lolita* 231.

137. Nabokov, *Lolita* 233.

138. Humbert's vulnerability to the ruse of style reappears in the "cryptogrammic paper chase" left for him by Clare Quilty. In a scene that echoes Adam Krug's protectiveness over his unique graphic style in *Bend Sinister*, Humbert uses the "peculiar t's, w's and l's" to identify his double, a man who otherwise seems a carbon copy of his personality: "The clues he left did not establish his identity but they reflected his personality." Nabokov, *Lolita* 249-51.

139. Pater, *Renaissance* 150.

140. Bush, "Tennis" 278.

141. Barnhiesel, *Cold War Modernists* 27.

142. Barnhiesel, *Cold War Modernists* 3-4.

143. For an influential account of this split, see McHale, *Postmodernist Fiction*.

144. On the retreat from postmodernism, see Hoberek, "Introduction: After Postmodernism" and Nealon, *Post-Postmodernism*. For review essays on scholarship in late modernist studies, see Thomas Davis "Late Modernism," and Afflerbach "Style, Ideology, and Autonomy."

145. Jameson, *Postmodernism* 355.

146. DeLillo, *Libra* 181. McCann, *Pinnacle* 170.

147. Mailer, *Papers* 184.

148. McCann, *Pinnacle* 142. Mailer, *Advertisements for Myself* 5, quoted in McCann *Pinnacle* 142. McCann, *Pinnacle* 142.

149. Mailer, *Papers* v.

150. Mailer, *Papers* 5.

151. Mailer, *Papers* 5. Thomas Schaub traces this notion in Mailer's writing from *Barbary Shore* through *Armies of the Night*; see *American Fiction* 74.

152. Depoe, *Ideological History* 55.

153. Depoe, *Ideological History* 55 (emphasis in original).

154. Kennedy, "Opening" 101.
155. Kennedy, "Opening" 101.
156. Kennedy, "Peaceful Revolution" 192.
157. Martin, "Arthur Miller" 176.
158. Marcuse, *One-Dimensional* 90.
159. Marcuse, *One-Dimensional* 93.
160. JFK's aggressive international interventions against Communism provided his administration a rhetorical means to compensate for a domestic agenda that, at least until 1963, remained cautious and conservative. Of course, the scrutiny of American race relations occasioned by this global ideological struggle would eventually make desegregation, in Mary Dudziak's memorable phrase, "a Cold War Imperative." See Dudziak, "Desegregation" and *Cold War Civil Rights*, esp. "Losing Control in Camelot."
161. On his administration's public relations and secrecy, see Hersch, *Dark Side*; Wills, *Kennedy Imprisonment*; Miroff, *Pragmatic Illusions*; and Mackenzie and Weisbrot, *Liberal Hour*.
162. Hersch, *Dark Side* 222.
163. Dugan and Newport, "Top Modern President."
164. For rankings among historians, see Hargrove, *The Power of the Modern Presidency* 3.
165. Schlesinger, *Imperial Presidency* 176.
166. Kennedy, "The Vital Center of Action" 20.
167. Kennedy made the power of the Presidency a central issue from the outset of his candidacy: "Not since the days of Woodrow Wilson," he remarked to the National Press Club in 1960, "has any candidate spoken on the Presidency itself before the votes have been irrevocably cast." "I have premised my campaign on the central issue of the Presidency itself," he insisted, "its powers, their use and their decline." "Kennedy's executive style," concludes Bruce Miroff, "was plainly keyed to power." Kennedy, "Vital Center" 17, 23. Miroff, *Pragmatic Illusions* 30.
168. McCann, *Pinnacle of Feeling* 11.
169. Theodore Roosevelt first established a consistent White House press corps, connecting the Executive and the American people. He then in turn invented the "techniques of public relations (the press conference, the backgrounder, the trial balloon, the deliberate leak)" that would allow future Presidents to carefully shape public opinion. When Woodrow Wilson reintroduced the State of the Union Address in 1914, he resumed a presidential practice that had been abandoned due to its monarchial overtones since the days of Thomas Jefferson. And during the Great Depression, FDR mobilized the power of radio through his hugely popular fireside chats, whose rhetoric helped establish "the American people" as a salient political category. McCann 17, 10.

170. McCann x, 18.
171. McCann 4, 6.
172. Hargrove, *Power* 11.
173. Henggeler, *Kennedy Persuasion* 8.
174. For a moving summary of this problem, see Ackerman, *Decline and Fall of the American Republic*.
175. This crisis in confidence led to a wave of revisionary studies on the presidency in the 1970s, many written by disgruntled liberal intellectuals who examined political concepts such as character and style with a newfound skepticism. See Hargrove, *Modern Presidency*; Reedy *Twilight of the Presidency*; and Schlesinger, *Imperial Presidency*. While LBJ and Nixon had their legacies tarnished for equivocations over Civil Rights and the escalating atrocities in Southeast Asia, however, this revisionist criticism directed little censure towards Kennedy. More critical studies did emerge later on; see note 161 above.
176. "Neoliberalism emerged as the New Deal's residuary legatee," argues Wolin, "and found its icon in JFK. Its proponents were willing to sacrifice some elements of social democracy in order to promote a 'strong state' for opposing Soviet communism abroad." Wolin, *Democracy Incorporated* ix, 221.
177. Mailer, *Papers* 202.

Conclusion

1. Friedman, *Two Lucky People* 24.
2. Lest the reader miss their cue, Friedman evokes his earlier episode, noting that "these lines . . . had been impressed on me" in "a not unrelated context." Friedman 206-7.
3. Naomi Klein, *Shock Doctrine* 65.
4. See David Harvey, *A Brief History of Neoliberalism*; Wendy Brown, *Undoing the Demos: Neoliberalism's Stealth Revolution*; and Klein, *The Shock Doctrine*.
5. Harvey x.
6. Taylor C. Boas and Jordan Gans-Morse, "Neoliberalism" 141.
7. Bruce Robbins, "Everything Is Not Neoliberalism" 840. "To bestow on any concept a divine ubiquity and omnipotence," Robbins complains, "is to guarantee in advance that the concept will be, like the deity, inscrutable." What's more, this critical conceit accepts "exactly what the champions of neoliberalism claim about the free market. The market is, and should be accepted as, sublime, immense, and almighty." Robbins 842.
8. As Mirowski and Plehwe note, Harvey's orthodox Marxist approach at time leads him to conflate neoliberalism with classical liberalism, as when he suggests that neoliberalism entails "a theory of political economic practices that proposes that human well-being can best be advanced by liberating individual entrepreneur-

ial freedoms and skills within an institutional framework characterized by strong private property rights, free markets, and free trade." Philip Mirowski and Dieter Plehwe, *The Road from Mont Pèlerin* 2. Brown likewise notes how Foucault's *Lectures* waver between distinguishing liberalism from neoliberalism and equating them as a natural continuity. Brown, *Undoing the Demos* 54.

9. Lippmann's book equivocates in its priorities: although he insists on maximizing a market freedom, which he continually refers to as the "division of labor," Lippmann also renews his critique of corporate power, warning that the "privilege of limited liability" and "perpetual succession" must be checked by law. Lippmann's faith in judicial regulation, but fear of executive power, represents an understandable if tenuous response to fascism's rise in the 1930s. Apparently, he was somewhat confused by his invitation to the conference. Walter Lippmann, *(An Inquiry into the Principles of) The Good Society* xi, 278.

10. It was not until later work by Chicago School thinkers like Friedman that neoliberals defined freedom as a "purely mechanical 'choice' that could be exercised in each and every sphere of life." Rob van Horn and Philip Mirowski, "The Rise of the Chicago School of Economics and the Birth of Neoliberalism," in Philip Mirowski and Dieter Plehwe. *The Road from Mont Pèlerin* 161-63.

11. Friedrich A. Hayek, *The Road to Serfdom* 45.

12. Hayek, *The Road to Serfdom* 78n4.

13. Bettina Benn Greaves, "Preface, 1985" vi.

14. The best general introductions to neoliberalism appear in Mirowski and Plehwe's *Road from Mont Pèlerin* and Naomi Klein's sprawling but commanding *Shock Doctrine*. Harvey's focus on class struggle in *Brief Introduction to Neoliberalism* and Brown's focus on modes of political and market reason in *Undoing the Demos* make these two studies rich and incisive yet more focused than those searching for a general introduction may require.

15. Brown, *Undoing the Demos* 53. See also Michel Foucault, *The Birth of Biopolitics*.

16. Brown, *Undoing the Demos* 53-54.

17. Philip Mirowski, "Postface: Defining Neoliberalism" 47.

18. Mirowski, "Postface" 425.

19. Mirowski, "Postface" 426.

20. John Dewey, *Art as Experience* 40.

21. Dewey, *Art as Experience* 40.

22. Dewey, *Art as Experience* 41.

23. Heritage Foundation, *Mandate for Leadership*, quoted in Carol A. Horton, *Race and the Making of American Liberalism* 214.

24. Anarchism and communization theory may have alternate political grammars, but whether these lie within the bounds of democratic governance remains a subject for dispute.

Bibliography

Aaron, Daniel. "Conservatism, Old and New." *American Quarterly* 6.2 (1954), 99-110.
———. *Writers on the Left: Episodes in American Literary Communism*. New York: Harcourt, Brace & World, 1961.
Abbot, Philip. "Are Three Generations of Radicals Enough? Self-Critique in the Novels of Tess Slesinger, Mary McCarthy, and Marge Piercy." *Review of Politics* 53.4 (Autumn, 1991), 602-26.
Ackerman, Bruce. *The Decline and Fall of the American Republic*. Cambridge, MA: Belknap Press of Harvard University Press, 2013.
Adams, Donald J. "Review of *The Unpossessed* by Tess Slesinger." *New York Times* 20 May 1934, sec. 6, p. 6.
Adarand Constructors, *Inc. v. Peña* 515 U.S. 200 (1995).
Address of Vice President Hubert H. Humphrey at the 25th Anniversary Banquet of *Christianity and Crisis*, New York City, February 25, 1966. 89th Congress, 2nd. sess. Congressional Record 112 pt. 4: 4503-8.
Adorno, Theodor. "Commitment." In *Aesthetics and Politics*, Adorno et al., 177-95. London: Verso, 2007.
Afflerbach, Ian. "Liberalism's Blind Judgment: Richard Wright's *Native Son* and the Politics of Reception." *MFS Modern Fiction Studies* 61.1 (Spring 2015), 90-113.
———. "On the Use and Abuse of Dostoevsky's *The Possessed* for Reading Tess Slesinger's *The Unpossessed*." *Notes and Queries* 259.1 (March 2014), 135-36.
———. "Style, Ideology, and Autonomy: Making Room for Late Modernism in the American Scene." *Literature Compass* 14.10 (2017): 10.1111/lic3.12408.
Agee, James, and Walker Evans. *Let Us Now Praise Famous Men*. 1941. Boston: Houghton Mifflin Company, 1960.
Agee, James. "Europe: Autumn Story." *Time* 15 Oct. 1954. In *Selected Journalism*, edited by Paul Ashdown, 149-52. Knoxville: University of Tennessee Press, 2005.
Allgeyer v. Louisiana. 165 US 578 (1897).
Allred, Jeff. *American Modernism and Depression Documentary*. Oxford, UK: Oxford University Press, 2010.

Althusser, Louis. *Lenin and Philosophy, and Other Essays.* Translated by Ben Brewster. NLB, London, 1971.

Amis, Kingsley. Review of *Lolita.* In *Nabokov: The Critical Heritage*, edited by Norman Page, 104-6. London: Routledge & Kegan Paul, 1982.

Anderson, Amanda. *Bleak Liberalism.* Chicago: University of Chicago Press, 2017.

———. "Postwar Aesthetics: The Case of Trilling and Adorno," *Critical Inquiry* 40 (2014), 418-38.

Appel, Alfred A., Jr., and Charles Newman. *Nabokov: Criticism, Reminiscences, Translations and Tributes.* Evanston, IL: Northwestern University Press, 1970.

Arendt, Hannah. "On the Nature of Totalitarianism: An Essay in Understanding." In *Essays in Understanding 1930-1945*, edited by Jerome Kohn, 328-60. New York: Harcourt Brace, 1994.

———. *The Origins of Totalitarianism.* 1948. New York: Harcourt Brace, 1976.

———. "Reflections on the Fate of the Union: Kennedy and After." *New York Review of Books* 1.9 (26 Dec. 1963).

———. "Understanding and Politics." In *Essays in Understanding 1930-1945*, edited by Jerome Kohn, 307-27. New York: Harcourt Brace & Company. 1994.

———. "What Is Authority?" In *Between Past and Future: Eight Exercises in Political Thought,* 91-141. New York: Penguin Books, 2006.

Arvidson, Heather. "Numb Modernism: Sentiment and the Intellectual Left in Tess Slesinger's *The Unpossessed." Twentieth Century Literature* 63.3 (Sept. 2017), 239-66.

Auden, W. H. "The Means of Grace." Review of *The Nature and Destiny of Man* by Reinhold Niebuhr. *The New Republic,* 2 June 1941. In *The Complete Works of W. H. Auden.* Vol. 2, *Prose: 1939-1948,* edited by Edward Mendelson, 131-34. Princeton, NJ: Princeton University Press, 2002.

———. "The Public v. the Late Mr William Butler Yeats," in *The Complete Works of W. H. Auden.* Vol. 2, *Prose: 1939-1948,* edited by Edward Mendelson, 3-7. Princeton, NJ: Princeton University Press, 2002.

Auspurger, Michael. *An Economy of Abundant Beauty: Fortune Magazine and Depression America.* Ithaca, NY: Cornell University Press, 2004.

Badger, Jonathan. *Sophocles and the Politics of Tragedy: Cities and Transcendence.* Routledge Innovations in Political Theory. New York: Routledge, 2013.

Bailyn, Bernard. *The Ideological Origins of the American Revolution.* Cambridge, MA: Harvard University Press, 1967.

Baldwin, James. "Everybody's Protest Novel." In *Notes of a Native Son,* 13-24. Boston: Beacon Press, 1983.

———. *The Evidence of Things Not Seen.* New York: Henry Holt and Company, 1985.

———. *Jimmy's Blues and Other Poems.* Boston: Beacon Press, 2014.

———. "Many Thousands Gone." In *Notes of a Native Son,* 25-46. Boston: Beacon Press, 1983.

Baldwin, James, Nathan Glazer, Sidney Hook, and Gunnar Myrdal. "Liberalism and the Negro: A Round-Table Discussion." *Commentary* (Mar. 1963), 25-42.

Balkin, Jack M., ed. *What Brown v. Board of Education Should Have Said*. New York: New York University Press, 2002.

Balridge, Letitia. *In the Kennedy Style*. New York: Doubleday, 1998.

Barnhiesel, Greg. *Cold War Modernists: Art, Literature, & American Cultural Diplomacy*. New York: Columbia University Press, 2015.

Baron, Dennis E. "The Syntax of Perception in Richard Wright's *Native Son*." *Language and Style* 9 (1976), 17-28.

Bates, Barclay W. "The Lost Path in *Death of a Salesman*." *Modern Drama* 11.2 (Summer 1968), 164-72.

Baxter, Charles. "Nabokov, Idolatry, and the Police State." *boundary 2* 5.3 (1977), 813-28.

Beisel, Nicola, and Tamara Kay. "Abortion, Race, and Gender in Nineteenth-Century America." *American Sociological Review* 69.4 (Aug. 2004), 498-518.

Bell, Bernard W. *The Afro-American Novel and Its Tradition*. Amherst: University of Massachusetts Press, 1987.

Bell, Daniel. *The End of Ideology: On the Exhaustion of Political Ideas in the Fifties*. Cambridge, MA: Harvard University Press, 1988.

Bell, Duncan. "What Is Liberalism?" *Political Theory* 42.6 (2014), 682-715.

Belloc, Hilaire. *An Essay on the Restoration of Property*. London: Distributist League, 1936.

Benston, Kimberly W. "The Veil of Black: (Un)Masking the Subject of African-American Modernism's *Native Son*." In *Richard Wright's Native Son*, edited by Harold Bloom, 43-73. Bloom's Modern Critical Interpretations. New York: Infobase Publishing, 2009.

Bentley, Eric. "The Innocence of Arthur Miller." In *The Crucible*, by Arthur Miller, edited by Gerald Weales, 204-9. New York: Penguin Books, 1996.

Bercovitch, Sacvan. *The American Jeremiad*. 1978. Madison: University of Wisconsin Press, 2012.

Bercovitch, Sacvan, and Myra Jehlen, eds. *Ideology and Classic American Literature*. Cambridge, MA: Harvard University Press, 1986.

Berlant, Lauren. "The Subject of True Feeling: Pain, Privacy, and Politics." In *Left Legalism/Left Critique*, edited by Wendy Brown and Janet Halley, 105-33. Durham, NC: Duke University Press, 2002.

Berle, Adolf A., Jr., and Gardiner C. Means. *The Modern Corporation and Private Property*. 1932. New York: Macmillan, 1936.

Berlin, Isaiah. "Two Concepts of Liberty." In *Liberty: Incorporating Four Essays on Liberty*, edited by Henry Hardy, 166-217. Oxford, UK: Oxford University Press, 2002.

Bethea, David M. "Style." In *The Garland Companion to Vladimir Nabokov*, edited by Vladimir E. Alexandrov, 696-704. New York: Garland, 1995.

Beye, Charles Rowan. *Ancient Greek Literature and Society.* Ithaca, NY: Cornell University Press, 1987.

Biagi, Shirley. "Forgive Me for Dying." *The Antioch Review* 35.2/3 (Spring-Summer 1977): 224-26.

Blair, Sara. "Modernism and the Politics of Culture." In *The Cambridge Companion to Modernism,* edited by Michael Levenson, 155-77. Cambridge: Cambridge University Press, 1999.

Blease W. L. *A Short History of English Liberalism.* London: Ernest Benn, 1913.

Boas, Taylor C., and Jordan Gans-Morse, "Neoliberalism: From New Liberal Philosophy to Anti-liberal Slogan." *Studies in Comparative International Development* 44 (2009), 137-61.

Bone, Robert A. *The Negro Novel in America.* New Haven, CT: Yale University Press, 1958.

Bonilla-Silva, Eduardo. *Racism without Racists: Color-Blind Racism and the Persistence of Racial Inequality in America.* Lanham, MD: Rowman & Littlefield, 2014.

Born, Daniel. *The Birth of Liberal Guilt in the English Novel: Charles Dickens to H.G. Wells.* Chapel Hill: University of North Carolina Press, 1995.

Bourdieu, Pierre. *The Field of Cultural Production: Essays on Art and Literature.* Edited by Randal Johnson. Columbia University Press: 1993.

——. *The Rules of Art: Genesis and Structure of the Literary Field.* Translated by Susan Emanuel. Stanford, CA: Stanford University Press, 1996.

Bourne, Randolph. "Twilight of Idols," in *The Radical Will: Selected Writings, 1911-1918,* edited by Olaf Hansen, 336-347. New York: Urizen Books, 1917.

——. "The War and the Intellectuals." 1917. In *War and the Intellectuals: Collected Essays 1915-1919,* edited by Carl Resek, 3-14. Indianapolis: Hackett, 1964.

Bowles, Hamish. *Jacqueline Kennedy: The White House Years.* New York: Bulfinch Press, 2001.

Boyd, Brian. *Vladimir Nabokov: The Russian Years.* London: Chatto & Windus, 1990.

Brandom, Robert, ed. *Rorty and His Critics.* Oxford, UK: Wiley-Blackwell, 2000.

Briggs v. Elliott. 132 F. Supp. 776 (E.D.S.C. 1955).

Brinkley, Alan. *The End of Reform: New Deal Liberalism in Recession and War.* New York: Knopf, 1995.

Brock, Clifton. *Americans for Democratic Action: Its Role in National Politics.* Washington, DC: Public Affairs Press, 1962.

Brown v. Board of Education. 347 U.S. 483. (1954).

Brown, Gillian. *Domestic Individualism: Imagining Self in Nineteenth-Century America.* Berkeley: University of California Press, 1990.

Brown, Stephanie. *The Postwar African American Novel: Protest and Discontent, 1945-1950.* Jackson: University Press of Mississippi, 2011.

Brown, Wendy. *States of Injury: Power and Freedom in Late Modernity.* Princeton, NJ: Princeton University Press, 1995.

———. *Undoing the Demos: Neoliberalism's Stealth Revolution*. New York: Zone Books, 2015.

Burke, Kenneth. *Attitudes towards History*. 1937. Berkeley: University of California Press, 1984.

Burke, Kenneth, and Malcolm Cowley. *The Selected Correspondence of Kenneth Burke and Malcolm Cowley, 1915-1981*. Berkeley: University of California Press, 1989.

———. "Synthetic Freedom." Review of *The Restoration of Property: An Essay on the Modern Crisis* by Hilaire Belloc. In *Equipment for Living: The Literary Reviews of Kenneth Burke*, edited by Nathaniel A. Rivers and Ryan P. Weber, 381-82. West Lafayette, IN: Parlor Press, 2010.

Bush, Ronald. "Tennis by the Book: *Lolita* and the Game of Modernist Fiction." In *Transitional Nabokov*, edited by Will Norman and Duncan White, 265-84. Bern: Peter Lang, 2009.

Butler, Judith. "A Carefully Crafted F**k You." Interview with Nathan Schneider. *Guernica* 15 Mar. 2010.

———. *Undoing Gender*. New York: Routledge, 2004.

Butler, Judith, and Athena Athanasiou. *Dispossession: The Performative in the Political*. Cambridge, UK: Polity Press, 2013.

Butler, Robert. *Native Son: The Emergence of a New Black Hero*. Boston: Twayne, 1991.

Caldwell, Erskine, and Margaret Bourke-White. *You Have Seen Their Faces*. Athens: University of Georgia Press, 1995.

Capers, Bennett. "On Justitia, Race, Gender, and Blindness." *Michigan Journal of Race and Law* 12 (2006), 203-33.

Carr, Leslie G. *"Color-Blind" Racism*. Thousand Oaks, CA: Sage Publications, 1997.

Castro, Joy. "'My Little Illegality': Abortion, Resistance, and Women Writers on the Left." In *The Novel and the American Left: Critical Essays on Depression-Era Fiction*, edited by Janet Galligani Casey, 16-34. Iowa City: University of Iowa Press, 2004.

Chambers, Whittaker. "Faith for a Lenten Age." *Time* 8 Mar. 1948, 70-76, 79.

Chase, Richard. *The American Novel and Its Tradition*. 1957. Baltimore: Johns Hopkins University Press, 1980.

———. *Herman Melville: A Critical Study*. New York: Macmillan, 1949.

———. "A Novel Is a Novel." *Kenyon Review* 14 (Autumn 1952), 678-84.

Chicago, *Milwaukee & St. Paul Railway Company v. Minnesota*. 134 US 418 (1890).

Ciepley, David. "Beyond Public and Private: Toward a Political Theory of the Corporation." *American Political Science Review* 107.1 (2013), 139-58.

———. *Liberalism in the Shadow of Totalitarianism*. Cambridge, MA: Harvard University Press, 2006.

Clark, Eleanor. "Old Glamour, New Gloom." *Theatre Chronicle, Partisan Review* 16.6 (June 1949): 631-635. In Arthur Miller, *Death of a Salesman*, 217-23. New York: Viking Critical Library, 1996.

Clark, Lorenne M. G., and Lynda Lange, eds. *The Sexism of Social and Political Theory: Women and Reproduction from Plato to Nietzsche*. Toronto: University of Toronto Press, 1979.

Coles, Robert. *Agee: His Life Remembered*, edited by Ross Spears and Jude Cassidy. New York: Holt, Rinehart and Winston, 1985,

Commons, John R. *The Legal Foundations of Capitalism*. New York: Macmillan, 1924.

Cornell, Drucilla. *The Imaginary Domain: Abortion, Pornography & Sexual Harassment*. New York: Routledge, 1995.

Cort, John C. "Contemporary Social Problems." Review of *Let Us Now Praise Famous Men*, by James Agee and Walker Evans. *Commonweal* 34 (12 Sept. 1941), 499-500.

Couturier, Maurice. "Annotating vs. Interpreting Nabokov: The Author as a Helper or a Screen?" *Cycnos* 24.1 (20 Mar. 2008). http://revel.unice.fr/cycnos/index.html?id=1034.

Crenshaw, Kimberlé Williams. "Color-Blind Dreams and Racial Nightmares: Reconfiguring Racism in the Post-Civil Rights Era." In *Birth of a Nation'hood: Gaze, Script, and Spectacle in the O. J. Simpson Case*, edited by Toni Morrison and Claudia Brodsky Lacour, 97-168. New York: Pantheon Books, 1997.

Crenshaw, Kimberlé Williams, et al. "Introduction." In *Critical Race Theory: The Key Writings That Formed the Movement*, xiii-xxxii. New York: New Press, 1995.

Curran v. Bosze, 41 Ill. 2d 473, 153 Ill.Dec. 213, 566 NE.2d 1319 (1990).

Darden, Christopher. *In Contempt*. New York: Regan Books, 1996.

Davis, Benjamin, Jr. Review of *Native Son*, by Richard Wright. In *Richard Wright: The Critical Reception*, edited by John M. Reilly, 68-76. New York: Franklin, 1978.

Davis, Hugh. *The Making of James Agee*. Knoxville: University of Tennessee Press, 2008.

Davis, Thomas S. "Late Modernism: British Literature at Midcentury." *Literature Compass* 9.4 (2012): 326-37.

Decker, Mark. "'A Lot Depends on What Judge We Have': *Native Son* and the Legal Means for Social Justice." In *Richard Wright's Native Son,* edited by Harold Bloom, 175-96. Bloom's Modern Critical Interpretations. New York: Infobase, 2009.

Delgado, Richard. "Liberal McCarthyism and the Origins of Critical Race Theory." In *Critical Race Theory: The Cutting Edge*, edited by Richard Delgado and Jean Stefanic, 38-46. Philadelphia: Temple University Press, 2013.

DeLillo, Don. *Libra*. 1988. New York: Penguin, 1991.

de Man, Paul. *Allegories of Reading: Figural Language in Rousseau, Nietzsche, Rilke, and Proust*. Hartford, CT: Yale University Press, 1979.

Denby, David. "A Famous Man." Review of *The Collected Works of James Agee*. *New Yorker* 6 Jan. 2009.

Denning, Michael. *The Cultural Front: The Laboring of American Culture in the Twentieth Century*. London: Verso, 1997.

Depoe, Stephen P. *Arthur M. Schlesinger, Jr., and the Ideological History of American Liberalism*. Tuscaloosa: University of Alabama Press, 1994.
Dewey, John. *Art as Experience*. In *The Later Works, 1925-1953*. Vol. 10, edited by Jo Ann Boydston, 1-352. Carbondale: Southern Illinois University Press, 1989.
———. *Freedom and Culture*. In *The Later Works, 1925-1953*. Vol. 13, edited by Jo Ann Boydston, 63-252. Carbondale: Southern Illinois University Press, 2008.
———. "How to Anchor Liberalism." In *The Later Works, 1925-1953*. Vol. 15, edited by Jo Ann Boydston, 248-50. Carbondale: Southern Illinois University Press, 1991.
———. *How We Think*. In *The Later Works, 1925-1953*. Vol. 8, edited by Jo Ann Boydston, 105-352. Carbondale: Southern Illinois University Press, 2008.
———. *Individualism Old and New*. In *The Later Works, 1925-1953*. Vol. 5, edited by Jo Ann Boydston, 41-124. Carbondale: Southern Illinois University Press, 2008.
———. *Liberalism and Social Action*. In *The Later Works, 1925-1953*. Vol. 11, edited by Jo Ann Boydston, 1-65. Carbondale: Southern Illinois University Press, 1991.
———. "The Need for a New Party." In *The Later Works, 1925-1953*. Vol. 6, edited by Jo Ann Boydston, 156-82. Carbondale: Southern Illinois University Press, 2008.
———. "Philosophy and Civilization." In *The Later Works, 1927-1928*. Vol. 3, edited by Jo Ann Boydston, 3-10. Carbondale: Southern Illinois University Press, 1984.
———. *The Public and Its Problems*. In *The Later Works, 1925-1953*. Vol. 2, edited by Jo Ann Boydston, 235-372. Carbondale: Southern Illinois University Press, 2008.
Dickstein, Morris. *Dancing in the Dark: A Cultural History of the Great Depression*. New York: W. W. Norton, 2009.
Dillon, Elizabeth Maddock. *The Gender of Freedom: Fictions of Liberalism and the Literary Public Sphere*. Stanford, CA: Stanford University Press, 2004.
Douzinas, Costas, and Lynda Nead. "Introduction." In *Law and the Image: The Authority of Art and the Aesthetics of Law*, edited by Costas Douzinas and Lynda Nead, 1-18. Chicago: University of Chicago Press, 1999.
Dragunoia, Dana. *Vladimir Nabokov and the Poetics of Liberalism*. Evanston, IL: Northwestern University Press, 2011.
Dudziak, Mary L. *Cold War Civil Rights: Race and the Image of American Democracy*. Princeton, NJ: Princeton University Press, 2000.
———. "Desegregation as a Cold War Imperative." *Stanford Law Review* 41.1 (1988), 61-120.
Dugan, Andrew, and Frank Newport. "American Rate JFK as Top Modern President." *Gallup* 15 Nov. 2013. http://www.gallup.com/poll/165902/americans-rate-jfk-top-modern-president.aspx.
Durantaye, Leland de la. "The Pattern of Cruelty and the Cruelty of Pattern in Vladimir Nabokov." *Cambridge Quarterly* 35.4 (2006), 301-26.

———. *Style Is Matter: The Moral Art of Vladimir Nabokov*. Ithaca, NY: Cornell University Press, 2007.

Edmunds, Susan Louise. "'Just Like Home': Richard Wright, Harriet Beecher Stowe, and the New Deal." *American Literature* 86.1 (2014), 61-86.

Eliot, T. S. *After Strange Gods*. New York: Harcourt, Brace, 1933.

———. *Christianity and Culture*. London: Harvest Books, 1967.

Ellison, Ralph. "The World and the Jug." In *Shadow and Act*, 107-43. London: Secker, 1967.

Evans, Walker. "James Agee in 1936." In James Agee and Walker Evans, *Let Us Now Praise Famous Men*, 5-7. Boston: Houghton Mifflin, 1960.

"Executive Order 10925, Establishing the President's Committee on Equal Employment Opportunity." 5 Mar. 1961.

"Experiment in Communication." Review of *Let Us Now Praise Famous Men* by James Agee and Walker Evans. *Time* 13 Oct. 1941, 667.

Fabre, Michel. *The Unfinished Quest of Richard Wright*. 1973. Translated by Isabel Barzun. Chicago: University of Illinois Press, 1993.

Fawcett, Edmund. *Liberalism: The Life of an Idea*. Princeton, NJ: Princeton University Press, 2014.

Felski, Rita. "Introduction." In *Rethinking Tragedy*, 1-28. Baltimore: Johns Hopkins University Press, 2008.

Ferrall, Charles. *Modernist Writing and Reactionary Politics*. Cambridge, UK: Cambridge University Press, 2001.

Filreis, Alan. *Modernism from Right to Left: Wallace Stevens, the Thirties, & Literary Radicalism*. Cambridge, UK: Cambridge University Press, 1994.

Fishburn, Katherine. *Richard Wright's Hero: The Faces of a Rebel-Victim*. Metuchen, NJ: Scarecrow, 1977.

Fitzgerald, Robert. "James Agee: A Memoir." *Kenyon Review* 30.5 (1968), 587-624.

Flaubert, Gustave. *The Letters of Gustave Flaubert*. Edited and translated by Francis Steegmuller. Cambridge, MA: Belknap Press, 1980.

Foley, Barbara. *Radical Representations: Politics and Form in U.S. Proletarian Fiction, 1929-1941*. Durham, NC: Duke University Press, 1993.

Foucault, Michel. *The Birth of Biopolitics*. Series: Lectures at the Collège de France 1978-1979. Edited by Michel Senellart. Translated by Graham Burchell. New York: Picador, 2008.

Fox, Richard Wightman. "Reinhold Niebuhr and the Emergence of the Liberal Realist Faith, 1930-1945." *Review of Politics* 38.2 (1976), 244-65.

———. "Reinhold Niebuhr: Self-Made Intellectual." *The Quarterly Journal of the Library of Congress* 40.1 (Winter 1983), 48-55.

———. "Tragedy, Responsibility, and the American Intellectual, 1925-1950." In *Lewis Mumford: Public Intellectual*, edited by Agatha C. Hughes and Thomas P. Hughes, 323-37. Oxford, UK: Oxford University Press, 1990.

Fraser, Steve, and Gary Gerstle, eds. *The Rise and Fall of the New Deal Order, 1930-1980*. Princeton, NJ: Princeton University Press, 1989.

Frederickson, Kathleen. *The Ploy of Instinct: Victorian Sciences of Nature and Sexuality in Liberal Governance*. New York: Fordham University Press, 2014.

Freeman, Joseph. Review of *The Unpossessed* by Tess Slesinger. *Daily Worker*. New York Edition. 2 June 1934, 7.

Friedman, Milton, and Rose D. Friedman. *Two Lucky People: Memoirs*. Chicago: University of Chicago Press, 1998.

Friedman, Susan Stanford. "Periodizing Modernism: Postcolonial Modernities and the Space/Time Borders of Modernist Studies." *Modernism/modernity* 13.3 (2006), 425-43.

Fromm, Erich. *Escape from Freedom*. 1941. New York: Avon Books, 1965.

Fukuyama, Francis. "The End of History?" *The National Interest* 16 (1989), 3-18.

Garcia, Jay. *Psychology Comes to Harlem: Rethinking the Race Question in Twentieth-Century America*. Baltimore: Johns Hopkins University Press, 2012.

Gassner, John. "*Death of a Salesman:* First Impressions, 1949." *Quarterly Journal of Speech* 35 (Feb. 1949), 289-94. In Arthur Miller, *Death of a Salesman*, 231-39. New York: Viking Critical Library, 1996.

Genter, Robert. "Toward a Theory of Rhetoric: Ralph Ellison, Kenneth Burke, and the Problem of Modernism." *Twentieth Century Literature* 48.2 (2002), 191-214.

Gerstle, Gary. "The Protean Character of American Liberalism." *American Historical Review* 99.4 (1994), 1043-73.

Gibson, Donald B. "Wright's Invisible Native Son." In *The Critical Response to Richard Wright*, edited by Robert J. Butler, 35-42. Westport, CT: Greenwood Press, 1995.

Gillette, Meg. "Bedside Manners in Dorothy Parker's 'Lady with a Lamp' and Kay Boyle's *My Next Bride*." *Studies in American Fiction* 35.2 (2007), 159-79.

———. "Making Modern Parents in Ernest Hemingway's 'Hills Like White Elephants' and Viña Delmar's *Bad Girl*." *MFS Modern Fiction Studies* 53.1 (2007), 50-69.

———. "Modern American Abortion Narratives and the Century of Silence." *Twentieth Century Literature* 58.4 (Winter 2012), 663-87.

Gillon, Steven M. *Politics and Vision: The ADA and American Liberalism, 1947-1985*. New York: Oxford University Press, 1987.

Glazer, Nathan. "New Light on the Authoritarian Personality: A Survey of Recent Research and Criticism." *Commentary* 17 (1954), 289-97.

Gold, Mike. "Why I Am a Communist." *New Masses* 8.3 (1932). In *Mike Gold: A Literary Anthology*, edited by Michael Folsom, 209-14. New York: International Publishers, 1972.

Goldstein, Philip. "Richard Wright's *Native Son*: From Naturalist Protest to Modernist Liberation and Beyond." In *New Directions in American Reception Study*, edited by Philip Goldstein and James L. Machor, 119-38. Oxford, UK: Oxford University Press, 2008.

Goldstone, Andrew. *Fictions of Autonomy: Modernism from Wilde to de Man*. Oxford, UK: Oxford University Press, 2013.

Gonzales v. Carhart. 550 US 124 (2007).

Goodlad, Lauren. *Victorian Literature and the Victorian State: Character and Governance in a Liberal Society*. Baltimore: Johns Hopkins University Press, 2003.

Gotanda, Neil. "A Critique of 'Our Constitution Is Color-Blind.'" *Stanford Law Review* 44.1 (1991), 1–68.

Grady, Hugh. "The Modernity of Western Tragedy: Genealogy of a Developing Anachronism." *PMLA* 129.4 (2014), 790–98.

Greaves, Bettina Benn. "Preface, 1985." In Ludwig von Mises, *Liberalism (Liberalismus) in the Classical Tradition*, v–viii. San Francisco: Cobden Press, 2002.

Green, David. *Shaping Political Consciousness: The Language of Politics in America from McKinley to Reagan*. Ithaca, NY: Cornell University Press, 1987.

Greenberg, Clement. "Modernist Painting." In *Clement Greenberg: Collected Essays and Criticism*. Vol. 4, edited by John O'Brien, 85–93. Chicago: University of Chicago Press, 1993.

Greif, Mark. *The Age of the Crisis of Man: Thought and Fiction in America, 1933–1973*. Princeton, NJ: Princeton University Press, 2015.

Griffin, Roger. *Modernism and Fascism: The Sense of a Beginning under Mussolini and Hitler*. New York: Palgrave, 2007.

Griswold v. Connecticut. 381 US 479 (1965).

Gross, Seymour L. "Dalton and Color-Blindness in *Native Son*." *Mississippi Quarterly* 27.1 (Winter 1973), 75–77.

Guinier, Lani. "From Racial Liberalism to Racial Literacy: Brown v. Board of Education and the Interest-Divergence Dilemma." *Journal of American History* 91.1 (June 2004), 92–118.

Gunnell, John G. "The Archeology of American Liberalism." *Journal of Political Ideologies* 6.2 (2001), 125–45.

Haag, Pamela. *Consent: Sexual Rights and the Transformation of American Liberalism*. Ithaca, NY: Cornell University Press, 1999.

Hadley, Elaine. *Living Liberalism: Practical Citizenship in Mid-Victorian Britain*. Chicago: University of Chicago Press, 2010.

———. "On a Darkling Plain: Victorian Liberalism and the Fantasy of Agency." *Victorian Studies* 48.1 (2005), 92–102.

Halberstam, David. *The Best and the Brightest*. 1972. New York: Ballantine Books, 1993.

Haney-Lopez, Ian. "Is the 'Post' in Postracial the 'Blind' in Colorblind?" *Cardozo Law Review* 32.3 (2011), 807–31.

———. "'A Nation of Minorities': Race, Ethnicity, and Reactionary Colorblindness." *Stanford Law Review* 59 (Feb. 2007), 985–1064.

Hardwick, Elizabeth. "Introduction" in Tess Slesinger, *The Unpossessed*, vii–xiv. New York: New York Review Books, 2002.

Hargrove, Erwin C. *The Power of the Modern Presidency*. New York: Alfred A. Knopf, 1974.

Harris, Cheryl L. "Whiteness as Property." *Harvard Law Review* 106.8 (June 1993), 1707-91.

Hartz, Louis. *The Liberal Tradition in America: An Interpretation of American Political Thought since the Revolution*. New York: Harcourt, Brace & World, 1955.

Harvey, David. *A Brief History of Neoliberalism*. Oxford, UK: Oxford University Press, 2007.

Hayek, Friedrich A. *The Road to Serfdom*. In *The Collected Works of F.A. Hayek*. Vol. 2, edited by Bruce Caldwell, 36-245. Chicago: University of Chicago Press, 2007.

Hegel, G. W. F. *Phenomenology of Spirit*. Translated by A. V. Miller. Oxford, UK: Oxford University Press, 1977.

Hegeman, Susan. *Patterns for America: Modernism and the Concept of Culture*. Princeton, NJ: Princeton University Press, 1999.

Heise, Michael. "Brown v. Board of Education, Footnote 11, and Multidisciplinarity." *Cornell Law Review* 90.279 (2005), 279-320.

Hellman, John. "Kennedy and Postwar Intellectual Culture." In *The Cambridge Companion to John F. Kennedy*, edited by Andrew Hoberek, 134-48. Cambridge, UK: Cambridge University Press.

———. *The Kennedy Obsession: The American Myth of JFK*. New York: Columbia University Press, 1997.

Henggeler, Paul R. *The Kennedy Persuasion: The Politics of Style since JFK*. Chicago: Ivan R. Dee, 1995.

Heritage Foundation, *Mandate for Leadership: Policy Management in a Conservative Administration*. Washington, DC: Heritage Foundation, 1981.

Hersey, John. "Agee." *New Yorker* 18 July 1988, 72-82.

Hersh, Seymour M. *The Dark Side of Camelot*. Boston: Back Bay Books, 1997.

Hilgart, John. "Valuable Damage: James Agee's Aesthetics of Use." *Arizona Quarterly* 52.4 (1996), 85-114.

Ho, Janice. "The Crisis of Liberalism and the Politics of Modernism." *Literature Compass* 8.1 (2011), 47-65.

———. *Nation and Citizenship in the Twentieth-Century British Novel*. Cambridge, UK: Cambridge University Press, 2015.

Hoberek, Andrew. "Introduction: After Postmodernism." *Twentieth Century Literature* 53.3 (Fall 2007), 233-47.

———. "Introduction: JFK and/as America." In *The Cambridge Companion to John F. Kennedy*, edited by Andrew Hoberek, 1-16. Cambridge, UK: Cambridge University Press.

Hobhouse, L. T. *Liberalism*. In *Liberalism and Other Writings*, edited by James Meadowcroft, 1-120. Cambridge, UK: Cambridge University Press, 1994.

Hobson, J. A. *The Crisis in Liberalism: New Issues of Democracy*. London: P. S. King, 1909.

Hofstadter, Richard. *The Age of Reform: From Bryan to F.D.R.* New York: Vintage Books, 1955.

———. *Anti-intellectualism in American Life*. New York: Alfred A. Knopf, 1966.

Hook, Sidney. "The New Failure of Nerve." *Partisan Review* 10.1 (Jan.-Feb. 1943), 2-23.

———. "Pragmatism and the Tragic Sense of Life." *Proceedings and Addresses of the American Philosophical Association* 33 (1959-60), 5-26.

Hoover, Herbert. *The Challenge to Liberty*. New York: Scribner's, 1934.

Horkheimer, Max, and Theodor W. Adorno. *Dialectic of Enlightenment: Philosophical Fragments*. Edited by Gunzelin Schmid Noerr. Translated by Edmund Jephcott. Stanford, CA: Stanford University Press, 2002.

Horton, Carol A. *Race and the Making of American Liberalism*. Oxford, UK: Oxford University Press, 2005.

Horton, Walter M. "The New Orthodoxy." *The American Scholar* 7.1 (Winter 1938), 3-11.

Howe, Irving. "Black Boys and Native Sons." In *Richard Wright's "Native Son": A Critical Handbook*, edited by Richard Abcarian, 135-43. Belmont, CA: Wadsworth, 1970.

———. "The Culture of Modernism." In *Decline of the New*, 3-33. New York: Horizon Press, 1970.

Hughes, Langston. "Justice." In *The Collected Poems of Langston Hughes*, edited by Arnold Rampersad and David Roessel, 31. New York: Alfred A. Knopf, 1994.

Humphreys, David. "The Aesthetics of Failure: James Agee's Tragic Sensibility." PhD diss. Case Western Reserve University, 1979.

Husock, Howard. "Popular Song." *Wilson Quarterly* 12.3 (1988), 48-65.

Hutchinson, Ben. *Modernism and Style*. London: Palgrave Macmillan, 2011.

Hyde, Alan. *Bodies of Law*. Princeton, NJ: Princeton University Press, 1997.

Irons, Peter. *A People's History of the Supreme Court*. New York: Penguin, 1999.

Jackson, Lawrence P. *The Indignant Generation: A Narrative History of African American Writers and Critics, 1934-1960*. Princeton, NJ: Princeton University Press, 2011.

Jackson, Walter A. *Gunnar Myrdal and America's Conscience: Social Engineering and Racial Liberalism, 1938-1987*. Chapel Hill: University of North Carolina Press, 1990.

Jameson, Fredric. *Fables of Aggression: Wyndham Lewis and the Modernist as Fascist*. Berkeley: University of California Press, 1979.

———. "Postmodernism and Consumer Society." In *Postmodernism and Its Discontents: Theories, Practices*, edited by E. Ann Kaplan, 13-29. London: Verso, 1988.

———. *Postmodernism: Or, the Cultural Logic of Late Capitalism*. Durham: Duke University Press, 1992.

———. *A Singular Modernity*. London: Verso, 2001.

Jay, Martin. "Must Justice Be Blind? The Challenge of Images to the Law." In *Law and the Image: The Authority of Art and the Aesthetics of Law*, edited by Costas Douzinas and Lynda Neads, 19-35. Chicago: University of Chicago Press, 1999.

Jerng, Mark. *Claiming Others: Transracial Adoption and National Belonging*. Minneapolis: University of Minnesota Press, 2010.

Johnson, Barbara. "Apostrophe, Animation, and Abortion." In *A World of Difference*, 184-99. Baltimore: Johns Hopkins University Press, 1987.

Joyce, Joyce Ann. *Richard Wright's Art of Tragedy*. Iowa City: University of Iowa Press, 1986.

"Joycean, *adj.* and *n.*" *The Oxford English Dictionary*. 2013. OED Online. Oxford University Press. 3 July 2014.

"Justice Harlan Concurring." *New York Times* 23 May 1954, 10E, cols. 1 and 2.

Karem, Jeff. *The Romance of Authenticity: The Cultural Politics of Regional and Ethnic Literatures*. Charlottesville: University of Virginia Press, 2004.

Kazin, Alfred. "The President and Other Intellectuals." *American Scholar* 30.4 (Autumn 1961), 498-516.

Keats, John. "Hyperion. A Fragment." In *The Complete Poems*, 283-306. New York: Penguin, 1988.

Kempton, Murray. *Part of Our Time: Some Ruins and Monuments of the Thirties*. New York: New York Review of Books, 1998.

Kennedy, John F. "The Definition of a Liberal." In *Let the Word Go Forth: The Speeches, Statements, and Writings of John F. Kennedy 1947 to 1963*, edited by Theodore C. Sorensen, 106-8. New York: Delacorte Press, 1988.

———. "The Opening of a New Frontier." In *Let the Word Go Forth: The Speeches, Statements, and Writings of John F. Kennedy 1947 to 1963*, edited by Theodore C. Sorensen, 96-102. New York: Delacorte Press, 1988.

———. "The Peaceful Revolution." In *Let the Word Go Forth: The Speeches, Statements, and Writings of John F. Kennedy 1947 to 1963*, edited by Theodore C. Sorensen, 192-96. New York: Delacorte Press, 1988.

———. "The Vital Center of Action." In *Let the Word Go Forth: The Speeches, Statements, and Writings of John F. Kennedy 1947 to 1963*, edited by Theodore C. Sorensen, 17-23. New York: Delacorte Press, 1988.

Kennedy, Randall. *For Discrimination: Race, Affirmative Action, and the Law*. New York: Pantheon, 2013.

Keynes, John Maynard. *The General Theory of Employment, Interest and Money*. New York: Harcourt, Brace & World, 1965.

Kimmage, Michael. *The Conservative Turn: Lionel Trilling, Whittaker Chambers, and the Lessons of Anti-Communism*. Cambridge, MA: Harvard University Press, 2009.

King, Desmond S., et al. *Still a House Divided: Race and Politics in Obama's America*. Princeton, NJ: Princeton University Press, 2011.

Kinnamon, Keneth. "How *Native Son* Was Born." In *Richard Wright: Critical Perspectives Past and Present*, edited by Henry Louis Gates Jr. and K. A. Appiah, 110-31. New York: Amistad, 1993.

———. "Introduction." In *New Essays on "Native Son,"* edited by Keneth Kinnamon, 1-33. Cambridge, UK: Cambridge University Press, 1990.

Kirsch, Adam. *Why Trilling Matters*. New Haven, CT: Yale University Press, 2011.

Klein, Naomi. *The Shock Doctrine: The Rise of Disaster Capitalism*. New York: Picador, 2007.

Kristeva, Julia. *Possessions*. Translated by Barbara Bray. New York: Columbia University Press, 1998.

Krupnick, Mark. *Lionel Trilling and the Fate of Cultural Criticism*. Evanston, IL: Northwestern University Press, 1986.

Krutch, Joseph Wood. *The Modern Temper*. 1929. New York: Harcourt Brace Jovanovich, 1957.

Kuklick, Bruce. "Myth and Symbol in American Studies." *American Quarterly* 24.4 (1972), 435-50.

Kull, Andrew. *The Color-Blind Constitution*. Cambridge, MA: Harvard University Press, 1992.

Larsen, Erling. "Let Us Not Now Praise Ourselves." Review of *Let Us Now Praise Famous Men* by James Agee and Walker Evans. *Carleton Miscellany* 2 (Winter 1961), 86-97.

Lasch, Christopher. *The New Radicalism in America (1889-1963): The Intellectual as a Social Type*. New York: Alfred A. Knopf, 1965.

LeGuin, Ursula K. *The Dispossessed*. New York: Avon Books, 1974.

Levenson, Michael, *Modernism and the Fate of Individuality*. Cambridge, UK: Cambridge University Press, 1991.

Lewis, Pericles. "Introduction." In *The Cambridge Introduction to Modernism*, edited by Pericles Lewis, 1-37. Cambridge, MA: Cambridge University Press, 2011.

———. *Modernism, Nationalism, and the Novel*. Cambridge, MA: Cambridge University Press, 2000.

"Liberalism and Tempo." *New York Times* 23 Oct. 1937, 16.

Lippmann, Walter. *(An Inquiry into the Principles of) The Good Society*. Boston: Little, Brown, 1937.

———. *Drift and Mastery: An Attempt to Diagnose the Current Unrest*. 1914. Madison: University of Wisconsin Press, 1985.

Locke, John. *Two Treatises of Government*. Edited by Peter Laslett. Cambridge, UK: Cambridge University Press, 1988.

Lokrantz, Jessie. *The Underside of the Weave. Some Stylistic Devices Used by Vladimir Nabokov*. Acta Universitatis Upsaliensis, Studia Anglistica Upsaliensia. Vol. 11. Uppsala, Sweden: Almquist & Wiksell, 1973.

Looper-Friedman, Susan E. "'Keep Your Laws Off My Body': Abortion Regulation and the Takings Clause." *New England Law Review* 29:2 (1995), 253-84.
Losurdo, Domenico. *Liberalism: A Counter-History*. London: Verso, 2014.
Lowi, Theodore J. *The End of Liberalism: The Second Republic of the United States*. New York: W. W. Norton, 1979.
Lucaites, John Louis. "Visualizing 'The People': Individualism vs. Collectivism in *Let Us Now Praise Famous Men*." *Quarterly Journal of Speech* 83.3 (Aug. 1997), 269-83.
Luker, Kristin. *Abortion and the Politics of Motherhood*. Berkeley: University of California Press, 1984.
Lustig, R. Jeffrey. *Corporate Liberalism: The Origins of Modern American Political Theory, 1890-1920*. Berkeley: University of California Press, 1982.
Macdonald, Dwight. "Death of a Poet." *New Yorker* 16 Nov. 1957, 204-21.
Mackenzie, G. Calvin, and Robert Weisbrot. *The Liberal Hour: Washington and the Politics of Change in the 1960s*. New York: Penguin Press, 2008.
MacKinnon, Catherine. *Feminism Unmodified: Discourses on Life and Law*. Cambridge, MA: Harvard University Press, 1987.
MacPherson, C. B. *The Political Theory of Possessive Individualism: Hobbes to Locke*. 1962. Oxford, UK: Oxford University Press, 1972.
Maharidge, Dale, and Michael Williamson. *And Their Children after Them*. New York: Pantheon, 1989.
Mailer, Norman. *Advertisements for Myself*. New York: G. P. Putnam's Sons, 1959.
——. *The Presidential Papers of Norman Mailer*. New York: Bantam, 1964.
Malachowski, Alan R., ed. *Reading Rorty: Critical Responses to Philosophy and the Mirror of Nature and Beyond*. Oxford, UK: Wiley-Blackwell, 1991.
Mangrum, Ben. *Land of Tomorrow: Postwar Fiction and the Crisis of American Liberalism*. Oxford, UK: Oxford University Press, 2018.
Marcuse, Herbert. *One-Dimensional Man*. Boston: Beacon Press, 1964.
Margolies, Edward. *The Art of Richard Wright*. Carbondale: Southern Illinois University Press, 1969.
Martin, Robert A. "Arthur Miller—Tragedy and Commitment." In *Conversations with Arthur Miller*, edited by Matthew C. Roudané, 173-76. Jackson: University of Mississippi Press, 1987.
Marx, John. *Geopolitics and the Global Anglophone Novel, 1890-2011*. Cambridge, UK: Cambridge University Press, 2011.
Mason, Robert. "Kennedy and the Conservatives." In *The Cambridge Companion to John F. Kennedy*, edited by Andrew Hoberek, 225-39. Cambridge, UK: Cambridge University Press.
"Masterpieces of the XXth Century," 1952, Allen Tate Papers, Box 16, "Congress for Cultural Freedom" folder, Purdue University Library.

Mattson, Kevin. *When America Was Great: The Fighting Faith of Postwar Liberalism*. New York: Routledge, 2004.

Matusow, Allen J. *The Unraveling of America: A History of Liberalism in the 1960s*. New York: Harper & Row, 1984.

McCann, Sean. *A Pinnacle of Feeling: American Literature and Presidential Government*. Princeton, NJ: Princeton University Press, 2008.

———. *Gumshoe Fiction: Hard-Boiled Crime Fiction and the Rise and Fall of New Deal Liberalism*. Durham, NC: Duke University Press, 2000.

McCleskey v. Kemp. 481 US 279 (1987).

McClintock, Anne. "Imperial Ghosting and National Tragedy: Revenants from Hiroshima and Indian Country in the War on Terror." *PMLA* 129.4 (2014), 819-29.

McGowan, John. *American Liberalism: An Interpretation for Our Time*. Chapel Hill: University of North Carolina Press, 2007.

McHale, Brian. *Postmodernist Fiction*. 1987. New York: Routledge, 2001.

McKeever, Porter. *Adlai Stevenson: His Life and Legacy*. New York: William Morrow, 1989.

McLoughlin, Kate. "Introduction: A Welcome from the Host." In *The Modernist Party*, edited by Kate McLoughlin, 1-24. Edinbugh, Scotland: Edinburgh University Press, 2013.

McNeely, Trevor. "Lo and Behold: Solving the *Lolita* Riddle." *Studies in the Novel* 21.2 (1989), 182-200.

Melamed, Jodi. *Represent and Destroy: Rationalizing Violence in the New Racial Capitalism*. Minneapolis: University of Minnesota Press, 2012.

Mendelman, Lisa. *Modern Sentimentalism: Affect, Irony, and Female Authorship in Interwar America*. Oxford, UK: Oxford University Press, 2020.

Merquior, J. G. *Liberalism Old and New*. Boston: Twayne, 1991.

Miller, Arthur. *Death of a Salesman*. 1949. New York: Viking Critical Library, 1996.

———. "On Social Plays." In *The Theater Essays of Arthur Miller*, edited by Robert A. Martin and Steven R. Centola, 51-63. New York: Da Capo Press, 1996.

———. "Tragedy and the Common Man." *New York Times* 27 Feb. 1949, sec. 2, 1, 3. In *The Theater Essays of Arthur Miller*, edited by Robert A. Martin and Steven R. Centola, 3-7. New York: Da Capo Press, 1996.

Miller, D. Quentin. *Re-viewing James Baldwin: Things Not Seen*. Philadelphia: Temple University Press, 2000.

Miller, Perry. *Errand into the Wilderness*. 1956. New York: Harper and Row, 1964.

———. *The New England Mind: From Colony to Province*. Cambridge, MA: Belknap Press, 1953.

———. *The New England Mind: The Seventeenth Century*. Cambridge, MA: Belknap Press, 1939.

Miller, Tyrus. "Documentary / Modernism: Convergence and Complementarity in the 1930s." *Modernism/modernity* 9.2 (2002), 226-41.

Mills, Charles. *Black Rights, White Wrongs: The Critique of Racial Liberalism*. Oxford, UK: Oxford University Press, 2017.
———. *The Racial Contract*. Ithaca: Cornell University Press, 1997.
———. "Racial Liberalism." *PMLA* 123.5 (2008), 1380-97.
Mills, C. Wright. "The Powerless People: The Role of the Intellectual in Society." *politics* 1.3 (Apr. 1944). In *The Politics of Truth: Selected Writings of C. Wright Mills*, edited by John H. Summers, 13-24. Oxford, UK: Oxford University Press, 2008.
Miroff, Bruce. *Pragmatic Illusions: The Presidential Politics of John F. Kennedy*. New York: David McKay, 1976.
Mirowski, Philip. "Postface: Defining Neoliberalism." In Philip Mirowski and Dieter Plehwe. *The Road from Mont Pèlerin: The Making of the Neoliberal Thought Collective*, 417-56. Cambridge, MA: Harvard University Press, 2009.
Mirowski, Philip, and Dieter Plehwe. *The Road from Mont Pèlerin: The Making of the Neoliberal Thought Collective*. Cambridge, MA: Harvard University Press, 2009.
Missouri ex rel. *Gaines v. Canada.* 305 US 337 (1938).
Mohr, James. *Abortion in America*. New York: Oxford University Press, 1978.
Moon, Donald J. *Constructing Community: Moral Pluralism and Tragic Conflicts*. Princeton, NJ: Princeton University Press, 1993.
Moore v. Regents of the University of California. 51 Cal. 3d 120, 271 Cal. Rptr. 146, 793 P.2d 479 (Cal. 1990).
Morgan, Stacy I. *Rethinking Social Realism: African American Art and Literature, 1930-1953*. Athens: University of Georgia Press, 2004.
Morgenthau, Hans J. "The Influence of Reinhold Niebuhr in American Political Life and Thought." In *Reinhold Niebuhr: A Prophetic Voice in Our Time*, edited by Harold R. Landon, 97-109. Greenwich, CT: Seabury Press, 1962.
Morris, Debra, and Ian Shapiro. "Editors' Introduction." In John Dewey, *The Political Writings*, edited by Debra Morris and Ian Shapiro, ix-xix. Indianapolis: Hackett Publishing, 1993.
Mottram, Eric. "Arthur Miller: The Development of a Political Dramatist in America." In *Arthur Miller: A Collection of Critical Essays*, edited by Robert W. Corrigan, 23-58. Englewood Cliffs, NJ: Prentice, 1969.
Mumford, Lewis. *Technics and Civilization*. New York: Harcourt, Brace, 1934.
Murakawa, Naomi. *The First Civil Right: How Liberals Built Prison America*. Studies in Postwar American Political Development. New York: Oxford University Press, 2014.
Murray, J. Middleton. *The Problem of Style*. Oxford: Oxford University Press, 1922.
Mussolini, Benito. *Fascism: Doctrine and Institutions*. Rome: Ardita, 1935.
Myrdal, Gunnar. *An American Dilemma: The Negro Problem and Modern Democracy*. New York: Harper & Brothers, 1944.
Nabers, Deak. "Past Using: James Baldwin and Civil Rights Law in the 1960s." *Yale Journal of Criticism* 18.2 (2005), 221-42.

Nabokov, Dmitri. "Revisiting Father's Room." *Encounter* (Oct 1972), 77-82.
Nabokov, Vladimir. *The Annotated Lolita*. 1955. Edited by Alfred Appel Jr. New York: McGraw-Hill, 1970.
———. *Bend Sinister*. 1947. New York: Vintage, 1990.
———. *Lectures on Literature*. New York: Harcourt Brace Jovanovich, 1980.
———. *Pnin*. 1957. New York: Vintage International, 1989.
———. *Strong Opinions*. New York: McGraw-Hill, 1973.
"Nabokovian, *adj*." *The Oxford English Dictionary*. 2013. OED Online. Oxford University Press. 3 July 2014.
Nagel, James. "Images of 'Vision' in *Native Son*." In *Critical Essays on Richard Wright's Native Son*, edited by Keneth Kinnamon, 86-93. New York: Hall, 1997.
Naiman, Eric. "Hermophobia (On Sexual Orientation and Reading Nabokov)." *Representations* 101.1 (2008), 116-43.
———. *Nabokov, Perversely*. Ithaca, NY: Cornell University Press, 2010.
Naveh, Eyal. *Reinhold Niebuhr and Non-Utopian Liberalism: Beyond Illusion and Despair*. Brighton, UK: Sussex Academic Press, 2002.
Nealon, Jeffrey. *Post-Postmodernism: Or, The Cultural Logic of Just-in-Time Capitalism*. Stanford, CA: Stanford University Press, 2012.
Nelson, Cary. *Repression and Recovery: Modern American Poetry and the Politics of Cultural Memory, 1910-1945*. Madison: University of Wisconsin Press, 1989.
Newfield, Jack, and Jeff Grenfield. "The Disrupted History of Populist Liberalism." In *The Liberal Tradition in Crisis: American Politics in the Sixties*, edited by Jerome M. Mileur, 36-45. Lexington, MA: D. C. Heath, 1974.
Niebuhr, Reinhold. *Beyond Tragedy*: *Essays on the Christian Interpretation of History*. 1937. New York: Charles Scribner's Sons, 1965.
———. "The Blindness of Liberalism." *Radical Religion* 1 (Autumn 1936), 4-5.
———. *The Children of Light and the Children of Darkness: A Vindication of Democracy and a Critique of Its Traditional Defense*. New York: Charles Scribner's Sons, 1944.
———. *The Irony of American History*. New York: Charles Scribner's Sons, 1952.
———. *Moral Man and Immoral Society*. 1932. New York: Charles Scribner's Sons, 1960.
———. "The Pathos of Liberalism." *The Nation* 11 Sept. 1935, 303.
Nietzsche, Friedrich. *The Birth of Tragedy*. Translated by Francis Golffing. New York: Anchor Books, 1956.
———. *The Twilight of the Idols, or, How to Philosophize with the Hammer*. Edited by Oscar Levy. Translated by Anthony M. Ludovici. Complete Works of Friedrich Nietzsche, Vol. 16. New York: Russell & Russell, 1964.
Nikolopoulou, Kalliopi. *Tragically Speaking: On the Use and Abuse of Theory for Life*. Lincoln: University of Nebraska Press, 2012.
Noel, Hans. *Political Ideologies and Political Parties in America*. Oxford, UK: Oxford University Press, 2013.

Norman, Will. *Transatlantic Aliens: Modernism, Exile, and Culture in Midcentury America*. Baltimore: Johns Hopkins University Press, 2016.

Norman, Will, and Duncan White, eds. *Transitional Nabokov*. Bern, Switzerland: Peter Lang, 2009.

North, Michael. *Novelty: A History of the New*. Chicago: University of Chicago Press, 2013.

———. *The Political Aesthetic of Yeats, Eliot, and Pound*. Cambridge, MA: Cambridge University Press, 1991.

North Carolina State Board of Education v. Swann. 402 US 43, 44 n.1 (1971).

Nowlin, Michael. "Ralph Ellison, James Baldwin, and the Liberal Imagination." *Arizona Quarterly* 60.2 (2004), 117-40.

O'Kelley, Charles R. T. "Berle and Veblen: An Intellectual Connection." *Seattle University Law Review* 34.4 (2011), 1317-50.

Paolucci, Anne, and Henry, eds. *Hegel on Tragedy*. Westport, CT: Praeger, 1978.

Pateman, Carole. *The Sexual Contract*. Cambridge, UK: Polity Press, 1988.

Pateman, Carole, and Charles Mills. *The Contract and Domination*. Cambridge, UK: Polity Press, 2007.

Pater, Walter. *Studies in the History of the Renaissance*. Oxford World Classics. Oxford, UK: Oxford, University Press. 2010.

Patterson, Annabel. *Early Modern Liberalism*. Cambridge, UK: Cambridge University Press, 1997.

Pease, Donald E., and Robyn Wiegman, eds. *The Futures of American Studies*. Durham, NC: Duke University Press, 2002.

Pells, Richard H. *Radical Visions and American Dreams: Culture and Social Thought in the Depression Years*. New York: Harper & Row, 1973.

Petchesky, Rosalind. *Abortion and Woman's Choice: The State, Sexuality, and Reproductive Freedom*. Boston: Northeastern University Press, 1990.

Phillips, Wendell. *National Anti-slavery Standard* 11 Feb. 1865, at 2, col. 4 (speech to Mass. Anti-Slavery Society 26 Jan. 1865).

Pifer, Ellen. *Nabokov and the Novel*. Cambridge, MA: Harvard University Press, 1980.

Pitzer, Andrea. *The Secret History of Vladimir Nabokov*. New York: Pegasus Books, 2014.

Plessy v. Ferguson. 163 US 537 (1896).

Pocock, J. G. A. *The Machiavellian Moment: Florentine Thought and the Atlantic Republican Tradition*. Princeton, NJ: Princeton University Press, 1975.

Poovey, Mary. "The Abortion Question and the Death of Man." In *Feminists Theorize the Political*, edited by Judith Butler and Joan W. Scott, 239-56. New York: Routledge, 1992.

Portelli, Alessandro. "Everybody's Healing Novel: *Native Son* and Its Contemporary Critical Context." *Mississippi Quarterly* 50.2 (1997), 255-65.

Posnock, Ross. *The Trial of Curiosity: Henry James, William James, and the Challenge of Modernity*. Oxford, UK: Oxford University Press, 1991.

Post, Robert C. *Prejudicial Appearances: The Logic of American Antidiscrimination Law*. Durham, NC: Duke University Press, 2001.

Pound, Ezra. *Guide to Kulchur*. 1938. New York: New Directions, 1970.

Powe, Lucas A., Jr. *The Warren Court and American Politics*. Cambridge, MA: Belknap Press of Harvard University Press, 2000.

Rabinowitz, Paula. *Labor & Desire: Women's Revolutionary Fiction in Depression America*. Chapel Hill: University of North Carolina Press, 1991.

———. *They Must Be Represented: The Politics of Documentary*. London: Verso, 1994. Print.

Rahv, Philip. Review of *The Unpossessed* by Tess Slesinger. *The New Masses* 11.9 (1934), 26-27.

Ramsey, Priscilla. "Blind Eyes, Blind Quests in Richard Wright's *Native Son*." *CLA* 24 (1971), 48-61.

Rancière, Jacques. *Mute Speech: Literature, Critical Theory, and Politics*. Translated by James Swenson. New York: Columbia University Press, 2011.

———. *The Politics of Aesthetics*. Translated by Gabriel Rockhill. London: Continuum, 2004.

Ransom, John Crowe. "The Understanding of Fiction." *Kenyon Review* 12 (Spring 1950), 189-218.

Rawls, John. *A Theory of Justice*. Cambridge, MA: Harvard University Press, 1971.

Reagan, Leslie. *When Abortion Was a Crime: Women, Medicine, and Law in the United States, 1867-1973*. Berkeley: University of California Press, 1997.

Reedy, George. *The Twilight of the Presidency*. New York: Mentor, 1971.

Regents of the University of California v. Bakke. 438 US 265 (1978).

Rhode, Deborah L. "Feminist Critical Theories." *Stanford Law Review* 42.3 (Feb. 1990), 617-38.

Rice, Daniel F. *Reinhold Niebuhr and John Dewey: An American Odyssey*. Albany: State University of New York Press, 1993.

Riesman, David, Nathan Glazer, and Reuel Denney. *The Lonely Crowd: A Study of the Changing American Character*. New York: Doubleday Anchor, 1954.

Robbins, Bruce. "Everything is Not Neoliberalism." Review of Neoliberalism and Contemporary Literary Culture, Mitchum Huels and Rachel Greenwald Smith, editors. *American Literary History* 31.4 (2019): 840-49.

———. *Upward Mobility: Toward a Literary History of the Welfare State*. Princeton, NJ: Princeton University Press, 2007.

Rodden, John, ed. *Lionel Trilling & the Critics: Opposing Selves*. Lincoln: University of Nebraska Press, 1999.

Rodman, Selden. "The Poetry of Poverty." Review of Let Us Now Praise Famous Men by James Agee and Walker Evans. *The Saturday Review* 23 Aug. 1943, 6.

Rodriques v. Furtado. 950 F.2d 805 (1st Cir. 1991).
Roe v. Wade. 410 US 159 (1973).
Roosevelt, Franklin D. "Address at Oglethorpe University, May 22, 1932." In *The Public Papers and Addresses of Franklin D. Roosevelt*, edited by Samuel I. Rosenman. Vol. 1, *The Genesis of the New Deal, 1928-1932*, 639-47. New York: Random House, 1938.
———. "Inaugural Address, March 4, 1933." In *The Public Papers and Addresses of Franklin D. Roosevelt*. Vol. 2, *The Year of Crisis, 1933*, edited by Samuel I. Rosenman, 11-16. New York: Random House, 1938.
Rorty, Richard. *Contingency, irony, and solidarity*. Cambridge, UK: Cambridge University Press, 1989.
Rosenblatt, Helena. *The Lost History of Liberalism: From Ancient Rome to the Twenty-First Century*. Princeton, NJ: Princeton University Press, 2018.
Rosler, Martha. "In, Around, and Afterthoughts (on Documentary Photography)." In *The Contest of Meaning: Critical Histories of Photography*, edited by Richard Bolton, 303-42. Cambridge: MIT Press, 1992.
Rotunda, Ronald. *The Politics of Language: Liberalism as Word and Symbol*. Iowa City: University of Iowa Press, 1986.
Rowe, John Carlos. *Afterlives of Modernism: Liberalism, Transnationalism, and Political Critique*. Hanover, NH: Dartmouth College Press, 2011.
Rowe, W. W. *Nabokov's Deceptive World*. New York: New York University Press, 1971.
Russell, Bertrand. *Principles of Social Reconstruction*. London: George Allen & Unwin, 1916.
Ryan, Alan. *John Dewey and the High Tide of American Liberalism*. New York: W. W. Norton, 1995.
Sandel, Michael, ed. *Liberalism and Its Critics*. New York: New York University Press, 1984.
Santa Clara County v. Southern Pacific Railroad Company. 118 US 394 (1886).
Santayana, George. "The Irony of Liberalism." In *Soliloquies in England and Later Soliloquies*, 178-89. New York: Charles Scribner's Sons, 1923.
———. "Liberalism and Culture." In *Soliloquies in England and Later Soliloquies*, 173-78. New York: Charles Scribner's Sons, 1923.
Saunders, Francis Stonor. *The Cultural Cold War: The CIA and the World of Arts and Letters*. New York: New Press, 1999.
Schaub, Thomas Hill. *American Fiction in the Cold War*. Madison: University of Wisconsin Press, 1991.
Schechner, Mark. "The Elusive Trilling." *The Nation* (Sept. 1977). In *Lionel Trilling & the Critics: Opposing Selves*, edited by John Rodden, 352-58. Lincoln: University of Nebraska Press, 1999.
Schickler, Eric. *Racial Realignment: The Transformation of American Liberalism, 1932-1965*. Princeton, NJ: Princeton University Press, 2016.

Schlesinger, Arthur, Jr. "The Future of Liberalism." *The Reporter* 3 May 1956. 8-11.
———. *The Imperial Presidency*. Boston: Houghton Mifflin, 1973.
———. *Kennedy or Nixon: Does It Make Any Difference?* New York: Macmillan, 1960.
———. *A Thousand Days: John F. Kennedy in the White House*. Greenwich, CT: Fawcett Crest, 1965.
———. *The Vital Center: The Politics of Freedom*. 1949. New Brunswick, NJ: Transaction Publishers, 1998.
Schmidt, Christopher W. "Brown and the Colorblind Constitution." *Cornell Law Review* 94.1 (Nov. 2008), 203-38.
Schoenbach, Lisi. *Pragmatic Modernism*. Oxford, UK: Oxford University Press, 2012.
Schultz, Kevin M. *Buckley and Mailer: The Difficult Friendship That Shaped the Sixties*. New York: W. W. Norton, 2015.
Scott, Daryl Michael. *Contempt and Pity: Social Policy and the Image of the Damaged Black Psyche, 1880-1996*. Chapel Hill: University of North Carolina Press, 1997.
Scott, Winfield. "Most 'Famous' Unknown Book in Contemporary Letters." *New York Herald Tribune Book Review* 9 Oct. 1960, 6.
Shakespeare, William. *King Lear*, edited by Barbara A. Mowat and Paul Werstine. Folger Library. New York: Washington Square Press, 1993.
Shannon, William. "The Kennedy Administration: The Early Months." *American Scholar* 30.4 (1961), 481-88.
Sharistanian, Janet. "Afterword." In Tess Slesinger, *The Unpossessed*, 359-86. New York: Feminist Press, 1984.
Shklar, Judith. "The Liberalism of Fear." In *Liberalism and the Moral Life,* edited by Nancy L. Rosenbaum, 21-38. Cambridge, MA: Harvard University Press, 1989.
Siegel, Paul N. "The Conclusion of Richard Wright's *Native Son*." In *Critical Essays on Richard Wright's* Native Son, edited by Keneth Kinnamon, 94-103. New York: Hall, 1997.
Siegel, Reva B. "Abortion as a Sex Equality Right: Its Basis in Feminist Theory." In *Mothers in Law: Feminist Theory and the Legal Regulation of Motherhood*, edited by Martha Albertson Fineman and Isabel Karpin, 43-72. New York: Columbia University Press, 1995.
———. "Discrimination in the Eyes of the Law: How 'Color Blindness' Discourse Disrupts and Rationalizes Social Stratification." In *Prejudicial Appearances: The Logic of American Antidiscrimination Law*, edited by Robert C. Post, 99-152. Durham, NC: Duke University Press, 2001.
Siraganian, Lisa. *Modernism and the Meaning of Corporate Persons*. Oxford: Oxford University Press, 2021.
———. "Dreiser's Anti-corporate Tools: Veil-Piercing and the Novel of Corporate Agency." *American Literary History* 30.2 (Summer 2018), 249-77.
———. *Modernism's Other Work: The Art Object's Political Life*. Oxford, UK: Oxford University Press, 2012.

Slesinger, Tess. "After the Party." In *On Being Told That Her Second Husband Has Taken His First Lover and Other Stories*, 21-62. 1935. Chicago: Elephant, 1962.
——. *The Unpossessed*. 1934. New York: New York Review Books, 2002.
Smith, Valerie. "Alienation and Creativity in *Native Son*." In *Richard Wright's Native Son*, edited by Harold Bloom, 105-14. Modern Critical Interpretations. New York: Chelsea, 1988.
——. *Self-Discovery and Authority in Afro-American Fiction*. Cambridge, MA: Harvard University Press, 1991.
Smith v. Allwright. 321 US 649 (1944).
Smyth v. Ames. 171 US 361 (1898).
Snyder, Brad. "How the Conservatives Canonized *Brown v. Board of Education*." *Rutgers Law Review* 52.2 (2000), 383-494.
Solinger, Rickie. *Beggars and Choosers: How the Politics of Choice Shapes Adoption, Abortion, and Welfare in the United States*. New York: Hill and Wang, 2002.
Sorensen, Theodore C. "Introduction." In *Let the Word Go Forth: The Speeches, Statements, and Writings of John F. Kennedy*, edited by Theodore C. Sorensen, 1-8. New York: Delacorte Press, 1988.
Spiegel, Alan. *James Agee and the Legend of Himself*. Columbia: University of Missouri Press, 1998.
Stanton, Kay. "Women and the American Dream of Death of a Salesman." In *Feminist Rereadings of Modern American Drama*, edited by June Schlueter, 67-102. Rutherford, NJ: Farleigh Dickinson Press, 1989.
Stearns, Harold. *Liberalism in America: Its Origin, Its Temporary Collapse, Its Future*. New York: Boni and Liverwright, 1919.
Stegner, Page. *Escape into Aesthetics: The Art of Vladimir Nabokov*. London: Eyre and Spottiswoode, 1976.
Steiner, George. "'Tragedy' Reconsidered." In *Rethinking Tragedy*, edited by Rita Felski, 29-44. Baltimore: Johns Hopkins University Press, 2008.
——. *The Death of Tragedy*. London: Faber and Faber, 1961.
Stevens, George. "Afraid to Grow Up." *Saturday Review of Literature* 10 (19 May 1934), 701.
Stigler, George J., and Claire Friedland. "The Literature of Economics: The Case of Berle and Means." *Journal of Law and Economics*, 26.2 (June 1983), 237-68.
Stormer, Nathan. *Articulating Life's Memory: U.S. Medical Rhetoric about Abortion in the Nineteenth Century*. Boston: Lexington Books, 2003.
Stott, William. *Documentary Expression and Thirties America*. New York: Oxford University Press, 1973.
Stratton, Matthew. *The Politics of Irony in American Modernism*. New York: Fordham University Press, 2014.
Sun, Emily. *Succeeding King Lear: Literature, Exposure, and the Possibility of Politics*. New York: Fordham University Press, 2010.

Susman, Warren. "The Thirties." *The Development of an American Culture*, edited by Stanley Coben and Lorman Ratner, 179-218. Englewood Cliffs, NJ: Prentice Hall, 1983.

Szalay, Michael. *Hip Figures: A Literary History of the Democratic Party*. Stanford, CA: Stanford University Press, 2012.

———. *New Deal Modernism: American Literature and the Invention of the Welfare State*. Durham, NC: Duke University Press, 2000.

Tate, Allen. *Reason in Madness: Critical Essays*. New York: Putnam, 1941.

Tennyson, Lord Alfred North. "You Ask Me, Why, tho' Ill at Ease." In *The Works of Alfred Lord Tennyson*, 119-20. Hertfordshire, UK: Wordsworth Editions, 2008.

Teres, Harvey M. *Renewing the Left: Politics, Imagination, and the New York Intellectuals*. New York: Oxford University Press, 1996.

Thomas, David Wayne. *Cultivating Victorians: Liberal Culture and the Aesthetic*. Philadelphia: University of Pennsylvania Press, 2004.

Toker, Leona. *Nabokov: The Mystery of Literary Structures*. Ithaca, NY: Cornell University Press, 1989.

Tourgée, Albion, and Jasper C. Walker. Brief for Plaintiff in Error. *Plessy v. Ferguson* 210 (1895). In *Landmark Briefs and Arguments of the Supreme Court of the United States: Constitutional Law*, edited by Philip B. Kurkland & Gerhard Casper, 27-80. Vol. 13. Arlington, VA: University Publications of America, 1975.

Trask, Michael. *Camp Sites: Sex, Politics, and Academic Style in Postwar America*. Stanford, CA: Stanford University Press, 2013.

Tremaine, Louis. "The Dissociated Sensibility of Bigger Thomas." In *Richard Wright's Native Son*, edited by Harold Bloom, 89-104. Modern Critical Interpretations. New York: Chelsea, 1988.

Trilling, Lionel. *E. M Forster*. New York: New Directions, 1943.

———. "Greatness with One Fault in It." *Kenyon Review* 4.1 (1942), 99-102.

———. "The Last Lover." In *Speaking of Literature and Society*, 322-42. New York: Harcourt Brace Jovanovich, 1980.

———. *The Liberal Imagination: Essays on Literature and Society*. New York: Charles Scribner's Sons, 1976.

———. *Matthew Arnold*. New York: Harcourt Brace Jovanovich, 1939.

———"A Novel of the Thirties." In *The Last Decade: Essays and Reviews, 1965-1975*, 3-24. New York: Harcourt Brace Jovanovich.

———. *The Opposing Self: Nine Essays in Criticism*. 1955. New York: Viking Press, 1969.

———. *Speaking of Literature and Society*, edited by Diana Trilling. New York: Harcourt Brace Jovanovich, 1980.

———. "A Tragic Situation." In *Richard Wright's 'Black Boy': A Casebook*, edited by William Andrews and Douglas Taylor, 37-40. New York: Oxford University Press, 2003.

Turner, Fred. *The Democratic Surround: Multimedia & American Liberalism from World War II to the Psychedelic Sixties*. Chicago: University of Chicago Press, 2013.
van den Brink, Bert. *The Tragedy of Liberalism: An Alternative Defense of a Political Tradition*. Albany: State University Press of New York, 2000.
van Horn, Rob, and Philip Mirowski, "The Rise of the Chicago School of Economics and the Birth of Neoliberalism." In *The Road from Mont Pèlerin: The Making of the Neoliberal Thought Collective*, edited by Philip Mirowski and Dieter Plehwe, 139-80. Cambridge, MA: Harvard University Press, 2009.
Veblen, Thorstein. *Absentee Ownership and Business Enterprise in Recent Times*. 1923. New Brunswick: Transaction Publishers, 1997.
———. *Theory of the Leisure Class*. 1899. New York: Penguin, 1979.
Vernant, Jean-Pierre, and Pierre Vidal-Naquet. *Myth and Tragedy in Ancient Greece*. Translated by Janet Lloyd. New York: Zone Books, 1988.
Vidal, Gore. "The Holy Family." In *Homage to Daniel Shays: Collected Essays, 1952-1972*. New York: Vintage Books, 1973.
———. *United States: Essays 1952-1992*. New York: Random House, 1995.
Vogel, Dan. "Willy Tyrannos." In *Willy Loman*, edited by Harold Bloom, 58-65. Major Literary Characters. New York: Chelsea House, 1991.
von Mises, Ludwig. *Liberalism (Liberalismus) in the Classical Tradition*. 1962. San Francisco: Cobden Press, 2002.
Wain, John. Review of *Lolita*, by Vladimir Nabokov. In *Nabokov: The Critical Heritage*, edited by Norman Page, 114. London: Routledge & Kegan Paul, 1982.
Wald, Alan M. "The Menorah Group Moves Left." *Jewish Social Studies* 38.3/4 (1976), 289-320.
———. *The New York Intellectuals: The Rise and Decline of the Anti-Stalinist Left from the 1930s to the 1980s*. Chapel Hill: University of North Carolina Press, 1987.
Walter, Brian D. "Two Organ-Grinders: Duality and Discontent in *Bend Sinister*." In *Discourse and Ideology in Nabokov's Prose*, edited by David H. J. Larmour, 24-40. London: Routledge, 2002.
Warshow, Robert. "The Liberal Conscience in *The Crucible*." In Arthur Miller, *The Crucible*, edited by Gerald Weales, 210-26. 1953. New York: Penguin Books, 1996.
Washington v. Davis. 426 US 229 (1976).
Watson, Mary Ann. "The Kennedy-Nixon Debates: The Launch of Television's Transformation of U.S. Politics and Popular Culture." In *The Cambridge Companion to John F. Kennedy*, edited by Andrew Hoberek, 45-58. Cambridge, UK: Cambridge University Press.
Watt, Ian. *The Rise of the Novel*. Berkeley: University of California Press, 1957.
Weales, Gerald. "Introduction." In Arthur Miller, *Death of a Salesman*, vii-xx. New York: Viking Critical Library, 1996.

Weiner, Rachel. "Va. State Sen. Stephen H. Martin criticized for 'host' comment in antiabortion Facebook post." *Washington Post* 25 Feb. 2014. http://www.washingtonpost.com/local/virginia-politics/virginia-senator-martin-criticized-for-host-in-anti-abortion-facebook-post/2014/02/25/f2b32d94-9e55-11e3-b8d8-94577ff66b28_story.html. Web access: 3 Mar. 2015.

Weingarten, Karen. *Abortion in the American Imagination: Before Life and Choice, 1880–1940*. New Brunswick, NJ: Rutgers University Press, 2014.

Werner, Craig. "Bigger's Blues: *Native Son* and the Articulation of Afro-American Modernism." In *New Essays on Native Son*, edited by Keneth Kinnamon, 117–52. Cambridge, UK: Cambridge University Press, 1990.

Wertham, Frederic. "An Unconscious Determinant in *Native Son*." *Journal of Clinical Psychopathology and Psychotherapy* 6 July 1944, 111–15.

West, Cornell. *The American Evasion of Philosophy: A Genealogy of Pragmatism*. Madison: University of Wisconsin Press, 1989.

Westbrook, Russell. *John Dewey and American Democracy*. Ithaca, NY: Cornell University Press, 1991.

Williams, Raymond. *Modern Tragedy*. 1966. Verso: London, 1979.

Williams, William Appleman. *The Tragedy of American Diplomacy*. 1959. New York: Norton, 1972.

Wills, Gary. *The Kennedy Imprisonment: A Meditation on Power*. Boston: Little, Brown, 1982.

———. "Richard Nixon: The Last Liberal." *Washington Monthly* (Oct 1970), 22–33.

Winning, Joanne. "'Ezra through the Open Door': The Parties of Natalie Barney, Adrienne Monnier, and Sylvia Beach as Lesbian Modernist Cultural Production." In *The Modernist Party*, edited by Kate McLoughlin, 127–46. Edinburgh, Scotland: Edinburgh University Press, 2013.

Wise, Gene. "'Paradigm Dramas' in American Studies: A Cultural and Institutional History of the Movement." *American Quarterly* 31.3 (1979), 293–337.

Wise, Tim. *Colorblind: The Rise of Post-Racial Politics and the Retreat from Racial Equity*. San Francisco: City Lights Books, 2010.

Wolin, Sheldon. *Democracy Incorporated: Managed Democracy and the Specter of Inverted Totalitarianism*. Princeton, NJ: Princeton University Press, 2008.

Wood, Gordon S. *The Creation of the American Republic, 1776–1787*. Chapel Hill: University of North Carolina Press, 1969.

Wood, Michael. *The Magician's Doubts: Nabokov and the Risks of Fiction*. Princeton, NJ: Princeton University Press, 1994.

Wright, Richard. "How 'Bigger' Was Born." In *Native Son*, 431–62. New York: Harper, 2005.

———. "Introduction." In St. Clair Drake and Horace R. Cayton, *Black Metropolis: A Study of Negro Life in a Northern City*, xvii–xxxiv. New York: Harper and Row, 1962.

———. *Native Son*. 1940. New York: Harper, 2005.
Young, James P. *Reconsidering American Liberalism: The Troubled Odyssey of the Liberal Idea*. Boulder, CO: Westview Press, 1996.
Žižek, Slavoj. *Did Somebody Say Totalitarianism? Five Interventions in the (Mis)use of a Notion*. London: Verso, 2001.
Zox-Weaver, Annalisa. *Women Modernists and Fascism*. Cambridge, UK: Cambridge University Press, 2011.

Index

Aaron, Daniel, 119
abortion. *See* reproductive rights/abortion
Abstract Expressionism, 138
abstraction, 2, 181
abstraction/embodiment dualism, 2, 10, 17, 22, 24, 36, 71, 105, 184
academic Left, 3, 182
adoption, transracial, 95-96
Adorno, Theodor W., 136, 143, 144, 223n15; *The Authoritarian Personality,* 74; "Commitment," 57; *Dialectic of Enlightenment,* 131-32
Advisory Council on the Arts, 155
aestheticism, 14, 57-58, 146, 159, 163
affirmative action, 68, 93-94, 95
African Americans: Black Arts movement, 96; cultural and political consciousness, 96; social psychology, 71-77; as voters, 67. *See also* color-blind law; racial liberalism
Agee, James, 14, 123, 130, 131, 139, 154, 216n65, 217n69; *A Death in the Family,* 119; on journalism, 217n73; social documentary critique, 106, 108-15, 118-19, 121-22, 130, 131; tragic sensibility, 28, 139, 217n73, 218n81, 218n82, 219n88. See also *Let Us Now Praise Famous Men*
alienation, 29, 42, 71, 138, 141, 145, 150, 152, 156, 159
Allport, Gordon, *The Nature of Prejudice,* 74
Alsop, Stewart, 153
ambiguity, 13, 24, 96, 97, 100, 128; of post-WWI intellectual discourse, 103, 115, 117, 118, 122
American Enterprise Institute, 182, 211n122
American Federation of Labor, 67

American liberalism: during 1930s, 3, 5, 9-10, 16-17, 104-5, 150; academic Left criticism, 3; core concepts, 1-2; definitions, 1-7, 56, 179, 180; Dewey on new liberalism, 5, 10, 12, 36, 114, 118, 122, 124, 160-61, 164, 178, 179, 181, 219n97, discursive origins, 14-23; as intellectual tradition, 1-4; new liberalism, 104, 115, 139, 186n18; Niebuhr on new liberalism, 6, 12, 28, 103, 104-5, 106, 123-28, 136, 179, 219n97; post-WWII, 6, 100, 103-36; reconstruction, 23-30, 183-84; reductive attacks on, 182-83; relationship with modernism, 4, 6, 11, 13; semantic erosion, 182, 183, 184; tragic sensibility, 129, 130. *See also* postwar liberalism
American Philosophy Association, 127
Americans for Democratic Action, 9, 67, 76, 77, 125, 126, 228n79
American studies, 11-12
Amis, Kingsley, 230n125
Anderson, Amanda, 3, 13, 18-19, 103, 117, 185n5
anti-communism, 15, 76, 123, 142, 145-46, 232n160
anti-liberalism, modernist, 7-9, 186n16, 186n21
Arendt, Hannah, 156-57, 226n30; *Origins of Totalitarianism,* 142, 149
art, modern, 181-82, 202n117; as aesthetic experience, 23-24; as ideological propaganda, 145-46, 167; as modernist aesthetic, 61-62; moral realism, 118; post-WWII literary critics' view, 115, 116-17;

art, modern (*continued*) style as principle of, 137-39; tensions, 115, 116-17; tragic complexities, 118. *See also* modernism; modern literature
Arvidson, Heather, 197n48, 201n104, 202n116
Athanasiou, Athena, *Dispossession: The Performative in the Political*, 55-56
Atlantic Monthly, 73
atomic bomb, 28, 103, 119, 124, 126
Auden, W. H., 8, 146
Auschwitz, 8-9, 28, 119
authoritarianism; individualism *vs.*, 143-44, 223n15; totalitarianism vs., 226n30
autonomy, 2; aesthetic, 163; intellectual, 143-44, 145-49, 150-51. *See also* individual autonomy
autonomy/dependence dualism, 10, 184

Badger, Jonathan, 129
Baldridge, Letitia, *In the Kennedy Style*, 155
Baldwin, James, 71, 92, 93, 96, 98, 99, 100, 116, 155; "Everybody's Protest Novel," 87, 100; *The Evidence of Things Not Seen*, 97, 100; "Many Thousands Gone," 87, 100, 209n93; on *Native Son*, 91; poetry, 97-98. *See also* N*ative Son*
Barnhiesel, Greg, *Cold War Modernists*, 138, 167
Baron, Dennis, 88
Barth, Karl, 123
Baudelaire, Charles, 116
Bay of Pigs invasion, 171
Beard, Charles, 103
Beckett, Samuel, *Endgame*, 137
Bell, Daniel, 103, 119
Bell, Duncan, 19
Bellow, Saul, 121, 155
Bentham, Jeremy, 18
Bentley, Eric, 133
Bercovitch, Sacvan: *The American Jeremiad*, 11; *Ideology and Classic American Literature* (ed.), 11
Berlin, Isaiah, 129; "Two Concepts of Liberty," 125
Berman, Russell, 8-9
Black Arts movement, 96
Blackmun, Harry, 94, 200n77

Blair, Sara, 8-9
Bland, Alden, *Behold a Cry*, 75
Blease, W. L., *Short History of English Liberalism*, 19
blindness metaphor: in Baldwin's works, 97-98; of liberalism, 104-5; in *Native Son* (Wright), 14, 26-27, 79-82, 85-86, 88-90, 96, 99-100, 208n77, 208n88
Bone, Robert, 73
Bonilla, Silva, 94-95
Bourke-White, Margaret, *You Have Seen Their Faces*, 107, 110
Bourne, Randolph, 41, 191n66; "The War and the Intellectuals," 40
Boyd, Brian, 160, 225n22
Brennan, William J., 94
Brenner, Anita, 37
Brooks, Cleanth, 117; *Understanding Poetry*, 115
Brooks, Van Wyck, 41
Brown, Lloyd, *Irony City*, 75
Brown, Wendy, 1-2, 10, 22, 50-51, 57, 90, 176, 180, 185n4
Brown v. Board of Education, 26, 68, 72, 77, 78, 79, 84, 91, 94, 203n6, 206n55, 207n56, 207n70, 208n80, 208n86
Burke, Kenneth, 25, 34-35, 36, 45-46, 56, 63, 183, 197n42; *Attitudes Toward History*, 42
Bush, Ronald, 165
Butler, Judith, 183; *Dispossession: The Performative in the Political*, 55-56

Caldwell, Erskine, 107; *You Have Seen Their Faces*, 107, 110
Cambridge Introduction to Modernism, 8
capitalism, 135-36, 138-39; consumer, 131-32; industrial, 41, 130. *See also* corporate capitalism
Carmichael, Stokely, 92
Cato Institute, 182, 211n122
Cayton, Horace, 73; *Black Metropolis*, 74
Central Intelligence Agency (CIA), 138, 145-46, 162, 171
Chambers, Whittaker, 123
character: democratic, 142-50; moral, 19, 83, 159; personality vs, 224n15; as political style, 151, 152, 153-54, 156, 169, 170-71, 172, 173; style as, 150, 164

character-formation, 6, 10, 27, 139; politics of, 140, 142-50, 151, 152. *See also* individual autonomy
Chase, Richard, *The American Novel and Its Tradition*, 115-16
Christian realism, 124
Ciepley, David, 33-34, 142
civil rights: 1930s-1940s, 67-68; affirmative action, 68, 93-94, 95; anti-communism and, 76; as Cold War issue, 232n160; conservatives' position, 182; Democratic Party's support, 76-77; economic reform and, 67; legislative support, 76-77; liberalism's support, 67-68, 218n81. *See also* color-blind law
Civil Rights Act of 1964, Title VII, 93
Clark, Eleanor, 133
Clark, Kenneth, 74, 76, 77-78, 92-93
Clark, Lorenne, 54
class consciousness, 25, 42, 114, 153
classical liberalism, 4-5, 10, 33, 135-36; decline/failure, 7-8, 16, 21-22, 23, 24, 25, 134, 178; equality/differences dualism, 92; neoliberalism and, 180; racial inequality and, 95; Republican Party and, 182-83
Clinton, Bill, 177
Cohen, Elliot, 37
Cold War, 8, 115, 123; cultural, 138-39, 167-68; segregation during, 76
Cold War liberal discourse, 3-4, 10-11, 15, 125-27, 141, 179; civil rights as issue during, 232n160; liberal democracy vs. totalitarianism, 142-50; modernist art/liberalism relationship, 138-39; modernist style, 137-74; Niebuhr's influence on, 10-11, 125, 126, 219n97; totalitarian vs. democratic character, 142-50; tragic sensibility, 28, 126
Coles, Robert, 126
color-blind law, 12, 14; *Brown v. Board of Education*, 26, 68, 72, 77, 78, 79, 84, 91, 94; conservative reactionaries' response, 68, 71, 87-96; disparate-impact laws, 94; Equal Protection Clause and, 51, 79, 84, 85, 91, 94; individualism and, 94-95; as liberal aporia, 96-97; *Native Son* as critique of, 79-100; neoconservatives's response, 93; *Plessy v. Ferguson*, 26, 68, 77, 78-79,

84; racial differences/racial equality under, 70, 71, 79, 82-83, 84, 86, 87, 90, 91, 93, 97; as racial liberalism ideal, 68-69, 77-87; white Americans' moral hypocrisy and, 84-85; white supremacy and, 83-84, 95
Commentary, 92, 93
communism, 8, 20, 41, 46, 64-65, 123, 197n41, 204n24, 202n117; anti-communism, 15, 76, 123, 142, 145-46
Communist Manifesto (Marx), 108, 113, 213n18
Communist Party, 64, 73, 205n25, 205n26, 209n97
conflict: individual autonomy *vs.* collective suffering, 112; modernism's preoccupation with, 13; in modern life, 19, 181-82; political, 45, 66; social, 42; tragic sensibility of, 105, 115, 117, 122, 125, 131
Congress for Cultural Freedom, 9, 125, 138, 146, 219n97
Congress of Industrial Organizations (CIO), 9, 67
Connolly, William, 129
conservatism, 172; color-blind law response, 68, 71, 87-96; of postwar liberal intellectuals, 122
constitutive dualisms, of liberalism, 2, 4, 6-7, 10, 13, 14, 22; abstraction/embodiment, 2, 10, 17, 22, 24, 36, 71, 105; anti-racism applications, 75-76; color-blind law and, 95-96; equality/difference, 2, 10, 22, 50, 105, 125, 174; frictions in, 118; gendered nature, 90; individual/social, 2, 24; individual/social dualism, 22, 184; liberty/necessity, 2, 50; modernist style and, 141; of politics, 129, 167-68; possessive individualism and, 36, 50-51; of post-WWII liberalism, 105-6; as public discourse, 172-73; public/private, 2, 10, 50, 105, 118, 160; racial liberalism and, 68, 71, 95-96; rights/needs, 2, 10, 184; of social documentaries, 112-13; unreconcilability, 160; value, 184
consumer culture, 147
consumerism, 138
contraceptives, 47, 48
contradiction, 115, 116, 118, 122
Cornell, Drucilla, 52

corporate capitalism, 173, 193n5, 193n7; neoliberalism and, 176, 178, 180-81, 183, 234n9; possessive individualism and, 23, 25, 33-34, 39, 40-41, 62, 196n37
Coulter, Ann, *How to Talk to a Liberal (If You Must),* 3
Couturier, Maurice, 140, 224n19
Crenshaw, Kimberlé Williams,
critical race theory, 2, 27, 68, 83, 90, 94, 193n102
critical theory, 2, 164
Croly, Herbert, 40
Cronkite, Walter, 168
cruelty, 29, 160, 161, 163, 164, 166
Cuban Missile Crisis, 171

Dalton, John, 82-83, 208n77
"Daltonism," 82-83, 208n77
Davis, Hugh, 108
Decker, Mark, 73
Declaration of Independence, 19
de la Durantaye, Leland, 160
DeLillo, Don, 168
de Man, Paul, 85
democratic character, totalitarianism vs., 142-50
Democratic Party, 153, 169; civil rights commitment, 76-77; Dixiecrats, 67, 77; "hip culture," 9, 228n80; political style, 140
Denby, David, 111
Denning, Michael, *The Cultural Front,* 9
Depoe, Stephen, 169
Derrida, Jacques, 161
Dewey, John, 5, 10, 12, 36, 103, 114, 116-17, 118, 122, 124, 160-61, 164, 178, 179, 181, 183, 216n51; *Art as Experience,* 22-24, 61-62; *Freedom and Culture,* 76; "How to Anchor Liberalism," 126-27; *How We Think,* 192n91; *Liberalism and Social Action,* 8, 17-18, 19, 22, 125-26, 198n57; Niebuhr and, 105, 129, 219n95, 219n97; on philosophy, 63; possessive individualism and, 25, 34-35, 46; on totalitarianism, 226n35
Dickens, Charles, 150; *Bleak House,* 13, 18, 224n18
Dickstein, Morris, 37
Dillon, Elizabeth Maddock, 13
documentation, of social and personal tragedy. *See* social documentaries

Dos Passos, John, 155, 213n17, 216n51
Dostoevsky, Fyodor, 69-70, 119, 123; 194n18, 195n22
Dragunoia, Dana, 160, 225n22
Drake, St Clair, *Black Metropolis,* 74

Eastman, Max, 37, 195n18
economics: post-Keynesian, 175-76, 177. *See also* corporate capitalism; free market
Eisenhower, Dwight, 116-17, 153, 155
Elia, Kazan, 155
Eliot, George, *Middlemarch,* 13
Eliot, T. S., 22, 116, 137, 145-46, 186n21; *After Strange Gods,* 7, 8
Ellison, Ralph, 71, 100, 121, 209n99; *An American Dilemma* review, 96; *Invisible Man,* 97, 212n155; "The World and the Jug," 98-99
"Emotional Health of Negroes, The," 74
Encounter, 138, 162
Engels, Friedrich, 42
equality, 4; abstract, 2, 24, 70, 75, 79, 90, 125
equality/difference dualism, 2, 22, 50, 105, 125, 174; racial, 70, 71, 79, 82-83, 86, 87, 90, 91, 93, 97
Esquire, 154
Euripides, 120
Evans, Walker, 214n37; *American Photographs,* 107; *Let Us Now Praise Famous Men,* 106-15, 120-21

Fadiman, Clifton, 37
fascism, 7, 8, 14, 20, 103
Faulkner, William, 121
Federal Art, Music, Theater, and Writers' Projects, 9, 107, 222n143
Felski, Rita, *The Limits of Critique,* 183
feminism, 49
feminist critical theory, 2, 36, 38, 53, 56-57, 185n4, 193n102
Fishburn, Katherine, 88
Fisher, Dorothy Canfield, 69-70
Fitzgerald, Robert, 120
Flaubert, Gustave, 137, 158
Ford, Henry, 123-24
Ford Foundation, 138
Fortune, 107, 217n73
Foster, Richard, 133

Index

Foucault, Michel, 3, 16; *The Birth of Biopolitics,* 179-80
Fourteenth Amendment, 34; Equal Protection Clause, 51, 79, 84, 85, 91, 94, 200n77
Fox, Richard Wightman, 123, 130-31
Frankfurter, Felix, 126
Frankfurt School, 132, 136, 170
free market, 7, 14-15, 16, 18, 20, 33, 41, 75, 135; neoliberalism and, 177-78, 179, 233n7, 234n9
Freud, Sigmund, 117-18
Friedman, Milton, 16, 175-76, 177, 179, 184, 234n10
Friedman, Susan Stanford, 17; "Periodizing Modernism," 14
Fromm, Erich, *Escape from Freedom,* 143
Frost, Robert, 155
Fukuyama, Francis, *The End of History and the Last Man,* 16

Galbraith, John Kenneth, 126, 146, 151, 228n79; *Affluent Society,* 150
Garcia, Jay, 96-97; *Psychology Comes to Harlem,* 74, 203n8
Gassner, John, 133
gender: as literary focus, 14; possessive individualism and, 35-39, 43-44, 49-50, 51-54, 57, 59, 63
Gerstle, Gary, 1
Gibson, Donald, 87-88
Gillette, Meg, 48
Gladstone, William, 18, 150
Glazer, Nathan, 92; *Affirmative Discrimination,* 93; *The Lonely Crowd,* 145, 154-55
Glenn, John, 155
Gold, Mike, "Why I Am a Communist," 7
Goldwater, Barry, 67
Gotanda, Neil, 91
Grant, Ulysses S., 20
Great Depression, 20-21, 104, 107; abortion during, 47-48; corporate capitalism, 41; liberalism during, 3-4, 10, 16, 25; possessive individualism during, 25-26; social documentaries, 107. *See also* New Deal; Roosevelt, Franklin D.
Great Society, 22, 182
Greenberg, Clement, 61
Grenfield, Jeff, 155
Guilbaut, Serge, 138

Haag, Pamela, 50
Habermas, Jürgen, 161
Hadley, Elaine, *Living Liberalism,* 18-19
Haney-Lopez, Ian, 79, 91, 94
Harberger, Arnold, 176
Hardwick, Elizabeth, 43
Hargrove, Erwin, *The Power of the Modern Presidency,* 172
Harlan, John Marshall, 26, 68, 78, 79, 84
Harris, Charles K., 62
Hartz, Louis, *The Liberal Tradition in America,* 15
Harvey, David, 176, 177
Hayek, Friedrich, 178; *The Road to Serfdom,* 179
Hegel, Georg Wilhelm Friedrich, 63; *Lectures on Fine Art,* 113
Hegeman, Susan, 111
Heidegger, Martin, 161
Hellman, John, 140, 154
Hemingway, Ernest, 38; "Hills Like White Elephants," 48; *The Old Man and the Sea,* 228n79
Herder, Johann Gottfried, 158
Heritage Foundation, 182, 211n122
Hilgart, John, 110
Himes, Chester, *If He Hollers Let Him Go,* 75
Hines, Lewis, 110
Hiroshima and Nagasaki, 28, 119, 124
Hiss, Alger, 123
Hitler, Adolf, 8, 103, 124, 139, 142, 149, 209n93
Hobbes, Thomas, 33
Hobhouse, L. T., *Liberalism,* 19
Hobson, J. A., 19
Hoffman, Abbie, 168
Hofstadter, Richard, 126, 152, 153
Holmes, Oliver Wendell, 73
Homer, 120
homophobia, 153, 154
homosexuality, 227n61
Hook, Sidney, 37, 38, 92, 103, 127
Hoover, Herbert, 20-21; *The Challenge to Liberty,* 20
Hoover Institution, 211n122
Horkheimer, Max, 136, 144; *Dialectic of Enlightenment,* 131-32
Horton, Carol, 84
Horton, William, 122

Houghton Mifflin, 114
House on Un-American Activities Committee, 12, 15, 123
Howe, Irving, 73, 209n99; "Black Boys and Native Sons," 98; *The Culture of Modernism*, 7
Hughes, Langston, 84; "Justice," 77
Humphrey, Hubert, 105, 123, 126, 127-28, 228n80
Hyde, Alan, 27, 51

Ibsen, Henrik, 136; *A Doll's House*, 132; *Enemy of the People*, 132
individual agency, 130-36
individual autonomy, 14-15, 16, 17-18, 139-40, 154, 221n131; relationship to intellect, 164; social dependence vs., 2, 24; in social documentaries, 28, 110-11; totalitarianism vs., 143-44, 145-49, 150-51; in tragic drama, 221n131
individualism, 1, 2, 20; authoritarianism vs., 143-44; color-blind law and, 94-95; free market, 41; Jeffersonian, 40; laissez-faire, 124; legal reactionary interpretation, 87, 91-92; political, 22; portrayal in *Native Son*, 99-100; post-WWII liberalism's concept of, 122. See also possessive individualism
individual rights, 4-5
individual/social dualism, 22, 184
intelligence, creative, 17, 23-24
International Labor Defense, 73
irony, 6, 10, 14, 24-26, 100, 103, 117, 181-82; of history, 140; liberal ironists, 159-68; as New Critics' keyword, 115; tragic, 28. See also under individual literary works

Jackson, Andrew, 172
Jackson, Lawrence, 71-72
Jackson, Walter, 75, 77
James, Henry, 117; *The Princess Casamassima*, 117-18
Jameson, Fredric, 61, 137-38, 167, 168
Jay, Martin, 82
Jefferson, Thomas, 40, 155
Jerng, Mark, 211n138
John Reed Clubs, 73
Johnson, Barbara, 56

Johnson, Lyndon B., 67, 222n143, 229n96, 233n175
Joyce, James, 116, 137, 141; *Finnegan's Wake*, 137; *Ulysses*, 58-59, 66, 201n103
Joyce, Joyce Ann, 88
Julius Rosenwald Fund, 69, 75, 203n10

Kafka, Franz, 116
Kazin, Alfred, 73; "President Kennedy and Other Intellectuals," 157
Keats, John, 117-18, 128, 180-81; "Ode on a Grecian Urn," 175-76, 181
Kempton, Murray, 38
Kennan, George F., 123
Kennedy, Jacqueline, 155
Kennedy, John F., 28-29, 93, 123, 140, 153-57, 158, 179, 185n2; assassination, 141, 159-60, 168; civil rights position, 171, 232n160; on liberalism, 151, 228n79; liberal totalitarianism and, 168-74; personal and political styles, 25, 29, 140, 141, 151, 153-57, 229n82, 229n84, 229n99, 230n103; *Profiles in Courage*, 153-54; use of irony, 155-56; *Why England Slept*, 153
Kennedy, Randall, 91, 94
Kent, Rockwell, 107
Keynes, John Maynard, *The General Theory of Employment, Interest and Money*, 175
Kierkegaard, Sören, 119, 123
King, Martin Luther, Jr., 92
King Lear (Shakespeare), 108-9, 113, 117, 133, 214n37, 215n40
Kinnamon, Keneth, 69-70, 75
Kirsch, Adam, 116
Klein, Naomi, 176
Kristeva, Julia, *Possessions*, 57
Kristol, Irving, 93
Krupnick, Mark, 118
Krutch, Joseph Wood, 213n6; *The Modern Temper*, 130-31
Ku Klux Klan, 73
Kull, Andrew, 68, 78, 79, 84

labor movement, anti-discrimination policies, 67
Labor Non-Partisan League, 67
laissez-faire: capitalism, 177-78; economics, 22, 40, 180; individualism, 20-21, 124; liberalism, 18, 19, 25, 40, 46, 180, 199n71

Lange, Dorothea, *American Exodus*, 107
Lange, Lynda, 54
Lasch, Christopher, 42, 167
leadership, heroic, 12, 29, 106-7, 140, 154, 155, 168-74
legal equality, race-blind. *See* color-blind law
legal realism, 73
LeGuin, Ursula K., *The Dispossessed*, 57
Let Us Now Praise Famous Men (Agee and Evans), 24-25, 28, 106-15, 118-19, 214n20, 214n36; as failure, 215n41; 1960 re-release, 28, 106, 120; tragic sensibility, 111-15, 120-22, 214n37; Trilling's praise for, 118-19, 122
liberal democracy, 7-8, 138-40, 163; totalitarianism *vs.*, 28-29, 142-50, 223n15
liberal ironists, 159-68
liberalism: core concepts, 1-2; historical presentation, 189n52. *See also* American liberalism; classical liberalism; neoliberalism; postwar liberalism
"Liberalism and the Negro" roundtable, 92, 93
liberal modernism, 6
Liberal Party, 18, 190n64
Liberal Republican Party, 20
liberals: definition, 160; right-wing stereotypes, 3
liberty, 2; positive and negative views on, 125
liberty/necessity dualism, 2, 50
Life, 107
Lincoln, Abraham, 172
Lippmann, Walter, 10, 22, 25, 34-35, 40, 41, 46, 49, 191n66; *(An Inquiry into the Principles of) The Good Society*, 178, 234n9; *Drift and Mastery*, 34, 46; Lippmann Colloquium, 178, 179-80
Locke, John, 2, 4, 17-18, 33, 41, 45, 54, 125, 186n10, 188n39; *Second Treatise on Government*, 19-20
Lucaites, John Louis, 107
Lucas, Curtis, *Third Ward Newark*, 75
Luce, Henry, 107, 108, 119, 120, 123, 217n69, 217n73, 219n88
Lukács, Georg, 114
Lustig, Jeffrey, 34, 41
lynching, 67, 73, 76-77

Macdonald, Dwight, "Death of a Poet," 119-20

MacKinnon, Catherine, 51
MacLeish, Archibald, 155
Macpherson, C. B., 33, 45
Mailer, Norman, 3, 14, 29, 121, 141, 156, 168-69, 173-74; *Advertisements for Myself*, 168; *Presidential Papers*, 169, 170-71; "Superman Comes to the Supermarket," 154, 169
Malcolm X, 92
Malraux, André, 155
Manchester School, 20
Mangrum, Ben, *Land of Tomorrow*, 10, 146-47
Marcuse, Herbert, *One-Dimensional Man*, 170
Marshall, Thurgood, 78, 94
Martin, Steve, 47, 49
Marx, Karl, 38, 42; *The Communist Manifesto*, 108, 113, 213n18
Marxism, 15, 42, 114, 124, 127, 198n53
mass culture, 152, 168, 221n132
mass media, 143-44; political tyranny relationship, 143-44; presidential use of, 171, 172, 173
Masterpieces of the Twentieth Century Festival, 146
McCann, Sean, 168; *A Pinnacle of Feeling*, 9, 172
McCarthy, Eugene, 222n143; 228n80
McCarthy, Joseph, 15, 118, 153, 222n143
McClintock, Anne, 128-29
McGowan, John, 185n8
McLean, Helen, 74
McLoughlin, Kate, *The Modernist Party*, 59
McNeely, Trevor, 165
Melamed, Jodi, 69, 71, 75, 76, 99
Melville, Herman, 115, 116
Mendelman, Lisa, 201n104
Mill, John Stuart, 18, 150, 161
Miller, Arthur, 14, 155, 169-70, 222n143; *Death of a Salesman*, 130, 132-36; essays, 133; on tragedy, 222n145
Miller, D. Quentin, 98
Miller, Perry, 126; *Errand into the Wilderness*, 11; *The New England Mind*, 11
Mills, C. Wright, 127; *White Collar: The American Middle Class*, 145
Mirowski, Philip, *Road from Mont Pèleri: The Making of the Neoliberal Thought Collective*, 178, 180-81, 234n14

modernism: end of, 167-68; late, 167-68; redefinition during Cold War, 138; relationship with liberalism, 4, 6, 11, 13; tragic liberal imagination and, 115-22. *See also* art, modern

modernist studies, 11-12

modern literature: liberal politics and, 7-14; social meaning, 24

Moon, Donald, 129

moral idealism, 123

moral realism, 5, 105, 106, 117, 118, 121-22, 123, 216n55

moral reform, 185n9

Morgenthau, Hans, 126

Motley, Willard, *Knock on Any Door,* 75

Mouffe, Chantal, 129

Moynihan, Daniel, 93

Mumford, Lewis, 34-35, 46; *Technics and Civilization,* 41-42; tragic sensibility and, 213n6

Murakawa, Naomi, 77

Murphy, Frank, 78

Murray, J. Middleton, 137

Mussolini, Benito, 7, 22, 178, 209n93

Myrdal, Gunnar, 92; *An American Dilemma,* 69, 72, 75-78, 96

NAACP, 68, 78, 206n54

Nabokov, Dmitri, 159-60, 225n22

Nabokov, Nicholas, 146, 147

Nabokov, Vladimir, 12, 14, 28-29, 159-60; *Bend Sinister,* 139, 142, 143-50, 151, 158, 160, 161, 164, 231n138; biographic criticism, 225n22; *Lectures on Literature,* 140, 224n18; as liberal humanist, 159, 225n22; as liberal ironist, 159-68; *Lolita,* 138, 141, 159-68, 230n125, 231n126, 231n138; *Pale Fire,* 167; *Pnin,* 139, 150-53, 157-59, 164; *Speak, Memory,* 140; style, 140-41, 146-50, 151-59, 224n18; 224n20

Naiman, Eric, 147, 148-49

National Endowment for the Arts, 155

Native Son (Wright), 68-100; Baldwin's and Ellison's critique, 96-97, 98, 100; blindness metaphor, 14, 26-27, 79-82, 85-86, 88-90, 96, 99-100, 208n77, 208n88; color-blind justice theme, 14, 82-87, 208n77; existential readings of, 209n97; influence on racial liberalism, 26-27, 68-69, 79-80,

99; irony, 24-25, 26, 87, 96, 99, 100; post-WWII criticism, 87-96, 98, 99, 116; as protest novel, 68-69, 74-75, 87, 116, 203n8, 204n15, 208-9n91; self-actualization/self-determination theme, 69-70, 87-96, 99-100, 204n15; sociological naturalism, 69-70, 84, 87, 97, 204n15; sociological protest in, 9, 71-77, 90, 99-100

naturalism: critique, 100; in *Let Us Now Praise Famous Men,* 112; liberal culture's identification with, 116; in *Native Son,* 70, 72, 84, 87, 97, 98

natural rights, 19, 22

Nazism, 73-74, 142, 146, 151, 158

neoconservatives, 93, 211n122

neoliberalism, 16, 30, 175-84, 233n8, 233n7, 233n176, 234n10, 234n14; corporate capitalism and, 176, 178, 180-81, 183, 234n9

New Criticism, 24, 115-16, 117, 137

New Deal, 64, 115, 126, 172; comparison with New Freedom and New Frontier, 185n2; cultural politics, 107; racial liberalism, 67, 90, 91; social documentaries, 106, 107, 108, 109, 119, 121, 130; social engineering policies, 75; social welfare policies, 9, 21, 22, 179-80, 182

New Freedom, 172, 185n2

New Frontier, 169, 185n2

New Left, 15

New Modernist Studies, 11

New Nationalism, 172

New Republic, 30, 40, 190n66

New Right, 15

New Yorker, 63, 119-20

New York intellectuals, 37

New York Times, 21, 78, 107, 133

Niebuhr, Reinhold, 67, 219n95, 219n96; *Beyond Tragedy,* 124; *Christianity and Crisis* (journal), 127-28; influence on John F. Kennedy, 140; *Irony and American History,* 126; *Moral Man and Immoral Society,* 124; *On the Nature and Destiny of Man,* 8; new liberalism and, 6, 12, 28, 103, 104-5, 106, 123-28, 136, 179, 219n97; tragic sensibility and. 213n6

Nietzsche, Friedrich, 21-22, 161, 192n86; *The Birth of Tragedy,* 112

Nixon, Richard, 154, 229n82, 233n175

Norman, Will, 11

Norris, Frank, *The Octopus*, 34
Nowlin, Michael, 100

Oakeshott, Michel, 129
Obama, Barack, 173
O'Connor, Sandra Day, 91
Odets, Clifford, 118-19
Offord, Carl, *The White Face*, 75
Olin, Jack M., 16
Olson, Elder, 133
O'Neill, Eugene, 132-33
Oppenheimer, Robert, 155
Ordoliberalism, 180
Orwell, George, *1984*, 142

paradox, 100, 103, 115-16
Paris Review, 140
Parrington, Vernon, *Main Currents in American Thought*, 11
Parson, Talcott, 126
parties (social gatherings), in modernist culture, 58-63, 65-66
Partisan Review, 100, 116, 127, 138, 217n69
Pateman, Carole, 49-50, 90
Pater, Walter, 137, 168
personhood, 12, 25, 33, 34, 56, 134
pessimism, 103, 104, 126, 130
Petry, Ann, *The Street*, 75
Phillips, Wendell, 78
Pitzer, Andrea, 160
Playboy, 140
Plehwe, Dieter, *Road from Mont Pèleri: The Making of the Neoliberal Thought Collective*, 178, 180-81, 234n14
Plessy, Homer, 78
Plessy v. Ferguson, 26, 68, 77, 78-79, 84, 206n55, 207n70
pluralism, 11, 129, 145
Pocock, J. G. A., 15
Podhoretz, Norman, 92, 93
political style, 12, 25, 28-29; Franklin D, Roosevelt, 21, 172; heroic leadership, 12, 29, 106-7, 140, 154, 155, 168-74; John F. Kennedy, 140, 141, 151, 153-57; personality and, 145, 150-51
politics: of character, 151, 152; constitutive dualisms of, 129, 167-68; left-*versus*-right spectrum, 3, 21, 186n22; liberal aesthetic, 139-40; of literature, 13-14; of style, 150-59

Pollock, Jackson, 138
Poovey, Mary, 51, 56
Portelli, Alessandro, 87
possessive individualism, 25-26, 33-66, 124-25, 185n9, 199n71; consumer capitalism and, 132; corporate capitalism and, 23, 25, 33-34, 39, 40-41, 62; in *Death of a Salesman*, 133-35; dispossession as antithesis, 35, 42-44, 45, 55-56, 57, 66; feminist critical theory, 56-57; gender and sexual politics of, 35-39, 43-44, 49-50, 51-54, 57, 59, 63; Niebuhr on, 127; pre-WWI, 33-34, 39-40; reproductive rights and, 35-39, 46-63, 174, 200n81
Post, Robert, 93
postmodernism, 167-68
poststructuralism, 2, 3, 16, 56, 63, 160, 164
postwar liberalism, 10-11, 103-36, 203n1; conservatism, 122; constitutive dualisms, 105-6; executive power relationship, 127-28; intellectuals' political status, 197n50; during Kennedy Administration, 153-57; style, 137-74; totalitarianism as focus, 142; tragic sensibility, 25, 103-22, 139. *See also* new liberalism
Pound, Ezra, 7, 22, 178, 186n21
pragmatism, 160
presidential power, 9, 127-28, 141; heroic leadership and, 12, 29, 106-7, 140, 154, 155, 168-74; liberal totalitarianism and, 168-74; mass media use and, 171, 232n167, 232n169; revisionary studies, 233n175
price theory, 175-76, 181
print culture, 12-13
Progressive era, 39-40, 110
Progressives, 20, 35, 41, 115; 190n64, 191n66
property relations, 12, 196n37
protest novels, 68-69, 74-75, 87, 116
Proust, Marcel, 116, 145-46
"Psychological Approach to Race Relations, The," 74
public/private dualism, 2, 50, 105, 118, 160

Rabinowitz, Paula, 112; *Labor & Desire*, 38
race: changing concepts of, 73-74; as literary focus, 14
race-blindness. *See* color-blind law

race novels, 68-69, 71, 74-75; narrative realism, 68-70, 75
racial classification, reparative, 87, 91, 93
racial differences, 82-83
racial equality: as reverse discrimination, 93, 182. *See also* equality/difference, racial
racial liberalism, 14, 25, 67-100, 210n108; 1960s<N>1990s, 92-100; African-American consciousness and, 96; Agee and, 218n81; *An American Dilemma* and, 72; color-blind law and, 68-69, 70-71, 77-87, 104; *Native Son* as foundational text, 68-69, 79-80, 99; sociological research and, 73-77; as white liberalism, 92-93; white moral hypocrisy and, 77, 79, 84-85
racism, 75-76, 90-91; color-blind law and, 68, 70-71; psychological effects, 72-75, 76, 77; structural/systemic, 83, 85, 94
radicalism, as literary focus, 14
Rahv, Phillip, 38
Ramsey, Priscilla, 81
Rancière, Jacques, 137
Ransom, John Crowe, 137
Rawls, John, 2; *A Theory of Justice*, 15-16
Reagan, Leslie, *When Abortion Was a Crime*, 48
Reagan, Ronald, 3, 177, 180, 182
realist novels, 13, 19
Regents of the University of California v. Bakke, 93-94
Rehnquist, William, 91
reproductive rights/abortion, 6, 12, 25, 198n60, 199n62; during 1930s, 26, 47-48, 199n74; conservatives' opposition, 182; intellectuals' attitudes toward, 54-56; legal decisions affecting, 51, 55, 93-94, 200n75, 200n80; possessive individualism and, 26, 35-39, 46-63, 174, 200n81
Republican Party, 3, 64, 156, 182-83
Reuther, Walter, 67
Riesman, David, 139, 153, 154, 164; *The Lonely Crowd*, 145, 154-55
rights/needs dualism, 2, 184
Riis, Jacob, 110
Rilke, Rainer Maria, 116
Robbins, Bruce: "Everything is Not Neoliberalism," 177; *Upward Mobility*, 9
Rockefeller Foundation, 69, 75
Roe v. Wade, 51, 55, 93-94, 200n77, 200n80

Rokeach, Milton, *The Open and Closed Mind*, 145
Roosevelt, Eleanor, 71, 76, 126
Roosevelt, Franklin D., 7, 172; "Brains Trust," 75; civil rights position, 67; fireside chats, 171, 232n169; liberalism, 20-22, 64-65, 124, 185n2; political style, 21, 172; rural poverty documentation, 107; welfare state policies, 21. *See also* New Deal
Roosevelt, Theodore, 172, 232n169
Rorty, Richard, 129, 141, 160; *Contingency, irony, and solidarity*, 141, 160-64, 166
Rosenblatt, Helena, *The Lost History of Liberalism*, 4-5
Rosenthal, Henry, 37
Rosler, Martha, 109-10
Rothstein, Arthur, 107
Rotunda, Ronald, 21
Rowe, John Carlos, *Afterlives of Modernism*, 12; 188n32
rural poverty, social documentaries. See *Let Us Now Praise Famous Men* (Agee and Evans)

Santayana, George, 21-22
Saunders, Frances Stonor, 138, 145-46
Schaub, Thomas, 103, 115
Schechner, Mark, 118
Schickler, Eric, *Racial Realignment: The Transformation of American Liberalism*, 67-68
Schiller, Friedrich, 61, 158
Schlesinger, Arthur, Jr., 6, 10, 28, 105, 123, 151, 153, 179; Americans for Democratic Action and, 125, 228n79; *Kennedy or Nixon: Does It Make Any Difference?*, 154; new liberalism and, 104, 150; *The Vital Center*, 15, 76, 142, 171-72
Schoenbach, Lisi, *Pragmatic Modernism*, 10, 192n87
segregation, 68, 72, 76, 91; *Brown v. Board of Education*, 26, 68, 72, 77, 78, 79, 84, 91, 94, 207n56, 207n70; *Plessy v. Ferguson*, 68, 77, 78-79, 84, 207n70; psychological effects, 72, 77-78, 84; *Regents of the University of California v. Bakke*, 93-94
sentimentalism, 201n104
Serviceman's Readjustment Act (1944) (GI Bill), 115
sexual contract, 49-50

Shaw, George Bernard, 118-19
Sherman Act, 34
Shklar, Judith, 1, 160
Siegel, Reva, 93
Simpson, O. J., 95
sin, 123, 124
Siraganian, Lisa, *Modernism's Other Work*, 10
Slesinger, Tess, 14, 27, 125, 194n15; "After the Party," 63-66; "Mother to Dinner," 37; style, 195n19; *Time: The Present*, 37; *The Unpossessed*, 25-26, 35-39, 43-47, 51-55, 57-66, 194n18
Smith, Adam, 18, 45, 180
Smith, Valerie, 88
Smith, William Gardner, *The Last of the Conquerors*, 75
social action, 126-27
social contract, 15-16, 49-50, 90
Social Darwinism, 72
social documentaries, 6, 12, 213n17; Agee's critique, 106, 108-15, 118-19, 121-22, 130, 131; constitutive dualisms, 112-13; individualism portrayed in, 110-11; of the New Deal, 28, 106; tragic sensibility of, 113-15. *See also* Bourke-White, Margaret, *You Have Seen Their Faces*; *Let Us Now Praise Famous Men* (Agee and Evans)
Social Gospel, 123-24
socialism, 20, 64
social media, 153
social protest culture, 100
social psychology, 145; of African Americans, 71-77; influence on Black protest novels, 96
social realism, 24, 117
Social Security Administration, 9
socioeconomic inequality, 90
sociological jurisprudence movement, 73, 205n28
sociological research, racial liberalism and, 73-77
Solow, Herbert, 37
Sophocles, 120
Sorensen, Theodore, 153-54
Southern Agrarians, 115
Soviet Union, 35, 41, 126, 138-39, 142, 169
Spiegel, Alan, 120
Stalin, Joseph, 103, 121, 124, 139, 149, 209n93

Stearns, Harold, "*Liberalism in America: Its Origin, Its Temporary Collapse, Its Future*," 40-41
Stegner, Page, 152
Steinbeck, John, 118-19; *The Grapes of Wrath*, 116
Steiner, George, *The Death of Tragedy*, 131
Stevenson, Adlai, 126, 140, 153, 154, 155
Stewart, Potter, 91
Stott, William, 107; *Documentary Expression in Thirties American*, 121-22
Stratton, Matthew, *The Politics of Irony in American Modernism*, 24, 212n155
Stryker, Roy, 107
Student Nonviolent Coordinating Committee, 96
style, modernist, 137-74; during Cold War, 137-74; decline, 137-38; heroic, 29; individualism and, 137-39; political power relationship, 141; politics of, 150-59; Trilling on, 150, 223n14
stylistics, 151
Sumner, Charles, 78
Sutherland, Robert, *Color, Class, and Personality*, 74
Szalay, Michael, 90, 156; *Hip Figures*, 9, 228n80; *New Deal Modernism*, 9

Tate, Allen, 115
Taylor, Paul, *American Exodus*, 107
tenant farmers, social documentaries. *See Let Us Now Praise Famous Men* (Agee and Evans)
Tennessee Valley Authority, 107
Tennyson, Alfred, 21
tension, as New Critics' keyword, 115
Thatcher, Margaret, 177, 180
Thirteenth Amendment, 79
Thomas, Clarence, 91, 94
Time, 107, 123, 219n88
totalitarianism, 87, 126, 127, 132, 139, 147-48, 149, 151-52, 159; comparison with tyranny, 226n30; individual autonomy *vs.*, 143-44, 145-49, 150-51; liberal, 168-74; liberal democracy *vs.*, 28-29, 142-50
Tourgée, Albion, 78
tragedy, as dramatic form, 130-36, 220n120, 221n131, 222n145

tragic sensibility: of Cold War, 126; of *Let Us Now Praise Famous Men* (Agee and Evans), 111-15, 119, 120-22, 154; of the liberal imagination, 115-22, 212n3, 213n6, 213n13; of liberalism, 129, 130; Miller on, 133; as moral realism, 117, 118; of Niebuhr, 123-28; political, 12; of post-WWII intellectual discourse, 103-22, 154; pre-WWII, 213n6; of social documentaries, 111-15, 122; of Trilling, 123; Trilling on, 117-18, 164

Trask, Michael, 151

Trilling, Diana, 155

Trilling, Lionel, 6, 37, 38, 76, 103, 104-5, 106, 116-18, 123, 128, 136, 139, 140, 154, 155, 162, 164; "An American Classic," 122; "Greatness with One Fault in It," 118-19; *The Liberal Imagination*, 100, 105-6, 117, 118; *Matthew Arnold*, 150; on moral realism, 216n55; on narrative style, 150, 223n14; new liberalism and, 28; *The Opposing Self*, 55; the tragic liberal imagination and, 115-22, 213n6

Truman, Harry S., 67, 76, 115, 123, 153, 228n80

Trump, Donald, 173

Turner, Fred, 145

Unamuno, Miguel de, 119

Union for Democratic Action, 67, 76

United Kingdom, liberalism development, 17-20

US Constitution, 171-72; color blind nature, 77-78, 91, 93, 94; color blindness, 68, 78-79

US Information Agency (USIA), 138, 145-46

US Supreme Court, 9; *Brown v. Board of Education*, 26, 68, 72, 77, 78-79, 84, 91, 94, 203n6, 207n56, 207n70, 208n80, 208n86; color-blind justice, 78-79, 94-95; *Curran v. Bosze*, 200n81; *Gonzales v Carhart*, 200n75; *Moore v. Regents of the University of California*, 200n81; *Plessy v. Ferguson*, 26, 68, 77, 78-79, 84, 206n55, 207n70; *Regents of the University of California v. Bakke*, 93-94; *Roe v. Wade*, 51, 55, 93-94, 200n77, 200n80; *Washington v. Davis*, 94

University of Virginia, Page-Barbour Lectures, 8

Unpossessed, The (Slesinger), 25-26, 35-39, 43-47, 51-55, 57-66; irony, 60-61, 62; "Missis Flinders" chapter, 37, 47-48, 54-55; party scene, 58-63; possession individualism theme, 57-58; republication, 195n20

van der Brink, Bert, 129, *The Tragedy of Liberalism*, 220n119

Vanity Fair, 37

Veblen, Thorstein, 34-35, 41, 57, 103, 196n38; *Theory of the Leisure Class*, 39-40, 196n26

Victorian liberalism, 13, 18-19, 21-22, 150

Vidal, Gore, 156

Vietnam War, 128, 173, 222n143, 233n175

Vogel, Dan, 133

von Mises, Ludwig, 178; *Liberalismus* or *The Free and Prosperous Commonwealth*, 179

Wald, Alan, 37, 38

Wallace, Henry, 77, 115, 228n80

Walter, Brian, 161

Walter Lippmann Colloquium, 178, 179-80

Warren, Earl, 68, 77, 84; "Footnote 11," 77-78

Warren, Robert Penn, 117, 155; *Understanding Fiction* (Warren), 115

Watt, Ian, 80

Weales, Gerald, 133

West, Cornel, 127

Weyl, Walter, 40

White, Byron, 94

white supremacy, 83-84, 90-91, 92, 96

Whyte, William, *The Organization Man, The*, 145

Wilde, Oscar, 137

Williams, Raymond, 132, 136

Williams, Tennessee, 132-33, 155

Williams, William Appleman, *The Tragedy of American Diplomacy*, 126

Wilson, Edmund, 155

Wilson, Woodrow, 7, 40, 172, 185n2, 191n66, 232n169

Wirth, Louis, 73

Wolin, Sheldon, 173

Wood, Michael, 158

Woolf, Virginia, 59

Works Progress Administration, 9, 71

World War I, 7-8, 35, 40-41, 167, 191n66
World War II, 7-8, 213n6; economic prosperity after, 150; liberalism after, 103-6
Wright, Richard, 12, 14, 99, 125, 134-35; *Black Boy,* 76; *Black Metropolis,* 212n153; *The God That Failed,* 73; "I Tried to Be a Communist," 73; politics, 73; on social work research, 74; tragic sensibility and, 213n6; *Uncle Tom's Children,* 71. See also *Native Son*

Yeats, William Butler, 116, 145-46, 186n21

www.ingramcontent.com/pod-product-compliance
Lightning Source LLC
Chambersburg PA
CBHW070235240426
43673CB00044B/1805